FOR THE SAKE OF
Argument

FOR THE SAKE OF
Argument

---

*Practical Reasoning, Character,
and the Ethics of Belief*

EUGENE GARVER

The University of Chicago Press

CHICAGO *&* LONDON

Eugene Garver is the

Regents Professor of

Philosophy at Saint

John's University in

Minnesota. He is the

author of *Aristotle's*

Rhetoric: An Art of

Character and *Machiavelli*

and the History of

Prudence, as well as

coeditor of *Pluralism in*

Theory and Practice:

Richard McKeon and

American Philosophy.

The University of Chicago Press, Chicago 60637

The University of Chicago Press, Ltd., London

© 2004 by The University of Chicago

All rights reserved. Published 2004

Printed in the United States of America

13 12 11 10 09 08 07 06 05 04   5 4 3 2 1

ISBN (cloth): 0-226-28396-8

ISBN (paper): 0-226-28397-6

Library of Congress Cataloging-in-Publication Data

Garver, Eugene

    For the sake of argument : practical reasoning,

character, and the ethics of belief / Eugene Garver.

      p.   cm.

    Includes bibliographical references and index.

    ISBN 0-226-28396-8   (cloth : alk. paper) —

    ISBN 0-226-28397-6   (pbk. : alk. paper)

    1. Persuasion (Rhetoric)   2. Reasoning.

3. Ethics.   4. Belief and doubt.   I. Title

P301.5.P47 G37   2004

808′.001—dc22

                         2003017900

To my mother

and in memory of my father

CONTENTS

ACKNOWLEDGMENTS

This book addresses questions about thought and character that bear on particular contemporary problems of democracy and expertise, the virtues of trust and friendship in a society of strangers. I explored some of the deep interrelations of thought and character already in my first two books, *Machiavelli and the History of Prudence* and *Aristotle's Rhetoric: An Art of Character.* Here I try to speak to those issues more directly and in my own voice, instead of through the practice of doing philosophy through meditating on a text. Machiavelli's *Prince* and Aristotle's *Rhetoric* have always attracted me because they straddle in different ways standard dichotomies between theoretical and practical texts, inviting us to think about different ways in which intelligence can be practical.

This book is part of my continuing attempt to bring Aristotle's *Rhetoric* to bear on contemporary problems of practical reason. As I will argue, it is a major flaw in the *Rhetoric* that while Aristotle thinks he can give useful advice to the speaker concerning how to persuade audiences, and to legislators concerning how to structure public deliberation, he has nothing to say about how audiences should listen.

Aristotle limits the maximum size of a polis to a group of people who can know each other. Mass democracy, representative democracy, universal human rights—all such things were far beyond his imagination. And yet I argue that friendship is a crucial ingredient in our being able to reason together even in such novel circumstances. There is a connection between the idea of friendship I try to develop in these pages and the friendships I am so pleased to acknowledge here.

I have been lucky in having many friends who have patiently and critically listened and responded to the arguments presented in these pages. Academic and professional friendships are strange things. They don't involve intimacy or necessarily even affection, but require respect and frankness, the desire to help someone else advance projects very different from one's own. Some of my closest friends, people with whom I can speak most honestly and deeply and who return to the favor, are people I see only intermittently. My experience verifies Aristotle's claims that one can only be true friends with a few people, and that such requires time, but rebuts his claim that friendship takes living together. (If these friendships are as deep as I think they are, they also rebut Aristotle's thesis that true friendship is possible only among the morally virtuous.) Friends have made this book better by giving selflessly their time and intelligence. Not only is this book the better for it, but so is my life.

The argument of the book as a whole took shape over the same time that I was writing and presenting what appear here as individual chapters. Audiences and readers of earlier versions have to be excessively careful listeners and readers to recognize those versions, since everything has been extensively rewritten several times over. Chapter 1, "Truth in Politics," was first conceived as part of a conference with that title at the University of Cape Town. The South African experience dramatically illustrated ways in which what might seem like interesting academic puzzles had practical import. It is easy for Americans not to face ways in which ideas indeed have consequences. Thanks go to the South African Research Foundation for a travel grant to attend the conference. I'm also grateful to the perceptive comments of Barbara Cassin and Philippe Salazar at the conference.

Chapter 2, "Confronting The Sophist," has a more complex history. I began thinking about the difference between reasoning and rationalizing, between rational and sophistic rhetoric, when faced with a practical problem of adjudicating between these competing concepts during litigation concerning a retention and tenure decision at my institution. I was gradually and reluctantly convinced that the more autobiographical presentation that I found psychologically satisfying would likely be misunderstood by a wider audience. James B. White offered compelling advice on how to eat my cake and have it too. Members of a faculty seminar at the University of Memphis read and discussed an intermediate version, as did the conference at the Collège Internationale de Philosophie, and a conference on intellectual history at Trinity College, Cambridge. I'm grateful to John A. Campbell, Nancy Struever, and once again to Salazar and Cassin, for intense discussions.

"*Brown v. Board of Education* as a Paradigm of Practical Reason," the third chapter, was presented at a Law, Culture, and the Humanities conference at Georgetown Law School. Among the discussants at that occasion, David Luban stands out for insightful and productive comments.

To skip a chapter, chapter 5, "Rhetorical Argument and Ethical Authority," was also presented at a Law, Culture, and the Humanities conference (at Wake Forest Law School) and then published in *Law and Critique* 10 (1999): 117–46. Many of my ideas about *Brown* were stimulated by my January term classes on *Brown* at Saint John's University, and by a presentation and discussion for the Ghanian Bar Association sponsored by the United States Information Service in Accra. That discussion taught me about how *Brown* stands as a paradigm in ways an American could not guess at.

A much earlier version of chapter 4, "The Ethical Criticism of Reasoning" appeared in *Philosophy and Rhetoric* 31 (1998): 107–30. I very much appreciate the support of that journal over the years. Almost twenty years of continuing conversation with Jonathan Adler was indispensable in leading me to directions and conclusions he doesn't like at all. Thinking about the issues in that paper taught me how even the most impractical academic sorts of arguments have crucial ethical dimensions.

I presented chapter 6, "The Will to Be Believed," at the University of Iowa and at Witwatersrand University. David Depew at Iowa was, as ever, especially helpful. A long discussion over coffee with Jonathan Shay deepened my understanding considerably.

Chapter 7, "Taking Reasoning Seriously," first appeared as "Rhetoric, Hermeneutics, and Prudence in the Interpretation of the Constitution," *Rhetoric and Hermeneutics in Our Time*, ed. Walter Jost and Michael Hyde (New Haven: Yale University Press, 1996), 171–95. Those editors, plus Phillip Bobbitt, Paul Kahn, and James White, not only improved the clarity of my thought but engaged in provocative discussions that pushed my thinking as far as I would allow. The final chapter, "Rhetoric, the Unity and Plurality of Practical Reason," contains materials first presented at Vanderbilt University, and extensively reworked since.

Many other friends provided assistance ranging from editorial suggestions to much more substantive reworkings. My colleagues at Saint John's, Jim Read, Scott Richardson, and Charles Wright gave helpful readings. Phil Keith and Wendy Olmsted gave exactly the editorial advice I needed at the right time, as did, once again, John Campbell and Jim White.

The University of Chicago Press, and most especially Doug Mitchell, helped me enormously in making this book as good as it could be. The referees—and I am now pleased to name Lenn Goodman and Stephen Turner and to thank them publicly—allowed me to construct a more integrated and more readable whole than I could have done on my own.

Rhetoric and Practical Reason

What role does practical reason play in our lives? What role *should* it play? Are claims to rationality liberating or oppressive? Not only have theories, ranging from psychoanalysis to legal realism, shown the power of irrationality, but simple historical evidence of the twentieth century gives little comfort to anyone hoping for the eventual triumph of reason. While at many crucial points in the past reasoning was seen as a powerful democratizing force, now we are often alerted to the way it stacks the deck in favor of some to the disadvantage of others. The rational is just a name for the weapons used by the powerful; its use covers the fact that persuasive power and deliberative ability are weapons too. Reason often seems either impotent or dangerous, or both.[1]

These worries about practical rationality are nothing new, but exploring practical reason by making rhetoric its central case is. That is what I shall undertake. For all the contemporary talk about discourse ethics and deliberative democracy, as well as, in earlier generations of the twentieth century, Dewey's talk about "communication" and Arendt's emphasis on "speech," surprisingly little attempt has been made to mine the history of rhetoric for insight into practical reason. For all the revivals of Aristotle and talk about *phronēsis* or practical wisdom, few have turned to the *Rhetoric* to deepen what Aristotle has to offer in the *Ethics*. The role of practical reasoning in our lives emerges when we deliberate together, persuade each other, are persuaded by each other, and consider how we should persuade and be persuaded.

I propose then to answer Anthony Kronman's question about rhetoric:

What must our condition be if the appeals that rhetoricians make to a real though contested truth and justice—appeals that transcend mere interest and power, like the arguments of mathematicians, but unlike them can never definitively be resolved—are to be possible at all? And what must the human condition be if the securing of our beliefs regarding truth and justice in the middle realm of politics and law is to depend upon an artful mobilization of the passions that is always also capable of producing the opposite result?[2]

What must our condition be if reason can be something other than a cover for manipulation or a working out of a neutral and universal theory? When the connection between reason and character is severed, the definitive resolutions of the mathematicians and the mere battle of interest and power are the only alternatives. Practical reason has its own integrity when who we are and how we think are intimately connected. Interrelations between who we are and how we think create the situation Socrates notes in the *Euthyphro* when he asks about the subjects where our differences cause "anger and hatred" (7b). Thinking in such situations is an inherently ethical act. Which hypotheses, for example, I can take seriously as policy recommendations says a lot about who I am. My character shows itself in the choices of lines of argument, of examples, of alternatives to argue against.

Without such a connection between thought and character, calculation, the more unemotional the better, serves given, irrational goals. Contemporary "rational choice" theory is a perfect example. By narrowing reason and placing ends outside discussion, such a vision of practical reason makes passion irrational, indistinguishable from prejudice and compulsion. Looking at the practices of persuasion will let us broaden the rational so that pathos and *ethos,* the two sources of conviction that Aristotle lists alongside reason (*logos*) (*Rhetoric* I.2.1356a5–20), are not irrational.

To act successfully, we have to act together. To act together, we must deliberate together. Therefore we have to persuade each other. "On any important decision we deliberate together because we do not trust ourselves" (*Nicomachean Ethics* III.3.1112b10–11). Therefore the good person must be good at deliberation and persuasion. Because practical wisdom requires persuasive power, such persuasive ability is a sign of practical wisdom. Like most signs, however, it can be manipulated and exploited. Therefore rhetoric can take on a life of its own and so become an opponent of practical wisdom. If rhetoric weren't essential to practical reason, it couldn't be mistaken for it, and it couldn't be exploited.

I propose to mine Aristotle's *Rhetoric* for help in coming to terms with our problems with practical reason. I have the great good fortune to be captivated by the *Rhetoric* but not to be a native speaker of classical Greek.

Therefore it comes as a continuing surprise to me that a single word in Greek, *pistis*, can be rightly translated as proof, argument, reasoning, persuasion, belief, trust, faith, conviction, obligation, and confidence. These essays are a meditation on the connections among those terms. I want to exploit the fact that the connections among the terms I listed are not immediate or smooth to a speaker of English. I have been inspired by the *Rhetoric*, but nothing in what follows turns on whether I have interpreted the *Rhetoric* accurately or not, and so I have minimized explicit references to it. I believe that what I'm doing adapts Aristotle's project to current circumstances, but what matters is the project of developing the ethical dimensions of practical reason through looking at rhetorical argument, not its provenance. In the *Ethics* and *Politics*, as well as the *Rhetoric*, Aristotle articulates a vision of practical reason and of rhetoric that ties thought and character together. He helps us see how we don't have to rest with a forced choice between the Platonic program which will save reason by removing it from human contamination and the sophistic and skeptical resignation to reason as a slave to the passions.[3]

Practical reason relies on the interrelation between thought and character, where the non-rhetorical alternatives make us choose between them. The distinction Richard Rorty draws between the methodical and the civilized frames my theme:

> In one sense . . . to be rational is to be methodical: that is, to have criteria for success laid down in advance. . . . The other meaning is "sane" or "reasonable" rather than "methodical." It names a set of moral virtues: tolerance, respect for the opinions of those around one, willingness to listen, reliance on persuasion rather than force. These are the virtues which members of a civilized society must possess if the society is to endure. In this sense of "rational," the word means something more like "civilized" than like "methodical."[4]

The two meanings pose a nice dilemma. Unless practical reason follows the scientific method by laying out neutral standards in advance, to call rationality a mark of civilization is simply to congratulate ourselves and look down on the opposition as irrational. But the methodical and the civil seem to have little in common. If we can't overcome that dilemma, then scientific reason and reasoning as a cover for desire will be the only alternatives.

Rhetoric shows how reason can be contingent, emotional, and interested without ceasing to be rational. I can argue rationally by appealing to your interests, prejudices, and emotions. I can be an advocate trying to win, and still engage you rationally. An ethical or an emotional argument can sometimes be more rational than an argument that tries to rely on reason alone. Therefore rhetoric allows reason to extend beyond what methodical or theoretical rationality can accomplish.

Rorty's question about the relation between the rational as civilized and as methodical would sound familiar to Aristotle, who positions practical wisdom and rhetorical ability, in both the *Ethics* and the *Rhetoric*, between Rorty's pair. Practical wisdom thinks about what lies beyond rules (*Ethics* VI.5.1140a28–30, II.2.1104a7–10). The *Rhetoric* begins: "Rhetoric is the counterpart of dialectic, since both are concerned with things that fall within the knowledge of everyone and belong to no separately defined science" (I.1.1354a1–3; see 1354b7–8). Rhetoric and dialectic are faculties that everyone—everyone civilized enough to count—possesses and exercises. Thus far both practical wisdom and rhetoric seem rational in the sense of civilized, but the *Rhetoric* then goes on to present itself as an *enthechnos methodos*. and the discussion of deliberation takes geometrical constructions as its model (*Ethics* VI.5.1140a28–30, *Rhetoric* I.1.154a11).

Because of its ties to the rational as civilized, practical rationality can never be the self-contained enterprise that science can be. But Aristotle doesn't draw the moral that therefore practical reason is inferior to scientific rationality. What it lacks by not being methodical, it compensates by connecting reason and character. When tied to character, practical reason rises above the instrumental. Newman's *Grammar of Assent* captures this Aristotelian picture of practical wisdom:

> In concrete reasonings we are in great measure thrown back into that condition, from which logic proposed to rescue us. We judge for ourselves, by our own lights, and on our own principles. . . . It is this distinction between ratiocination *as the exercise of a living faculty in the individual intellect,* and mere skill in argumentative science, which is the true interpretation of the prejudice which exists against logic in the popular mind, and of the animadversions which are leveled against it, as that its formulas make a pedant and a *doctrinaire,* that it never makes converts, that it leads to rationalism, that Englishmen are too practical to be logical, that an ounce of common-sense goes farther than many cartloads of logic, that Laputa is the land of logicians, and the like.[5]

Understanding practical reasoning as "the exercise of a living faculty in the individual intellect" is the purpose of this book. Reasoning as the exercise of a living faculty is ethical reasoning. We shouldn't infer that when method fails us, reason fails us too. Like eros, praxis is a great leveler.

I propose to make sense out of the relation between thought and character, *logos* and *ethos*, by adopting as a proof-texts Aristotle's remark in the *Ethics*:

> Friendship would seem to hold cities together, and legislators would seem to be more concerned about it than about justice. For concord would seem to be similar to friendship and legislators aim at concord above all, while they try above all to expel civil conflict, which is enmity. Further, if people are friends, they have no need of justice, but if they are just they need friendship in addition; and the justice that is most just seems to belong to friendship. (VIII.1.1155a22–29)

Starting in the first chapter, I will take issue with the modern view that bargaining between strangers should be the model for practical reason, and instead take deliberation between friends for my paradigm. Like friendship and unlike justice, practical reason is not rule-governed, not, in Rorty's term, methodical. Justice might make claims of universality, but practical reason, like friendship, is context-sensitive without becoming irrational. The Platonic hope of replacing ethical reasoning by the certainties of science aspires to substitute the neutrality and objectivity of justice for the informal and negotiable bonds of friendship. Aristotle's pair, justice and friendship, relate to each other as Rorty's methodical relates to the civilized. Practical reason and rhetoric can flourish when the civilized has enough power to resist reduction to the methodical.

Broadening the rational beyond the instrumental requires us to find practical resources within our own lives, not in high theory. I want to display an attractive and live alternative to reducing practical reason to instrumental reason. At issue is how to speak, to listen, and to create conditions in which rationality is thickened from the instrumental to the ethical. What ethical qualities are engendered by the practice of reasoning, and especially by the practice of reasoning with others and trying to persuade them? What are the conditions in which thought and character support each other?

Thought and character support each other and practical rationality functions well where friendship flourishes. Although philosophers from Hume through Rawls have explored the circumstances of justice, the circumstances of friendship need equal attention.[6] Political friendship enables the ethical virtues of practical reasoning to develop and succeed.

It is a great failing of Aristotle that he does not consider the circumstances of friendship. The *Rhetoric* looks at how speakers do and should persuade but says almost nothing about the conditions under which the better argument wins and reason prevails. He doesn't match his advice to speakers with corresponding advice to how to listen. If everything is as it ought to be, the *Rhetoric* will work. But we need to know how everything ought to be, and how to recognize good rhetoric when we see it.

Why should we take bargaining with strangers as the paradigm for practical reason, and to think that we must live with justice and not with friendship? The rational as methodical, like bargaining with strangers, has an important place in our practical lives, but not at the center. Even in a large, diverse, and bureaucratic community such as the United States, we can find ethical and friendly argument at work. I will argue that the desegregation decision, *Brown v. Board of Education,* is a profound act of friendship among the citizens of the United States. In chapter 1 I look at the Truth and Reconciliation Commission in South Africa, where I find ethical argument and friendship in an even more unlikely place than in race relations in the United States. Political friendship does not replace justice with the friendship of intimates: we all know the bitterness of civil war and of enmities within families, and all have the experience that honesty and productive discussion is sometimes more possible with strangers than with intimates. The conception of friendship and its place in practical reasoning should not be read as idealizing the parochial or the traditional.

For present purposes, I want to reduce the *Rhetoric* to three simple theses. First, the heart of the art of persuasion is reasoning:

> Those who have composed arts of speech have worked on only a small part of the subject; for only *pisteis* [proofs] are artistic (other things are supplementary), and these writers say nothing about enthymemes, which is the "body" of persuasion (*sōma tēs pistēus*), while they give most of their attention to matters external to the subject, for verbal attack and pity and anger and such emotions do not relate to fact but are appeals to the juryman. (I.1.1354a11–17)

If I get you to do what I want by tainting your water supply, I haven't persuaded you of anything. If my manipulations of your emotions make your assent involuntary, then you aren't persuaded either. There is no community between us, no rationality in our interchange, and so no civility.

Second, while reasoning is the essence of persuasion, *ethos*, character, is the most authoritative source of belief. When Aristotle says that *ethos* is the most authoritative source of belief he means that it both is and ought to be the most persuasive. A commitment to rationality commits us to trust in and to be persuaded by character:

> [There is persuasion] through character (*ethos*) whenever the speech is spoken in such a way as to make the speaker worthy of credence (*axiopiston*); for we believe (*pisteuomen*) fair-minded people to a greater extent and more quickly [than we do others] on all subjects in general and completely so in cases where there is not exact knowledge (*akribes*) but room for doubt. . . . Character is almost the controlling factor in persuasion. (I.2.1356a5–13)

Third, however, *ethos* derives its authority from reasoning. The *ethos* of pre-existent reputation, of tradition or charisma, might be persuasive, but an *ethos* created by the speech rationally integrates is and ought. Having a trustworthy and credible character emerges through the practice of reasoned argument. The more rational and ethical a speaker, the friendlier the relations between speaker and hearer. Conversely, the friendlier we are, the more we understand emotional appeals as rational. Aristotle's relation between friendship and justice is a model for the relation between character and thought. Friendship exceeds justice, especially legal justice, but is never unjust. *Ethos* exceeds reason but is never irrational. The road to political friendship is through justice, and the road to rhetorical *ethos* is through reasoning:

> But this confidence must be due to the speech (logos) itself, not to any preconceived idea of the speaker's character. For it is not the case, as some writers of rhetorical treatises lay down in their "art," that the worth of the orator in no way contributes to his powers of persuasion; on the contrary, *ethos* constitutes the most authoritative means of proof (*pistis*). (I.2.1356a8–13; emphasis mine)

I propose to present examples of practical reasoning as the exercise of a living faculty, and to look for the enabling and destroying conditions of ethical argument. I draw many of my examples from legal argument because law is such a rich field for the interactions of the rational and the ethical. In law, at least the appearance of rationality is obligatory. We can ask how superficial that appearance is, as I will do in chapter 2. South Africa's Truth and Reconciliation Commission, the U.S. Supreme Court's decision in *Brown v. Board of Education,* and Phillip Bobbitt's pluralism of constitutional interpretation are a series of moments in which legal reasoning becomes ethical by concerning itself not only with what the law says but with how the law represents justice. We abandon the certainties of method for the ethical gains of friendship, and so we find out what the law is by determining what the law should be. Legalism, aiming at agreement, and seeking a modus vivendi or law without friendship require ethical virtues of self-restraint. Aiming at truth and friendly justice require virtues of commitment that are more fully rational and ethical than the virtues of self-restraint.

This book contains four pairs of essays–that is, four more concrete chapters in each instance followed by another chapter that draws generalizations from the examples in the prior chapter. The first pair of essays (chapters 1 and 2) looks at the first thesis I impute to the *Rhetoric,* that persuasion is essentially reasoning. The next pair turns to the second thesis—*ethos,* and not reasoning itself, is the most authoritative source of belief. The third pair develops the final thesis: authoritative *ethos* is itself a function of reasoning. In the last two chapters, I turn away from Aristotle to a feature of practical reasoning unique to modern democracies, to explore the question of what practical reason should look like when it reasons about incommensurable goods, with irreducibly plural methods for reasoning. Here is a quick précis of the eight chapters that follow.

1. Aristotle, as I noted, places friendship alongside justice as fundamental to communities. Yet modern liberal democracies claim to make room for diversity and freedom through living by justice alone, relegating friendship to private life. They see obvious advantages to a politics of justice without friendship that allows communities to be more heterogeneous and private life to flourish. But there are costs too.

Practical reason has different virtues and objectives depending on whether the community aims at truth or agreement. "Truth in Politics: Ethical Argument, Ethical Knowledge, and Ethical Truth" starts from the description of liberal societies as communities that aim at agreement rather than truth, and looks at the South African Truth and Reconciliation Commission to wonder about the meanings of justice and friendship in contexts which test democracy. Agreement looks easier to achieve than truth. The greater the diversity and instability of a community, the more plausible it may seem to limit oneself to achieving agreement. But what happens to community when truth and friendship erupt as competitors to agreement and justice? Both truth and agreement can destabilize communities. Communities can fail through excessive and through insufficient ambition.

Civic and rhetorical friendship is not the friendship of love between intimates, but still is friendship and not just a formal legal relation between strangers or enemies. Confining one's aim to agreement can be unstable, and so contemporary democracy continually searches for something between law and eros, between the negative respect of leaving each other alone and the overbearing lack of privacy and autonomy of a theocracy or family. Instead of insisting that democracy only concern itself with agreement, rhetorical friendship shows how to accommodate truth claims without losing freedom.

2. No one is against friendship, I suppose, but these are not easy times in which to defend rationality. From consumer advertising to Supreme Court rulings, it certainly looks as though reason plays little role in most people's choices. How can one decide between the competing claims of, on the one hand, practical reason based on Aristotle's *Rhetoric,* which upholds the centrality of reason, and, on the other, the assertions of the sophists who proclaim that images, emotions, and style are all.

"Confronting the Sophist" presents the contest between rational and sophistic rhetoric as a paradigmatically philosophical dispute. Neither side can refute the other. Neither can simply prove its own value by pointing to neutral empirical evidence. Still, there are ethical reasons for preferring a rhetoric centering on reasoning over a rhetoric of emotion. "Confronting the Sophist" contains lessons for philosophy and for rhetoric. It shows the rhetorician how the apparent advantages of the sophist are overrated. It shows the philosopher how ethically to adjudicate between incommensurable competing paradigms when purely logical decisions between them are impossible.

3. The next chapter, "*Brown v. Board of Education* as a Paradigm of Practical Reason," turns to the second thesis I impute to the *Rhetoric.* Excellent practical reasoning needs ethical virtues and not only logical skills, both on the part of the speaker and the hearers. Rationality, including scientific reasoning, might require certain minimal intellectual virtues, such as honesty, but if practical reason involves ethical qualities in more profound ways than that, how can practical reason still be rational?

Brown shows how reason generates an *ethos* which then exceeds reason. Practical reasoning generates an ethical surplus that allows us to affirm and be committed to more than reason alone would allow. The *Brown* decision was justified by a premise about the place of education in contemporary society, and so was limited to desegregation in education. But the *ethos* of the opinion quickly justified further antidiscrimination rulings. It opened up a new role for courts, government, and community that went far beyond the initial desegregation order. Far from being lawless, I regard the decision as a perfect example of what ethical reasoning looks like at its best.

My analysis of *Brown* will show how practical reason can generate conclusions more powerful than the premises from which we infer the conclusions. Sometimes that ampliative character means that a conclusion will be more general than the premises that lead to it, sometimes more particular. Often the conclusion will be more firmly held than its premises. If practical reason has such power, then it is not a second-best form of thinking that we only resort to when we can't think more scientifically.

4. "The Ethical Criticism of Reasoning" looks more generally at chapter 3's idea of an ethical surplus and ampliative reasoning. Since it is hard to generalize about how ethical reasoning works, I turn to the easier job of showing how ethical virtues are at work in our judgments of the practical reasoning of others. Part of the resistance to the ethical criticism of reasoning comes from supposing that ethical criticism must be directed at people, not at reasoning, and that reasoning itself is subject only to rational analysis. Moral properties apply to people, logical properties to statements and the connections among them. Seeing how reasoning can be the subject of ethical judgment will improve the practice of the ethical criticism of reasoning.

As Aristotle himself observed, one can become unethical by being too logical (*Rhetoric* III.17.1418a37–b1). To treat a practical problem as a purely technical one can be an ethical error. But it does not follow that therefore to be ethical is to be illogical. There is a difference between an argument which claims that a conclusion follows from the nature of the good—a purely logical claim—and an argument which shows me *inferring* that same conclusion because of my *commitment* to the good—a demonstration that is simultaneously logical and ethical. I make clear my own character and moral purpose in my argumentative choices, but I am not on that account being illogical. Logic relates propositions, while *ethos* relates assertions of propositions to each other. Ethical necessity replaces logical necessity. In this way, a rhetorical understanding of practical reasoning can be as rigorous as a purely logical understanding without sacrificing the context-sensitivity of ethical analysis.

5. "Rhetorical Argument and Ethical Authority" returns to *Brown v. Board*

of Education to show how argument creates rational authority. Authority is an example of an ethical phenomenon that is not well treated if taken as either purely rational or irrational and emotional, but which makes sense when treated ethically. Throughout the book, I try to explore the conditions under which there is an ethically principled distinction between reasoning and rationalizing. Here I ask whether there is a principled distinction between authority and force. The Court, having neither sword nor purse, effects obedience through persuasion. Sometimes authority is a given, but in *Brown* the Court creates its own authority through a rationally constructed *ethos*. Courts can certainly command through manipulating the emotions, provoking guilt, anger, or pride, but such authority rarely commands respect. Courts can become authoritative through reason alone, for example by showing that their judgment follows necessarily and ineluctably from the text of the Constitution, but such purely rational demonstrations often backfire and create mistrust. *Brown*, though, is an ethical argument, not an emotional manipulation or a purely logical argument.

Rationally created authority lasts longer than authority accorded because of the office, vindicating Aristotle's claim that *ethos* created by argument is more powerful than any authority given by something else, such as prestige or perceived benefits. *Brown* is an avowedly ethical argument. The Court creates authority by refusing to pretend that its authority results automatically from the transmission of authority from a more authoritative source in preexistent constitutional law, and instead shows that its authority derives from the force of its argument.

6. "The Will to Be Believed" examines trust. Like authority, trust is unintelligible when considered in terms of a false choice between its being cognitive or emotive. I look at trust by looking at the philosopher who most seriously examines the question of why I should want to be trusted, Adam Smith. Trust, as an ethical yet rationally based phenomenon, thus extends Aristotelian *ethos* to circumstances Aristotle could not imagine. Just as one can forfeit trust by appearing too logical, one can lose trust by relying on antecedent reputation instead of trust that one earns. The fact that I desire to be trusted not only for the benefits it brings, not only for instrumental reasons, shows how we value practical reason and character on noninstrumental grounds.

7. Chapter 1 characterizes modern democracies as aiming at agreement rather than truth, but one could also describe them as communities organized around plural ultimate values. Neither that pluralism of values nor

the parallel recognition of the legitimacy of plural modes of argument and interpretation has a counterpart in Aristotle. They belong to the *ethos* of the modern democratic community. "Taking Reasoning Seriously: Rhetoric, Hermeneutics, and Pluralism in the Interpretation of the Constitution" examines practical reason through the example of Philip Bobbitt's theory of constitutional interpretation.

Practical reason has autonomy when it is not a second-best form of thinking that we only resort to when we can't think more scientifically. Practical reason offers resources for living with plurality not available to reason alone. The existence of plural legitimate modes of interpreting the Constitution is not a scandal but a responsible way of coming to terms with plural and conflicting values. Plural values and ways of thinking set the problem for contemporary ethical argument, and ethical reasoning is superior to theoretical reasoning when it comes to arguing about plural and conflicting values.

8. The final chapter, "Rhetoric and the Unity of Practical Reason," draws on the work of Richard Rorty to think about philosophy and rhetoric as projects of practical reason. I place Rorty's attacks on philosophy in the context of the classical three genres of rhetoric, deliberative, forensic, and epideictic, with their characteristic emphases on the useful, the just, and the noble. In addition to rationality as methodical and as civilized, Rorty recognizes a third, called philosophy, which he thinks is a bad idea. He fails to see how the two more evident forms of practical reasoning, instrumental reasoning and tolerant reasonableness, depend for their rationality on philosophy, that is, on making reasoning its own end and the end of one's actions.

Aristotle says that facility in rhetoric will make no one wiser (I.2.1356a32–34). He agrees with Newman that there are no experts in practical reason. As Charles Taylor puts it, "If theory can transform practice, then it can be tested in the quality of the practice it informs. What makes a theory right is that it brings practice out in the clear; that its adoption makes possible what is in some sense a more effective practice."[7] Acts of rational and ethical persuasion do exist, and understanding them can help us make public life more coherent. I have tried to articulate a civic and rhetorical *ethos* of putting reason first, an image of friendship that does not depend on racial or credal identity but on shared activity. My own ethical purpose is to invite readers into a certain form of community in which trust and commitment are intelligible and desirable forms of life.

CHAPTER 1

Truth in Politics

ETHICAL ARGUMENT, ETHICAL KNOWLEDGE,

AND ETHICAL TRUTH

Dans l'aimitié comme dans l'amour on est souvent plus heureux
par les choses qu'on ignore que par celles que l'on sait.
La Rochefoucauld, *Réflexion morale* § 441

Political Friendship and Liberal Democracy

Aristotle does not give solutions to modern political problems. His world was so different from ours that I see little risk of falling for the fantasy that he speaks directly to us. I can't imagine someone today saying, in the words I quoted in the Introduction, that "legislators seem to be more concerned about friendship than about justice." The modern state appears to have figured out ways of living without friendship. The *Federalist* explains that the Constitution provides a system of accountability founded on mistrust rather than trust, on the assumption that neither ruler nor ruled will be virtuous. Kant tells us that we can have a just constitution for a nation of devils. Liberalism dispenses with friendship and virtue to found communities on rights and thus on a form of justice that can do without friendship. Practical reason suited to liberal democracy is formal, not substantive, rationality; its marks are publicity, neutrality, impersonality, and universality.

Periodically—and the South African revolution is one of those times— the richer form of community associated with friendship rather than justice alone has its revenge. If philosophy begins with wonder and requires leisure, practical wisdom often emerges from crises, from the daunting practical problems South Africa faced, or, to point to other examples I will use, from the American crisis over slavery and the civil war, and from the belated commitment to equality that began with *Brown v. Board of Education* and led to reflections on the nature of constitutional interpretation. Periodically, when trust breaks down, we rediscover that even minimal communities of strangers depend on trust. Even Rorty's rationality as method depends on the rational as civil, as many recent discoveries that the rule of law requires civil society attest. The South African revolution and the activities of its Truth and Reconciliation Commission might seem the last place to find friendship, but I regard those activities as a profound act of friendship. What could friendship and truth mean in conditions that revealed what Archbishop Tutu called "the depths of depravity"?

Liberalism began as an alternative to religious civil war. The need for justice and stability in such conditions limited rationality to impersonal evidence and neutral ways of thinking. Practical reason coordinates free individuals, so devises ways of getting along with the minimum of coercion. The success of liberal democracy depends on lowering one's ambitions from seeking truth to settling for agreement. Truth has too much divisive potential to be a subject for political deliberation. Insisting on truth breaches civility. Hobbes puts it this way: "This right reason, which is the law, is no otherwise certainly right than by our making it so by our approbation of it and voluntary subjection to it."[1] Thus Rawls says that "reasonable persons . . . are not moved by the general good as such but desire for its own sake a social world in which they, as free and equal, can cooperate with others on terms all can accept."[2] Rorty thinks that pragmatism generalizes this insight from politics to rationality overall as pragmatists "hope to blur . . . the contrast between what makes beliefs true and what makes them conducive to human happiness."[3] Contemporary communities get along by looking for agreement and consensus instead of truth. They reasonably assume that "what everybody knows" really is true, and so take agreement as a reason to stop deliberating. "The more consensus becomes the test of a belief, the less important is the belief's source."[4] The more consensus becomes the test of a belief, the less important is the belief's truth.

Where older forms of toleration let live in peace people with opinions thought to be false, now tolerance becomes indifference, a smaller ethical challenge. Different people see some things differently, and that by itself need not threaten the community.[5] For this reason Cass Sunstein advises that we should be reluctant "to attack one another's most basic or defining commitments, at least if it is not necessary to do so in order to decide particular controversies." We can then "seek agreement on what to do rather than exactly how to think."[6] Looking for agreement instead of truth allows liberal societies to incorporate a diversity of citizens.

Political theorists often describe liberalism as a bracketing of the good and the priority of the right to the good: allegiance to the good would necessarily be coercive, and we instead should find a structure of society we can all live with, but which will probably not engage our primary loyalty. Arriving at a common solution is more important than hitting the correct answer. The law decides which side of the road everyone will drive on so that we can decide on the important things in life for ourselves.

Advocates of the priority of the right over the good assume that societies organized around the good start from an agreed on or imposed idea of what is best. Such societies draw no strong distinction between public and private, and lack the toleration which is part of the meaning of rationality. I find the distinction between truth and agreement a more fruitful taxonomy because truth and agreement are goals, not starting points. Toleration and reasonableness will mean something different in communities that aim at truth, but such communities need be no more authoritarian or unreasonable than those that aim at agreement. Different organizing purposes require different sorts of intellectual virtues.[7]

Modern democracy, by aiming at agreement, abandons friendship for justice. I am interested in the times when that strategy fails through being insufficiently ambitious, because those times can teach us a lot about practical reason and its virtues. The South African Truth and Reconciliation Commission (TRC) discovered the need for truth, as did the United States in the Civil War. For example, where Douglas argued that slavery was a subject on which we had to agree to disagree, Lincoln thought that the continued existence of the nation depended on its embracing truth, not agreement, about slavery. The nation had to commit itself to the truth of the proposition that all men are created equal. Lincoln saw that aiming at consensus rather than truth was divisive. As Martin Luther King Jr. put it, "The Negro's great stumbling block in his stride toward freedom is not the White Citizen's Councilor or Ku Klux Klanner, but the white moderate, who is more devoted to 'order' than to justice."[8]

Leaders of the South African TRC, unlike their counterparts in other countries, tried to pursue truth and reconciliation together rather than choose peace over truth. Since it often seems that an excessive desire for truth would hinder national reconciliation, the dominant solution in Eastern Europe was to avoid full confrontation with the truths of the past in order to foster reconciliation for the future.[9] Aiming at agreement looked friendlier than aiming at truth. In South Africa, the old ruling class, the perpetrators and beneficiaries of injustice, urged that truth was too dangerous, and that peace came from forgetting. Perpetrators usually have a shorter memory than victims. Hence the ominous meaning of my epigram: in friendship, as in love, we are sometimes happier because of the things we don't know than because of what we know.

The liberal orientation to agreement rather than truth sometimes aims too low. Settling for agreement can be disruptive, while committing oneself to truth can lead to national unity. A too quick declaration of reconciliation could prevent the emergence of important truths, and of deeper forms of friendship. That may have been the experience of the United States after the Civil War, and especially after Reconstruction was abandoned in 1876. Many citizens were exhausted by the brief struggle for true justice, and opted for order instead. Racial subordination became part of the American *ethos,* and, apart from the abolition of legal slavery, the South won the Civil War as the federal government remained weak and the South's story of the war became the received version.[10] The TRC depended on the hope that full inquiry into the truth would make reconciliation and justice deeper and more permanent, without residual suspicions of what we are holding back from knowing. In the words of Archbishop Tutu,

> Some have been upset by the suggestion that the work of the Truth and Reconciliation Commission could have resulted in making people angrier and race relations more difficult, as indicated by a recent survey. It would be naïve in the extreme to imagine that people would not be appalled by the ghastly revelations that the Commission has brought about. It would have been bizarre if this had not happened. What is amazing is that the vast majority of the people of this land, those who form the bulk of the victims of the policies of the past, have said they believe that reconciliation is possible. The trouble is that there are erroneous notions of what reconciliation is all about. Reconciliation is not about being cosy; it is not about pretending that things were other than they were. Reconciliation based on falsehood, on not facing up to reality, is not reconciliation at all.[11]

Sometimes the truth makes us free. Sometimes loss of memory allows us to live together. Sometimes it will be a shared mythical past. There is, therefore, no single relation that truth and agreement must take. There are risks in all directions.

Truth and Truths

The TRC expanded the number of ways of confronting practical disagreement beyond the three standard alternatives of (1) finding which opinion is true, (2) searching for consensus, or (3) exercising the strategies for indifference, toleration, or privatization that let us live with disagreement, by thinking that none of the options really is true, they are only true for someone. The TRC pointed to a fourth possibility: multiple truths. Pluralism creates an ethical middle ground between negative respect and the positive love of intimates, between rights and politeness, between instrumental rationality between strangers and the sort of friendship and love that dissolves personal identity, the love which Plato thought essential to a good state but which Aristotle thought reduced political association to a family. We find this middle ground in the intellectual virtues of political friendship and trust. What is persuasive is persuasive to someone (*Rhetoric* I.2.1356b26–9); why not take that a step further and say that what is true is true for someone? Or must that attempted step be a plunge into relativism?

The Truth and Reconciliation Commission sometimes left multiple narratives and accounts stand without deciding which gets the title of truth, and without reducing all of them to something less than a claim of truth. Sometimes eliminating some discourse as false would have been more than bad manners; at other times, to let an account stand without contradiction would have been injurious. Deciding what to do with plural accounts requires virtues of friendship and justice.

Victims of apartheid gained a moral standing by having their stories heard. They became part of a moral community.[12] Their desires and cries of pain became interests that had to be included in any political calculus. Nothing would have been achieved by challenging those stories against conflicting accounts. And yet simply to think of them as stories with expressive value and not truth would be to fail to take them seriously. That would be the interpretation of "true for them" that reduces pluralism to relativism, and would reduce our ethical relations to politeness, the respect we owe to strangers.[13] The Commission often acted under the maxim that any freely offered account, especially if expressed by the oppressed, must be taken as true. Unless the victims' stories were heard as true, the victims could not gain moral standing. Consequently the TRC "rejected the popular assumption that there are only two options to be considered when talking about truth—namely factual, objective information or subjective opinions."

Instead, it named four kinds of truth: factual, objective information, "personal or narrative truth, social or dialogue truth, and healing or restorative truth."[14] They rediscovered the fact that rhetorical arguments are always persuasive to someone, and yet rhetorical contests are contests over truth, not what is true in someone's opinion. The TRC faced the most delicate practical problem of how to take an account seriously without thereby embracing it. The TRC revived the old correlation between truth and goodness, and combined it with the modern recognition of a diversity of goods to yield a diversity of truths. Formal conceptions of practical reason are inadequate for these further senses of truth.

The complicated relations between truth and justice are exemplified in the following extract from Antjie Krog's *Country of My Skull:*

> Now that people are able to tell their stories, the lid of the Pandora's box is lifted; for the first time these individual truths sound unhindered in the ears of all South Africans. The black people in the audience are seldom upset. They have known the truth for years. The whites are often disconcerted: they didn't realize the magnitude of the outrage, the "depth of depravity" as Tutu calls it.
>
> Where does the truth lie? What does it have to do with reconciliation and justice?
>
> "For me, justice lies in the fact that everything is being laid out on the same table," says my colleague Mondli. "The truth that rules our fears, our deeds, and our dreams is coming to light. From now on you don't only see a smiling black man in front of you, but you also know what I carry inside of me. I've always known it—now also you know."
>
> "And reconciliation?"
>
> "Reconciliation will only be possible when the dignity of black people has been restored and when whites become compassionate. Reconciliation and amnesty I don't find important. That people are able to tell their stories—that's the important thing."[15]

Truth is the condition for membership in the community. Perpetrators, beneficiaries, and victims of "the depth of depravity" cannot live together without facing the truth together. Truth is less a correspondence between statement and reality than a relation between speaker and hearer. This is the connection between truth and trust that will be a theme throughout this book. True relations between speaker and hearer are supple enough to allow for single truths, truths relative to individuals or groups, and multiple truths. Plural truth is an ethical option.

We quickly discover that, however important it is that "people are able to tell their stories," more is needed. Aristotle pictured the political speaker as reasoning from and about common opinion. He didn't imagine that politics would include a contest over which opinions counted as common opinions. Such a struggle for common meaning and power must be rhetorical.

Including more and more truths and truth tellers within the community cannot always work. Testimony accusing someone of a crime could not simply be accepted as true because it was offered sincerely and by someone who was poor and oppressed. When accepting an account has consequences, such as awarding monetary compensation or sending someone to prison, judicial canons of evidence had to decide between conflicting accounts. Krog places a dilemma in the hands of those presiding at the TRC: "The leader of testimony has two tasks: to steer the testimony in a direction that will yield enough facts of use to the Commission; and to let the testimony unfold as spontaneously as possible, so that there can be healing and renewed self-respect."[16] Spontaneity and utility are both desirable, but not always compatible. Devotion to spontaneity alone lets multiple accounts stand without trying to resolve their differences, and if an argument can't be contested, it isn't an argument but an assertion. On the other hand, "facts of use to the Commission" are usually accounts taken as exclusively true, and judicial canons of evidence can stack the deck in favor of the old regime.

The philosophical issue of absolutism and relativism here becomes a concrete and real issue. Is community fostered, and truth and justice pursued, by respecting a multiplicity of true accounts or by deciding on a single representation of reality? Whether truth is one or many is not a metaphysical issue but an ethical one of the relation between truth and reconciliation, an issue illustrated by the following long extract from early in *Country of My Skull:*

And the idea of truth. Even if it's not spelt with a capital. . . . Nadine Gordimer once asked a black writer: "Why do you always picture a white woman lounging next to a swimming pool? We are not all like that!" He replied: "Because we perceive you like that." Gordimer admits that she has to take cognizance of that truth.

One morning, when I was still a lecturer at a training college for black teachers, a young comrade arrived. He refused to enter my class.

He called Afrikaans a colonial language. "What is English then?" I asked. "English was born in the centre of Africa," he said with great conviction. "It was brought here by Umkhonto we Sizwe." That was his truth. And I, as his teacher, had to deal with this truth that was shaping his life, his viewpoints, his actions.

Will a Commission be sensitive to the word "truth"?

If its interest in truth is linked only to amnesty and compensation, then it will have chosen not truth, but justice. If it sees truth as the widest possible compilation of people's perceptions, stories, myths and experiences, it will have chosen to restore memory and foster a new humanity, and perhaps that is justice in its deepest sense.[17]

I can see the point to calling the stereotype of a white person a truth, but the African origin of English seems to me, at best, a strongly held belief. Krog is right not to be dismissive of a student's beliefs that shape "his life, his viewpoints, his actions." In the Introduction I pointed to ethical reasoning embodying intimate connections between who we are and what we think. Simply to reject what someone thinks can be a rejection of the person as well. Thinking of the black stereotype of whites as a truth means accepting it as a perspective on reality worth taking into account. It would trivialize the claim to take it relativistically as "true from someone's point of view." But thinking of the African origins of English as true seems to mean nothing more than treating the person with such a belief with respect.[18] The grade inflation of extending the honorific, true, to such an idea leads nowhere. To call it "true for him" is patronizing. There is a serious ethical problem of how to treat the assertion that English comes out of Africa, similar to the issue of how I can be friends with someone who I am convinced is wrong.

Partisans and beneficiaries of the old regime often criticized the TRC for allowing unsubstantiated claims to stand. They claimed that the possibility of compensation gave a powerful incentive for lying. The pursuit of truth must be disinterested. According to theoretical measures of rationality, interest pollutes discourse and thought. Thinking of practical reason rhetorically allows us to see how traditional methods for establishing truth could stifle the free expression necessary to develop a full picture of the past. Judicial canons of evidence stack the deck in favor of the old regime. People only speak the truth when they have incentives to do so.

The dilemma of interest and reason is perfectly expressed in a commentary on another country's truth commission, Ariel Dorfman's play, *Death and the Maiden.* Paulina, a victim of torture in Chile, interrogates her torturer in front of her husband, a lawyer asked to head their country's new truth commission. She points a gun at both of them, to try to force the torturer to confess and to get her husband to choose sides. The husband says: "While you point [the gun] at me, there is no possible dialogue." She replies, "On the contrary, as soon as I stop pointing it at you, all dialogue will automatically terminate. If I put it down you'll use your strength to win the argument."[19]

Dorfman dramatizes the way coercion can both engender and hinder discovery. Practical reason is autonomous when truth and interest are compatible. In the Introduction I claimed that rhetoric will allow reason to be contingent, emotional, and interested without ceasing to be rational. Dorfman demands that his audience exercise practical wisdom to figure out how speakers can be motivated and interested and yet audiences can still make judgments of truth.

Common Knowledge and "Being of One Mind"

My initial quotation from Aristotle claiming that friendship is more important to communities than justice challenges the life of liberalism. Liberals think that a community aiming at truth and friendship will be monolithic and coercive, while overcoming the need for friendship constitutes progress. Without friendship we can have moral and political relations, such as respect, with a broader range of people. The South African revolution had to make a single nation out of people who speak eleven official languages, with linguistic issues so politically charged that the Sharpeville massacre began with protests over school language policy. Whites, coloreds, Indians, and blacks were legally separated, and the white minority owned almost all the material resources. Given the extreme diversity and heterogeneity of citizens of the new South Africa, one would think that this is a situation calling for liberal justice rather than Aristotelian friendship.

Aristotle would regard the liberal community not as a community in his sense at all but as an alliance, a peace treaty, or a commercial treaty. Fellow citizens in his political community "care about each other's virtue" (*Politics* III.9.1280b7). In such a community I must take account not only of the fact that you want something, but I have to think about whether what you want is actually good. Liberalism revolted against Aristotelianism to reject that orientation to truth and not only agreement. Liberals thought that to care about one another's virtue was to impose my values on you. A liberal state governed by instrumental rationality teaches us that through working together, dividing our labor and exchanging goods, each of us can get more of what we want. I care about which things you think are good because I can deliberate about which of your desires I can satisfy at what price. I don't care whether what the things you want—cigarettes, golf courses whose fertilizer runoff poisons habitat downstream, or the freedom from having to see homosexual or interracial couples—are truly good or not.

Because I care whether what my friends desire really is good, though, truth is dangerous and so potentially disruptive. How many people I can allow to care about what is good for me limits how many friends I can have. But Aristotle's political friendship—as opposed to the friendship he describes in the *Ethics*—isn't as scary as that. Concord and political friendship are crucially limited to "advantage and with what affects life" (IX.6.1167b3–4). The things about which a community must have one mind are limited to the objects of deliberation.

> *Homonoia* [literally being of one mind] is not merely sharing a belief, since this might happen among people who do not know each other. Nor are people said to be in concord (*homonoia*) when they agree about just anything, e.g. on astronomical questions, since concord on these questions is not a feature of friendship. Rather a city is said to be in concord when [its citizens] agree about what is advantageous, make the same decision, and act on their common resolution. (*Ethics* IX.6.1167a22–30; see VI.5.1140b13–19)

Limiting such democratic agreement to the practical, Aristotle answers the question of what we have to have in common to be a community. The limit of concord to practical knowledge creates a connection between "being of one mind" and friendship. While liberalism seems more modest and less ambitious than Aristotle's community aiming at friendship and truth, it paradoxically requires more extensive sorts of being of one mind. The TRC's goal of producing a common history and a common *ethos* for the new South Africa sounds totalitarian in contrast to liberal freedom of each to understand the past and present in his or her own way, but in other ways aiming at truth is liberating.

To set off South Africa's solution to how to live together without the usual sources of commonality, consider by contrast the efforts of E. D. Hirsch. Hirsch wrote a series of very influential books which claimed that citizenship depends on common education, which in turn depends on common knowledge among citizens. If we don't have to share values, we do have to share facts. These facts are not the weighty truths about history the TRC was trying to establish, but far more mundane conditions for understanding each other. They are common because they are shared, and unobjectionable because they're so trivial. In *Rhetoric* I.2 Aristotle appeals to what everyone knows: "To prove that Dorieus was the victor in a contest at which the prize was a crown, it is enough to say that he won a victory at the Olympic games; there is no need to add that the prize at the Olympic games is a crown, for everybody knows it" (1357a).[20]

Unless people know that the prize at the Olympic games is a crown, they cannot participate in civic life; they aren't part of "everyone." I remember once reading a story, in the *New Yorker* I think, about a woman reporting to her psychiatrist about a very torrid love affair she was having with Jerry Lewis. Her doctor was very well-trained and intelligent, but since he grew up in the Philippines, he did not know that Jerry Lewis was an actor, and therefore the woman's story was a fantasy. The lack of common background knowledge prevented him from treating her properly. Everyone in America must know that George Washington was the first president, that he chopped down a cherry tree, and that crossing the Delaware was an important event in the Revolutionary War. I can't remember what its importance was, but that does not disqualify me from citizenship. When you refer to Washington crossing the Delaware I know what you are referring to. Knowing such facts allows us to understand each other. These mythical events might carry no cognitive content or emotional impact for me at all, but Hirsch maintains that I still must recognize them in order to understand common political arguments. Anyone who has ever lived in more than one country can see the appeal of what Hirsch is claiming. I can understand the French language perfectly, yet sometimes get terribly confused in France because I do not know the French equivalents of George Washington chopping down a cherry tree. Hirsch produced book after book containing long lists of things everyone needed to know.[21]

Hirsch's point is a liberal one. The things we all need to know are trivial. They don't commit us to any particular political position, so this is far from an agreement on a creed. They are simply the banal shared understandings that we all presume and rarely make explicit. They don't even have to be true, so long as everyone understands them. Washington never did chop down a cherry tree. It is a fable invented a few generations later as part of a campaign to deify the first president. We possess this civic knowledge in the way we know a language. English is no more the language of truth than Tswana, but for us to get along in America, everyone must speak English.

The recent popular studies that claim to prove that religious belief is good for your health say nothing about the truth or even the content of those beliefs. (Apparently, religious belief leads to well-being in a way that is second only to having pets.) If so, religious beliefs are like the "knowledge" that George Washington chopped down a cherry tree, or that English originated in central Africa.

At its extreme, this picture of democracy resting on agreement rather than truth is embodied in Richard Rorty's idea of conversation. The enemy of civilization is seriousness. Like the Enlightenment polemics against "enthusiasm," Rorty thinks that serious people cannot be part of a community, since they insist on being right. We should not adjudicate among our differences but should celebrate them, in epideictic rhetoric, just as we celebrate the variety of fictions in great literature.[22]

Sometimes, the truth of a religious or political belief matters. Maybe Rorty's joshing is the right strategy to speak with the person who believes that English comes from central Africa, but what about the person who believes that apartheid is divinely sanctioned or that torture and terror in the name of anticommunism are irreproachable? Once I realize that someone believes that English comes from central Africa because English, unlike Afrikaans, is the language of freedom, is joshing still the best strategy?

The story of the South African revolution more makes it tempting to present the relation between truth and agreement as a Kuhnian narrative. In normal communities, people work toward agreement. Persuasion based on common opinion works happily there. There are no epistemological crises of members of that community wondering whether their agreements track truth.[23] Periodic revolutionary movements, such as the South African revolution, present disruptive truths which destroy the existing community. Since normal communities define what counts as rational, these injections of truth are never rational. They are emotional appeals that ask the powerful to take seriously the pains of the victims or the needs of the neglected. After the revolution, these new truths become domesticated, civilized, and rationalized. Truth becomes commonplace. The community returns to a new stable existence founded in a new set of agreements. The TRC was an instrument in that normalization process.

On this account, revolution and community are antitheses and there are no communities of truth, only of agreement. Hobbes's sovereign defines right and wrong, just and unjust. New sovereigns define truth again for the community, but until they succeed in becoming sovereign, they offer not truth but force. On that picture, competing interests, tastes, and desires can co-exist within a community, but competing truths live in a state of nature toward each other. The modern state is an alternative to civil war because it reduces truth claims, and claims to justice and other values, to interests, tastes, and desires.[24]

Friendship versus Justice: Ethos versus Logos

As well as the South African experience seems to fit Kuhn's model, finding truth outside community has a cost. Only defining knowledge within the community makes political and social life transparent. Only common knowledge allows citizens to know what the consequences, conditions, and meanings of their acts are. In words of Charles Taylor I quoted in the Introduction, "if theory can transform practice, then it can be tested in the quality of the practice it informs. What makes a theory right is that it brings practice out in the clear; that its adoption makes possible what is in some sense a more effective practice."[25] The TRC faced the practical problem of finding a way to talk about knowledge and truth by finding within the community and its opinions the resources for distinguishing between knowledge and prejudice.

Bishop Tutu's remarks on the practical task of facing history is a nice contrast to Hirsch's idea that we need common knowledge. Instead of a single set of true beliefs, we have a "new, shared, and ceaselessly debated memory." Such memory resembles Aristotle's *homonoia* limited to common practical knowledge:

In moving away from the discredited governing consciousness of the past, we will need to build a new, shared, and ceaselessly debated memory of that past. . . . This talk of shared memory must not be misunderstood or mystified. It is not the creation of a post apartheid *volk* or a stifling homogeneous nationhood; not a new fatherland. Nor is it merely the equivalent of every individual's mental ability to retain facts and arguments at the front of her consciousness. Such analogies between individual and collective memory are unhelpful. Rather, shared memory, in the intended sense, is a process of historical accountability.[26]

Aiming at agreement may avoid civil war, but the prejudices of the powerful get toconstitute common knowledge. Claims about truth and not merely agreement usually come, as in both the examples of the South Africa TRC and the American struggles for racial justice, from excluded outsiders rejecting the myths that reject them. Outsiders naturally feel the loss of truth more heavily than the powerful. The powerful have no reason not to be satisfied with agreement. Rorty's liberal strategy of privatizing disagreement gives comfort, against his own intentions, to the powerful.[27]

Outsiders face the rhetorical task of convincing those who identify truth with common opinion that there are other measures of truth. Such outsiders are, paradoxically, the last people rulers usually regard as friends. But the turn to truth reconstitutes community in the name of friendship and not only justice. It might seem that friendship is more exclusive and so conservative than justice. Since justice is formal, it can be more inclusive and progressive. But if truth and reconciliation need each other, then the TRC's search for truth can be an act of friendship. Broadening practical reason to include relations of friendship as well as justice between speaker and hearer, rulers and ruled, develops ways of talking about knowledge and truth that do not go outside the community. Aiming at truth is one of the circumstances of friendship.

Whatever the merits of Kuhn's story in science, in practical reason ethical argument aims at truth within a community, and so his assumption that rationality means standards of publicity, neutrality, and universality commits us to reasoning without *ethos,* truth without community, rationality as methodical rather than civilized. Such reason is stable, but vulnerable to periodic overthrow when someone unmasks its self-justifying status as a myth. The victims of apartheid did not think that they were behaving irrationally when they violated community values in which blacks should silently defer to whites.

The Three Sources of Conviction: Logos, Pathos, and Ethos: Friendship Makes Pathos and Ethos Rational

Modern psychology—and the modern world which that psychology describes—encourages us to think solely in terms of a choice between the rational and the emotional. If those are the alternatives, then the Kuhnian vision of periodic alternation between rational argument about agreement and irrational appeals to truth makes sense. Only emotional appeals to pity, guilt, or sympathy can break through a consensus on what counts as rational.

Aristotle, however, offers a trio, *ethos, logos,* and *pathos,* instead of a simpler distinction of the rational and the irrational. Ethical argument, not logos or pathos, allows us to move from justice to friendship, and from agreement to truth, and so lets us conceive the search for truth rather than agreement as a rational activity.

Truth always potentially disrupts community. But, just as there is a difference in rhetoric between the kind of *ethos* produced by argument and *ethos* as preexistent reputation, so there is a difference between an appeal to truths which trumps public reason—because of my position, or because of my suffering, you must defer to what I say—and appeals to truths which expand public reason, and so do not destroy community but deepen it. A community organized around the search for truth need not be a more closed community than one aiming at agreement.

The TRC replaced the false official opinions that held together the old South Africa with new truths it found by being more inclusive about what counts as the rational. It was of course more inclusive in terms of who had a voice. That was the easy part. It had to be more profoundly inclusive, including emotional and ethical appeals. The friendlier we are, the more my emotional and ethical appeals can be rational. The more we are strangers, or enemies, or the more we simply mistrust each other, the more those same emotional and ethical appeals are illegitimate, and the more rhetoric must be confined to logic, and our goals limited to agreement and justice. The scope of rationality increases when there are friendly relations between speaker and hearer.

Through political friendship, practical reason can aim at truth while staying committed to public argument because ethical arguments can be more powerful and more rational than arguments from reason alone: that is the thesis that animates my entire book. In situations of suspicion and mistrust which set the problem that liberalism was designed to solve, appeals to character and emotion are appeals to prejudice and authority, obstacles to finding truth. The ability to express ethical arguments and the ability to hear persuasive appeals as ethical arguments are among the chief circumstances of friendship.[28]

The friendlier we are, the more our emotional and ethical appeals are rational and argumentative rather than irrational appeals to personal experience or authority. Without friendship, potentially rational appeals are perceived as emotional and so as potentially coercive. What counts as a conversation-stopper and what as a contribution to deliberation cannot be determined outside of context, and so Rawls's gag rules against comprehensive views and similar calls for self-restraint only preach to the converted. Whether emotional and ethical appeals are licit depends on how friendly we are, but at the same time friendship in the relevant political sense depends on our having this broader sense of rationality that includes the emotional and the ethical. With a broader sense of rationality, we can see the concern for truth as a form of common reasoning and not as its own form of violence.[29]

Once I see you as a fellow-citizen, and not as a noisy and needy outsider, your formerly irrational pleas become reasonable proposals. People whom I hear as rational are my political friends. Jonathan Shay shows the importance of trust and ethical communication in a description that bears on the South African problem:

> Democratic process embodies the apparent contradiction of *safe struggle*. . . .
>
> Democratic process entails debate, persuasion, and compromise. These all presuppose *the trustworthiness of words*. The moral dimension of severe trauma, the betrayal of "what's right," obliterates the capacity for trust. The customary meanings of words are exchanged for new ones; fair offers from opponents are scrutinized for traps; every smile conceals a dagger.
>
> Unhealed combat trauma—and I suspect unhealed severe trauma from any source—destroys the unnoticed substructure of democracy, the cognitive and social capacities that enable a group of people to freely construct a cohesive narrative of their own future.[30]

"Safe struggle" epitomizes such civic rhetoric's dual emphasis on trying towin the argument while also remaining limited to friendly and just relations between speaker and audience. Without trust in "the trustworthiness of words," we will hear everyone as a sophist using words to manipulate us. "Every smile conceals a dagger." Rhetorical relations of speaking and hearing can be basic to trust in general, and rhetorical acts of virtue, treating one's audience as beings to reason with and not to manipulate, can be the basis for ethical relations in general.

Of course there are practical and material background conditions that have to be in place for persuasion to be received as the giving of reasons rather than manipulation. But equally the trustworthiness of words can create trust and community in broader ways. This is the "the unnoticed substructure of democracy, the cognitive and social capacities that enable a group of people to freely construct a cohesive narrative of their own future." That cohesive narrative is the project of the TRC.

Since the interrelations among *ethos,* pathos, and logos will be fundamental to so much of my argument, I want to clarify those terms and the idea of ethical argument before returning to the specifics of the TRC. I try to persuade you to vote for candidate X by reminding you of the reasons you gave for supporting candidate Y. I could be using any of those three modes of proof: (1) My appeal to precedent could be a logical argument of consistency. (2) It could be an emotional appeal if I try to get you to commit to something you would otherwise resist. You should be shamed by the tacit implication that you were not really committed to the reasons you proffered for candidate Y, but were really motivated by envy or resentment, or party loyalty. We all like to think that we are reasoning, not merely rationalizing to cover an irrational preference. You will vote my way so that you can feel the emotions you would like to feel. (3) I can appeal to those same reasons ethically if I take your commitments and principles seriously, and join with you in reasoning from them. I am appealing to your *ethos,* your character. To do so successfully, I must manifest and risk my own *ethos.*

Now the stakes are higher. You must trust me to a degree far greater than the trust a speaker needs to make a rational or emotional appeal. Such an ethical argument does not aim at consistency, as in either the logical argument or the emotional appeal to shame, but at reliability and integrity. My appeal to a specific audience in this case is not a concession to its weakness, or an occasion for manipulation. Aristotelian *homonoia* occurs when I join with you in exploring the implications of your principles. Persuading you that your commitments entail voting for Y, unlike shaming you into doing it, is subject to rational assessment. What could otherwise be an emotional appeal becomes ethical. When it does, it becomes rational.

A more sophisticated example shows what difference it makes whether we conceive of consistency as logical, emotional, or ethical. Ethically, it is a powerful argument. Logically or emotionally, it does not work very well at all:

> We were strangers [in Egypt], so we must treat strangers kindly. The inference belongs not to logic but to sympathy. Yet it grounds a law of constitutional scope, not a psychological claim. Sympathy might

breed cruelty or contempt, as Spinoza showed. Or it might be over-ruled by spite or vengeance, chauvinism or fear. But here it is trans-muted to a categorical moral demand. Thus the reference to God. "Ye were strangers . . ." gives the sentimental motive, which only intentions can interpret; but "I am the Lord thy God" states the reason and guides the intention.[31]

Only ethical appeals to "sympathy" can "ground a law of constitutional scope," not strictly emotional or logical considerations. Only with the idea of ethical argument can we make sense of such an important argument as: We were strangers [in Egypt], so we must treat strangers kindly.

I display my own *ethos* in tracing the ethical implications of your beliefs. Ethical argument creates essentially civic relations between people. Reason be-comes thickened from consistency to integrity. The emotions become thick-ened and rationalized, too. They are no longer involuntary responses, as in the feeling of shame in my narrative, but become responses you, the audience, take responsibility for because I join with you in evaluating them. If you don't vote for candidate *X,* you should feel ashamed of your vote for *Y.*

Ethical arguments hold communities of truth together by expanding the range of appeals that will count as rational. But I don't want to oversell *ethos* as a panacea. There are certain aspects of community-building that only *ethos* can do. Hence its importance, and hence the loss when it is neglected. But each of Aristotle's three sources of proof, logos, *ethos* and pathos, can be used to make a community more open or more closed. Each can be used in the name of progressive and retrograde causes.

Thus, Nietzsche talks about reasoning as a weapon of the weak, to be used against people who are strong enough not to need to give reasons. The strong never apologize; never explain. On the other hand, being rational is a mark of a ruling class, who rely on calm reason instead of the messy emotionalism of outsiders, whether women or other groups that the power-ful want to think of less civilized.[32]

Just as the purely rational can sometimes insure the stability of communi-ties, sometimes restrict entrance into communities, and sometimes provide access to the weak, so both *ethos* and pathos can be sometimes community building and sometimes community destroying. Consider, on pathos, these lines from Justice Brennan: "The framers [of the U.S. Constitution] operated within a political and moral universe that had experienced arbitrary passion as the greatest affront to the dignity of the citizen. . . . In our own time, . . .

the greatest threat . . . is formal reason severed from the insights of passion."[33] Intensity of emotion can gain hearing for a cause where reason alone produces indifference. Protest movements such as those seeking to prohibit the sale of alcohol or the practice of abortion, or in favor of vegetarianism, depend on shocking the feelings, not on rational appeals. On the other hand, feelings of offense and outrage have been used to justify the status quo, as in laws against interracial marriage or homosexuality.

And so too for *ethos*. Ethical arguments are both useful and dangerous. They can constitute and can destroy communities. Character and trust have been used to defend privilege against outsiders. "Trust me. I know what is best." What everybody knows defines the *ethos* of the community, but as we've seen what everybody knows can be false. Common knowledge does not always deserve the name of knowledge. On the other hand, personal testimony has often been used by outsiders to gain a hearing. Compelling testimony establishes its own *ethos*. While established and reputable opinions seem to limit practical reasoning to agreement instead of truth, the word of outsiders presents personal experience that seems to supersede reasoning in the name of truths accessible by more noble methods than rational calculation to agreement—the appeal of the Kuhnian framework. Thus the TRC had peculiar problems when they could not consistently follow their policy of deferring to the poor and powerless as privileged witnesses to truth. They upheld that general rule as an ethical principle, but also had to acknowledge that the powerless often had the same motives to evade and deny the truth as the powerful.

Character, Aristotle says, is the most authoritative source of belief. Character as a source of belief, whether the *ethos* which comprises aristocratic privilege and accumulated experience or the experience of the victim, sets the boundaries within which reasoning might then work. The *ethos* of the community sets the ends toward which we deliberate, since the common opinions of the community determine which appeals will be persuasive. Because of this finality, sometimes the ethical is another name for prejudice; sometimes it is truly a form of knowledge that cannot be reduced to the purely rational. The problem the South African revolution and the TRC faced was this: if *ethos* is given and beyond criticism, how can it be changed? How can it be changed without appeal to sources or standards of truth outside the community itself?

Formal logic is universal and so does not have to worry about relations between speaker and hearer. That is its strength and its weakness. Ethical argument allows us to raise the crucial question of what is worth listening to. What *should* I hear? What *can* I hear? One person might feel great pain at being excluded from military service because he is a homosexual, while another feels equally great pain when she learns that gays are allowed to serve in our military. We still have to answer the political question of which feelings of pain deserve our attention. It is only the *ethos* of the community that can decide which emotions, and which reasons, we should listen to.[34]

I take it as a real deficiency in Aristotle's *Rhetoric* that while he talks about the rhetorical virtues of speakers, he had nothing to say about the virtues of an audience. The TRC presented unavoidable problems about how to listen, how to hear the cries of pain, the demands for recognition, the plurality of languages, the confessions and defenses of perpetrators, the nuances of different degrees of guilt and victimhood. It became evident that the virtues of the audience in this case were more than intellectual, more than emotional. Listening challenged the *ethos* of each member of the audience and of the community as a whole.

Since the concrete results of the Commission were findings of amnesty, or its denial, and recommendations for compensation, it looks as though one should judge the success or failure of the TRC by the standards of judicial rhetoric, determining the truth of the past in order to find guilt or innocence, justice or injustice. Instead, we should judge the TRC as a successful instance of epideictic rhetoric, proclaiming the values of a community and reconstituting community, remaking the community in accordance with its declared values. Just as the Gettysburg Address talked about the past and future as part of an epideictic expression of *ethos* and values, connecting birth and new birth to death and sacrifice, so the TRC placed deliberation about the future and judgment of the past in the epideictic context of announcing what the new South Africa was. When it succeeds, epideictic rhetoric closes any gap between appearance and reality, between agreement and truth. As I will show in the final section of this chapter, democratic self-knowledge unfolds itself in successful epideictic rhetoric.[35]

Rhetorical Friendship

Liberalism assumes that modern states are characterized by a diversity that makes appeals to *ethos* and pathos unpersuasive and sometimes coercive. Liberals would tell the TRC to keep reasoning as formal as possible just because South Africa's citizens had so little in common. The more diverse the community the more limited rationality must be. But in a context such as the South African revolution, limiting oneself to formal rationality is self-defeating. Just when we need *ethos* the most, we cannot have it or use it. The TRC is an important counterexample to the liberal self-restriction of practical reason.

Aristotle's great idea—the third thesis in my Introduction—is that the *ethos* that is, and ought to be, the most powerful and authoritative source of belief must be an *ethos* created by the argument (*Rhetoric* I.2.1356a5–13). That is, the friendship and trust constituted by and in argument is better than friendship and trust that comes from other sources such as common blood, a common creed, or shared preferences. A purely argumentative *ethos* and trust might seem more limited and so less valuable and powerful. This book is an invitation to reverse that judgment.

If we are talking about relying on a preexisting *ethos* of reputation or shared beliefs, then of course homogeneity and consensus are necessary for making ethical appeals, as they are for simple comprehension. This is the appeal of Hirsch's liberal strategy. On the other hand, if by *ethos* we mean *ethos* created by the argument itself, then that need for uniformity disappears. Aristotle is as concerned in his own way as we are about making political communities out of heterogeneous populations without requiring unity of either blood or creed. Such political communities flourish only when *homonoia*, being of one mind, is restricted to the common activity of reasoning, and not shared beliefs. We need to share dispositions to act, that is, to share *practical* knowledge.[36] Communities need a common *ethos*, not a common logos.

Rhetorically, we don't trust in people who agree with us, or who look like us, but trust in people whom we think are engaged with us in a common project. Trust and *ethos* that come from argument alone can be more politically valuable than trust and *ethos* grounded in what seem to be more solid and real factors. The more we trust in reasoning, the less we need to worry about shared ends, shared values, and presupposed truths. The more we trust in reasoning, the less has to be off-limits to our disputes and deliberations.

Limiting *ethos* to rational *ethos* offers a way of understanding trust and friendship that avoids the awkwardness of imposing Aristotelian ethical concerns on modern liberal democracies. If friendship means presenting one's beliefs, desires, and values as arguments and charitably interpreting another's appeals as arguments, then it does not have to extend past the rhetorical situation itself. Rhetorically, caring about one another's virtue means treating each other as engaged in a common enterprise of reasoned deliberation.

Rhetorically, when friendship is tied to argument, it is also limited to argument. We do not have to yearn for Aristotle's imagined polis. Caring about one another's virtue, making political participation into a positive good—these can be interpreted rhetorically so that they do not carry connotations of community inappropriate for pluralistic democracy. This sort of friendship does not mean affection, just as good will (*eunoia*), a crucial component of political friendship in Aristotle, need not involve "intensity or desire" (*Ethics* IX.6.1166b30–1167a12). We can be friendlier in rhetorical and rational terms with strangers with whom we are working than with intimates and family. We have to be guarded in our conversations with friends and family, because we fear they will take things personally, while we can be honest and open with strangers because we expect them to take what we say at face value and not look for hidden motives. Rhetorical friendship means treating each other as rational agents. Treating each other rationally takes more than a formal method. It takes intellectual virtues, ways of thinking that engage the entire person, his or her character. The friendlier we are, the more I interpret what you say charitably and rationally.

Interest and Ethos versus Sympathy

Since the TRC hearings were such an emotionally powerful experience for all concerned, it might seem that an understanding of truth and community centering on reasoning and character must fail to do it justice. When Aristotelian rhetoric makes reasoning and argument the center of persuasion, and makes *ethos* the most authoritative of the three sources of persuasion, doesn't he denigrate and minimize the role of the emotions? Starting with the Stoics, it has seemed attractive to replace an ethics and rhetoric that center on interest and citizenship with a more ecumenical ethics and rhetoric of sympathy.[37]

I think that the charge of a neglect or denigration of the emotions by practical reason is a half truth worth sorting out. The *Rhetoric* itself obviously does not neglect the emotions. After establishing the primacy of reason, Aristotle explores in detail a series of emotions in Book II, with none of the hesitation one might expect from the polemics at the start of Book I. Subordinate to argument, pathos becomes not only part of a rational system of production of arguments but in addition becomes subject to rational normative criteria of appropriateness. The passions subordinate to argument are not bodily affections, but are limited to emotions with rational content of desert, justice, and expectations. "The orator persuades through his hearers, when they are led into *pathos* by his *logos*" (1356a14).

But whatever Aristotle does in the *Rhetoric*, the accusation against its slighting of the power and value of the passions still carries weight. It is a charge we should look at closely, because, however unusual the TRC may have been, the South African experience of outsiders challenging common opinion in the name of truth is one that we can expect liberal democracies to have to face frequently in the future. In the *Ethics* someone can only have full ethical relations with fellow citizens, that is, adult, male, property-holding sons of citizens. The better the state, the more restricted citizenship is, and so the more limited the number of people with whom I can have full ethical relations.

No wonder Aristotle is often thought an inappropriate source of practical wisdom for contemporary problems. There are no moral relationships to humanity in general. Correspondingly, all the emotions discussed in the *Rhetoric* are specifically civic emotions. The *Rhetoric* shows me how to have ethical relations with people with whom I can talk and to whom I can listen. Ethical relationships are necessarily reciprocal. There can be inequalities of power, wealth, and intelligence, but there must be an equality of citizenship.

This ethical and rhetorical vision obviously lacks connections with people who cannot reciprocate. At best, helpless and speechless people have others who speak for them, in the way that the Aristotelian citizen can have indirect and derivative moral relationships with women, children, and slaves. Therefore Aristotle can easily give in the temptation to describe such people as emotional rather than rational, and thus as less than fully human. Whatever its uses in ancient Athens, a morality and a rhetoric restricted to fellow citizens seems too narrow for today's moral problems. Therefore, the reasoning goes, we should look to sympathy to extend our moral boundaries to address contemporary problems. We need more pathos, not more reason or *ethos*.[38]

What does Aristotle have to offer instead of the attractive idea that sympathy and benevolence are at the root of both morality and rhetoric? To deliberate together, we have to have a shared interest, a shared end. That is *homonoia* or concord. For me to accord you citizenship in my moral community, I have to be convinced that we share interests. Then we can deliberate together and so be of one mind, and so be political friends. In South African terms, I have to be convinced that we—black and white, privileged and poor, former perpetrators, beneficiaries, and victims—share a future. Whites had to believe that blacks would not treat them as they were treated.[39]

In South Africa, the cold calculations of interest arguably made a more solid ground for community, for truth and reconciliation, than sympathy. The sufferings and oppression of blacks were always there for whites to see, but sympathy only became an active and powerful force when whites had no choice but to listen to blacks. This necessity was not a product of sympathy but of interest. At that point, the history of injustices became part of democratic knowledge.[40]

The shared interest that makes deliberation possible may seem a weak reed in comparison with sympathy as a bond of the community of moral concern, so we need to argue more carefully here. Even if calculation finally made whites open the boundaries of their moral community in South Africa, there had to be emotional responses that, overtly or not, did the real work. Sympathy can overcome the shortcomings of an ethics that ends at the borders of community by including the excluded. Sympathy not only has these moral advantages. It is also supposed to underlie persuasion itself, as you share my pain, indignation, and hope. Sympathy seems morally and rhetorically more powerful than interest and *ethos* precisely because it does not depend on reciprocity.

Those attractions of sympathy are too good to be true. Sympathy means finding someone sympathetic. They are suffering. We are not, although we feel their pain. Valorizing sympathy in this way can lead to competition for the title of victim. Prior to 1989 both sides in South Africa appealed for the sympathy of the United States and Western Europe by presenting itself as besieged and threatened in a sea of violent and ruthless enemies, blacks by the white rulers of apartheid and whites by the encircling black and communist regimes nearby. Appeals to sympathy lead naturally to an arms race in competitive victimization. "Of all the words which console and reassure men, justice is the only one which the oppressor does not dare to pronounce, while humanity is on the lips of all tyrants."[41]

The advantages and disadvantages of sympathy are contrary to those of reciprocity. Sympathy widens our moral circles. But its power reminds me of certain strands of Christianity. The poor are always with us. We have a special obligation to the poor. All such moral concern assumes that there is Us, the Christians, and Them, the poor. "Ressentiment fixes the identities of the injured and the injuring as social positions and codifies as well the meanings of their actions against all possibilities of indeterminacy, ambiguity, and struggle for resignification or repositioning."[42] But although sympathy creates an apparently wider field for moral relationships than does reciprocity, citizenship, and interest, it is burdened by its asymmetrical nature. Civic rhetoric and civic morality exclude the voices of outsiders, while a rhetoric and morality of sympathy runs the danger of condescension. In the long run, I'd rather be a citizen than be the object of your pity. In the next chapter I will talk about the difficulties of comparing different conceptions of rhetoric, so I don't want to advertise this quick comparison of an ethics and rhetoric of reason and interest with a rhetoric and ethics of sympathy as decisive. But I do maintain that what might seem an obvious reason to abandon Aristotle's emphasis on reason and *ethos* is not decisive either. The TRC impressively avoided fixing positions in the way invited by a rhetoric of sympathy.

Democratic Knowledge

Practical reason starts from the *ethos* of a community, not from private, expert knowledge. When it works well, practical reason develops that given *ethos*, makes it into something better. Consider again the difference between how Douglas and Lincoln appealed to the *ethos* of their community in making arguments about the expansion of slavery. Douglas thought that the will of the people, what everybody knows, should be dispositive. Since citizens disagreed about slavery, we should privatize the disagreement, let different people hold different truths. Lincoln maintained that the nation had to commit itself to the truth of the proposition that all men are created equal. He didn't criticize Douglas's appeal to the will of the people from some transcendent standpoint. Equality was not a truth imported from outside the community, but part of the American *ethos*, although certainly not something that could be revealed by public opinion polls. In Rousseau's terms, Douglas appealed to the will of all, Lincoln to the general will.

Lincoln shows that practical reasoning based on *ethos* need not be conservative. Both Lincoln and Douglas argued from the *ethos* of the nation, but Lincoln shows that drawing on the *ethos* of the community for the premises of an argument is not confined to speaking by telling the audience what they want to hear. In later chapters I will show how practical inference, in drawing out implications of what someone believes, can lead to discoveries and implications not anticipated by those who hold the original beliefs. Practical reason will be ampliative. We can rely on the authority of a text or other source of legitimacy without becoming the passive organ of transmission for that authority. That a speaker base his or her *ethos* on that of the audience can increase, not decrease, the possibilities of argument for the speaker.

Lincoln drew his premise in the Gettysburg Address that all men are created equal from the Declaration of Independence. But nothing was fixed about what dedication to such a proposition committed the nation to. He acknowledged the indeterminacy of such an *ethos* by observing in the Second Inaugural that both sides in the civil war read the same Bible and prayed to the same God. His *ethos* relied on argument to transform the shared dedication to equality into a new commitment to abolish slavery, a new birth of freedom. Americans have been arguing ever since concerning what more we are committed to, whether to a color blind Constitution or a color blind society, when those two are not identical. The scope of commitment will be the subject of chapter 3.

Temporarily and occasionally, as in Lincoln's speeches and actions, in judicial decisions such as *Brown,* and executive orders such as Truman's desegregating the Armed Forces, the *ethos* of a leader makes the *ethos* of the community determinate. Ethical leadership, as in Lincoln's case, is not alien wisdom imposed on a passive audience. It is the realization, in the argument of the speaker, of the *ethos* of the community. That *ethos* is transformed as it is realized.

In similar ways, the TRC developed its country's democratic *ethos.* Successful epideictic rhetoric is a development of self-knowledge. If South Africa had become democratic simply by expanding the franchise, the number of interests represented would have been increased. The past would be ignored, and people would settle down to the business of making money. The TRC permitted a more profound transformation. It changed the *ethos* of the country by changing its common or democratic knowledge.

Democratic or public knowledge is not knowledge that everyone has. Normally, if I know something I also know that I know. But what might be an automatic transition for individuals is different for communities. There are things that each of us might know, but which *we* do not know because it is not public knowledge, not democratic knowledge, not a part of what Vico and more recently Gadamer called *sensus communis.*[43] If we cannot acknowledge that we know something, it cannot figure in our deliberations. There is an extensive literature on the difference between public and private preferences, but the relation between private and public knowledge has not been explored in analogous ways. Yet, as Dewey puts it, "the primary problem of the public [is] to achieve such recognition of itself as will give it weight."[44] Self-knowledge is an ethical problem requiring intellectual virtues oriented to discovering truth.

When each citizen knows something, then epideictic rhetoric, through symbolic affirmations and rituals, including ritual trials, can convert knowledge from something that each person knows to something that everybody knows and which therefore can figure in deliberations. Widely distributed knowledge becomes shared knowledge, a rhetorical and rational version of Rousseau's conversion of the will of all into the general will.[45]

Making common knowledge truly common is the function of epideictic rhetoric, as opposed to the deliberative rhetoric that calculates means to an end and judicial or forensic rhetoric that determines guilt or innocence in the past. It concerns collective responsibility as opposed to individual guilt. As Robert Meister puts it, "Is the sharing of guilt for the crimes that one did not commit more important to the moral foundation of national recovery than accountability for the crimes that actually occurred? Must there be consensus on the *truth?*"[46] I can know that the government uses torture, but my knowledge is transformed when I find that you know it as well. Like the Eichmann trial, the TRC created such public knowledge of something that many private individuals already knew. As Madison puts it in *Federalist* 49, "If it be true that all governments rest on opinion, it is no less true that the strength of opinion in each individual, and its practical influence on his conduct, depends much on the number which he supposes to have entertained the same opinion."

Many of the failures of social science come from a neglect of the difference between what each knows and what all know. Public opinion surveys can measure the opinions of each, but how those are summed into the opinion of all cannot be known in advance. The difference between the knowledge of all and democratic knowledge creates the apparent discontinuities of political revolutions, from Iran to South Africa. Each knew something, but if it wasn't public knowledge, it wasn't known by the community. Suddenly each realized that everyone else knew too. Then common opinion was radically different from what it had just been. Hence too both the truth and the falsity of the after the fact claims that "we didn't know" so common after the Holocaust. Many individuals are not in a position to know something, even when they have adequate evidence, without public knowledge they can adhere to. Making explicit what everybody knows, saying what goes without saying, can transform the subject-matter of political deliberations and the range of political options.[47]

> We that come from the old order—or the majority of us—are horrified by the stories that victims of gross human rights violations have told over the past year. We are horrified and feel betrayed. . . . We feel our dignity impaired. That things like these were possible, right under our noses. How could this have happened? We are victims of the cruelest fraud committed against us! . . . But the experience of those who come from the struggle, those who were on the receiving end of these things, the things that horrify us . . . this pain can help us soften in our own indignity at the betrayal. . . . If we want to make a contribution to the future of a healthy South Africa, of a country where they can be us and we can be them, where we can all be us— then we will have to endure the larger pain of sharing their pain. Then we must get beyond the luxury of wallowing in our own pain.[48]

Democratic knowledge has as its counterpart democratic ignorance. Just as communities that aim at consensus also are communities in which we agree to disagree, so democratic knowledge is never complete, and requires democratic ignorance as a complement. Each of us might know something that we as a community cannot know, and so cannot use as the basis for deliberations. We need such ignorance most clearly in judicial contexts. There are truths that are not admissible as evidence. If I am trying to prove that you are a rapist, I may not be allowed to show photographs of the violent effects of the assault in question, since they say nothing about whether you are guilty. In legal language, the "prejudicial effect" of these truths outweighs their "probative value." But we also exclude some things that each of us knows from deliberative rhetoric. Each of us might know that women live longer than men, and that white Americans live longer than black Americans. However, as a public we are ignorant of these data. We cannot use them, for example, as the basis for arguing that women should pay more into retirement accounts than men, or that blacks should pay more than whites for medical insurance. We are democratically ignorant of these facts, as of many other facts about race, gender, and class. Maybe we should be. But whether we should be or not, the reasons we can share depend not only on what the reasons are but on who we are. In all these cases, their likely prejudicial effects may outweigh any value of using them as the basis for deliberations. Democratic ignorance is often the realm of the private. And so juries are routinely told to ignore something they just heard. This is not a demand of amnesia but that something not become common knowledge.[49]

To take another example, it may be that Congressional investigations without judicial procedural safeguards can discover facts that more formal methods cannot find. But often repugnance at those inquiries says that here are some facts that are not worth knowing, not at the cost of using such methods. What democracies know and what they do not know, what they should know and should not know, is an ethical question. The TRC constantly had to face the possibility that some truths should remain untold. "What you believe to be true depends on who you believe yourself to be."[50]

What we know is transformed when it changes from what each knows to what everybody knows. Brute desires give way to rational desires. Dewey puts this transformation this way:

> In justifying our actions and our requests to one another we normally make our case by explaining why it is that we want a certain thing rather than merely citing the fact that we do prefer it and indicating the strength of our preference. In a situation in which there is real disagreement over what is to be done, to be willing to say only, "I prefer . . ." amounts to deliberate incommunicativeness or even imperiousness.[51]

Selfish preferences are replaced by judgments about what is best for all. Moving from being an isolated "I" to being part of a "We," even if I do so in order to get something from you, is a civilizing process. I am civilized by having to persuade you. The rhetorical activities of deliberation, judgment, and celebration make our desires and opinions ethical as much as they make them rational, as they make a plurality of people into a community.

The TRC made South Africa better by making truth public. Private knowledge of atrocities became public. Blacks typically said, "We already know these things," while many whites said: "We didn't know." Both sets of people were transformed when the past became common knowledge. However, there is no rule that we should always aim at truth, not agreement, at single rather than multiple truth, at agreement over agreeing to disagree, or even knowledge over ignorance. And so the ominous truth of my epigram. If friendships are sometimes enhanced by ignorance, it is often just the kind of ignorance I am describing here, where both friends may themselves know something, but, by leaving it unsaid, stop the knowledge from being shared, reciprocal knowledge.[52]

But this idea of democratic knowledge, as well as democratic agreement, gives grounds for hope as well. Krog quotes a remark about the TRC that expresses this hope: "Truth does not bring back the dead, but releases them from silence."[53] What we know and who we are vary together, recalling my earlier claim that truth is not only a relation between propositions and the facts they represent but a relation between speakers and hearers. We aren't done bringing truth to a community when each becomes aware of something. The community as a whole must do the knowing. When such common knowledge emerges, so does friendship and a common *ethos*. The interesting rhetorical challenge for truth in politics is to move from something which each of us knows to something that *we* know.

The TRC was an exercise in practical rationality. Through it, South Africa persuaded itself that it was a democratic nation, and so became one. The rationality was exercised by the witnesses and judges of the TRC, and equally by the national audience who daily listened to reports and testimony in person throughout the country and on the radio. The nation and the TRC's judges were constantly making decisions about how to discover and present the truth about the past, deciding how to avoid having to choose between truth and community, and figuring out how to make the truth the possession of the community and not of individual powerful or powerless speakers. They needed to decide whether in each case to accept multiple truths, insist on a single truth, or settle for agreement.

Making these decisions well depends on democratic friendship and ethical argument. The friendlier we are, the more the rationality of our transaction is elevated from agreement to truth, and from the instrumental to the rational. The more rational I am, the more the world is rational to me. The good research scientist sees the world as more law-governed than the rest of us can. For practical reason, increase in rationality consists in seeing more of persuasion as rational. The more appeals, by oneself or another, to emotion and character are rational, the more rational I am. But I cannot become more rational by fiat or in isolation. The increase in rationality is a communal job.

The TRC was a democratic achievement. The South African people learned how to speak and listen in new ways. They built a community out of such discourse. The constitution of a community which aimed at truth and not agreement did not solve all the frightening problems of race, of poverty, of emigration and immigration, in South Africa. Rationality and friendship can only do so much, because there is more to the world than our opinions and arguments.

What does the TRC teach us about the circumstances of friendship? First, friendly relations between speaker and audience consist in speakers treating hearers rationally, and audiences hearing speakers as presenting rational appeals. Second, there is a circularity between the way friendship increases as we treat emotional and ethical appeals as rational, and the way expanding the rational to include the emotional and ethical increases friendship. Finally, the circumstances of friendship include the ambition of aiming at truth and not simply agreement.

CHAPTER 2

Confronting the Sophist

The central issue of philosophy and critical thought since the eighteenth century has always been, still is, and will, I hope, remain the question: What is this Reason that we use? What are its historical effects? What are its limits, and what are its dangers? How can we exist as rational beings, fortunately committed to practicing a rationality that is unfortunately crisscrossed by intrinsic dangers? One should remain as close to this question as possible, keeping in mind that it is both central and extremely difficult to resolve.[1]

The instrumental conception of reason is often tied to the claim that reason is a historical artifact, but the claim that reason is a mere servant of power misunderstands the historical basis of reason, and, above all, the meaning or living and thinking within a culture. The easy assimilation of reason to an instrument of raw power forgets that debates over abstract concepts like equality and liberty are always simultaneously attempts to understand and define what is more or less reasonable. They are collective exercises in the historical creation and development of reason. Viewed through a purely instrumentalist lens we forget the extent to which intellectual disputes are exactly what they purport to be—*attempts by the members of a culture to discover and name what is true and false, better and worse, efficacious and inefficacious.*[2]

In the last chapter I tried to show how we can learn about practical rationality from the Truth and Reconciliation Commission process. The TRC confronted deep philosophical problems, of relativism, of what sort of unity a community must be, in practically urgent form. It found political friendship in an unexpected place, and it showed how with friendship rationality can expand to include *ethos* and pathos, and how a community can aim at truth as well as agreement.

But of course one could tell other, more cynical, stories about the TRC. White South Africans realized that they would have to share power, and mostly tried to share as little as possible. Black South Africans saw that they were going to be full citizens, at least legally, and did what they could to acquire full economic and political power. Both sides fought for power, but made it appear that they were struggling for legitimate power. Instead of directly fighting over power they fought over the meaning of history. The appearance of rationality was just a cover for interest and desire.[3] In chapter 1 I showed how South Africans struggled to find common ground between incommensurable visions of the identity of their community. Now I want to look at the philosophical issues of incommensurability between competing accounts of the place of practical reason within such struggles.

A Forced Confrontation

My account of the TRC featured a conception of rhetoric that makes reasoning central. A competing cynical account could see all persuasion as manipulation. Judging between these two competing narratives about South Africa means judging between two competing pictures of rhetoric and reason. We quickly find ourselves facing philosophical issues of incommensurability and judgment: can one claim fairly that one incommensurable alternative is superior to another? Must one choose between truth and victory, or can they be compatible? Is the limitation of rhetoric to argument an arbitrary, or moralistic, restriction, or is it empowering? Is rhetoric rational or manipulative?

I can't think of a better example of the philosophical problems of judging between incommensurables than that between a philosophy that remakes rhetoric in its image as a rational procedure, and a rhetoric that envelops all and remakes philosophy into just another way in which people manipulate images to dominate one other. The ancient and perennial quarrel between philosophy and rhetoric is a prime example of a confrontation between incommensurable and incomparable alternatives. Two forms of rhetoric face off, one rooted in reasoning and the other in emotion, images, and style. How can we choose between them? From within, each mode of thinking seems self-evident, and proposed alternatives seem obviously false or unintelligible. To compare them is an act of judgment that makes them into objects. But ultimate orientations or modes of thinking are ways of looking and acting; they are not objects to look at, and so judging between them makes them into something they are not. To judge between incommensurable modes of thought is not a good way to make friends.

Yet comparisons between incommensurable ultimates are not only impossible, they are also inevitable. The student who forcefully claims that the questions I ask in philosophy classes have no right answers, that his opinions about philosophy are his own and cannot be judged by another—incommensurability par excellence—will quickly contest an unfavorable grade. Whether a verdict in a tenure case can be appealed turns on whether the committee making the judgment reasoned from evidence or was influenced, consciously or not, by powerful images and emotions. As intellectual systems, basic modes of thinking may be incommensurable. But as ways of living, they have to be comparable.

The quarrel between rhetoric and philosophy is not only ancient; it is all around us in the *Kulturkämpfe* that like to make political debates into metaphysical issues. From the legal realists a few generations ago through contemporary feminist and critical legal studies, many people see legal argument as a deceptive form covering more fundamental political and irrational motives, while their opponents see the "external" influences these partisans celebrate as factors that legal institutions should minimize or expel. Each looks naive to the other, always a good sign of incommensurability. Some people see political deliberation as a sincere effort to use reasoning to formulate the best course of action while others see it as a way each of us tries to get as much for ourselves as we can and give up as little as possible. Is there a principled difference between practical wisdom and cleverness or cunning, between reasoning and rationalization?[4]

We already have a superb example of the confrontation between two visions of rhetoric and philosophy, one which brings to attention the philosophic issues involved in incommensurable confrontations. Plato's *Gorgias* illustrates how the two sides fail to share even the most basic premises or criteria for a successful argument. Socrates and Callicles see each other as ridiculous (484e1, e3, 485a7, 509b4–5), and as promoting an activity fit only for children (484c) or slaves. Socrates says that the discourse of each is disciplined by two loves, and the objects of love seem beyond dispute. In such a case, the "common experience" Socrates and Callicles is both common and incommensurable:

> If human beings didn't share common experiences, some sharing one, others sharing another, but one of us had some unique experience not shared by others, it wouldn't be easy for him to communicate what he experienced to the other. I say this because I realize that you and I are both now actually sharing a common experience: each of the two of us is a lover of two objects, I of Alcibiades, Clinias' son, and of

philosophy, and you of the people (*demos*) of Athens and of Demos who's the son of Pyrilampes. (*Gorgias* 481d)

This chapter is an exercise in imagination. I want to invite Aristotle to replace Socrates in the conversation and see what kind of confrontation there could be between the sophists as Plato represents them and the arguments about rhetoric that Aristotle supplies in the *Rhetoric*.[5] Socrates forces us to choose between aiming at truth and aiming at victory. Speaking for Plato, James White frames the problem this way:

> One cannot be a propagandist in the service of truth or an advocate in the service of justice, for the character and the motives are wrong. And character and motives are for these purposes everything, for "truth" and "justice" are not abstract absolutes, to be attained or not in materially measurable ways; these are words that defined shared motives out of which a community and a culture can be built and a character made for the individual and his world. They express an attitude, imply a process, and promise a community.[6]

Aristotle has learned from that battle of incommensurables and sees the two goals of truth and victory as compatible. There are certainly ways of aiming at victory incompatible with seeking the truth, and he as much as Plato holds the sophists guilty of that (*Metaphysics* IV.2.1004b18–27), but trying to persuade an audience can be an epistemically and ethically respectable activity. Getting an audience to do what I want on the basis of *their* beliefs can be respectable, as I argued in my example of the ethical variation on *ad hominem* arguments in the first chapter. Sometimes the fact that we are trying to persuade someone to advance our own interests corrupts our reasoning, and our relations to the audience, and sometimes it enhances both our thought and our relationships.

I turn to Aristotle because he asks us to pay a smaller price to abandon sophistic than Socrates demanded. While the sophists debunk any distinction between internal and external factors, such as the distinction between reasons that should influence our practical decisions and emotions that should not, and while Socrates' response was to fix such a distinction metaphysically, Aristotle allows us to draw such a line while always recognizing that it is a historically conditioned distinction, liable to contest and development. That we do not have to choose between aiming at winning and aiming at truth is prefigured in his account of humans as political animals:

> Speech is for making clear what is beneficial or harmful, and hence also what is just or unjust. For it is peculiar to human beings, in comparison to the other animals, that they alone have perception of what is good or bad, just or unjust, and the rest. And it is community in these that makes a household and a state. (*Politics* I.2.1253a13–19)

People have the power of speech, and so can communicate not only about pleasure and pain but advantage and disadvantage and *therefore* the just and the unjust. Justice is not a set of concerns different in kind from the useful, and the true is not set off in a realm distinct from the strategic. We perceive and talk about justice because we perceive and talk about the useful and the harmful. Aristotle differs from Plato in thinking that we can aim at effectiveness and at rightness together.[7]

Thus James White sees true community as transforming the incompatibility between the desire for victory and for truth into a permanent tension characteristic of communities of friendship:

> The function of the law is to maintain a language that keeps alive this very tension between fact and ideal, expediency and justice, self and other; this tension is in fact essential to the practice of talking about what justice requires. You can see this tension in my own defense of law: when I say that the lawyer makes the "best case" that can be made in the circumstances, does that mean the case that is most persuasive or most just? You would draw a sharp line between them; I would not say that they are the same, but I would say that the answer to that question is always, or almost always, unclear. For to be the "most just" argument it must be a workable one; to be workable, it must be just, at least in the sense that it must maintain the possibility, essential to the existence of self and community, of appealing to ideals that limit the will.[8]

Aristotle's conception of friendship develops a conception of rhetoric that is true to White's "tension."

This, then, is a confrontation between Aristotle and the Callicles of Plato's *Gorgias*. Two incommensurable visions of rhetoric, Aristotelian and sophistic, face each other. One makes reasoning fundamental and the other sees persuasion revolving around images, emotion, and style. Aristotle opens the *Rhetoric* by opposing his art of rhetoric, which has reasoning at the center, to the arts of the sophists who claim that all persuasion is emotional manipulation and for whom all reasoning is rationalization. Aristotle sees internal connections between *pistis* as a rhetorical argument and *pistis* as the state of belief in the audience:

Artistic method [for rhetoric] is concerned with *pisteis,* and since *pistis* is a sort of demonstration (for we most believe [*pisteuomen*] when we suppose something to have been demonstrated) and rhetorical demonstration is an enthymeme (and this is, generally speaking, the strongest [*kuriōetaton*] of the *pisteis*) and the enthymeme is a sort of reasoning. (*Rhetoric* I.1.1355a3–7)

All opinion (*doxa*) requires conviction (*pistis*), conviction implies being persuaded (*pepeithai*), and persuasion implies discourse (*logos*). Conviction (*pistis*) belongs to no beasts, whereas appearance (*phantasia*) belongs to many of them. Every belief follows conviction, conviction follows being persuaded, persuasion follows reason. . . . There are beasts who have the possibility of imagination, but none are disposed to reason. (*De Anima* III.3.428a19–24)

Aristotle himself does not take the sophists seriously as Plato does. He thinks that they are so philosophically uninteresting that any practical dangers they present are not worth extended thought. Simply making laws against speakers getting off the point will do. If only we could have such confidence today. We see abundant evidence that sophistic works. After all, there are many flourishing Departments of Communication and programs in English Composition that proceed along sophistical lines. The town I live in recently hired someone from a Communication Department who is a putative expert in "visioning" to help them with planning future growth. Educators and businesses vote with dollars that sophistic is the right model of persuasion. Advertising agencies and political consultants, jury consultants and flamboyant defense attorneys make a lot more money selling their talents than I do. When Callicles claims that philosophy is all right for the young as part of liberal education, but that real men use sophistic, he has a lot of evidence on his side. With all that track record of success, shouldn't an impartial jury believe the sophist who claims that all persuasion works through the power of images, not argument, and shouldn't we regard claims about rational persuasion as naive and self-serving? If Aristotelian rhetoric is right, why am I not rich? The sophistic race to the bottom seems to beat the Aristotelian race to the top every time.

Philosophical Dimensions of the Confrontation

The contested nature of success makes trying to adjudicate between kinds of rhetoric difficult, a sure sign of a confrontation between incommensurables. Politicians and advertisers who rely on sophistic rhetoric can point to its successes. Aristotelian rhetoric points to a different form of success. It's Willie Horton on one side, and Burke, Lincoln, and Churchill on the other.[9] With nothing at stake we can afford to praise and admire a rhetoric based on reasoning, but when it counts, people line up on the sophistical side.[10] Lincoln lost the senatorial election to Douglas, and Churchill's Munich Agreement speech and Burke's Conciliation Speech were also on the losing side. We'd like to think of ourselves as engaged in rational rhetoric, but when things really count, have to fall back on sophistic. "In public people praise above all what is just and fine, in private they wish for useful things" (*Rhetoric* II.23.1399a29–30).

The contest between Aristotle and the sophists is a paradigmatically philosophical argument. Here are two theories fighting not only for knowledge but for power, the power to diminish the significance of inconvenient contrary evidence, the power to denigrate and discount, and sometimes discipline and punish, audiences who do not behave as the theory predicts and mandates. In such incommensurable confrontations, the power to speak can be the power to silence.[11]

In such a confrontation between incommensurables, no purely empirical refutation will work. If it had, one of these would have disappeared long ago. We can, though, make an ethical, as opposed to an empirical, choice between these incommensurable alternatives. While weighing empirical evidence allows experts to decide, displaying ethical grounds for the choice between conceptions of rhetoric keeps that choice in the hands of the relevant political audience.

Because success is contested, it is tempting to choose between them by claiming that a preferred vision of rhetoric leads to morally or politically superior results. There is, though, no correlation between conceptions of rhetoric and political outcomes. While at many crucial points in the past reason was seen as a powerful democratizing force, now we are often told that it stacks the deck in favor of those privileged by cultural or economic status. Kenneth Burke was right when he said that "the history of debunking is interwoven with the history of liberalism,"[12] but that association has salience only when the debunkers are opposed to the powerful, not when those in power denigrate rationality to keep outsiders out. Sometimes sophistic stands on the side of the dispossessed, the outsiders, rebelling against formal rules of law and argument which serve only to reinforce existing status and relations of power. But the South African example suggests that sophistic can equally be used on the other side, as whites used the language of pluralism and basic rights to defend traditional privilege, much as creationists and holocaust deniers use the language of free and open debate to claim an equal standing between sense and nonsense. Rational rhetoric can be used to topple the privileges of those whose rhetoric depends on deference and similar retrograde emotions. Argumentative and emotional rhetoric can both be used in the service of both progressive and reactionary causes.[13]

Empirical evidence doesn't settle the matter, nor does partisanship. There is a third unhelpful way of contrasting rational and sophistic rhetoric, by making the issues between them supposedly follow from ontological or epistemological differences. It is question-begging to argue for the superiority of rational rhetoric on the grounds of some ontological or epistemological high theory about the nature of reality or whether truth should be spelled with a capital letter or not, the tactic often adopted by defenders of Western civilization and "Enlightenment rationality" against the insurgent postmodernist multiculturalists.[14] Such "proofs" not only are never persuasive except to the converted; they should not be. These claims about reality and knowledge follow from rhetorical practices, and do not ground them. Arguing about whether reality exists is simply a way of raising one's voice, not elevating the things talked about.

In the absence of such decisive evidence, what is one to do? There can be no purely empirical proof of the superiority of one or another form of rhetoric, but that doesn't mean that empirical evidence is beside the point. The way each paradigm points to evidence is itself revealing. In pointing to its successes, the sophist offers two distinct sorts of proof for the claim that persuasion works sophistically. First, people think persuasion works that way, and so they pay the sophist. Second, scientific, empirical tests show that the sorts of strategies and tactics the sophists practice and teach actually work.

Neither of these proofs is decisive, because the idea of success is ambiguous. Aristotle distinguishes internal from external criteria for success; the sophists rely solely on the latter: "The function of rhetoric is not to persuade but to find out the available means of persuasion in each case, as is true of all the other arts; for neither is it the function of medicine to create health but to promote this as much as possible; for it is nevertheless possible to treat well those who cannot recover health" (I.1.1355b10–13). Aristotelian arts have internal criteria for success. Rhetoric fulfills its function by relying on argument. There might be no disputing the fact that some audience voted for the sophistic speaker, but no agreement at all on the significance of that fact.

Aristotle says that to rely on the audience as the measure of success corrupts the audience (*Rhetoric* I.1.1354a24), an argument reminiscent of Socrates' claim in the *Gorgias* that while Callicles thinks he is ruling the many, they are in fact ruling him. Not only do the two conceptions of rhetoric have different ideas of success, but they also differently interpret the other set of data, what people think goes on in persuasion. Sophists point to the fact that *speakers* believe that powerful images will do the trick, and so clients line up to hire them. Aristotelians point to the fact that *audiences* believe that they are consenting rationally to one appeal over another.

On its understanding of the nature of persuasion, the truth of sophistic lies in the fact that the same content, the same message, will be received more favorably if packaged and delivered by the sophist than if someone else tries to persuade. Thus Gorgias claims that he can get patients to take their medicine better than his brother the physician (459a–b). For such a conception to be testable, the persuasive powers of form and content must be separable. Therefore sophists turn to kinds of persuasion like advertising, where there are no differences between competing products, and the decision to buy one or the other depends only on form alone. We can only really know that the content is the same when the content is too unimportant to matter.

Sophistic can make a case for its superiority only when things don't matter. But separating form from content is much more contestable, more theory-laden, when content does count. To presume that the same words, delivered by different speakers, convey the same message, begs important ethical and political questions and makes metaphysical assumptions about sameness and identity. I can testify personally that the "same" words, drawn from the "same Bible," sound and mean something completely different when they are a reading from the Old Testament during a Catholic mass and when they are a reading from the Hebrew Bible in a synagogue. The "same" argument that I should give money to help former Russians settle in Israel is a different argument when it comes from my Rabbi or from Pat Robertson. Consider these remarks of Dewey:

> Even when the words remain the same, they mean something very different when they are uttered by a minority struggling against

repressive measures, and when expressed by a group that has attained power and then uses ideas that were once weapons of emancipation as instruments for keeping the power and wealth they have obtained. Ideas that at one time are means of producing social change have not the same meaning when they are used as means of preventing social change.[15]

For sophistic to be testable, two speakers must try to persuade with the same message, and the victory has to go to the one who better uses sophistic technique. But this standard for success is very odd, both rhetorically and ethically. For it to be a meaningful test, one has to assume that since sophistic works when nothing is at stake, then it will work all the more when the decision matters. Gorgias says that he teaches the ability to persuade the ignorant. Why should such a power have anything to do with persuading our equals? When choosing between things that are indifferent, I allow myself to be charmed by skillful persuasive appeals. I let free my fantasies that buying this car will let me compete for a better class of women. But when I think about the safety of my child in the back seat, I make my decisions very differently. Why think that a method of persuasion efficacious when I do not care about the issue should be a model for persuasion in general? A couple of pages ago it looked like we use sophistic whenever the result really matters to us, where we can't afford the luxury and fastidiousness of Aristotelian reliance on argument. For the sophistic proof of its superiority to work, that perception has to be reversed.

Holding content constant is a strange procedure. If a man teaches successfully by using a certain technique, yet a woman fails while doing the same thing, then, the argument goes, the students are engaged in sex discrimination. The claim presupposes that if a man does something successfully and a woman cannot, the same technique *should* have the same result. If it does not, the audience is at fault. I emphasize "should" to question the elision from a prediction to an assertion of right and desert. Where the sophist claimed to defer to the audience and formulate a system of persuasion based on what really works, it turns out that when something doesn't work, the audience bears the blame. Aristotle can claim without violating his own way of thinking that when audiences are not moved by arguments, they are corrupt, but sophists are not supposed to make such criticisms of their audiences. Not if the judgment of the audience is the measure of success. Therefore the proof of the truth of sophistic is not purely empirical. Nothing ever is.

Two Definitions of Rhetoric

Aristotle was wiser than Plato in not trying to refute the sophists. Refuting the sophists is as impossible or as pointless as refuting the skeptic. To defend reason by using reason comforts only the converted. However, once unproductive arguments about empirical success are cleared away, it is possible to defeat the sophists and uphold rationality on *ethical* grounds.

For Aristotle, according to those lines about the function of rhetoric I just quoted, rhetoricians fulfill their function not by persuading but by finding in any case the available means of persuasion. Sophists fulfill their function by persuading. Each definition is logically defensible. Neither leads to contradictions. Rhetoricians who limit themselves to argument have the advantages and disadvantages of such limitations, compared to the sophist who recognizes no limitations at all. Here is an ethical issue which Aristotelian and sophistic rhetoric can join.

At first the limitation to argument seems to be an unfair restriction, trying to persuade with one hand tied behind one's back, compared to the sophist who will do anything to win. If the goal and function of rhetoric is to persuade, then limiting oneself to argument is arbitrary, since under that definition there is nothing inherently superior about persuading through argument compared to other methods of persuasion. To prefer argument seems to appeal to an external standard which valorizes reason and denigrates emotion. Isn't that the Enlightenment prejudice against emotion, against women, against the local and the traditional from which the sophists are going to liberate us? The rhetorician limiting persuasion to argument is fastidious in a world that calls for no such restraint. Hence the sophist fights on the side of progress and can look at the Aristotelian as engaged in a nostalgic defense of his own ineffectuality. The Aristotelian rhetorician merely tries to assert moral superiority in the light of practical impotence. So the sophistic side of the issue.

On the other hand, in the right political circumstances, the limitation to rational methods can be liberating rather than restricting. If I limit myself to argument, I can engage in relations of friendship, justice, equality with the hearers. *Only* by limiting myself to argument can I have *ethical* relations with my audience, since the only rational form of *ethos* is one created through argument.[16]

In *Rhetoric* I.1 Aristotle says that the sophists neglected argument for the emotions *and* that they had no idea of *ethos.* It is one of Aristotle's most profound insights that those two go together. The limitation of the art of rhetoric to argument does not exclude rational appeals to emotion, as Aristotle shows in *Rhetoric* II. The limitation of the art of rhetoric to argument not only does not exclude *ethos,* it makes appeals to *ethos* possible. Apart from argumentative and rational relations between speaker and audience, the only kind of character or *ethos* a speaker can have is reputation. Without the limitation to argument that Aristotle insists on I must be the audience's master or its slave. I can have commercial relations, or military relations, but not ethical ones. The sophist can do anything to win, but the very lack of limits means that his "everything" is in fact not comprehensive. It cannot include things that are only available if one limits oneself to argument. One cannot be friends with someone who will do anything to win.

On this count, I find Aristotelian rhetoric ethically superior because it can have ethical relations between speaker and hearer. Rational rhetoric creates and sustains community, while sophistic cannot. It is ethically superior because it does not base its claims on the flimsy idea of success that I tried to discount in the first section, but relies on this more sophisticated criterion instead. It looked as though Aristotelian rhetoric, with its fastidious self-limitation to argument, is a luxury we might wish we could afford, but which we abandon as soon as the stakes start to matter. Now it looks like it's just the other way around, another sure sign of incommensurability.

There is a complication, though. For Aristotle, rhetoricians fulfill their function not by persuading but by finding in any case the available means of persuasion. But if that function were not at least indirectly related to persuasion, Aristotelian rhetoric would be refuted practically. If the rhetorician never or only rarely succeeded in actually persuading an audience, or succeeded only when no one cared about the outcome, the value of the art would be undermined. There is no simple answer to how much failure Aristotle's art of rhetoric can tolerate. That depends on many contingent factors, including the prestige, the honor, of rhetoric, the perceived value of deliberation. But there must be some regularity in the relation between finding the available means of persuasion and actually persuading. Doctors who successfully find the available means of healing but whose patients usually die have to have some other selling points or they will eventually lose their business. Judges whose findings of law are manifestly unjust undermine the rule of law.[17] The Aristotelian need not beat the sophist on his own terms, since we have seen how contestable and ambiguous such ideas of success are, but she cannot be consistently defeated either.

Comparing the two definitions of rhetoric gives the first ethical reason to prefer Aristotle's picture of rhetoric. The sophist has his own ethical reasons for preferring sophistic. The sophist acknowledges that his rhetoric does not sustain community. The whole point is to smash convention and rely on modes of persuasion that are not sanctioned by the ruling class, although advertisers and political consultants are equally adept at using the same techniques for less laudable purposes. The sophist dissociates himself from such uses, while pointing to them to show the power of rhetoric.

Aristotle defined rhetoric as the ability to find the available means of persuasion, and contrasted the rational methods that constituted that art with other possible ways of convincing someone. But in one way his analogy to medicine does not go far enough. His art of rhetoric is a practical rather than a productive art. We measure the excellence of other arts by their products, while evaluating rhetoric practically and ethically. Hence the permanent tension expressed in the questions of whether rhetorical facility requires ethical goodness, whether it teaches such goodness, or whether rhetorical excellence and practical wisdom are independent of each other, the permanent tension expressed earlier in my quotation from James White. These issues are not present for the other, productive, arts like medicine. The physician who limits himself to the medical art and the healer who will do anything to make her patient healthy are both measured ultimately against the health of the patient. The Aristotelian and sophistic rhetorician are tested not only by success in persuasion, but by the kind of relations between speaker and audience each engenders. We can fairly ask both argumentative and sophistic rhetoric about the sort of person one becomes by practicing them, and about the sort of community one creates in persuading one way or another.

Reflexivity as a Test

Earlier I noted that the two forms of rhetoric both appeal to data about how people in fact think persuasion works. The sophist relies on the fact that people think that others are persuaded through emotional appeals and powerful images. We look around that see others being manipulated and persuaded by images, emotion, and style. On the other hand, we look inward and think that *we* are persuaded by reason. The Aristotelian takes that introspection seriously and points to the fact that we often think that we are persuaded rationally. We encountered this Aristotelian point in the first chapter with its distinction between communities that aim at truth and those that aim at agreement. Even if we must ultimately define truth in terms of a final agreement, à la Peirce, truth and agreement constitute distinct ends.[18]

Because sophistic theories take the third-person point view, they are anti-reflexive. We might think that others are manipulable "wantons," to use Harry Frankfurt's nice term, but have trouble thinking of ourselves that way. Sophistic rhetoric must either claim that self-persuasion, deliberation, and decision are different in kind from persuasion, deliberation, and decision in interpersonal contexts, or it must think that self-persuasion is as irrational as the interpersonal case supposedly is.

To recall some familiar topoi from arguments against the legal realists, sophists can make predictions about how people will decide, but those predictions are no aid in deliberations about how one should decide. The advocate can view legal argument sophistically, as a set of predictions about which appeals will move which judges. But a judge cannot think of his or her own decisions in this way. No pathway connects a third-person point of view which centers on prediction or explanation to a first-person deliberative decision.[19] Thus the ancient sophists taught their students how to argue both sides of a question, but this facility did not lead to a valuing of the power of reason but to doubting that reasoning is actually doing any work apart from covering up the prejudices and interests that really determined which side one thought was right.

This asymmetry between prediction and deliberation does not refute the sophist. Indeed, the sophist can reply that that is exactly the point: I may *think* that I am deliberating by considering evidence and arguments, but I am in fact being moved in predictable ways, and so predictably will react one way to a male candidate and another when faced with a female in similar circumstances.

To the sophist, the Aristotelian rhetorician depends on a naive psychology that assumes that my mental processes are available to inspection and correction. A more sophisticated psychology shows that how I make decisions has nothing to do with how I think I decide. Sophistic rhetoric can be a science, since it makes predictions that can be confirmed or refuted. If self-deception is pervasive, then the lack of reflexivity, the fact that I cannot make up my mind according to sophistic theories but can only use them to persuade others, is no surprise and no defect. Marx and Freud should make us suspicious of the claims to self-knowledge of someone who claims to decide according to the best argument. Aristotelian rhetoric is instead a set of archaic beliefs resting on folk psychology, and it uses the gap between deliberation and prediction as a way of avoiding the kind of scientific tests to which sophistic is open.

While logically possible, the lack of reflexivity is an ethical defect. The theory has the ethical consequence of making the speaker, or whoever holds the theory, exempt from the processes to which the rest of us are bound. Such expert knowledge destroys community. When self-knowledge is impossible, it is impossible for the community to know itself. As we saw in chapter 1, only with common knowledge is political and social life transparent.

Even if persuasion really proceeds by manipulating images and passions, the person being persuaded still believes that he is responding to reasoning. Maybe when you say, "This is good," you really mean, "I like this a lot. You should too." But for me to be persuaded to like it too, I have to believe that you think that it is good, not that you like it and are recommending that I like it too. Maybe sophistic precepts are true. "Put your most important points first—or last." "A picture is worth a thousand words." But if such advice is valid, reality must always be hidden by false appearances. What an audience thinks is going on must have nothing to do with the actual persuasion taking place. No one can think: "Since this speaker put her most important points first, he has persuaded me." I cannot be persuaded by someone's reputation unless I think that the reputation is well grounded and that the person is really trustworthy. Which does the work, the rational appearance or the emotional reality?[20]

Even if the appearance of rationality is a false appearance, it still has to be explained. Maybe the student faced with a powerful presence in a female teacher interprets her power as authoritarian and domineering, where he would regard such power in a male teacher as a comforting sign of the authority teachers should have. But the student must think that he is responding to someone who is authoritarian and domineering. He cannot see himself wrongly interpreting as authoritarian and domineering someone who has an overwhelming amount of knowledge and presence. Therefore the sophist who wants to persuade me through images and irrational appeals has to pretend and convince me that he is persuading me through argument. For his emotional appeals to succeed, I cannot be aware of them. Such rhetoric is inherently deceptive, even if the deceptions are done with good will and for my own good.

This lack of continuity between first- and third-person views of persuasion is a serious ethical flaw. All friendship, Aristotle argues, is founded on self-friendship or self-love. "It is therefore because the good man has these various feelings towards himself and because he feels towards his friend in the same way as towards himself (for a friend is another self), that friendship is also thought to consist in one or other of these feelings, and the possession of them is thought to be the test of the friend" (*Ethics* IX.4.1166a30–33). As

I argue in detail in "The Will to Be Believed," we cannot trust someone who does not trust him or herself. Similarly, persuasion is rooted in the possibility of self-persuasion. Political deliberation depends on the deliberation that each engages in to make ethical as well as political decisions. A theory of rhetoric that on principle cannot account for how we deliberate and decide not only is incapable of generating communicative relationships that are friendly, just, and open, but such a theory has no room for selves at all. A theory that cannot be applied reflexively is ethically weak. It is practically weak too.

Therefore, the distinction between the third-person and first-person visions of persuasion diminishes the power of the sophist. Justice Cardozo once remarked, "I don't worry any more about whether I can influence the vote of the other Justices. I'm satisfied now if I can get myself to vote right."[21] Someone who thinks himself expert at moving others by predicting how they will respond to different stimuli becomes inept at argument, since he can only be using argument, not arguing, and therefore appears clever, not rational.[22] The power of a sophistic theory of communication becomes self-defeating. A speaker so aware of his superiority to his audience cannot respect the audience, and therefore will not be respected by it.

The rationality of rhetoric is present whenever there are standards beyond power. Whenever there are such standards, there is a difference between reasoning and rationalizing, and we can tell practical wisdom apart from cleverness. Clearly there are circumstances in which there is no such difference, and no standards beyond power. Without a difference between persuasion and manipulation, between reasoning and rationalizing, there is no reason to claim that persuasion is better than force. Being forced to do something leaves my insides intact in a way that being manipulated does not, so if I have to choose between the two, I would rather be forced. If persuasion is superior to force, it has to be possible for me to be persuaded while keeping my integrity.

The contest between rational and sophistic rhetoric is a permanent one because rationality never gives off sure signs, not even in circumstances with a difference between reasoning and rationalizing. In discussing the vice of boastfulness, Aristotle says that those who boast for the sake of "profit claim to have qualities that gratify other people and that allow someone to avoid detection when he claims to be what he is not—a prophet, a philosopher (*sophon*), or a doctor, for instance" (*Ethics* IV.7.1127b19–21). Socrates was mistaken for a sophist, and Plato's dialogues, from the *Apology* to the *Sophist*, illustrate the difficulties of telling philosophers and sophists apart.

The Descriptive and the Normative

I said above that the predictions of sophistic rhetoric give no help to deliberations about how to decide between the paradigms because they offer no connection between how we are persuaded and how we *should* be persuaded. (Because there is no connection, sophists have no way of successfully answering Socrates' question of whether they teach virtue. Gorgias offers to teach virtue along the way to any remedial students, but there is no connection between teaching rhetoric and teaching virtue.) If persuasion is irrational, then asking how one should decide is as pointless as asking how the planets should revolve. Sophistic theory makes normative questions otiose.

That is inadequate. Maybe when I persuade others, I want to know how I can do it, but when I want to persuade myself, or decide whom to believe, I want to know how I *should* be persuaded. In sophistic, such normative questions are left to the desires of the speaker, or some other coercive source.[23]

The *Rhetoric,* by contrast, is simultaneously about how persuasion works and about how it should work. There is no gap between "is" and "ought" because his rhetoric is a rhetoric of argument and reasoning. To the extent that rhetoric is an art of reasoning, it can be both prescriptive and normative. The "better" argument should be persuasive. Both the rhetorician and the statesman have to insure that the best argument will in fact be persuasive. The statesman does his best to make ought and is coincide by, for example, legislating against speakers getting off the point. Such a legislator, in effect, tries to create Habermas's "ideal speech situation" in which the better argument wins. The speaker makes the best argument win by the act of arguing. A good argument sustains the conditions under which arguments that should persuade do in fact persuade. The sophist will try to convince us that nothing is at stake, so that nothing but irrelevant emotions can govern our decision. If I am faced with competing rhetoricians, and need to decide which way to vote, choosing the better argument locates me and the competing rhetoricians within a political community of justice and friendship. Faced with the same competition in the absence of argument, choice becomes whim. This is an ethical reason for preferring argumentative rhetoric.

The sophistic case looks least plausible for the deliberations that Aristotle makes central to rhetoric. Maybe there is no determinate truth about the past; it's all a battle of interpretations. Some versions of history show how slaves were happier before emancipation, and others show abolition as progress. Maybe different communities have different ideas about goodness, and we cannot get outside those communal judgments to say that communities that think that some people are naturally born to govern and others to be ruled are wrong. But when it comes to deciding what to do about the future, few would maintain that if people think something is useful, then it is useful. The sophistic claim that there is no difference between reasoning and rationalizing makes little sense for deliberation about the future.

If deliberation is the genre of rhetoric that the sophist cannot account for, *ethos* is the source of conviction invisible to the sophist. It is the crucial case of the coincidence of the descriptive and the normative. In general, perhaps, the person with the best reputation is the most credible and most likely to win an argument. Such generalization can be countered, in good rhetorical fashion, by the contrary consideration that someone for whom the audience has low expectations can outdo the speaker with a reputation for eloquence and debating skills. There is no connection in either case between the normative and the descriptive. Consider instead, though, the *ethos* that Aristotle says is produced by the cogency of the argument itself. The speaker and speech with such an *ethos ought* to be the most persuasive (I.2.1356a5). To say that *ethos* "is the controlling factor in persuasion" says less that *ethos* always succeeds in persuading an audience than that it should be decisive.

The Ultimate Verdict of the Rhetorical Audience

Both Aristotelians and sophists can claim that their version of rhetoric is correct because most people think it is. The appeal to the audience is an ethical proof which asks people to decide between the two partisans on the only basis available, a popular judgment that is at once rational and emotional, disinterested and committed. What do most people think? Aristotle, again, points to the fact that when I am persuaded, I think I am responding to reason. The sophists, again, can point to the fact that others think that you are persuaded through the manipulation of images and emotions. Consequently, each has to account for the phenomena which the other makes basic. The Aristotelian must explain why rhetoricians believe that they are effective through the transmission of images and emotions. The sophist must explain why audiences think they are persuaded by reason.

Again, I think this shows how the dispute between Aristotelian and sophistic rhetoric is a paradigmatically philosophical dispute, not to be settled by simple appeals to evidence. Both sides are immune to refutation. Yet we must sometimes decide between them. On the sophistic account, people who are persuaded are systematically wrong about how and why they are persuaded. That doesn't refute the sophists; it only makes them experts, and makes the rest of us fallible and prone to mistakes. Expertise makes ethical relations between speaker and audience unnecessary.

If, on the other side, when I am persuaded I think that I am persuaded through argument, it will be it harder to have expertise and specialized knowledge. As a strategy for professional self-advancement, Aristotelian rhetoric is self-defeating. Since rational rhetoric centers on argument and reason, it is not a matter of expertise. Facility in the art of rhetoric, Aristotle says, will make no one any wiser (I.2.1356a32–34). He could have added that it won't make anyone rich either. An audience can then fairly ask, If the rhetorician does not know more than I do, why should I listen to and be persuaded by her? The rhetorician not only has trouble attracting clients, which we already knew, but has trouble presenting herself as worth believing.

As we will see, the answer will be ethical. But at this point I want to ask how each can account for the others' appearances, the Aristotelian for the fact that emotional appeals seem to work and the sophist for the fact that people believe they are persuaded by the best reason. That looks like a dispute that invites question-begging.

The sophist has a large job to do. It is one thing to make the general claim that the most effective way of moving people emotionally is by their believing that they are being moved by reason. It is quite another to give some more detailed accounts of how *these emotions* are best effected by *these reasons*, or how these reasons best conceal the emotional processes that are truly effecting the persuasion. If I am moved emotionally when I am persuaded, but I think I am moved by argument, a full sophistic account must not only explain why these passions move me as they do, but why these particular passions are accompanied by the illusion that I am moved by these particular rational appeals. Maybe such a detailed accounting can be done, although I have never seen much of an attempt. If some sophist were to do it, this ethical confrontation would become much more sophisticated than I can make it by myself. I doubt that such a fine-grained analysis is possible.

Sophistic theory needs what John Mackie called "error theory."[24] Ethics, Mackie says, isn't about any real qualities in the world. But for me to respond to ethical appeals, I must believe that ethics is about such real qualities. Therefore ethical theory must account not only for the reality—what is really going on when people respond to ethical ideas and qualities—but also the appearance, the beliefs people actually have about how ethics supposedly works. I wait for the sophist to do the same, not only explain how people are moved by emotion, but how people think they are moved by argument, by some arguments more than others.

The sophist need not accept this challenge. He can say instead that when the emotions are powerful enough and the sophist skillful enough, it does not matter what is going on in my consciousness. Any arguments might be on the surface, but they are not part of a causal chain that connects speaker and hearer. Arguments simply help the speaker distract attention from the real persuasive work that is going on, much as the magician's patter and extraneous showmanship distract attention from the hand movements that the audience cannot be aware of.

I would hope for a more powerful argument on the part of the sophist. Surely at least part of the time the arguments on the surface are part of the causal story. The sophist will use certain arguments because they will produce certain specific emotional effects. Argument is then a means to the emotional effects that effect persuasion.

For the sophist, reasoning has no special status among the devices which one might use to persuade. Reasoning is a means, either to mask the real persuasion going on, or to effect persuasion. People are for or against capital punishment because of feelings of justice, outrage, or sympathy, and arguments either hide the operations of those passions or are means of stimulating them.

Reasoning, the sophist can further say, is an especially efficacious means of persuasion because whenever I am persuaded, I think that I am being persuaded by reason. I like to think of myself as rational. The more I think that I am being persuaded by reason, the more powerfully I can be moved by emotion. When I believe that my preferences are irrational, I am less secure and ardent than if I think that I come by my opinion rationally. I do not have to be defensive about my feelings for capital punishment if I believe that they are rationally grounded.

That, I believe, is the strongest defense the sophist can mount on the charge of being unable to account for the discrepancy between appearance and reality. The problem with this line of argument follows from my earlier point about the lack of reflexivity. I can want to be persuaded. I cannot want to be manipulated. I can recognize that you are trying to persuade me because you want to sell me something or get me to vote your way. I find nothing objectionable in that. Persuasion depends on my understanding and my emotions being permeable and open to influence from outside. I can recognize that I should be open in that way. I am not insulted or harmed if I know that you regard me as an object of persuasion. But I am insulted and harmed by being regarded as manipulated. In persuasion, you need my cooperation to persuade me. In acting ethically, I must treat you as an ethical agent. I certainly prefer to be treated as one. The rhetorician shows that treating others as ethical agents is ethically and rhetorically superior.

The sophist then cannot do a good job of accounting for the common opinion that we are and want to be persuaded by reason. Aristotelian rhetoric has no corresponding trouble explaining the power, and ethical value, of emotional appeals. It is sometimes irrational to exclude the emotions. Sometimes someone's rationality is enhanced through appeals to guilt or shame, to anger or to indignation. As Aristotle says, "fear makes people deliberate" (*Rhetoric* II.5.1383a9). The emotions Aristotle explores in *Rhetoric* II.2–11 create civic, rational, and normative ties among speakers, the people they talk about, and the audiences they appeal to.

The Active Audience

And so a final ethical issue is joined here. Both sides agree that being persuaded is a form of being acted upon and is to that extent passive. But they differ on how to interpret that passivity. Both sides can agree that persuasion depends on my understanding and my emotions being permeable and open to influence from outside. They differ because Aristotle sees that being persuaded, unlike being suntanned or being crushed, requires active participation by the person being persuaded (see *Metaphysics* V.12.1019a15–18). In the *Discourse on the Origins of Inequality,* Rousseau argues that no one can be made to obey who does not himself wish to rule; successful persuasion and even domination relies on the desires and values of the person being persuaded. Similarly, Socrates in the *Phaedo* explains that when the soul is imprisoned in the body, it often cooperates in its own incarceration by judging the true and the false by pleasure and pain (83a). The passive event of being persuaded takes a lot of activity in the audience, and such activity is indeed cooperation with the speaker. Even in most emotional manipulation, the audience's rational faculty is an active, even if unknowing, partner in being persuaded. Being persuaded takes complicity.[25]

I learned personally about how active one must be in order to be persuaded the first time I had acupuncture. I was skeptical about whether sticking needles in my body could cure asthma, and wondered whether it wasn't an instance in which the will to believe, rather than any medical art, effected the cure. I was told to take off my shirt and lie down in one of the doctor's rooms. While I was waiting, there was nothing to look at except an acupuncture chart on the wall. It was a chart for a horse. I do not believe that horses are relieved of arthritis by being persuaded that the doctor is curing them. Placebos do not work on horses. I was therefore persuaded that acupuncture really worked, and worked physiologically rather than through my being persuaded. The equine chart told me that acupuncture worked on my body, not my mind, and that no participation or cooperation on my part was required. It may have taken the persuasion of the equine acupuncture chart to allow me to be treated medically rather than rhetorically, but once that rhetoric through images did its job, the rest of the asthma cure took no participation on my part. I did not have a rhetorical relationship to my doctor, but a purely medical one.

Horses, I assumed, are a poor audience for rhetoric. Therefore, I concluded—I had a lot of time waiting for the doctor—being persuaded, in contrast to being drugged or put in balance—or whatever acupuncture is supposed to do—by needles, takes a lot of cooperation by the audience. My being convinced by the chart may have been a completely irrational and emotional event, but only rational beings are capable of such passive and even sophistic persuasion.

Sophistic rhetoric works, when it does, in part because people believe that it works. We are manipulated by advertising because we know how advertising is supposed to work, and go along with it when it does work. Advertising does not work unless we understand its conventions. We consent to be manipulated when we agree that the best performance should win. We buy a product as a way of paying tribute to the craft values of the advertisement. Just as I do not believe that horses are cured by placebos, I doubt that they are charmed by seduction. I don't really believe that buying that car will make me more attractive to women, but I enjoy the idea and am willing to pay the price for the pleasure the idea gives me.[26] It may be passive, but this is a learned and trained passivity. I am told that in some European countries politicians never smile. A smiling politician might win the affection and trust of an American audience, and the audience might have no idea that they are persuaded by the smile rather than the quality of his policy proposals. But my unconsciously being won over by a smile is conventional.

Sophists from Callicles on have missed the conventional and cooperative nature of rhetorical persuasion. In a state of nature, persuasion is of no value and only force and its threat works. The sophist imagines a world of masters and slaves, a state of nature without ethical relations between speaker and hearer. If speaker and hearer are related conventionally, then there are ethical relations, including justice and friendship, even while people are trying to sell me something or get me to follow them into battle. The abuse of justice and friendship is different from their absence. When I am manipulated, my rationality is not circumvented. It is exploited.

The fact that rhetoric is conventional does not refute the sophists, but it is ethically troublesome. Sophistic must occlude the conventional nature of persuasion. Hobbes mastered the rhetorical lesson that language is a convention whose efficacy and authority depends on its seeming to be natural and inevitable. It is therefore inherently deceptive. Particular acts of persuasion need not be deceptive: speaker and hearer can both be aware of the sorts of appeals being proffered, as in the case where I enjoy an advertisement so much that I buy the product. But for the persuasion to be successful, its conventional nature cannot be evident.

Ethical versus Theoretical Superiority

I said earlier that if one version of rhetoric could be decisively refuted, it would have disappeared long ago. The ethical comparison of incommensurables lets us understand the permanence of conflict without that barring us from taking sides. This confrontation between incommensurables is productive because each side can learn from the other without losing its own identity.

Rhetoric based on reasoning is ethically superior to persuasion rooted in emotion. But if rational rhetoric is so attractive, why doesn't it have more adherents? All along we've seen a couple of reasons that will not go away. First, rational rhetoric does not always seem as attractive as it should because reliance on reason seems constraining. In both this chapter and my earlier consideration of the South African revolution I have shown how the limitations of rhetoric to argument can be liberating as well as constraining. But sometimes those limitations not only appear but in fact are constraining.

Similarly, maintaining that reason is the heart of rhetoric seems naive, and sometimes is naive. Reasoning seems weak compared to the other weapons that the sophist can use. I want to gesture briefly to Machiavelli to respond to this charge. I see Machiavelli as the Aristotelian rhetorician who has, unlike Aristotle, taken the sophistic challenge seriously and learned from it. There is a principled difference between reasoning and merely using reason. Yet, we always need to remember, that boundary is contested and moveable. The rational is always liable to be a term of self-congratulation. The Machiavellian prince is a persuader. He must command the loyalty of his subjects. While Machiavelli teaches the prince how to appeal to the emotions of his subjects, he also shows the prince how to rely on an *ethos* he constructs for himself, since the usurper Machiavelli is writing for cannot depend on the preexistent deference and loyalty due to the hereditary ruler. A rich form of practical rationality is necessary to manipulate the emotions that will constitute loyalty. The usurper must act like a prince, but he must teach his subjects to recognize that he is acting like a prince. The prince knows well that his subjects must be active participants in their subjugation. They must be forced to believe, but it is still *belief* that they are coerced into.[27]

Machiavelli shows something else that the Aristotelian can learn from the sophist. Socrates, and I think Aristotle with him, seems to think that pandering is easy. Convincing someone that he really ought to do what is right is difficult, but telling people what they want to hear is easy. On this count, Socrates and Aristotle are naive. Especially in competitive situations, speaking to an audience's prejudices and aiming at their satisfaction takes skill and hard work. Aristotle may be right, especially by his own criteria, that there is no art of delivery (*Rhetoric* III.1.1404a3), that arrangement is easy. But even if sophistic goals are not amenable to artistic treatment, they still require cleverness. Machiavelli convinces the potential usurper to brave moral censure and the risks of failure by reversing the holding of conventional morality that vicious and base action is easy, while upholding the right in the face of temptation is difficult. He on the contrary demonstrates that it is easy to be good. All you have to do is not care about consequences. It is hard, though, to be, by conventional standards, bad. All that goodness takes is innocence. The Machiavellian alternative takes intelligence and hard work. Machiavelli convinces his audience to do bad by making it seem difficult, and therefore potentially glorious. The Aristotelian rhetorician could well learn that sophistic, ignoble as it may be, still takes skill and work.

The ethical considerations I have amassed in favor of rational rhetoric are not neutral considerations. Sometimes I am in situations in which I must resort to sophistic. These are situations in which there can be no principled distinction between reasoning and rationalization. Thucydides' example of when words lose their meaning describes a situation in which moderation looks like weakness, for example.[28] If I thought that moderation was the right strategy, I might have to disguise it to get it adopted. But, although I would sometimes argue sophistically, I would rather enter into mutual relations, based on speech, than force or fraud.

While rational rhetoric is ethically superior to emotional rhetoric, it still can be abused. Both reason and emotion can be used in good and bad causes. This confrontation shows us how to reformulate the issue. What can only reason do? What can only emotion do? What—and this will be the subject for succeeding chapters—can only *ethos* do? Rational rhetoric is superior because there are ways of acting and ways of being part of a community that are only available to someone who uses this full art of rhetoric, and not the truncated, sophistic version.

I have no expectation that my ethical arguments will convince people to shut down Departments of Communication, advertising agencies, and political consultants. I hope my debunking of their empirical claims can shift the dispute to more interesting and choiceworthy grounds. A rational life is better than a life of force, fraud, tradition, or fantasy, the alternatives to reasoning. It would be wrong to conclude that, since I have shown the power of a rhetoric based on rationality and the poverty of theoretical elaborations of sophistic, we should, like Aristotle after he has disposed of the sophists in the first chapter of the *Rhetoric,* go on about our business of thinking through the implications of rational rhetoric without further concern for the sophistic deflation of reason. Only in some circumstances can we make a principled distinction between reasoning and rationalizing. Those situations are never permanent. They require constant maintenance.

Sophistic arguments remind us that assertions of rationality, like claims of neutrality and universality, benefit some and disadvantage others, and so are always subject to abuse, and to contestation. Deciding who is reasonable and how to recognize the reasonable person is always a historically nuanced decision, full of dangers of assimilating the reasonable to things we are comfortable with. The sophistic challenge to rationality shows the need for practical work in finding the conditions that support, engender, and maintain practical rationality. Being, as Aristotle says, political animals might be our nature. But we still have to fight to sustain the conditions in which we can exercise that humanity.

CHAPTER 3

Brown v. Board of Education as a Paradigm of Practical Reason

Part of the explanation for the primacy of ethos *is that in order for moral convictions to have force within the life of concrete societies, ethical intuitions must possess a great deal more self-certainty than they could possibly gather from merely theoretical demonstrations. (An insight of this kind is present in Hegel's and Nietzsche's analyses of Socrates, whose very appearance is seen as a symptom of moral decline within the polis.) As even Habermas concedes, "the difference between what we always claim for our rationality and what we are actually able to explicate as rational can in principle never be eliminated." But for the demands of situated praxis, this is simply not enough. One must act as if unreflectively, embodying a sure sense of what is good and right; one must command a kind of practical assurance that even the strictest, most rigorous set of arguments fails to supply. This is something made available only by character and habituation, never by rational argument as such. As an Aristotelian would say, in order to live virtuously and to make the right choices, one's soul must be shaped by certain habits of virtuous conduct, in a way that renders superfluous recourse to strict arguments. Judged by these purposes, the achievements of theory always fall short.*[1]

When Earl Warren arrived in Washington to become Chief Justice, Hugo Black advised him to read Aristotle's *Rhetoric*. There is no evidence about why Black gave this advice, what he thought someone could learn from the *Rhetoric*. There is no evidence that Warren took the advice, and, if he read the *Rhetoric*, whether he got anything out of it. But the performance of the Warren Court embodies something central to the *Rhetoric* in a magisterial way. The Warren Court's first important decision, *Brown v. Board of Education*, illustrates the complex interrelation between character and practical reasoning that lies at the heart of the *Rhetoric*.[2]

Supreme Court jurisprudence in cases such as *Brown* seems to violate the simplest strictures of logic, and so does not deserve to be called reasoning at all. The problem in the first two chapters was separating off rhetorical reasoning from sophistic. The apparently illogical nature of practical reasoning invites a confrontation not with sophistic but with the program of measuring practical reason by the standards of scientific rationality.

In the first two chapters I was concerned with vindicating Aristotle's claim that reasoning is the body of persuasion. We already saw that that thesis implicated the further thesis that *ethos* was the most persuasive of rational proofs. In this pair of chapters we will see how rational *ethos* can do things that reasoning by itself cannot do. We will see how legal reasoning becomes ethical when it thinks not only about what the law says but about how the law represents justice. As we saw in the first chapter, *ethos* is engaged more fully in reasoning that aims at truth than in reasoning that seeks agreement. Here we will see *ethos* engaged most fully in reasoning aiming at justice rather than mere lawfulness. In the final two chapters, I will be able to describe ethical reasoning as reasoning about ends and not simply means.

Brown *and Its Implications*

Here is the problem. *Brown* derives the unlawfulness of school segregation from the centrality of education in contemporary American life. It argues that depriving children of equal education denies them equal citizenship, and claims that separate education could not be equal. It is not discrimination as such that violated the equal protection clause of the Fourteenth Amendment, but discrimination in public education:

> We must consider public education in the light of its full development and its present place in American life throughout the Nation. Only in this way can it be determined if segregation in public schools deprives these plaintiffs of the equal protection of the laws. . . . In these days, it is doubtful that any child may reasonably be expected to succeed in life if he is denied the opportunity of an education. Such an opportunity, where the state has undertaken to provide it, is a right which must be made available to all on equal terms.
>
> We conclude that *in the field of public education* the doctrine of "separate but equal" has no place. Separate *educational* facilities are inherently unequal. (emphasis mine)[3]

The Court followed that case, though, with a series of decisions that extended the holding far beyond education. Since schools had to be integrated, drinking fountains, swimming pools, golf courses, public housing, and other public facilities could not remain segregated. Many of these decisions were proclaimed *per curiam:* the Court announced a conclusion without giving any reasons at all, apart from naming *Brown* as the authority.

The Fourteenth Amendment implies *Brown. Brown* implies further desegregation orders, culminating in the wonderfully titled *Loving v. Virginia,* which outlawed antimiscegenation laws. Equality requires desegregated schools, but integrated schools in turn imply something new about equality. The premise from which *Brown* was derived, the centrality of education, dropped out of the later cases.

If *Brown* needs a premise about education, then school desegregation doesn't simply follow from the nature of equality. But if *Brown* depends on education, then it can't imply that segregated drinking fountains are unconstitutional. The Fourteenth Amendment itself does not imply *Loving.* State laws prohibiting interracial marriage arguably did not discriminate at all, since they equally prohibited blacks from marrying whites and whites from marrying blacks. In logic, if *p* implies *q* and *q* implies *r,* then *p* implies *r.* If *p* does not imply *r,* then we can infer either that *p* did not imply *q* or that *q* did not imply *r. Brown* cannot make the connection between the Fourteenth Amendment and *Loving* any stronger. Logical validity is in that sense closed. Does legal reasoning have nothing to do with logical implication? If so, should it be called legal "reasoning"?

How is *Brown* an intermediary between equal protection and the unconstitutionality of antimiscegenation laws?[4] *Brown*'s critics claimed that integration in schools would lead inevitably to the ultimate horror of interracial sex and marriage. The critics' prediction came true. Were the defenders of *Brown* disingenuous in denying the implication?

Rhetorical and ethical arguments exist in time, while logical arguments do not. This chapter and the next ask how reasoning can exist in time. How can *Brown* initially be controversial, and then seem inevitable? The implications of given assumptions vary over time. While variable, the range of implication is not indeterminate as the sophists maintain. Practical reason and *ethos* limits to the range of implications. Otherwise, there is the danger that while *p* implied *q, q* now implies *not-p.* Some believe that that is exactly what happened in the civil rights cases, in a supposed movement from desegregation to taking race into account in affirmative action. But if legal reasoning can violate this simple rule of logic, truly anything goes.

Logically, either *Brown* is right under the Fourteenth Amendment or it is not. It could not *become* right because of *Sweatt and Painter,* earlier cases that found segregation unconstitutional in graduate schools and law schools. Segregation in the public schools could not become wrong because segregation in graduate schools and law schools was first ruled to be wrong. In the same way, the antimiscegenation laws finally ruled unconstitutional in *Loving* could not be in violation of the Fourteenth Amendment after *Brown* but not before. And similarly for the other extensions of the rejection of "separate but equal" beyond education. After all, why would the Court issue its rulings *per curiam* if it had some reasoning to back them up? This process does not look like reasoning but some irrational principle of inertia, similarity, or least resistance, or a calculation of what judges or the public will accept.[5]

The difficulty of understanding the sequence of civil rights cases as a rational process can suggest interpreting the sequence as case-to-case reasoning.[6] If the Court's only audience were the parties in front of it, common law reasoning might be adequate. But the Supreme Court not only speaks to the parties in a dispute, identifying winners and losers. It speaks to lower courts, other governmental agents, and the people, to give them guidance about what to do. The Court also speaks to the public to convince them that the decision is legitimate by convincing them that it speaks *for* them. "When justices interpret the Constitution, they speak for their community, not for themselves."[7] Legitimacy is a more demanding standard than the finality required by the first audience or the predictability and guidance demanded by the second. Rhetoric forces us to be attentive to who is reasoning to whom.

Given this broadest audience and this last purpose for judicial reasoning, the thinking must be more than case to case. Warren had it right when he said that "the opinions [in *Brown* and its companion, *Bolling v. Sharpe*] should be short, readable by the lay public, non-rhetorical, unemotional and, above all, non-accusatory."[8] The opinions need to be readable by the lay public because it is they who decide whether the opinion is legitimate, and this particular opinion had to be legitimate in order to be successful. Warren's eyes were so fixed on this widest audience that the actual parties to the case became an afterthought, as remedy was separating from the finding of injury, and eventually giving rise to the ruling that schools had to be integrated "with all deliberate speed," in spite of the fact that gradual integration meant the continued violation of "personal and present" rights of schoolchildren.[9]

Warren's decision to make the opinion "non-accusatory" appears to violate Aristotle's advice that judicial rhetoric should be about guilt and innocence, and so different from deliberative rhetoric which focuses on the useful and the harmful, and from epideictic rhetoric about good and evil apart from particular actions. Because of the separation of verdict from remedy, the *Brown* decision is not judicial rhetoric but an epideictic declaration that equality and antidiscrimination are fundamental American Constitutional values. That judgment had consequences for judgments about the past and future, but it itself was a statement not about who is guilty, or about what is to be done, but about Constitutional *ethos*. Its epideictic nature connects *Brown* back to Lincoln and forward to the TRC.[10]

Brown and its progeny form a paradigm of ethical reasoning, a paradigm of the Aristotelian interrelation between reason and *ethos*. While rational *ethos* is produced by argument, it allows practical reasoning to go further than reasoning itself could go. *Brown* will be a paradigm of what I quoted Newman in the Introduction calling practical reason "the exercise of a living faculty in the individual intellect."

Ethical Surplus and Ampliative Reasoning

Ethos allows practical reason to reach conclusions that reason could not authorize by itself. It generates an ethical surplus which makes practical reasoning legitimately ampliative. The conclusion is stronger than the premises that lead to it. Such increase is impossible under a purely deductive conception of rationality. Other modes of thought, such as induction and abduction, or inference to the best explanation, have their own resources for producing conclusions that are more firmly held and which extend more widely than their premises, and successful poetic works use probability and verisimilitude to lead to novel and unexpected events that carry with them a sense of inevitability. There is no general method for thinking to be ampliative. *Ethos* offers the ampliative resources for practical reasoning.

Because the Justices abandon the reliance on education in subsequent decisions, Supreme Court jurisprudence cannot be interpreted through a deductive model. But the inference that it must therefore be case to case or irrational relies on a false dilemma. I want to suggest ethical argument as a *tertium quid* between the security of an algorithmic method for deciding cases and the flexibility and novelty of case-to-case or analogical reasoning. The civil rights cases need a higher standard of legitimacy than case-to-case reasoning can provide without answering to a false god of theoretical reason.

Consider the judge deciding whether to extend *Brown* to interracial marriage in *Loving*. Is only the holding relevant, as would be true if it were case-to-case reasoning? The judge would then have to decide whether the new case is "similar" enough to the existing precedent to justify a ruling. Or is the original rationale and meaning still relevant? There is nothing about public education in a case challenging antimiscegenation laws. What does *Brown* have, beyond the finding that separate but equal schools are inherently unequal, that leads to further decisions?

As a chain of deductions, the line from the Fourteenth Amendment through *Brown* to *Loving* fails. *Brown* relied on the place of education in society. That justification does no work in the further cases. *Brown* transmits something more than the holding and less than the reasoning to further cases. The meaning of *Brown*—its *ethos*—survives in the ethical surplus of the argument. That ethical surplus is the antidiscrimination model by which it commits the Court to desegregation beyond schools. *Brown*'s meaning is its understanding of equality and discrimination. That understanding led to the later decisions.[11]

Logic and Practical Inference

The judge asks himself or herself, To what does *Brown* commit the Court? Drawing consequences is not reducible to logical implication because a judge's decisions are enforceable. They have force behind them.[12] The judge cannot draw all the implications logic authorizes because logic cannot pay attention to separation of powers, to the relation between deciding controversies, guiding other public agents, and stating ideals that embody legitimacy. The judge is ethically constrained.

The range of ethically admissible implications is not reducible to calculation of what will be accepted. Sophistic rhetoric always draws that implication from the irreducibility of practical reasoning to logic, as Stephen Douglas's interpreted the American *ethos* in chapter 1. A judge can draw whatever implications the audience will accept. It takes an expert in public opinion to determine whether antimiscegenation laws are unconstitutional. Rhetoric is then a contest of wills, either a matter of what the clever speaker can impose on an audience, or how to win by telling the audience what they want to hear. Once again we face the question of whether there is a principled distinction between reasoning and rationalizing.

Some arguments succeed by reasoning alone. Not all argument, even all practical argument, should be ethical. But some arguments succeed, still *qua* argument, through the ethical effect of making the hearer trust the speaker. Because of the quality of someone's arguments, we come to trust and rely on those arguments and on the person who asserts them and draws the inferences. The argument alone might lead to a conclusion, but because those arguments make us trust the speaker, we draw a stronger conclusion than that warranted by the evidence alone—the ethical surplus. The ethical surplus gives meaning to Aristotle's claim that *ethos* is the most powerful means of securing belief. It is the self-certainty Beiner talked about in the epigraph to this chapter. Ethical argument allowed the Court to derive a conclusion in *Brown* that was about more than education.

Ethical argument and the ethical surplus are necessary in practical arguments and decisions because practical judgment is always uncertain. We never have strong enough evidence to authorize and justify a practical decision beyond the possibility of rebuttal and error. There are time constraints. Evidence is limited and partial and there are costs to obtaining more, so that it can be irrational to go beyond partial evidence. Yet, although practical conclusions are rarely compelled and certain, practical decisions should not therefore always be hesitant. They often have to be definitive for us to act successfully. Unless a decision is arbitrary, it must be generated by something as strong and definitive as the decision itself. *Ethos* provides something adequate for moral and practical certainty. That is the indispensable role of *ethos*. Theory and reason alone cannot provide the kind of closure that practice, and so practical reason, need.

Once *ethos* leads past argument to a practical decision, that *ethos* is always available to take practical reasoning further. Thus we get to the result in *Brown* through ethical reasoning, and *Brown* then leaves us with an ethical surplus for future practical reasoning about equality and discrimination. All reasoning must come to an end somewhere. Ethical reasoning comes to an end at the *ethos* of speaker and hearer, the confident assumption of responsibility on the part of the Court speaking for the public whose sense of equality and justice is the ultimate ground for *Brown*. The ethically reliable is a better basis for action than the logically certain or the arbitrary and willful.

Ethical reasoning gives us tools for handling precedent more subtly than the advocates of pure logic, such as devotees of "original intent," propose. The Court famously had to confront the fact that the same Congress that adopted the Fourteenth Amendment also approved segregated public schools in the District of Columbia. The Court recognized that that approval did not settle the issue the Court faced almost a hundred years later. Not only was the historical record ambiguous, but it could not be dispositive because the meaning of education had changed.

"An additional reason for the inconclusive nature of the Amendment's history, with respect to segregated schools, is the status of public education at that time." Here is a nice example of the hermeneutic circle that argues against the idea, contained in the official narrative offered by the Court, that first they decide whether the historical record, or text, or something else that might be authoritative, settles the matter, and only if it does not will they turn to the less secure and possibly less legitimate mode of reasoning that looks to justice and fairness. If the historical record gave them what they wanted, they would have found it unambiguous. Because history did not yield a satisfactory result, the Justices declared that it was ambiguous. The changing status of public education makes the history inconclusive.[13]

The authors of the Fourteenth Amendment may well have presupposed that segregation was legal, but that is different from saying that the Amendment implies or commits the country to segregation. There is a difference, an ethical difference, between asserting a proposition and merely presupposing it without either asserting it or questioning it. *The Merchant of Venice* presupposes anti-Semitic attitudes, but whether it endorses them is another question. The existence of capital punishment is presupposed by the Constitution, but that is not the same as saying that the Constitution asserts its legitimacy.[14] The distinction between a presupposition and a premise is invisible from the point of view of logic, but an ethical analysis of reasoning can treat it rationally. Warren's dismissal of history hinges on taking something that was thought to be a premise—segregated public schools are consistent with equal protection—and making into a presupposition instead.

Ethos and Ethical Reasoning

The Court courageously faced a dilemma. It had to present a reasoned opinion in order to secure legitimacy. But it had to state a moral principle more powerful than any backing that it could offer. Whatever reasoning it offered would fall short of being fully compelling. A decision as monumental as *Brown* must be self-supporting. It must be an ethical decision because nothing is superior to *ethos*. The Court made education central to citizenship so that it could derive the holding directly from the Fourteenth Amendment without the standard intermediaries of either legislative history or judicial precedent. It needed to show the people that it took responsibility for the decision. The *Brown* decision was an act of commitment.

Had the *Brown* decision been more "reasoned," with more explicit ties of judgment to text and precedent, it would have been less persuasive. Something as fundamental as the nation's commitment to equality cannot stand or fall with legislative history or prior and lesser decisions. What looks like tactical advice on Aristotle's part shows how *ethos* is ultimately self-grounding:

> Do not seek enthymemes about everything; otherwise you do what some of the philosophers do whose syllogisms draw better known and more plausible conclusions than their premises. And when you would create pathos, do not speak in enthymemes; for the enthymeme either knocks out the pathos or is spoken in vain. . . . Nor should you seek an enthymeme when the speech is being "ethical"; for logical demonstration (*logos*) has neither *ethos* nor moral purpose (*prohairesis*). Maxims should be used both in a narration and in a proof; for they are "ethical" (*ethikon*): "I have given [the money] though knowing one should not trust." (*Rhetoric* III.17.1418a10–21)

The brevity of the *Brown* opinion, which critics quickly characterized as "containing almost no law," is part of its persuasiveness because it is part of its legitimacy. So is the fact that it addresses the lay public, and that it is "unemotional" and "unrhetorical."

The Court could have written an opinion of nothing but footnotes, that is, constructed an opinion that deduced the violation of equal protection from constitutional text, history, and precedent, but for a case as monumental as *Brown* such a deduction would have been perceived as the Court hiding behind legal precedent and not taking responsibility for the decision. Finding the history inconclusive makes the Justices more responsible for their opinion. The Court presents the opinion as ethically necessary and inevitable precisely because it is not necessary and inevitable by narrow logical and legal criteria.

Look again at some of the language in the crucial paragraph I quoted earlier. This time I italicize a few words to emphasize its ethical necessity:

> We *cannot* turn the clock back to 1868 when the Amendment was adopted, or even to 1896 when *Plessy v. Ferguson* was written. We *must* consider public education in the light of its full development and its

present place in American life throughout the Nation. *Only* in this way can it be determined if segregation in public schools deprives these plaintiffs of the equal protection of the laws.

Integration has become ethically necessary. It is an undeniable implication of equal protection. The argument has generated its own ethical necessity.

It was, therefore, not disingenuous of the supporters of *Brown* to deny the attack that claimed that school desegregation would lead, as it did, if not to "miscegenation" at least to overthrowing laws that supported it. The supporters of *Brown,* including the Court and the NAACP, could not even know what implications *Brown* should have for school desegregation. School desegregation was declared unconstitutional before anyone had a clear idea of how to overcome it. In similar ways, Lincoln emancipated some slaves, and eventually saw the Civil War as abolishing slavery in general, without any clear idea of the future relations between the races in the this country. He, like many antislavery advocates, held to the fantasy of repatriation to Africa in spite of the complete absence of evidence for its plausibility solely because he could not imagine any realistic futures after abolition.[15] Practical reason takes place in time. Deciding one practical issue creates new ones. Those new problems are unanticipated consequences of solving the old questions.

New problems might be foreseeable, but we can't fully deliberate about them until we face them as real practical predicaments. As MacIntyre puts it:

It is a Cartesian error . . . to suppose that first by an initial act of apprehension we can comprehend the full meaning of the premises of a deductive system and the only secondly proceed to inquire what follows from them. In fact, it is only insofar as we understand what follows from those premises that we understand the premises themselves. . . . The moral life is a journey towards the discovery of first principles as an end, the full disclosure of which is, in both senses of "end," the end of that journey, so that it is in a strict sense only at the end that we know whether or not at the beginning we did in fact know what the true beginning was.[16]

In a similar vein, and to recall the South African achievement of the first chapter, here is Albie Sachs:

We give the last word to freedom, yet we know not what it is. This is the central irony of the deep and passionate struggle in South Africa—

that it is for something that exists only in relation to what it seeks to eliminate.[17]

Brown was an ethical argument. Moreover, it was the basis of further ethical arguments as the principle of equality spread to cases beyond education. Its conclusion, that separate but equal is impossible is stronger than the arguments that lead to the conclusion. The conclusion *should* be stronger in ethical arguments. It is inevitable that people will criticize the arguments while agreeing with the result in such a monumental case.[18] The conclusion is not only more firmly held than the arguments that lead to it, it is also more general than those arguments. *Ethos* goes further than reasoning alone can. The sources of the conclusion—the role of education, Constitutional text and history, case law—are not powerful enough or decisive enough to generate the verdict.

This is an ampliative argument with an ethical surplus. The greater the burden of *ethos,* the less is law needed as a set of premises. Warren draws on the American *ethos* by reference to the role of education in citizenship, which allows him to avoid tackling the questions of whether the Fourteenth Amendment has changed meanings since enactment or since *Plessy. Brown* enunciated an ethical principle. Its self-standing independence of context, history, and text made it indeterminate just how far the conclusion, that racial separation is inherently an instance of inequality, extends. Unlike a logical implication, we can always contest the reach of further ethical implications. Education requires equality. If so, what else follows? The *per curiam* decisions are corollaries. They require no argument because ethically *Brown* makes them self-evident.

Legal reasoning becomes ethical when it thinks about how the law represents justice. We find out what the law is by determining what the law should be. Aiming at agreement and seeking a modus vivendi or law without friendship requires ethical virtues of self-restraint. Aiming at truth and friendly justice require virtues of commitment. Such virtues are more fully rational and ethical than the virtues of self-restraint. Earlier I noted that *Brown* had to manifest ethical reasoning because it had to speak to *and for* the American people and command not simply acquiescence but fidelity. A judge must take responsibility and must manifest commitments in making a ruling on the law as the representation of justice. In situations that do not call for ethical reasoning, we can say that "the law" or "the Constitution" or "history" requires a given decision, but in ethical reasoning the speaker or author *makes* the decision, and so takes responsibility and exhibits commitment. The Justices in *Brown* acknowledged that they were responsible, which of course opened them to the criticism that they were making rather than following law.

In ethical reasoning, sometimes more is less. I quoted Aristotle earlier saying that too much rationality can make a speech unethical (III.17.1418a37–b1). The reasoning in *Brown* becomes ethical by being less determined by text and history. It is not less logical, but it is less logically determined so that the Justices can take responsibility for their decision. Taking responsibility does not mean being willful or arbitrary. The Justices engage in Constitutional interpretation. But they do not pretend that the Constitution is simply speaking through them.

Instead of thinking of the Constitution as a contract, consider it "as a representation of what Americans as a people are: Its purpose is not to enforce an agreement from the past but to enable Americans to think constructively about the values and relationships that characterize them as a people."[19] Deriving what the Constitution means for a given case, as the Justices had to do in *Brown*, is not applying a rule to a case but realizing "the values and relationships that characterize them as a people" in a given case. Ethical reasoning in constitutional law proceeds from the Constitution as a written text that "represents" the people. Such ethical reasoning does not depart from the text into the Justices' own values, or the Justices' sense of the values of the public. Friendship does not negate the law but fulfills it. For the purposes of constitutional reasoning, judges find the American *ethos* in the Constitution, and not in public opinion polls or the preferences of legislators. Lincoln expressed the relation between democratic government and democratic culture as the relation between the Constitution and the Declaration of Independence.[20]

Aristotle distinguishes rhetorical and practical reasoning from logic by reminding us that what is persuasive is always persuasive to someone (I.2.1356b28). But we learned in the last chapter whether an argument is persuasive or not does not depend on whether a given audience is in fact persuaded. Whether *Brown* in fact secured obedience is a different question from whether it appropriately establishes the legitimacy of the decision. The question is not how persuasive people found *Brown*, but whether the Court found the best possible arguments for the unconstitutionality of segregation, and in particular whether the ethical quality of their arguments improved the quality of the decision. In spite of continuing resistance to integration, it is one sign of the success of *Brown* that when antimiscegenation laws were finally found unconstitutional, that decision was met with silence and acquiescence.[21]

Not only is what is persuasive always persuasive to someone, but what inferences are allowed from given premises is also relative to the audience, and no less rational for that. *Ethos* enters into the inferences we draw as well as the premises we start from. It is the speaker's arguments, and not only his or her premises, that make reasoning ethical. Ethical reasoning is not only ethical in its premises, conclusions, and purposes, but is ethical in the reasoning itself. What inferences follow is relative to the audience in such a way that the reasoning itself gets to be called ethical. Thus Aristotle says that rhetorical arguments must be short, as Warren wanted *Brown* to be. The distance between premise and conclusion must be short, since it has to be traveled by the audience (II.22.1395b28; cf. I.2.1357a21, III.10.1410b10–26, II.23.1400b31–34, III.18.1419a18, *Topics* I.11.105a8–10). That rhetorical arguments should be short is not a concession to weary or flighty listeners, but a recognition of the irreducibility of rhetorical argument to logic or dialectic. If I assert a given proposition, I am committed, in dialectic, to all its logical consequences. There is consequently no *ethos* in dialectic or logic. "Mathematical works do not have an ethos because they do not show deliberative choice (for they do not have a [moral] purpose), but the Socratic dialogues do (for they speak of such things)" (*Rhetoric* III.15.1417a19–21). There is no *ethos* in mathematics, Aristotle claims, because my character is not at stake in my mathematical reasoning. The *Topics* shows how to exploit this commitment by enabling dialectical arguers to trip up their opponents, by showing, as Socrates often does, the undesirable implications of their propositions. The *Rhetoric* sees the rhetorical situation not as a confrontation between opponents, as the *Topics* does, but as the construction of a relationship between speaker and hearers.

The ethical terms of that relationship between speaker and audience are violated if a speaker tries to draw consequences that are too remote, but what counts as too remote is a matter for negotiation and trust between speaker and hearer. There is no mathematical measure for an inference being too long or an implication too remote; an argument is too long when it is unfriendly. In dialectic, a speaker bears responsibility for all the implications of his assertions, which makes the *Topics* so much more agonistic than the *Rhetoric*. In the *Rhetoric*, responsibility for the implications of one's assertions is an ethical responsibility, limited by ethical considerations of proximity and probability. The path from the Fourteenth Amendment to *Loving* might be too great, but when we travel via Brown our assertions follow ethically from one another.

Ethical argument runs beyond what purely logical argument can supply. *Brown* would have been a weaker argument had the Justices tried to support their case with more textual arguments, more history, more evidence about the harm segregation caused children. Presenting such additional argument suggests that if the text, or the history, or the psychological evidence, had gone the other way, then segregation would be constitutional.[22] *Brown* is ethically self-sufficient. If the psychological evidence had been other than it was, *Brown* would still have been right, so its justice doesn't depend on social science findings. If the legislative history of the Fourteenth Amendment were different, that would not affect the rightness of *Brown* either.

Taken to an extreme, the suggestion that *ethos* and ethical argument are sometimes weakened by the attempt to derive a conclusion by logic alone leads to the idea that the ultimate ethical argument would offer no reasoning at all, much as *Brown* was criticized for containing "almost no law." The ultimate ethical argument is the announcement of a *per curiam* decision, where *everything* is tacit. The companion case, *Bolling v. Sharpe,* which ruled against segregated schools in the District of Columbia, comes close. There was no Fourteenth Amendment at hand to rule on schools in the District of Columbia, but the Court barely paused on that inconvenience. Consider these lines, which are central to the decision in *Bolling:*

> The Fifth Amendment, which is applicable to the District of Columbia, does not contain an equal protection clause as does the Fourteenth Amendment which applies only to the states. But the concepts of equal protection and due process, both stemming from our American ideal of fairness, are not mutually exclusive. The "equal protection of the laws" is a more explicit safeguard of prohibited unfairness than "due process of law," and, therefore, we do not imply that the two are always interchangeable phrases. But, as this Court has recognized, discrimination may be so unjustifiable as to be violative of due process.[23]

Nothing could be a more purely ethical argument. Constitutional text does not seem to help; legislative history is on the wrong side. Here is a logically weak rationale for an ethically strong conclusion, and Warren signals the weakness by the double negative, "not mutually exclusive." *Brown* has changed the meaning of the Fifth Amendment. "Reverse incorporation," applying implications from the Fourteen to the Fifth Amendment, makes the Court's reasoning the ultimate ground for the decision. Practical reasoning creates *ethos*. The authority for *Bolling* is *Brown*.

What follows from the unconstitutionality of legally required school segregation? The question is not what follows logically, but what implications are we committed to drawing. More precisely, the question is which implications the Court is committed to drawing for the rest of us. Here is an important similarity between ethical argument and ethics in a more familiar sense. Which consequences of my actions I am responsible for changes with social and technological changes: am I today responsible for the size of my family in a way that previous generations were not? Am I responsible for pollution in Nigeria or violations of human rights in Afghanistan? Is the state responsible for private preferences of racial separation? What counts as foreseeable consequences, what counts as intended, will vary with technological changes and also with changes in political organization and political expectations.[24] I am claiming the same variability for the ethical implications of assertions and principles. Which implications of my assertions I am responsible for will vary. People are always tempted to infer from the fact that these implications are not logically required to the conclusion that it's all a matter of politics or force or something else irrational. But this variability does not mean irrationality but marks the flexibility associated with practical reason. There are ties of responsibility between me and only some of the direct and indirect consequences of my action. Similarly, there are ties of implication between my assertion and only some of its implications. So it doesn't violate logic to say that in 1953 antimiscegenation laws were not violations of equal protection, but a dozen years after *Brown* they were.

Which implications of my assertions I am responsible for varies with my own role and position. The *ethos* of a speaker is his own, and he is responsible for it. At the same time the speaker derives his *ethos*, via argument, from the audience. He cannot simply ask himself what he is committed to by his argument, but has to ask what the argument commits the audience to.[25] Again, this is not a prediction of how much the audience will put up with, how far they will go, but an assessment of a commitment's strength. The Supreme Court can declare that the nation is committed to equality so that it must find legal segregation of public schools at variance with its fundamental commitments and therefore unconstitutional. Neither the Court nor the public knows at that time whether this commitment extends to integration, or simply to banning legal segregation. No one knows in advance of actual decisions: that is their ampliative and ethical nature. Court and country have to decide, case by case, what happens to the commitment to equality when it conflicts with other basic values, freedom of association, freedom from government interference, federalism, competing interpretations of equality and equal protection. *Brown* only outlawed legal school segregation. But the Southern strategy of making school selection "voluntary" and a matter for "individual choice" was so transparently an evasion that the Court saw itself committed to integration. The meaning of ethical commitments, unlike the scope of logical implications, emerges through such confrontations and controversies. As Rorty puts it, "assumptions become visible *as* assumptions only if we can make the contradictories of those assumptions sound plausible."[26]

Commitment is an ethical act. Logic relates one proposition to another. Ethical reasoning relates the assertion of one proposition to the assertion of another. Logical validity consists in the transmission of truth from premises to conclusions. As we will see in more detail in the next chapter, ethical validity consists in the transmission of commitments from premises to conclusions.

Ethical reasoning is therefore no less rational, although more variable and dependent on circumstances, than logic itself. I am not necessarily committed to all the logical implications of a principle. I can also be committed to implications that go beyond strictly logical implications. Focusing only on the former leads to talk about judicial restraint and "passive virtues."[27] Focusing only on the latter leads to talk about judicial activism. This conception of ethical reasoning allows us to avoid those simplicities. *Ethos* consists in those implications a speaker can draw and those which an audience can accept.

Brown overrules *Plessy*. But, as ethical argument, *Brown* also overrules Harlan's dissent in *Plessy*. Harlan said that white superiority did not justify racial subordination. But his color-blind Constitution is different from Warren's. Harlan distinguished political equality from social equality:

> The white race deems itself to be the dominant race in this country. And so it is, in prestige, in achievements, in education, in wealth and in power. So, I doubt not, it will continue to be for all time, if it remains true to its great heritage and holds fast to the principles of constitutional liberty. But in view of the Constitution, in the eyes of the law, there is in this country no superior, dominant, ruling class of citizens.

There is no caste here. Our Constitution is color-blind. (*Plessy*, 163 U.S. at 559 [Harlan, dissenting])

Brown declared the unconstitutionality of racial subordination, and announced that the unconstitutionality of racial subordination implied that assertions of racial superiority were un-American. It therefore rejected Harlan's distinction between social and political equality, opening up a new set of questions about the relation of government to social equality. Like any revolution, it raised questions that could not be articulated before. *Brown* created this problem in part by refusing to argue historically. Since the correctness of its decision did not depend on history, there was no historical context in which to determine its scope. Hence all the *per curiam* decisions. Hence the stopping point at economic equality in *San Antonio Independent School District et al. v. Rodriguez et al.*, which denied that inequality in education due to the system of taxation violated the equal protection clause of the constitution.[28] According to the current American *ethos*, political equality is different from economic equality.

The Creativity of Brown

The ethical surplus of *Brown* transformed the way we look at all sorts of cases not obviously connected to school desegregation. The ethical surplus—the *meaning* of *Brown* as opposed both to its justification and its holding—is a new understanding of equal protection which made traditional lines between public and private, state action and individual choice, political equality and social equality, no longer constitutionally privileged or even intelligible. Thus the power of *Brown* comes out in what Paul Gewirtz calls the "triumph of the antidiscrimination model . . . more and more areas of social life are now viewed as raising a problem of 'discrimination'—rather than viewed as raising some other kind of problem, or raising no problem at all."[29]

In addition to its holding, *Brown* added an interpretation of equality that persisted through subsequent cases. Equality becomes a substantive and not only an adjective modifying protection, as *Brown* and the Warren Court make equality central to interpretation of the Constitution.[30] Not only does its ethical force lead us to see all sorts of racial inequalities as instances of discrimination, but discrimination as the meaning of equality transforms the meaning of sexual equality, equality among the generations, and equality for the disabled. As Gewirtz points out, religious inequalities are not viewed as problems of establishment and free exercise but as issues of discrimination, so that even the school prayer cases followed from *Brown*. While *Loving* affected people of all races equally, it was still an instance of discrimination and a denial of equal protection just because of this understanding of equality from *Brown*. The antidiscrimination model meant that *Brown* not only led to *Loving*, but to *Baker v. Carr* and *Reynolds v. Sims*, the "one man, one vote" decisions that led to redistricting of state legislatures. Since districting to reduce black representation was a denial of equal protection, so was any form of districting short of "one man, one vote," even when race was not involved. Facially neutral public policies whose disparate impact raised suspicions of denial of equal protection led to *Furman*, invalidating all capital punishment practices. Prior to *Brown*, a plaintiff had to show that a given practice of inequality and racial separation denied equal protection. Once *Brown* was decided, the burden of proof shifted and the state then had to show why a given practice of racial separation or inequality did not violate equal protection.[31] Warren's insistence that the decision be "non-accusatory" allowed the burden of proof to shift by asserting the existence of discrimination without anyone necessarily doing the discriminating. The more the public sees the Court speaking with an *ethos* it can identify as the public *ethos*, the more easily it concedes and assents to these more remote conclusions. *Brown* created new circumstances of friendship.

Ethical argument is never illogical. It depends on logic, and then goes beyond what it is logically authorized to conclude. There is a difference between an argument which claims that a conclusion follows from the nature of the good—a purely logical claim—and an argument which shows me inferring that same conclusion because of my commitment to the good—a demonstration that is simultaneously logical and ethical. The logical relation is among propositions; the ethical relation is among the assertions of propositions. Those relations are not necessarily in competition with each other. The further I go in drawing conclusions beyond what is logically authorized, the more responsibility I am taking on my own decisions and commitments. The ethical is therefore always in danger of becoming merely assertive and authoritarian, as the purely logical can become amoral and mechanical. Brown serves as a paradigm of what ethical reasoning looks like when it is successful. It is as deserving of our attention and respect as the standard paradigms of practical and rhetorical reasoning, Pericles' Funeral Oration, Burke's Conciliation speech, Federalist 10, or the Gettysburg Address.[32]

CHAPTER 4

The Ethical Criticism
of Reasoning

Men are so constituted that what they conceive by the pure intellect, they
defend only with the intellect and reason, whereas if they think something
because of some affects of the heart, they also defend it
with those affects.
Spinoza, *Theological-Political Treatise*, chap. 7

Our task is to broaden our reasoning to make it capable of grasping
what, in ourselves and others, precedes
and exceeds reason.
Merleau-Ponty[1]

The last chapter gave an example of ethical argument in action. As in earlier chapters, we saw how friendship increases the reach of rationality, and
how *ethos* can be generated by argument and yet exceed it. One conclusion
I draw from that example, as well as the example of the TRC in the first
chapter, is that ethical argument is both ubiquitous and unacknowledged.
At our best moments, we argue ethically. Yet our theories of practical reason
rarely do justice to those moments. In thinking about practical reason, we
constantly fall back on distinctions between the cognitive and the emotive,
between belief and desire, and so inadvertently reduce practical reasoning
to its instrumental form. Because ethical argument is both ubiquitous and
unacknowledged, this project is neither prescriptive nor descriptive. Instead
I point to exemplary performances of practical reason, and both their continuities with and their differences from the universal human practices of deliberating about what to do, making determinations about responsibility,
and praising and blaming people and actions. Here I will start by looking
at one example of someone engaging in ethical argument, not acknowledging
it, and for that reason doing it poorly. Understanding our practices of ethical
argument can improve them.

Ethical Aspects of Rationality

There is nothing controversial in saying that a reasoner's character is an entrance requirement for an argument to be worth listening to. "Because Hugo Black was a member of the Ku Klux Klan, his arguments against segregation have some initial credibility." "Because Thurgood Marshall personally suffered the injustices of racism, we should listen to his arguments against it." "Clarence Thomas has repeatedly benefited from affirmative action programs. If he's against them, I should pay special attention."

But many would argue that an entrance requirement is all it is. There is all the difference in the world between having a reason to listen to someone and having a reason to accept what someone says. Because you have shown yourself to be open-minded and thoughtful, I will take your proposal seriously. But it is all logic after that. Open-mindedness is no guarantee of truth. Once I start listening, the merits of your arguments then stand on their own. Once the ethical boundary has been crossed, character cannot be counted again, this time as a reason for assenting to an argument. Taking your claims and arguments seriously means looking at them as reasoning, and that in turn means abandoning the ethical criteria that gained you the initial hearing. If I see the argument as connected to your personal qualities, I am not taking it seriously as an argument. I am deferring to you, or patronizing you, instead. If the victim's voice, as with Marshall, and the convert's experience, Black—and Thomas too?—have special claims to a hearing, the hearing itself should be a rational affair. "Arguments are to be accepted by authority of the speaker's reasons, not by reason of the speaker's authority."[2] People, that is, have ethical qualities. Arguments have logical qualities.[3]

I want to challenge this two-stage picture, in which we first use ethical criteria to judge a reasoner, and then judge the reasoning using logical standards. The two-stage picture is reminiscent of the distinction in philosophy of science between contexts of discovery and of justification. The criteria for taking a hypothesis seriously enough to test it are distinct from the criteria for accepting it. But in practical reason, the difference between contexts of discovery and of justification disappears. We are always in the equivalent of the context of discovery.

Understanding other people's ethical arguments is a central ethical activity, yet what Philip Bobbitt says about ethical constitutional argument is apposite for practical argument in general:

There is an almost utter absence of the discussion of ethical arguments *as arguments* in the teaching of constitutional law. Either they are instead regarded as disreputable reflections of the moral and political positions of the judge who lacks sufficient willpower to keep them properly cabined or they are indulged by both the cynical and the sentimental for being what "real" judging is all about, having little to do with the competition of arguments *per se*.[4]

As Bobbitt's language suggests, the two-stage picture presupposes a psychology in which human beings are made up of reason and emotion. Aristotle's remark that there are three sources of persuasion, reason, emotion, and *ethos*, points to a richer psychology than a forced choice between reason and emotion. In such a psychology, reason need not be formal. We respond and evaluate ethical arguments ethically. To judge an ethical argument takes intellectual virtues, those same intellectual virtues that are the subject of our ethical judgments.

The theses that arguments have ethical properties and that assessing those qualities is an ethical act are controversial. Assessing arguments ethically seems to make our evaluations personal or subjective, a function, as Bobbitt suggests, of weakness of will. I maintain, on the contrary, that the existence of ethical arguments shows that judgments can be ethical without being irrational. When ethical predicates apply to arguments rather than arguers, the ethical qualities of argument are not merely threshold conditions but constitutive criteria that make something a good or bad argument. Ethical qualities give pieces of reasoning their identity and nature. Practical arguments have ethical conditions of success and failure. So much attention has been given to showing the rationality of ethics that it is worthy looking at the opposite: the ethical dimensions of rationality.[5]

One barrier to accepting my claim that purpose and context are part of the argument's identity and description is that logic studies the identity and validity of arguments, taking no notice of purpose and context, so that if we look at the ethical qualities of arguments, we aren't looking at them as arguments. But we have no trouble seeing purpose and context as defining activities other than reasoning: what is from the outside the "same action" is different depending on who does it, for what reason, and in what circumstances. There is a difference between an action done because the agent sees it as the right thing to do and that action done for the sake of money or reputation. Who is acting on whom, for what purpose, and in what institutional setting are part of what the action is, and not just circumstances surrounding something self-contained called the action. The circumstances of an action are part of its essence, of what it is. I claim the same for practical argument. This chapter is a generalization from the example of *Brown* in the last chapter in which we saw how ethical argument could go beyond logic without being illogical.

A Hermeneutic Example

Reasoning is an ethical act. Even reasoning which is not directly practical has ethical dimensions because all thinking goes on in some context for some purpose. There are institutions, such as the sciences, which can sometimes ignore the context and purpose of thought, but that abstraction is not the default position, as theories of logic sometimes suppose. My students know well that my demand that they present reasons for their opinions is an ethical demand, which is why they resist it. Some—without needing Nietzsche to tell them—initially take it as an assault on their integrity that I demand reasons from them. They realize that my demand creates an ethically distinctive kind of community, the opposite of a community governed by tradition or force.[6]

To see what such a rational and friendly community looks like, I begin with two examples, one of an argument that is not itself directly practical, which does not urge anyone to do anything, and the second the more narrowly practical arguing of an advocate. For the first, consider the following extracts from a scholar, Julia Annas, analyzing Aristotle's arguments about human nature. Her comments are neither personal and ethical criticisms of a person named Aristotle, nor logical criticisms of his arguments. Annas's language is more vivid than most philosophy articles, which is why I chose it, but it can serve as a representative anecdote for the unnoticed importance of ethical judgments of philosophical arguments:

> It is fair to regard Aristotle as open to criticism for not having thought more carefully about the relationship between his uses of nature in the physical works and his uses of it in the ethical and political works. (733–34)

> One passage in book 7 has a wider significance than Aristotle realizes for his view of political virtue. . . . Aristotle is refusing to find it incompatible with virtue to serve others in menial kinds of ways, as long as one does not have a menial or servile attitude. Aristotle unfortunately

does not realize that this point undermines much of his assumption about the importance of the conventional content of political virtue. (747)

Aristotle does not seem clear about the difference between these two lines of thought about the education of citizens; hence, perhaps, some of his wavering about whether certain forms of training are harmful in themselves or only when done beyond a certain point. (748)

Aristotle slides into allowing this fact to play the role of a natural fact in his construction of the ideal polis, because he fails to consider that it could have been otherwise. (749)

In Aristotle's own terms injustice is produced by political discrimination which is not based upon natural inequalities. I do not think that we should rush to berate Aristotle for this; it is something which in our own case we can easily find ourselves doing. (750)[7]

Aristotle has not thought "carefully" enough. His lack of moral imagination makes him fail "to consider that [social arrangements] could have been otherwise." Lamenting that he "unfortunately does not realize" that his refusal to find virtue incompatible with service to others "undermines" the conventionality of virtue goes beyond accusations of inconsistency. Judging that he "does not seem clear about the difference between this two lines of thought" goes beyond finding his words and arguments ambiguous. Annas's verdict of forgiveness in the last sentence is an ethical judgment.

I draw the moral that judgments about character play a role in understanding, formulating, and judging philosophic arguments. Such ethical criticism can be done well or badly. But philosophy is not praxis, so I want to move to a further example. In ethical arguments, our ethical judgments are not just legitimate but central. To develop these claims, let me turn to my second example.

Ethical Consistency, Hypocrisy, and Integrity

Consider someone who argues against bilingual education on the grounds that the purpose of the American school system is to unify the nation by providing a common education and culture, but who at the same time advocates public aid to parochial schools, in spite of the fact that part of the point of religious schools is to offer a culture and education different from the rest of the country. As with my initial glance at Supreme Court Justices, charges of formal inconsistency are beside the point, since it always possible in such cases to argue that the two policies are distinct in ways that makes their joint advocacy consistent. The real question is not one of logical inconsistency or consistency but of their ethical counterparts such as hypocrisy and integrity. "The excellent person is of one mind with himself, and desires the same things in his whole soul" (*Ethics* IX.4.1166a13). Do properties such as hypocrisy and integrity apply to reasoning or only to people?[8]

Therefore an obvious question: Why isn't ethical integrity reducible to logical consistency, and practical thinking to theoretical reason? If we lived in a Platonic dreamworld in which all values were reducible to a single good, and in which knowing the good told us what to do, then the logical consistency of an argument and the ethical wholeness of a person would be the same. We could reason through bi-conditionals between the true and the good. Politics could be reduced to a science, and practical reasoning to logic. The fact that thinking is done by people would be an insignificant accident. Aristotle nicely criticizes this reduction:

> If one were to abstract and posit absolute knowledge and its negation . . . , there would be no difference between absolute knowledge and another person's knowing instead of oneself; but that is like another person's living instead of oneself, whereas perceiving and knowing oneself is reasonably more desirable. (*Eudemian Ethics* VII.12.1244b29–34)

Logically, what is true for me is true for you. Impersonality is a sign of truth. Ethically, what I should do is as much as function of who I am as of the way the world is. When I look at your practical arguments, I do not judge them as eternal objects held up to logical standards. I look at how appropriate to circumstances they are. Practical reasoning, unlike theoretical rationality, presupposes that knowing what is best does not automatically dictate what is to be done. Practical reasoning must make decisions in the light of evidence that is in principle incomplete, and its decisions concern a future that is partly up to us. For these reasons, logical consistency and ethical integrity are not identical. As Bernard Williams puts it, "Where conflict needs to be overcome, this 'need' is not of a purely logical character, nor a requirement of pure rationality, but rather a kind of social or personal need, the pressure of which will be felt in some historical circumstances rather than others."[9] Ethical integrity is not reducible to logical consistency. It will be our prime example of how *ethos* is rooted in reason yet can exceed it, as political friendship is rooted in justice yet exceeds it.

Practical judgments are judgments of people and their reasons. The more practical the argument, the more fully ethical is my interpretation and evaluation of it. I read Annas as scolding Aristotle as a promising yet recalcitrant, and ultimately obstinate, student. It is hard for me to imagine a community that includes the three of us. I therefore see her analysis as an ethical failure. In truly practical cases ethical standards become dominant because not only am I judging the ethical character of the arguments and their author, as Annas does Aristotle, but my own character too is at stake. In thinking about education policy, I want to maintain my own ethical integrity, and I try to do so through looking at the ethical integrity, and other ethical properties, of someone else's arguments.

Suppose I am committed to bilingual education, and want to know whether I should by that fact consider myself also committed to public aid for parochial schools, which I have doubts about. Logical consistency gives no help here. I can consistently advocate bilingual education and either oppose or support state aid to religious schools. I encounter someone who maintains that religious differences deserve deference in a way that other preferences and practices, such as speaking a language other than English, do not. He opposes bilingual education yet supports state aid to religious schools. He defends his apparent inconsistency by arguing that religious differences are not only not compatible with citizenship but are built into the very idea of American citizenship. Linguistic differences, on the contrary, are divisive because they are not part of what it is to be an American.

This seems to me practical reasoning worth considering. I have to decide if this argument, and its consequent difference in policy recommendations for bilingual education and public aid to parochial schools, is an argument with integrity that I should ultimately assent to. To endorse a practical argument is to commit myself to action. My judgment is ethical; its subject is reasoning. Christine Korsgaard puts the difference between reason and *ethos* this way:

Rational necessity is not the same as logical necessity. . . . If all women are mortal, and I am a woman, then it necessarily follows that I am mortal. That is *logical necessity.* But if I *believe* that all women are mortal, and I *believe* that I am mortal, then I *ought* to conclude that I am mortal. The necessity embodied in that use of "ought" is *rational necessity.* If I am *guided* by reason, that I will conclude that I am mortal. But of course it is not inevitable that I will do so; perhaps the horror of contemplating my own mortality will make me irrational.[10]

Objections to My Thesis

These examples show that we in fact use ethical criteria in judging arguments, and not just in judging people to decide whether we should listen to their arguments at all. When we use ethical qualities to assess reasoning, we impute these ethical qualities to the argument, not only the people making the argument. That by itself says nothing about whether, when, and how we *should* employ ethical criteria in assessing arguments. Maybe if we knew more about bilingual or parochial education, we could make purely logical decisions. But when *ethos* goes where reason alone cannot, then practical argument has its own integrity and isn't just the way we are fated to argue because we don't know better. *Brown* was such an example. The Court didn't engage in ethical argument because it couldn't do better, as might be the case in my examples, but because it was right to argue ethically to reach a just conclusion. Comparing the excellence of *Brown* with the merely necessary nature of ethical reasoning in my examples raises some serious objections to the idea of ethical ampliative reasoning. Overcoming these difficulties will help us engage in ethical argument reflectively and with confidence.

These objections are reminiscent of the topoi in chapter 2 for comparing the rational and sophistic rhetorician. There the opponent of practical reason was the sophist who regarded all argument as a cover for advancing interests and satisfying desires. Here ethical arguments are under assault from those who think that thought and character are and ought to be distinct and that ethical considerations can only contaminate reason.

1. Ethical criteria seem to make the quality of argument relative, not universal. The same argument can be good or bad depending on who is asserting it. As the lines from Dewey I quoted in the second chapter suggest, the same propositions uttered by a different speaker might constitute a different argument. I noted before that we accept that the agent and his purposes and beliefs can be part of the definition and identity of an action—the just person giving the right change to the child performs a different action from the shopkeeper who gives the right change because he thinks it will be good for business—but resist doing the same for arguments. We think that reasoning,

unlike action, must be the same from the inside and the outside. The autonomy of reasoning depends on the independence of validity and other structural qualities from purpose.

We should, according to this objection, treat actions and reasons differently. Arguments have forms independent of purpose, while an action's form—its identity and nature—depends on its purpose. The beauty of logic is the independence of its formal structures from any purposes for which they can be deployed. Logical analysis and evaluation of arguments can be impartial and nonpartisan. The great appeal of restricting the understanding and assessment of argument to purely logical, as opposed to ethical, standards is that logical reasoning is self-contained and neutral. Once that self-contained nature is lost, it seems that anything goes, and relativism looms. I can reject the advocates of public aid to religious schools because I don't like their conclusions, and not for the sorts of neutral reasoning logic offers. A neutral conception of logic has the same appeal as does a neutral forum of justice that abstracts from competing conceptions of the good, enabling people who otherwise disagree to engage in public assessment of proposals without having to agree on all kinds of other premises.

My initial example of Justices Marshall, Black, and Thomas was intended to produce a tension between logical and ethical evaluation. I assume that many of my readers are likely to regard Marshall and Black as men of integrity and Thomas as a hypocritical opportunist. Yet both Black and Thomas exhibit a difference between how they live and how they argue. That discrepancy can be read either as hypocrisy or as the experience of a convert which thereby should be accorded greater weight. (Similarly, Marshall's consistency can either be the harmony of argument with experience or the special pleading of a partisan.) The same lack of consistency which causes people to admire Black for rising above his own experience seems to many people in Thomas's case to be ambition and a desire to please a new set of masters. If this isn't abandoning rational standards for assessing argument and retreating to personal judgments, what is?

2. The qualities which make someone trustworthy seem harder to assess and easier to fake and to abuse than logical properties. When an argument looks logical, that is usually because it is logical. But when an argument seems to embody ethical qualities such as practical wisdom or good will, it may be that someone wanted to make it look ethical. Logical fallacies are easier to detect than ethical failures.

The appearance/reality distinction raises questions about the relation between argumentative *ethos* and "real character" that are a theme of this book. These are questions about which Aristotle has nothing to say. The ambivalent status of rhetorical *ethos* is reflected in ordinary language. *Ethos* produced by argument is artificial, the product of intelligence; at the same time artful and so maybe merely apparent. That ambivalence is the tension between the rational as methodical and as civilized that has been our concern all along. Rational *ethos* can supplement and can threaten more "natural" forms of *ethos*. This objection forces us to come to terms with those two sides of rhetorical *ethos*. Judge Posner makes the same point in the context of judicial recusal:

> American judges today are subject to exquisitely refined and elaborate rules on disqualification for conflict of interest. The tiniest conflict is disqualifying. This would make no sense if legal reasoning (including the resolution of factual disputes) were as transparent and reproducible as scientific reasoning and experimentation, for then an erroneous decision would be perceived and corrected and the judge ridiculed for having yielded to temptation. So there is an evident lack of confidence in the ability to detect judicial errors.[11]

The proliferation of rules to detect and remove conflict of interest implies that *ethos* is in the eye of the beholder. There are no sure tests for a lack of ethical integrity as there are for lack of logical cogency. Logical failures are fallacies, things that look like valid reasoning but are not. Ethical failures are flatterers, the arguments of people who look like friends but are not (*Rhetoric* I.11.1374a17–24; see *Politics* V.11.1314a4, *Ethics* IV.7.1127b19–21).

3. There are paradoxes in reflexive argument that follow from the preceding objection. In chapter 2 I argued for the superiority of ethical argument to sophistic because we could reason with ourselves, while a sophistic picture of rhetoric could not account for such phenomena. Here, though, in comparison to theoretical reason, it looks as though ethical argument fails to be reflexive. The impartiality of logical analysis and the self-contained nature of the object of logical analysis imply that logical analysis is equally available to all, and that to know what is wrong with an argument is in principle to able to improve it. I can evaluate my own argument, but what do I look at to assess my own character? One of the purposes of argument analysis and evaluation is self-improvement. Learning to argue better seems a reasonable goal, while improving one's character through argument analysis is more far-fetched.

4. We hesitate to admit ethical criticism of arguments because being logical and being ethical seem at odds. I mentioned at the start that taking the claims of the victim or the convert seriously meant to look at arguments as arguments, while to give them special weight because of the experience of the arguer was to fail to take them seriously, but to patronize instead. "I fought in the Pacific. Don't tell me dropping the bombs on Japan wasn't necessary" is not an impressive argument. To take an appeal on trust is *not* to engage in reasoning. To present careful reasoning is to remove character from the process. Approaching mathematics as a limit, the more logical some reasoning is, the less ethical, and conversely. Logical norms have nothing ethical in them. We fall back on assessments of character when knowledge is not an option. Even if there are times when *ethos* and rationality seem to go together, at other times they don't:

And do not speak from calculation (*dianoias*), as they do nowadays, but from moral principle (*prohaireseos*): [not] "I desired it" and "For I chose this" [but] "Even if I gain nothing, it is better so." The first [two examples] are the words of a man of practical wisdom (*phronimou*), the last of a good one (*agathou*); for the quality of a practical man consists in pursuing his own advantage, that of a good man in pursuing the honorable. (*Rhetoric* III.16.1417a24–28)

Replies to Objections: That Logical Analysis Is Better than Ethical Analysis

I want to use each objection to enrich the idea of ethical argument. We have already seen some hints of how ethical integrity can be founded on logical consistency yet exceed it, and in my replies to these objections, I will show some ethical counterparts to other logical predicates. The first objection said that if purpose is part of the definition of a piece of reasoning, then what is logically a single argument will be understood and evaluated differently depending on who is arguing to whom, and evaluated by whom.

Because purpose and context are part of a practical argument, an additional premise that might make an argument stronger logically can weaken it ethically. Jefferson, Lincoln, and Reagan all at times acted *ultra vires*. By justifying his actions through citing the precedent of earlier presidents made Reagan's argument logically stronger than Jefferson's or Lincoln's, since he has a premise available that they did not. "Jefferson and Lincoln were great presidents; they did things that exceeded what they were authorized to do, and indeed in direct defiance of congressional mandates. Therefore you should not criticize my actions on constitutional grounds."

Ethically, though, Reagan's citation of precedent weakens his argument. It implies that he no longer has to consider counterarguments, as Jefferson and Lincoln did, because of what his predecessors did.[12] Which alternative arguments one rejects, and how they are rejected, as well which arguments are endorsed and which possible lines of argument are ignored, is subject to ethical judgment. An argument is an ethical act because it embodies such choices. In criticizing Reagan's argument, I am not disputing his use of precedents on the grounds that Jefferson's and Lincoln's situations are not comparable. The object of my criticism is his *asserting* the precedent, not the precedent itself. The assertion of such an argument is itself an ethical act.

Jefferson and Lincoln justified their extraconstitutional actions by arguments from emergency and necessity. Such arguments recognize that there is a prima facie case against their actions, and so acknowledge loss as well as gain in their necessary and defensible acts. To argue simply from precedent denies any serious objections to one's actions. It is to act outside the law with contempt for the law rather than to act outside the law while still respecting the law. Asserting precedent destroys friendship between president and public. (For the same reason, Operation Rescue's citation of Martin Luther King's acts as precedent puts their actions on a lower moral plane than King's.) While the truth of premises is outside the scope of logical analysis, the *choice* of premises falls within the scope of ethical criticism. Ethical integrity, unlike logical consistency, requires an attitude toward rejected reasons as well as toward the premises that lead to a conclusion. Speakers have to practice and audiences have to recognize such ethical integrity. It is one of the circumstances of friendship.

Therefore, it is right to apply the same sort of context-relative standards to practical arguments as we do to actions, including purpose and context in their evaluation. Justice without friendship applies to strangers. I can be just toward you without knowing anything about who you are. In the same way, logical argument speaks to no one in particular. That is its strength and its weakness. On the other hand, I cannot be friendly toward you, or act with the justice that Aristotle sees as embodying friendship, without knowing you. I cannot address you ethically without being a specific human being talking to other specific human beings. Justice abstracts from persons.

Friendship cannot follow justice in this regard. Ethical argument includes speaker, hearer, and purpose as part of its identity.

But the objection still stands: if purpose and context are part of the argument, how do we avoid making understanding and evaluating reasoning into a partisan activity? Can rhetoric have neutral, or at least nonpartisan, criteria for evaluation as logic does?

This objection forces a very useful clarification of the idea of ethical properties of argument. The partisan does not criticize the ethical properties of arguments, but aims criticism at the properties of arguers, or the effects of arguments, or at other considerations external to argument itself. If I reject the advocate of public aid to parochial schools who opposes bilingual education simply because I prefer another combination of policies, no ethical criticism of arguments is involved.

It is external criticism to attack someone's conclusions because one disagrees with them. It is internal ethical criticism to attack someone for how he divides arguments into those he endorses, those he relies on for precedent, those he considers but ultimately rejects, those he considers illegitimate, and those that would never even occur to someone of his character. The varieties of goodness requires a more fine-grained ethical set of relations between propositions and people than just affirmation and denial.

One place where that more fine-grained analysis is useful is conditional reasoning. Accepting something "for the sake of argument" is a free act without commitments in scientific reasoning; not so for practical reason. Since slavery is not a live issue in the United States today, we can look at Aristotle's arguments by accepting some of his premises for the sake of argument. Because the subjection of women is a live issue, to examine his arguments on women for the sake of argument is itself to make them into live possibilities.[13] Hume nicely captures the difference between logical and ethical conditionals this way:

> Whatever speculative errors may be found in the polite writings of any age or country. . . . There needs but a certain turn of thought or imagination to make us enter into all the opinions which then prevailed, and relish the sentiments or conclusions derived from them. . . . [But the] case is not the same with moral principles as with speculative opinions. . . . I cannot, nor is it proper I should, enter into such sentiments . . . and where a man is confident of the rectitude of that moral

standard by which he judges, he is justly jealous of it, and will not pervert the sentiments of his heart for a moment, in complaisance to any writer whatsoever.[14]

In the first chapter, I drew attention to the difference between each person thinking someone and everyone thinking it, the difference between thinking something and saying it in public. So here. In a political debate, merely to suggest something in order to reject it does not leave the debate unchanged. Something mentioned and then rejected has a different status in public debate from something that was never mentioned at all. Something can become a practical possibility, a possible object of choice, by being mentioned and denied. To say "*I* would never propose doing away with all race-based preferences" is not the same as not proposing it. Decisions about which lines of argument to advance, which to entertain, which to refute, and which to ignore are part of what I understand and judge in following the proposed argument. Those choices are matter for ethical assessment. As Stephen Carter puts it, "available choices are not simply available choices. A culture defines itself in large part by what it chooses to make available."[15]

Ethos differs from reason by itself as I take responsibility for what I say. That is why Reagan and Operation Rescue weakened their arguments by appealing to precedent. As David Luban puts it: "One can too easily end up studying the beliefs of others, which means there is nothing at risk for the self."[16] Reagan's arguments were ethically disreputable because, in great contrast to the Warren Court in *Brown*, he used precedent to avoid putting anything "at risk for the self."

Speakers take responsibility in various ways for their arguments. Such an ethic of responsibility is missing from purely logical treatments. The ethical conditional of accepting something for the sake of argument shows how the central ethical phenomena of reliability and trust take more subtle relations than consistency and implication. Consequently, ethical arguments require appropriate intellectual virtues and not simply method. Kronman captures the virtuous prerequisites for the ethical conditionals I introduced with the quotation from Hume this way: "The sort of imaginative sympathy that deliberation requires combines two opposite-seeming dispositions, that of compassion on the one hand, and that of detachment, on the other. . . . It is difficult to be compassionate, and often just as difficult to be detached, but what is most difficult of all is to be both at once."[17] The contrast between ethical and logical analysis helps here. Logic comes to us already detached from the reasoner. I have to work to detach myself from my ethical commitments. That work is ethical work. The variations on supposing something "for the sake of argument" are among the ethical and logical methods of detachment.

Along similar lines, arguing against a straw man violates no logical rules. The validity of an argument is the same whether it is directed against views actually held by an opponent or against a caricature. But ethically it is not the same argument and does not have the same value. When an argument is not well motivated, it fails to treat an opponent with adequate respect and charity. These are intellectual virtues related to friendship that can be imputed to an argument. They are part of the *ethos* of an argument. Good controversial arguments have worthy targets and treat their targets as worthy opponents.

Apparent Reasoning versus Apparent Character

The next objection was that the qualities which make someone trustworthy seemed harder to assess accurately than logical properties, and easier to fake, easier to present in order to be persuasive. To put the objection succinctly, apparent reasoning really is reasoning, while apparent character is only apparently character.

I think that both sides of that claim are overstated. Consider, first, how much time we spend as teachers telling students how to look rational: present footnotes that not only offer evidence for particular assertions but show *bona fides;* carefully consider arguments against one's own favored thesis; have a calm and detached, balanced, dispassionate, voice. Open-mindedness, judicious weighing of evidence and alternative hypotheses—these are the marks of rationality. Our students learn to look rational. Teaching the appearance of rationality is a justified pedagogical tactic, because often one learns to be rational by learning how to seem rational, just as we become courageous by first acting courageously. Arts of appearance and imitation are not always arts of deception and concealing.[18]

On the other hand, it is easy to lose sight of how hard and costly it is to fake trustworthiness. Often the best way to look like we are committed to truth rather than to winning the argument is by having such a commitment. I tell my students that a good paper shows that its author cares about the subject. Since, I explain, they are not skilled enough to fake such devotion, they have to *be* interested. Our true character is often manifested—and developed—in the choices we make about how to appear ethical. "She's not really a bad person; she's just arguing that way in order to win." "Yes, but even in order to win I wouldn't argue that way. Those tactical choices reveal the sort of person she is."[19]

As I suggested before, character is revealed not only in the choices we make, and not only in the respect and allegiance we display for good reasons on which we cannot act, but also in the lines of reasoning that we do not even consider. Just as democratic knowledge has as its counterpart democratic ignorance, so we reveal our *ethos* in the things we are attentive to and those that we don't notice. The complexity of moral decisions has its argumentative parallel here. Emotions such as guilt and regret show that rejected practical reasons are not discarded as rejected theoretical reasons are. We feel these emotions toward good we can act toward.[20] Similarly, our attitudes toward rejected reasons display our argumentative *ethos*. That Reagan did not reject his violations of rule of law tells against him ethically, although not logically.

Similarly, Socrates frequently uses shame as a way of testing belief. Someone does not mean what he says if he is ashamed to admit the implications of this statements. Hippocrates would be shamed if people thought he was a sophist; shouldn't he therefore be ashamed to study with Protagoras? If he would be ashamed, is that not a reason not to go to Protagoras? Shame is a property of practical beliefs that can be transmitted from consequent to antecedent: if p implies q, and if I would be ashamed to assent to q, I can continue to maintain p only with difficulty and discomfort. Here is a kind of character which is argumentative, not personal, and which would be quite difficult to fake.

Purely logically, there is supposition and there is affirmation. There are no logical states intermediate between assuming a proposition for the sake of argument and simply asserting it. Ethically, there are many possible intermediate positions, including suggesting, inviting, entertaining, and seducing. It is a logical fallacy to mistake a supposition for an affirmation, but it is an *ethical* failing to disregard or misunderstand the degree of affirmation involved, mistaking detached understanding for sympathy, sympathy for agreement, reluctant assent for endorsement. Hume is right to show that assuming something for the sake of argument is different in philosophy and in practical argument. Living tentatively and arguing tentatively are not the same. For example, in the case of *Mozert v. Hawkins County Board of Education*, the plaintiff claimed that the presentation in the schools of alternate lives to the one that she was teaching her children amounted to endorsement.

If her children saw the possibility that people other than fundamentalist Christians lived decent lives, then the children's faith would be undermined. What is to me the exploration of alternate possibilities is to the plaintiff endorsement because she did not want her children even to consider these as possibilities that are not options for them. It takes great ethical judgment to adjudicate between these differing views of possibility and consideration for the sake of argument.[21] Similarly, many parents think that sex education and condom distribution in schools sends a message of endorsement, even if the schools say otherwise; other parents feel that way about posting the Ten Commandments or filling the halls with vending machines. How can we judge who has the message right?

Let me give one further example of the role of ethical criteria in assessing arguments. Following the First World War, there were many serious inquiries concerning whether the war could be blamed on something called the German national character. Few parallel arguments were offered after the Second World War. What accounts for the change? No new evidence about the existence of national characters, but new evidence about the uses and consequences of such arguments. People became more aware of the dangers and abuses of a type of argument, and the argument consequently lost its appeal, although it periodically resurfaces, generally as a sign of incomprehension, as in talk about "the Arab mind," or, a few years ago, about "Asian values." The decline of talk about national character creates new difficulties for understanding the *ethos* of a community as we become aware of the abuses of such talk. This is a fine example of what in chapter 1 I called democratic ignorance. There is no logical reason for arguments from national character to lose their appeal because of the consequences of some people employing them. So much the worse for logic.

The Paradox of Reflection and Self-Improvement

The next objection was the paradox of reflection. I can analyze and evaluate my own argument in the same way I try to understand someone else's, but what do I look at to assess my own *ethos?* There seems to be a direct connection between understanding an argument and knowing how to improve it, but it seems easy to understand ethical defects in argument without being able to do anything at all about them.

The paradox comes from the fact that logic is supposed to be impersonal, while character is by definition personal. Therefore it does not matter whether a given argument is mine or yours, but the parallel assertion for character is not false but incoherent. That is the reason why knowing what is wrong with an argument tells you all you can know about improving it, while there can be gaps between diagnosis and treatment for character. Correcting a logical argument has nothing to do with the fact that it is mine.

It is certainly easier to see the flaws in other people's reasoning than in one's own, but that applies equally to ethical and logical errors. It is easier to give advice than to take it, but it is not obviously easier to give *good* advice than to take it. The same factors that make it hard to improve our own reasoning make it hard to improve character. That is as it should be.

We can use this response to build on my earlier sketch of the ethical idea of conditionals. Logically, "If I steal this car, I risk being put in jail," is equivalent to "Either I don't steal it, or I risk being put in jail." It seems to have as a logical consequence, "If I accept the risk, I can steal the car." The law's treatment of punishment and desert becomes a prediction of probable punishment, in Holmes's "bad man's view of law." It is an ethical inference drawn by a bad character. The same hypothetical, "If I steal this car, I risk being put in jail," does not invite the good man to consider whether the reward is worth the risk. Here character is revealed in premises and implications we do not consider because they are outside the range of our possible choices. If I find myself approaching the law as the bad man does, ethical criticism could help me to realize it and improve the ethical quality of my reasoning. The debates within moral philosophy about whether one is responsible for one's character reappear here. I ask myself, what *ethos* do I display in this argument? Is it an *ethos* I want to show? What *ethos* am I imputing to the community in my argument? Is that an *ethos* I want to reinforce? By thinking about what *ethos* I want to show, I can make choices about what *ethos* I want to have. Therefore, if these are reasonable questions, reflection is not paradoxical.

Logos and Ethos in Conflict

The final objection was that there had better not be an ethical evaluation of arguments, because the more ethical, the less logical an argument is—it becomes less an argument and more an appeal to an audience's prejudices and sentiments, as the victim's voice and the convert's experience often are. Conversely, the more logical an argument, the less ethical. People who judge an argument about the existence of God by whether believing would help them to live a better life would be inserting an inappropriate ethical judgment where only logic belongs. "Religious people are happy, so I'll become religious." Keeping the boundaries between *ethos* and reasoning intact is responsible, both ethically and logically.

The first reply to this objection is to agree to a sense in which, in practical matters, the more logical an argument is, the less ethical. But where mathematical arguments are not ethical, excessively logical appeals in practical matters are *un*ethical. For example, former judge Robert Bork caused people to mistrust him through his claims that reasoning is not only sufficient for good decisions, but that anything else was an indication of the judge "making things up" or injecting "subjective values" into the process and thereby corrupting the decision. His reasoning backfired. Just as the ancient sophists' emphasis on finding arguments on both sides of any dispute created mistrust, so here it is possible to fail ethically by being too rational. When someone uses reason alone where *ethos* is called for, reason is perceived as cleverness.[22]

Bork claimed that anything other than logic was preference. Being methodical was the only way to be rational. But the public saw his own purely logical arguments as unethical. Not only did his reasoning look disconnected from the beliefs and values of the public, but he declared that it had no connection to his own values. The public then saw his lack of *ethos* as a fatal lack of self-knowledge as well. Substituting reasoning alone for character denies personal responsibility by purporting to remove agency and present oneself as part of a chain of necessary connections. Claiming to rely on reason alone is to hide one's own commitments and act as though practical reasoning was an inferential relation between propositions, not between the assertion of propositions. If jurisprudence is an ethical rather than a mathematical matter, the exclusion of *ethos* is itself unethical and untrustworthy.

To return again to my example of bilingual education and public financial support for church schools, the perfectly predictable advocate might be logically consistent, but would anyone trust such a person? Logical consistency producing mistrust is a perfect example of reasoning destroying character. One could safely predict that Strom Thurmond will respond in the same way to every civil rights initiative from the integration of the Armed Forces in 1948 to the present: "This time they've gone too far!" Consistency can be a way of failing to come to terms with the particulars of the practical situation. Pursuit of the logical value of consistency can indicate a lack of integrity. Someone who, with apparent consistency, supported both state support

for parochial schools and bilingual education is not obviously more trustworthy and believable than someone opposed to one or the other of those
policies.

In matters of praxis, to live by reason alone and exclude *ethos* is unethical.
The more one is following rules, the less character is engaged. But if the
more logical an argument is, the less ethical, could we become more ethical
by being *less logical* and less rational?

We can avoid that implication by recalling the idea of ethical surplus and
ampliative reasoning from chapter 3. One can become unethical by being
too logical, but it does not follow that therefore to be ethical is to be illogical.
The crucial distinction is between an argument which claims that a conclusion follows from the nature of the good—a purely logical claim—and an
argument which shows me *inferring* that same conclusion because of my
commitment to the good—a demonstration that is simultaneously logical
and ethical. I make my own character and moral purpose clear, but I am
not on that account being illogical. The logical relation is among propositions; the ethical relation is among the assertions of propositions, and those
relations are not necessarily in competition with each other. Ethical reasoning involves the assumption of responsibility and commitment. Thus Robert
Cover says that "the transformation of interpretation into legal meaning begins when someone accepts the demands of interpretation and, through the
personal act of commitment, affirms the position taken." That personal act
is an act of rhetorical friendship, and so he continues: "Creation of legal
meaning entails . . . the subjective commitment to an objectified understanding of a demand. It entails the disengagement of the self from the 'object'
of law, and at the same time requires an engagement to that object as a
faithful 'other.'"[23]

To think of ethical relations as matters of commitment, reliability, and
integrity is to see ethical argument as not illogical but as a development of
the logical beyond the reach of reason alone. Not only is ethical reasoning
ampliative, but *ethos* gives us the ability to reason about concrete particulars.
Aristotle attributes to both practical wisdom and to the art of rhetoric the
ability to apprehend and treat rationally particulars that seem beyond the
reach of reason. "We call people practically wise about some [restricted area]
whenever they calculate well to promote some excellent end, in an area
where there is no *technē*" (*Ethics* VI.5.1140a28–30). "The assemblyman and
the juryman are actually judging present and specific cases (*peri parontōn
kai aphorismenōn*)" (*Rhetoric* I.1.1354b7–8). In both rhetoric and practical

wisdom, *ethos* allows reason to go beyond the limits of reason. This is integrity, not consistency. It is how we judge the Supreme Court Justices I listed at the start of the chapter.

An ethical relation among the assertions of propositions ties form to purpose without being illogical. Because practical reason is reason first of all, it does not have its own logic. The ethical relations among assertions, and other propositional attitudes, does not set up a conception of form at odds with the purely logical one. Propositions have relations of consistency and implication with each other, while assertions have relations of integrity, justice, and friendship.[24]

What, finally, is then the relation between logical consistency and ethical integrity, between logical assertion and ethical endorsement? Consistency depends on a single world, while integrity is the unity of a single agent. Integrity is not an irrational final resting place of argument, but the ultimate yet still rational court of appeal. Logically, the world can contain people in conflict with each other. Ethically, my character and the character of the community can include contradictory values, contradictory beliefs about the world, even contradictory proposals about what to do, so long as there is a nonarbitrary means of acting on their basis. Such integrity is ethical, but relies on logical abilities and habits. The virtues of integrity are intellectual virtues.

Ethical Argument and Intellectual Virtue

I have been looking at how we judge other people's arguments. But my conclusions have significant bearing on how practical reason itself operates. The connections practical reason draws among assertions tracks the connections that logic draws among propositions. Sometimes this tracking takes the form of motivation, sometimes the transmission of an emotion, such as shame, from conditional to consequence. Because practical reason is reason first of all, it does not have its own "logic." It is not like desires, which need not obey the law of noncontradiction.

The rational structure of ethical argument has a richness that resists reduction to method. Ethical integrity can be more sensitive to particulars than logical consistency. Integrity is a virtue while consistency is simply a minimal condition of intelligibility. The *ethos* of hypothetical and conditional reasoning involves virtues of sympathy and detachment not present in logic. Logic is monotonic and closed. Additional true premises, that is, can only strengthen and never weaken a logical argument, but they can have that effect ethically. Each time we compare an ethical relation between assertions to its logical counterpart that relates propositions to each other, the terms of comparison resemble the difference between friendship and justice. Seeing that friendship is not rule-governed is not a reason to call it irrational, and the same holds for ethical reasoning and ethical persuasion. Rorty's identification of the rational with the civilized need not imply a loosening of the meaning of rationality. Intellectual virtues are in some ways more flexible than logic alone, and in other ways more demanding.

The challenge in this chapter has been to see ethical and practical reasoning as something other than a second-best form of thinking that we are doomed to fall back on when theoretical reasoning fails us. That picture of the relation of theory to practice fails when we see how *ethos* can exceed reason without ever becoming irrational. Theoretical reason fits the world, while practical reason fits a self with integrity. While in my series of objections the reflexive application of the ethical assessment of arguments may have seemed to be a refutation, I see the greatest use of such assessment as an aid to ethical self-knowledge. Earlier I pointed to the biblical argument "We were strangers in Egypt, so we must treat strangers kindly" as a paradigm of ethical argument. I want to end this chapter by quoting Jonathan Shay on a modern variant of such an ethical argument:

> When Lincoln wrote, "As I would not be a *slave,* so I would not be a *master,*" he did not claim any rational compulsion for what he would not be. The vision of a good life for a human being is an ethical choice and cannot be coerced. It can only be called forth by persuasion, education, and welcoming appeal.[25]

CHAPTER 5

Rhetorical Argument and Ethical Authority

The desire to narrate is the desire to represent authority, whose legitimacy depends on establishing certain grounding facts.

Narrative is the literary genre for the objectification of value.

Legal argument is a struggle for the privilege of recounting the past. To the victor goes the right to infuse a constitutional clause, or a statute, or a series of prior decisions with the meaning that it will henceforth bear by recounting its circumstances of origin and assigning its place in history.[1]

In the first four chapters I tried to make intelligible in a contemporary context the first two theses I derive from Aristotle's *Rhetoric,* that reasoning is the center of persuasion and that *ethos* is the most powerful means of persuasion. The first two chapters showed what it meant for reasoning to be the center of persuasion and for persuasion to be the central case of practical reason. The third and fourth chapters let us see how *ethos* allows reasoning to go beyond itself. If practical reason can go where theory cannot, it is not a second-best that we have to use when theory fails us. In this chapter and the next I turn to the third grand thesis, that the *ethos* that is most authoritative is an *ethos* produced by reasoning. In this chapter I will look at authority as an ethical phenomenon, and in the next show how trust functions ethically. Practical reason is the source of rational authority and trust. The healthy functioning of authority and trust is one of the prime circumstances of friendship.

Narrative versus Argument, Ethos versus Logos

After defending practical reason against the sophists and against those who would subordinate it to theory, I want to continue my project of articulating ethical reasoning by defending practical rationality, this time against its friends. Narrative has recently become popular as an antidote or supplement to argument. Argument is sterile and inert, and at the same time, paradoxically, compelling and hence violent, while narrative establishes relationships of friendship and trust between author and audience, rather than the more authoritarian sounds of a pure argument.

Narrative is a contemporary way of talking about what Aristotle calls example, the rhetorical equivalent of induction. Enthymeme and example are the two equally important kinds of rhetorical reasoning:

> In the case of persuasion through proving or seeming to prove something, just as in dialectic there is on the one hand induction and on the other the syllogism and the apparent syllogism, so the situation is similar in rhetoric; for the example is an induction, the enthymeme a syllogism. . . . All speakers produce logical persuasion by means of paradigms or enthymemes and by nothing other than these. (*Rhetoric* I.2.1356a35–b6)

The logical structure of reasoning with examples, like the logical structure of induction, is less visible than the logical structure of enthymematic reasoning, but its ethical nature is even more powerful. Character reveals itself, we have seen, in which lines of argument to follow, which to reject, and which to ignore. But character shows itself even more directly in our choices of examples and authorities. Narrative offers possibilities for recognizing and developing ethical argument. In particular, narrative can create the crucial kinds of character, trust and authority.

Narrative can create *ethos*. But we shouldn't oversell it. Richard Posner is right when he says, "narrative is a literary technique and there is nothing inherently egalitarian in literary technique." I argued in the second chapter that there is nothing about either rational or emotional rhetoric that will always put the one or the other on the side of progress or reaction, however these are defined. Similarly, there is nothing ethically superior about narrative as opposed to argument. Rhetorical induction is not morally superior to deduction.[2]

To think that narrative is ethically superior to argument misinterprets a profound truth. The great appeal of narrative and examples is that they are obviously and immediately ethical. Practical reasoning can be the manifestation of a pure rationality that has nothing ethical about it. "Logos has neither *ethos* nor moral purpose (*prohairesis*)" (III.15.1417a19–21). I can use reasoning to avoid responsibility and commitment. The goal of rhetorical argument is to make discourse ethical, making it civilized and not just methodical. Narrative is well suited to that task. One's choice of examples cannot help making discourse ethical by revealing character. I can offer a narrative in which Operation Rescue is part of a story that began with Vietnam War protests. If I do, I can blame the left for Operation Rescue. Alternatively, I could tell a story that starts with the Civil Rights demonstrations and ends with Operation Rescue. We all, in retrospect, participated in those Civil Rights demonstrations—thus goes our official myth—so that more extensive narrative would not prove that the left is to blame. Unlike arguments, narratives are never ethically innocent.

The revival of narrative puts us in a position to face a question Aristotle did not think about. The *Rhetoric* looks at individual acts of persuasion. But practical discourse never starts from a clean slate. Acts of practical reason are interventions into a field already filled with people and arguments. From the first chapter we have seen connections between the *ethos* of the community to an *ethos* of a speaker, and authority is one of the names we have for that connection. Just as the Greek word *pistis* applies to people whom we believe and trust and equally to propositions that we believe, authority too applies to people as well as propositions. Someone can be *an* authority, and someone else can be *in authority*.[3] Just as *ethos* can be either created by speech or by such externals as antecedent reputation or the trappings of power, so there are rational and irrational authorities. There can be personal authority with no propositional content or claims to truth: charisma is a standard name for such authority. Here there is no propositional content and no reason. At the other limit, one can have allegiance to a text without venerating its source, as for example is probably the case for most people with regard to the Fourteenth Amendment. Equal protection is part of the American national *ethos* but is a purely impersonal source of authority. The rightness of equal protection, not its source, makes it authoritative. The most interesting issues of authority come in neither of those cases but where there is an intersection between the personal and the propositional. This is the field of the ethical. Michael Moore puts it this way:

Authority is usually thought of as an attribute possessed by persons. . . . Yet . . . to grant authority to someone is to grant authority to something which that person says, does, or thinks. Otherwise, there is no way that an authority can enter our practical reasoning, for she is not us; only a norm derived from her orders, wishes, exemplary behavior, or general rules can enter our practical reasoning.[4]

Authority and trust, the subject of my next chapter, are ideal subjects for ethical consideration. Both can be created by any of Aristotle's trio of logos, pathos, and *ethos*. Both can be created by *ethos* in the sense of reputation or the *ethos* that comes from argument. I want to show how the trust and authority that come from argumentative *ethos* are ethically superior to trust and authority that come from either logos or pathos. In any case, trust and authority present an obvious problem. In chapter 3 I showed how in *Brown* the conclusion, segregated public education was unconstitutional, took on a life of its own independent of the premises that got us to that conclusion. Authority and trust are ethical relations that take on a life of their own that is more powerful than the considerations that lead us to obey an authority or trust someone. How can we make sense of their ampliative nature?

An Example of an Ethical Mistake

Before showing how ethical argument can successfully create authority, I want to explore narrative and ethical authority by looking at an especially maladroit narrative which destroyed credibility and authority. In the oral arguments for *Bolling v. Sharpe*, the companion case to *Brown v. Board of Education*, the counsel for the District of Columbia urged the Court to uphold the constitutionality of segregated schools in the district. As Richard Kluger puts it, Milton Korman "reviewed the congressional statutes that he said evidenced beyond doubt the lawmakers' intention to authorize a dual school system" at the same time that Congress was passing the Fourteenth Amendment.[5] Korman needed to make sure that the Court did not simply ignore legislative intent and decide the case on other grounds, so he made the historical record seem as unambiguous as possible.

Korman's narrative showed that segregation was legal in the minds of the authors of the Fourteenth Amendment. This narrative functions logically, providing reasons to accept the speaker's conclusion. Showing that the authors of the Fourteenth Amendment thought that segregation was legal is as much as reasoning, including narrative, can do. It isn't enough. It is one thing to show that the intent of the authors of the Fourteenth Amendment did not include outlawing segregated schools. It is another thing to convince the Justices that that demonstration should be dispositive. For that, reasoning is not enough and one needs *ethos*. One has to show that it is *right* to be guided by legislative intent in this case. That is, one has to show that that intent has *authority* over the decision the Justices are about to make.

If rhetoric allows us to frame arguments on both sides of a practical question, then argument by itself leaves the decision indeterminate. The greater the power of reasoning to produce arguments on both sides, the greater the need for *ethos* to lead to a determinate conclusion. Practical intelligence lets us see both sides of any issue, and leaves us needing to decide when faced with more cogent arguments than we can assent to. The gap between the legitimate and the just, between the reasonable or plausible and the rationally compelling, is an ethical one. It cannot be bridged logically but only ethically.

An argument from authority is one way to bridge the gap, because it can make an audience recognize an argument not only as possible and plausible but as convincing and decisive. Quoting an earlier Court decision is one device for moving an audience from recognizing a legitimate argument based on legislative intent to a definitive decision based on that argument. Such quotations serve the same function, and are a species of, what Aristotle calls maxims. Narratives can make arguments ethical, but maxims, Aristotle says, are even better at it. A good argument from authority can be even more useful in bridging the ethical gap between legitimacy and a final decision than a good narrative. Many of the benefits of narrative that attract people today were in Aristotle's eyes the benefits of maxims:

> One should also speak maxims . . . whenever the speaker's character is going to be made to seem better or the maxim is stated with *pathos*. (*Rhetoric* II.21.1395a21)

> A maxim makes the speech "ethical." Speeches have character insofar as deliberative choice is clear, and all maxims accomplish this because one speaking a maxim makes a general statement about preferences, so that if the maxims are morally good, they make the speaker seem to have a good character. (II.21.1395b13–17)

> Nor should you seek an enthymeme when the speech is being "ethical"; for logical demonstration (*logos*) has neither *ethos* nor moral purpose. Maxims should be used both in a narration and in a proof; for they are "ethical." (III.17.1418a18–20)

Citations of authority, like Aristotle's maxims, make one's argument ethical. The difference between legitimacy and justice is the difference we encountered in the last chapter between an argument as a relation among propositions and an argument as a relation among attitudes one takes toward propositions, attitudes that include consent, assent, and commitment.[6] Rhetorical situations frequently present us with incomplete evidence, pressures for making a decision in a timely way, conflicting possibilities and values, and, yet, the need for decision. One way an advocate can make one set of considerations seem weightier than others is by appealing to authority. Such appeals are ethical because they weight our choices.

Here is the quotation Korman used to buttress his argument:

> No one, we presume, supposes that any change in public opinion or feeling, in relation to this unfortunate race, in the civilized nations of Europe or in this country, should induce the Court to give to the words of the Constitution a more liberal construction in their favor than they were intended to bear when the instrument was framed and adopted.

Korman quotes a prior Supreme Court chief justice, in a majority opinion, reminding the Court that they had a duty to follow legislative intent. Authority is made by the combination of the right moral sentiments, which this passage expresses, and the utterance being made by someone in the right position, which this passage also has going for it. His argument from authority is an argument and not an authoritarian substitute for argument.

Kluger continues his account of the oral argument: "Supreme Court decisions, [Korman] went on quoting, could never be 'the mere reflex of the popular opinion or passion of the day.' Unfortunately, in seeking to stiffen the courage of the Justices . . . , Milton Korman had chosen to cite to them the most denounced and discredited decision in all the annals of the Supreme Court—*Dred Scott v. Sanford*." Kluger reports that this was such an "astonishing gaffe" that the NAACP attorneys were "elbowing each other with disbelief at the counsel table."[7] Earlier I said that one's choice of examples and authorities reveals one's character. Korman's choice of examples reveals *bad* character, not—it should be obvious in this case—bad character of Milton Korman the person, but of Korman the persuader.

But just why was Korman's citation of Taney's opinion in *Dred Scott* such a gaffe? *That* it was a mistake seems obvious, but I think the reasons behind its failure shed interesting light on the nature of rhetorical argument and the construction of credibility and authority. Kluger does not make much of this incident, since it had nothing to do with the decision the Court eventually made. But I think it's worth a closer look. If the study of rhetoric teaches anything, it is that we have to distinguish between failures to persuade, which can depend on all sorts of things that have nothing to do with the speaker's craft, and the artistic and ethical failures that are the legitimate focus of rhetorical criticism. In chapter 2 I explored Aristotle's careful definition of rhetoric as the art of finding the available means of persuasion, rather than persuading. There is a difference between achieving that end and succeeding at persuading a given audience. If Korman was simply guilty of miscalculating the Court's prejudices, that may be a blunder, but is of no theoretical interest. By looking more closely at this "gaffe" we can see something more about how narratives and arguments create, and destroy, authority and, with it, belief and confidence. The intertextual relations between the majority opinion in *Dred Scott,* Korman's brief, and the subsequent decision offer a way get at the richness required.[8]

One reason to think that quoting Taney is a more complicated sort of mistake is that the Court itself quoted him, although not *Dred Scott,* but in *Cooper v. Aaron,* the case that affirms the supremacy of the Supreme Court's interpretation of the Constitution over that of Governer Faubus, only a few years after *Brown* and *Bolling:* "Chief Justice Taney, speaking for a unanimous Court in 1859, said that this requirement [of judicial supremacy in Article VI] reflected the framers' 'anxiety to preserve it [the Constitution] in full force, in all its powers, and to guard against resistance to or evasion of its authority on the part of a State'" (358 U.S. 1 [1958] at 18–19). No one objected to the Court quoting Taney, so exactly what Korman did wrong needs a closer look.

Korman's is a model argument from authority, appealing to authority to create authority for itself. It is part of the nature of authority that it can be transmitted in this way, in a fashion parallel to the way in which valid inference transmits truth from premises to conclusion. One becomes an authority by credibly citing authorities. The authority of law is linked to the social practice of citing and arguing from authorities.[9] Korman might have profited from Aristotle's advice that "speaking in maxims is appropriate to those older in years and on subjects of which one is experienced, since to use maxims is unseemly for one too young, as is storytelling; and on a matter in which one is inexperienced it is silly and shows lack of education" (*Rhetoric* II.21.1395a). For someone in Korman's position to cite Taney to the Supreme Court is to hide behind an authority rather than argue from it. Using a high authority gives one's argument *gravitas,* but one has to have a certain *gravitas* oneself to use such authority. "The acknowledgment of anything by better men is more authoritative than if made by worse men" (Plato, *Sophist* 246d).

Korman does not claim that because Taney ruled as he did, the current Justices had no choice in the matter. Taney's words were in the first place not the decision but a refutation of a supposed counterargument, and as such they would not be binding on later Justices. But in addition, Taney's decision had itself been overruled by the Civil War and the Amendments that followed. Therefore his words never had institutional authority, and even if they had, that authority was lost by the break in continuity that Constitutional Amendments constitute.[10] Korman's argument is an argument from authority, not an argument from binding precedent.

Korman's argument rebuts a passive sense of authority, in which, as Hart puts it, authority involves a "surrender of judgment" in which someone acts according to the authority's "will instead of his own as a guide to action and so to take it in place of any deliberation or reasoning of his own."[11] That passive sense of authority makes the idea of arguments from authority merely a Pickwickian sense of argument. It is a decision to forgo deciding. Korman and the opposing counsel from the NAACP had presented all the possible arguments, and it would be improper for the Court to rely on anything but those arguments in making its decision. When the Court recognizes authority, it does not surrender its judgment. There should be no antinomy between authority and autonomy, because we decide to be compelled. In chapter 2 I contrasted the senses of passivity in sophistic and rational rhetoric, and that distinction is at play here: when I defer to an authority, deference is an action on my part, sometimes more voluntary, sometimes less, sometimes intelligently done, sometimes not.

Yet while the citation from Taney is not a citation of precedent as a substitute for thinking, it is not an argument from reason alone. The earlier opinion serves as a witness to the truth of Korman's claim and the validity of his reasoning. Authority is neither purely rational—if that were the case we could do without citations altogether—nor a matter of pure power—the Justices are persuaded not only by the fact of past Supreme Court majority opinions but by what they say.

Korman was free from the imputation that to follow Taney in this regard was to be committed to the substance of his decision in *Dred Scott*. The Thirteenth Amendment had taken care of that. The Justices were therefore free to take this quotation as Korman intended it, as a stylistically admirable and relevant framing of a familiar point that fidelity to the Constitution is fidelity to its authors' intent. It is a maxim, expressing in a particular value general terms. "Maxims should be used both in a narration and in a proof; for they are 'ethical' (*ethikon*)" (III.17.1418a10–21). So what went wrong?

The Justices in 1952, as at any other time, could never disagree with the content of Taney's dictum. No one ever declares himself against original meaning. They just change the subject. "Faced with the need to change its mind, the Court simply asks a different question."[12] But if the Justices agreed with the sentiment expressed by Taney and quoted by Korman, such agreement was overwhelmed by the fact that they had to distance themselves from the source. Korman wanted to associate himself with earlier rulings of the Court so that the current Court could associate itself with him. If he could convince the Court to see itself as part of a narrative that included the Constitution, an earlier statement by a Chief Justice, and Korman himself, then he and the Court would be on the same side, and he would win the case. Ethical argument creates authority by creating a narrative in which speaker and audience are in the same ethical community. That ethical community is what Aristotle means by ethical friendship. Korman and the current Supreme Court are of "one mind" with each other. Recall the line I quoted in chapter 1: "Concord (*homonoia*, being of one mind) then, is political friendship (*philia*) . . . for it is concerned with advantage and with what affects life" (*Ethics* IX.6.1167b3–4). By relying on someone else's knowledge, I can become part of a community with him. I join a community by sharing the democratic knowledge of chapter 1, and can do so through choosing to defer to an authority.

The citation of Taney is a rhetorical failure because it is an *ethical* failure. It is a pure case of a rhetorical ethical failure, since there is no reason to infer from this mistake to anything about Korman the person. His performance is an ethical failure because authority has two sides, what is said and who says it. Taney functions as an unwelcome witness. Korman wanted to establish a narrative in which there was a continuity from the Constitution, to past Supreme Court rulings, to his own pleadings, to the Justices' decision. The Justices wanted to be part of a narrative that included the Constitution and past Supreme Court rulings, but that narrative could not include Taney. Ethically, to cite *Dred Scott* is to re-fight the Civil War by proposing a smooth narrative instead of a discontinuity. We saw in the last chapter that the transmission of *ethos* from premise to conclusion is not identical to logical transmission. The Justices needed to be part of a narrative that included themselves and the Constitution, but which either explicitly excluded Taney or from which he was simply and silently absent. If they cannot be part of the same narrative with Taney, then they cannot be in the same narrative with Korman. Since Korman trusts Taney enough to cite him as an authority, the Justices cannot trust Korman. Korman's argument failed ethically because he mentioned something unspeakable. The Court will not reward Korman for putting them in an impossible position.

How could Korman have done anything so obtuse? I think the most reasonable hypothesis is that he mistakenly supposed that the Court's decision was a logical one, rather than an ethical one, and that therefore he did not worry about who is in what narrative with whom. It is a violation of decorum to suppose that an ethical decision is really a logical one, to be decided by purely logical argument. It is an ethical failure that rightly causes mistrust.

Korman could easily have missed this point because there is no rule that all Supreme Court decisions must be ethical rather than logical. Sometimes simply showing that the Constitution or precedent demands a certain decision is enough. One can, through logic, recognize that one's hands are tied. Sometimes one will welcome being told that one's hands are tied. Sometimes we are glad to avoid responsibility and to believe that a decision has been forced on us by necessity. But for a decision as revolutionary as *Brown* it would be disingenuous to pretend that it directly and obviously followed from either Constitutional text or precedent. Because they have to take responsibility for this decision, the decision has to be ethical. Therefore they have to be persuaded ethically. Korman misunderstood the Court's job just at the moment the Court was recognizing and reconceiving its own role as an authority in relation both to the Constitution and to the people, since *Brown* was a moment when the Court chose to speak directly to the people.

Ethos and Authority

The Justices in *Bolling* faced a common problem of practical reasoning. They were presented with arguments that led to conflicting conclusions, and they had to decide what to do. To rely on anything other than the reasons that were presented would be arbitrary. And yet the reasons presented are not adequate to justify a unique conclusion. Logic has run out, but we are committed to relying on logic alone. *Ethos* is the solution to the dilemma, since we have seen that rhetorical reasoning can produce an ethical surplus, that *ethos* based on reasoning can go where reasoning itself cannot. There is no further evidence or argument that takes a judge from conflicting arguments to a definite decision. The only responsible *ethos* is an *ethos* that is nothing but argument, yet goes past argument.

More concretely, the Justices in *Bolling* and *Brown* faced arguments from history, from constitutional text, from consequences, among others. It would be unjust and irrational of them to appeal to anything other than that evidence to decide among the competing arguments. That is where authority can help.

While it is a commonplace of modern philosophy that one cannot decide to believe, we do decide to undertake obligations. We freely bind ourselves. We decide that something is convincing. We can decide to be convinced and choose to find a line of reasoning compelling.[13] This is the essence of rational authority, deciding that something is compelling and taking responsibility for that decision.

An argument from authority, then, is a means of crossing the ethical gap between a legitimate argument and a definitive conclusion. The Court's decision that *Brown* and *Bolling* should be covered by the same line of reasoning, in spite of being rooted in two distinct parts of the Constitution, is an ethical decision. This conception of authority as a means of crossing the ethical gap between a legitimate argument and a definitive conclusion makes sense of a feature of judicial reasoning that is often a source of cynicism. Judges may rationally reach different conclusions, and each judge may struggle with her own doubts and conflicts, but when it comes time to write an opinion, each judge writes as though his or her decision is ineluctable, necessary, and inevitable.

That change of mood makes sense. Sometimes the careful balancing of reasons is a charade, but sometimes it isn't. If there are many possible legitimate arguments, reason alone cannot be enough to lead to a single conclusion. The judicial decision is supposed to be just, and not merely final. It is not hypocrisy for someone to reach a decision after considered and nuanced deliberation, but then write an opinion that presents the decision as inevitable. Before it was not inevitable, but now it is.[14] While reason alone cannot compel a conclusion, we don't give up and say: there are many legitimate arguments here, so we fill flip a coin, or operate under a rule that a plaintiff, or the state, always wins unless all the arguments are on the other side. A just decision in a context of plural legitimate arguments must be ethical and must involve *ethos*.

Behind this ritualized dance of carefully balanced reasons followed by a decisive judgment lies something that both judges and their audience must believe in order to find the assertion of authority morally convincing, rather than just a power that they must defer to. As Robert Hariman glosses Kenneth Burke: "All action is structured according to the essential ingredients of drama. Meaning is created through staged performances of conflict and resolution before an audience. Power is constituted by the persuasive communication of principles of order amidst changing situations."[15] The key sentence for our purposes is the second: *Meaning is created through staged performances of conflict and resolution before an audience.* Unless both conflict and resolution are believably staged, an audience will not voluntarily submit to authority. Drama and narrative produce an ethically satisfying exercise of authority. The narrative of allying oneself with previous authorities is part of that drama. We not only stage conflict and resolution; we stage our connections to the past and to the *ethos* of the community. Opinions are more convincing when a necessary and compelling decision is presented after an apparently fair presentation of opposed reasoning. Such opinions present not only the right decision but the right decision rightly arrived at. Why should such drama and narrative be convincing?

As *ethos* goes beyond pure reasoning, practical reason leads to definitive judgments in the light of incomplete evidence and competing arguments. The ethical decisiveness of a judgment can take many appearances. There are times when one wants to appear purely rational, to show that one's fidelity to history or to text is a function of reason alone, for example, when one is likely to be accused of partisanship. The self making the judgment disappears and one presents the decision as purely logical. There are other times when it is important to show that one is making a choice and taking responsibility for a decision, as in *Brown* and even more emphatically in *Cooper v. Aaron,* where the Court had to defend its function of saying "what the law is" against the contrary assertion of authority by Arkansas' Governor Faubus. Authority functions differently in those different circumstances. There are two sides to a rational decision, its rationality and the fact that it is a decision. Where the emphasis falls is a tactical decision.

Since we have an obligation to obey a judicial decision, why should it matter whether the reasoning behind the decision is compelling? We have to obey anyway, but citizens in a democracy obey reasons by participating in the democratic narrative of authority. "In this society, we say that we live under a government of laws, not men; we *expect* judges to write opinions that will persuade us, time and again, that this is so. And judges oblige us. Given our legal culture, this rhetorical strategy makes sense. Judges do not

have forces at their disposal to enforce the orders they give; they must persuade those whom they would order to comply."[16]

The existence of a gap, to be filled by ethical argument, is the source of
the debate between positivists, who think that only discretion, or will, can
cross that gap, and those, like Ronald Dworkin, who propose to fill the gap
with principles. *Ethos* can overcome those alternatives. The Justices must
decide to find one line of reasoning compelling. The gap between seeing
something as a legitimate argument and as a decisive, dispositive, just, and
compelling argument makes possible legitimate differences of opinion in
which judges reach a decision about probabilities and then are forcefully
committed to that decision. As Joseph Vining puts it, "The authoritative
statement is a clue to what one oneself believes."[17] Not all practical decisions,
and not all Supreme Court decisions, must be ethical. But when decisions
are in this sense ethical, Justices, like the rest of us, accept responsibility for
recognizing an authority.[18]

We are not all Supreme Court justices, but we all make ethical decisions
within such contexts of responsibility and authority. We *choose* to cross the
gap between legitimacy and justice. Nothing can compel us. Therefore reason alone is not enough and the move from legitimacy to justice is an ethical
act for which narrative is central. We don't make ethical decisions by pretending to be isolated Cartesian doubters who only accept reasons we have
generated by ourselves. We make decisions through weighing the reasons
we are presented with. We decide to acknowledge an authority. Deciding to
be compelled is a central unrecognized feature of our moral lives. Indeed,
deciding to be compelled is a condition of being a responsible and ethical
agent.[19]

We choose to find a reason compelling. A judicial opinion which weighs
opposing considerations and then forcefully announces a decision is a dramatic performance of the ethical act of encountering and then bridging the
gap between legitimacy and justice. When I find that decision authoritative,
I reenact the decision by following the reasoning. The rituals of reenactment
that dramatize our choosing to find a reason compelling are presented in
these remarks of Charles Fried:

> To accept another's reasoning is to follow along with it. At the least,
> this requires that the reasoning exhibit the kind of steadiness and com-
> mitment we aspire to in our own reasoning. In the sphere of public
> authority, this need is even more urgent. It is not just that we wish

for evidence that the public reasoner is indeed reasoning, as we would if we were considering her for, say, a post as an editor, but we demand that she commit to reason for us, in a way that we are invited to follow as she goes along, and so the public manifestation, the rituals of reasoning are owed as much as the substance.[20]

Choosing to be compelled is a paradox, since if something is truly compelling, that normally means that it is not up to us to find it compelling or not. If I am compelled to get off my bicycle because of a flat tire, I do not have a choice about it. If the cogency of a mathematical proof compels me to reach a certain conclusion, the whole point of the cogency of reasoning is that I have no choice in the matter. That is why Arendt says that "truth, namely, the truths we call self-evident, compel the mind, and . . . this coercion, though it needs no violence to be effective, is stronger than persuasion and argument."[21] Arendt's formulation makes sense only if we forget that the compulsion of self-evident truths can be the product of persuasion and argument. She is right to notice that the ethical coercion by successful rhetorical argument can be as powerful and compelling as physical coercion or the necessity of a mathematical proof. One of the attractions of narrative has been a rejection of the picture of argument as compelling in a way that denies responsibility and commitment on the part of the audience. But we now see that finding an argument compelling does not reduce my autonomy.

The more rational a commitment, the more ethical it is. The more one consciously chooses among alternatives, the more committed one becomes. As Justice Douglas put it, "confidence based on understanding is more enduring than confidence based on awe."[22] The more rational I find a decision, the more committed I will be. Democracy is a gamble that Douglas is right: unthinking obedience is weaker than obedience given through choice. *Ethos* based on reasoning is, as it ought to be, more powerful than other sorts of *ethos*. Democratic faith is trust in rhetorical argument.

There is no loss of autonomy in acknowledging an authority, no loss of autonomy in acting rationally or ethically. As Robert Cover said:

Creation of legal meaning entails subjective commitment to an objectified understanding of a demand. It entails the disengagement of the self from the "object" of law, and at the same time requires an engagement to that object as a faithful "other." The metaphor of separation permits the allegory of dedication. This objectification of the norms to which one is committed frequently, perhaps always, entails a narrative—a story of how the law, now object, came to be, and more importantly, how it came to be one's own. Narrative is the literary genre for the objectification of value.[23]

The idea of freely accepting an authority is implicit in Aristotle's definition of rhetoric that I discussed in chapter 2. Rhetoric is the art of finding the available means of persuasion. It is not an art of persuading. The speaker's job is to present compelling arguments, not compelling the audience. The audience will decide to be compelled by deciding that those arguments are compelling. The fact that we choose to be compelled shows how authority is created in the rhetorical act of persuading someone that one is an authority or is in authority. Korman's argument is a failed attempt to constitute oneself as an authority through argument. Other arguments succeed in creating authority. Such creation is rational and ethical.

Careful balancing of reasons followed by decisive judgment: that is a dramatic reenactment of the decision to find something compelling. As history turns the present into past, it turns contingencies into necessities. Thus, as *Brown* recedes into the past, it looks more and more inevitable, while at the time it was quite a near thing. In the case of authority and commitment, we make history by contingencies being willed into necessities.[24]

When I recognize an authority, I choose to find something compelling. In making that choice and commitment, I consider the putative authority's reasons as reasons. Once I make the choice, I am committed to the authority's decision. Therefore it appears that the reasoning is lost to be replaced by force. I think that that analysis is wrong. The reasons which I find binding in following an authority are, as Joseph Raz notes, the kinds of reasons I find binding otherwise.[25] Authority differs from force on just this point. If I rely on an authority to decide that in this case I should follow precedent, or the letter of the law, that authority is intelligible to me because following precedent, or the letter of the law, is something I otherwise recognize as legitimate. Authority gives weight to some reasons over others, but for authority to be rational, the things it gives weight to have to be reasons.

If I am bound by the rulings or decisions of an authority, then the same kind of reasons that could lead to my own decision lead to the authority's prior rulings. Any other form of authority is truly heteronomous. If I am faced with an argument that leads to one conclusion because of history, and another argument that leads to a distinct conclusion because of the plain meaning of the text, I can rationally decide that a given authority compels me to decide in favor of plain meaning. I cannot rationally decide that an authority compels me to decide in favor the richer litigant, or the more sympathetic cause.

But if I rely on the authority because it presents a rational appeal, what is the difference between obeying an authority and simply obeying an argument? What's the difference between employing a methodological rule that original intention is dispositive and relying on the authority of Taney in *Dred Scott*, which serves as a premise to get the same conclusion?[26]

In following Taney as a rational authority, I reenact his reasoning. Yet my reasoning is *re*-enactment. That is what makes Taney an authority. I am bound by the original reasoning, and do not start over and engage in my own reasoning. I can think for myself through reenacting someone else's reasoning. The autonomy of practical reason need not be antinomian. Being part of a community through reenacting the reasoning of an authority is a practice that is often misunderstood when viewed from the outside. I often find that I think best about difficult issues by thinking through Aristotle's arguments. Aristotle's arguments serve as narratives, arguments, and maxims that make my own thinking more sharp and productive. People who are not part of the same philosophical interpretive community can read my uses of Aristotle as arguments from authority, or even citations of authority in place of argument. Reasoning from authority is a practice that can expand the scope of community and friendship, but any particular example of reenacting an authority's reasoning can always be a contested example. There are no sure signs of reasoning rather than deferring to authority.

Authority bridges the ethical gap between a legitimate and possible consideration and a decisive decision. Whether something is authoritative is not an all or nothing question but is often a matter of degree. Does the Ninth Amendment have less authority than the First? Did Warren Burger have less authority than Earl Warren? There are parts of the Constitution, such as the privileges and immunities clause or the guarantee of republican form of government, that seem to have no authority at all in deciding whether a law is constitutional. These parts of the Constitution are, because of developments of history, purely aspirational values without connection to deliberation and decisions about particular policies and cases. They have only epideictic, not deliberative or judicial, use.[27]

To move a little outside the Constitution, the Declaration of Independence has no binding legal status, and has only rarely been explicitly cited as an authority in constitutional adjudication, but it could well have other authoritative functions. The Declaration sits nicely somewhere between the rational authority Aristotle's texts have for me and the legal authority of the Constitution, which can command obedience and threaten painful sanctions in a way nonlegal texts cannot. The Declaration of Independence shows that there is a continuum between a purely intellectual authority and a compelling legal one. But in all these examples, the decision to acknowledge and obey an authority is not simply a choice between the alternatives of total acceptance and complete rejection: I can follow an authority grudgingly, or I can endorse as well as obey the decision.

Consider, for example, the way that *Plessy v. Ferguson* remained authoritative for sixty years. It was an authority until explicitly overruled. But as its reasoning was discredited, it became a less authoritative authority. As it looked more arbitrary and less rational, the range of matters over which it had authority declined. In the last ten years of its authority, its scope was restricted from segregation in general back to the railroad cars that were at issue in the case. It was read as controlling a smaller and smaller set of cases, and as its scope declined, so did its authority. The narrative history of the decline of the authority of *Plessy* shows that authority is not all or nothing, and so the reasons behind an authoritative decision are a part of our reasons for obeying it, and for how we obey it. The more rational the authority looks, the more powerful. The decline of *Plessy* proves Aristotle's claim that rational *ethos* is and ought to be the most authoritative sort of *ethos*.[28]

Instead of thinking that the authority's reasons are lost when one obeys an authority, my picture accords with Friedrich's remark that authority requires "a very particular kind of relationship to reason, . . . the potentiality of reasoned elaboration,"[29] a potentiality which the idea of reenactment captures. This more rational and less passive sense of authority is Justice Souter's understanding of authority in *Casey:*

> The Court must take care to speak and act in ways that allow people to accept its decisions on the terms the Court claims for them, as grounded truly in principle, not as compromises with social and political pressures having, as such, no bearing on the principled choices that the Court is obliged to make. Thus, the Court's legitimacy depends on making legally principled decisions under circumstances in which their principled character is sufficiently plausible to be accepted by the Nation.[30]

Ethical Attitudes: Supposition, Presupposition, and Affirmation

The ethical uses of argument provide a resolution to the paradox of authority and the obligation to obey the law. If the authority of law derives from the moral goodness of what it commands, then, as Raz puts it, "its weight or strictness reflects" the weight of those moral considerations. "But if so, then the obligation to obey the law is at best redundant. . . . It is at best a mere shadow of other moral duties. It adds nothing to them. Since the obligation to obey exists only in a just state, it is at best redundant."[31] In a paradox familiar to theologians trying to understand the goodness of divine commands, the more reasons there are to obey the ruling, the less reason there is to obey because it is a ruling. In other words, the more rational a command, the less it is a command. In a similar way, I have wondered why, if when consenting to an authority, we rationally consent to the authority's reasons, whether the authority itself isn't dispensable. Maybe I wouldn't pay so much attention to equal protection were it not a phrase in the Constitution, but now that I do adhere to it as a value, it is equality, and not its presence in the Constitution, that leads to my decisions. Like an emotionally moving narrative, an authority serves a preliminary function of putting me in a position to listen to reason. But it is reason I should listen to.

The ethical uses of argument dissolve this paradox. I do not lose autonomy by choosing to obey an authority. *Ethos,* recall, goes beyond argument but can cite no reasons that are not already present in the argument. An authority provides a reasoned decision. Those who follow the authority can follow the reasoning and adopt it for their own. To obey is to follow: that is the nature of authority. In cases of rational authority and arguments from authority, to obey is to follow the reasoning of the authority. To follow someone's reasoning is to reenact it and become committed to it as one's own. My example from the arguments over *Bolling v. Sharpe* shows how narratives make use of the transitive nature of authority, when Korman cites Taney's authority in order to establish his own authority and win the authority of the Court. Such transference is not a delegation of power but makes authoritative reasoning one's own.[32]

This view of rational authority also shows why the passive understanding of authority, in which reason and authority are opposed, is wrong. Such a view of authority assumes that to act as a free moral agent and to think for oneself is to ignore everyone else's thinking. Instead of that dichotomy between reason and authority, I would point to the difference between understanding someone else's reasoning and choosing to be committed to it. I exercise and expand my rational powers by understanding and following your reasoning. I exercise intellectual virtue by choosing to be committed to it. Above I said that there is a difference between the purely logical claim that a conclusion follows from some premises and the act, simultaneously logical and ethical, of inferring that same conclusion because of my commitment to the good. That difference is crucial here in understanding the ethical acts of creating and following an authority.

Ethos goes farther than pure rationality because there are more than two possible ethical propositional attitudes. Propositions are either true or false. Logically, arguments are either valid or not. Ethically, there is a wider variety of options. As we've seen, a proposition can be embraced or rejected, but it can also be supposed for the sake of argument, to see where it leads. It can be held at arm's length. It can be treated with respect but not deference. It can be heard politely or enthusiastically. I can obey an authority grudgingly by simply deferring to its superior force or wisdom without making any connections between the reasons I obey and the reasons, if any, that led to the authoritative rule. I can obey the authority somewhat more willingly if I understand and acknowledge the reasoning behind the rule without adopting it as my own. In such case I not only recognize the authority of the person or institution making the ruling, but also the legitimacy, and to that extent the authority, of the ruling itself. I take the authority as rational, but not as providing reasons that I choose to adopt. Finally, I can obey authority most fully and most rationally when I reenact and commit myself to the reasons. It may be that those are reasons I never would have proposed for myself without the authoritative presence of the authority. Authority is not an all or nothing decision because there are things I can do with a proposition other than affirm or deny it. In the government brief on *Brown,* Elman argued that the Court could "construe the congressional acts regarding separate schools in the district as neither approving nor disapproving of segregation but merely as assuming its practice."[33] Since ethical argument is about assertions of propositions, not the propositions themselves, the practical reasoner has flexibility. I can't simply do whatever I like, but I can, through argument, convert an endorsement into an acknowledgement. As we already saw in chapter 3, I can convert an assertion into a presupposition. Rational authorities give me more to reason about.

But what has happened to friendship? Authority carries connotations of inequality, friendship implications of equality. Rational authority faces a paradox: If we respect an authority because of the reasons it embodies, why not simply be moved by the reasons? The more rational an authority, the more the authority seems a dispensable vehicle for transmitting the reasons. Friendship has a parallel paradox. If my friendship for you is not irrational, I love you because of, say, your unfailing honesty in the face of strong temptations of betrayal. When I have such a reason, there is always the suspicion that I don't love you but the honesty in you. I care about you because I value your honesty. Therefore it's not you I care about but that honesty. Friendship means valuing you as more than a vehicle for delivering the qualities I value.[34]

Authority and friendship, then, can both be concrete realizations of rationality. Rhetorical rationality is always embodied. The appeal of narrative, and the power of examples and maxims for Aristotle, come from the way practical reason works best when it is concrete. I understand the value of honesty better by having an honest friend than by deriving an abstract justification for honesty. Similarly, I understand the value of equal protection by submitting to the authority of the Constitution than by trying to appreciate equal protection on its own. Friendship, unlike a purely formal relationship governed by contract, allows parties to change without destroying the relationship. With a friendly relation to authoritative texts, the Constitution can become a living document. Like friendship, authority makes practical wisdom into a virtue and not simply a skill.

The authority of the Constitution, along with the practices of constitutional adjudication, is more than a good example of how reasoning from authority works. As we will see in detail in chapter 7, the existence of a written constitution makes possible a democratic community as a rhetorical community of argument and reasoning rather than a community of common blood or history. Like the common experience of confronting the past in chapter 1, sharing and arguing over a common written constitution widens the scope of *homonoia* and friendship.

Authority and Trust

Arisotle's *Rhetoric* teaches the speaker how to persuade. It shows the citizen how to reflect on the practices of persuasion to understand the place of persuasion in deliberation and action. The *Rhetoric* is silent on how to be persuaded. It does not offer lessons in how intelligently to be persuaded. Therefore, as I mentioned, it is not attentive, as we need to be, to the circumstances of friendship. It has little to say about the institutional conditions in which rational friendship can flourish, as opposed to circumstances that invite a hermeneutics of suspicion or a rationality fit for bargaining with strangers. In chapter 2 I showed how we could distinguish within rhetoric between reasoning and rationalizing. Here there is a parallel difference between being persuaded by an argument from authority and being the passive object of authoritarian force.[35]

It is in my interest to be convinced well. As we saw in chapter 2, people like to think of themselves as rational and as convinced rationally. I need to think that being convinced is both my own decision and the best decision. The autonomy of practical reason, then, does not imply the isolation and self-sufficiency of my individual practical reasoning. Therefore I situate myself within a community of argument, under the assumption that I will make the best decision I can in the light of other reasoners. "On any important decision we deliberate together because we do not trust ourselves" (*Ethics* III.3.1112b10–11). An account of practical reason has to have room for the intellectual virtue of listening to people who know more than I do, intelligently binding oneself to authority. Aristotle's own *Ethics* and *Rhetoric* are incomplete because he shows the virtue of giving good advice, but not of listening to it. Practical reasoning is not reasoning from scratch but engaging critically with authorities, including authoritative texts.

This orientation toward authority and rhetoric itself is radically different from that of the contemporary critical thinking movement which teaches us how to avoid being tricked, which itself is parallel to the conception of philosophy as intellectual hygiene or therapy. Those initiatives reflect the common and sophistic assumption that most people who try to persuade us are out to get us to do something we don't want to do, the assumption that we live in a society of self-interested strangers. The art of being persuaded is mostly an art of not being persuaded, a rational equivalent of defensive driving. We begin with a hermeneutics of suspicion. We need to be on guard against manipulation.

Most of the time, that could be the appropriate strategy. There are more sophists than Aristotelian rhetoricians out there. But we pay a price for adopting that strategy. There are possible human connections of friendship and respect that become unavailable with that attitude. The virtues of persuasion, belief, commitment, and conviction are only available when we treat each other rationally. Presenting and listening to arguments from authority are a way to treat each other rationally. The idea of authority broadens friendship by making room for rational relations between unequals, the relations I can have toward people who know more than me or who deserve deference and respect on other grounds. There are virtues of authority, both of being an authority and of responding to one. Ethical authority consists in rhetorical transactions between authors and audiences in which the words can defend themselves, can talk back. I become rational by treating you rationally. I become rational by responding to you as though you are treating me rationally. Reasoning as, in Newman's phrase, "the exercise of a living faculty in the individual intellect," is reasoning within a community. The living faculty in the individual intellect is intelligible only within an existing structure of authorities.

Aristotle's thesis that *ethos* is the most authoritative source of conviction has led us to look at narrative and authority, examples and maxims. We become ethical agents by becoming full citizens of a rational community, a community that can include texts and exemplars of the past. Thus there is something very sensible behind the revival of narrative. It is a movement toward inclusion. In earlier chapters I showed how as rationality increases, appeals that were formerly emotional and irrational become rational. Although any argumentative technique can be used for both good and bad causes, there is at least the potential for greater inclusion of excluded people as ethical argument and friendship expand the range of admissible persuasive appeals. Examples and maxims expand rationality beyond where the reason alone can go. The revival of narrative invites us to look at facets of practical reason that are not subject to method. To be rational as a member of a community is to argue from civic materials, from examples, sayings, and authorities we can all endorse. Just as the civilized side of rationality is beyond method, so too is it friendly beyond the determinations of legal justice. This exploration of authority shows how political friendship is possible with someone who knows more than me, or is for some other reason in a superior position to me. I can defer to your arguments without going further and deferring to you. That is, I resist the inference from your rational *ethos*, the superiority of your arguments, to your *ethos* in general, that is, your superiority as such. Friendship and the limitation of *ethos* to what is generated by argument allows us avoid reducing all relations between authors and readers to arithmetic equality.

In the next chapter, I will take this argument one step further. Authority is a special case of the more general ethical phenomenon of trust. Like authority, trust can be created or destroyed by reasoning. From the first chapter on, I have shown how practical truth is less a correspondence between statement and reality than a relation between speaker and hearer, and I have played on the fact that *pistis* can fairly translated by three different adjectives in a *trustworthy* speaker, a *cogent* argument, and a *convinced* audience. That identification of *pistis* with trust is the subject of "The Will To Be Believed."

CHAPTER 6

The Will to Be Believed

In the last chapter I looked at the rhetorical and ethical problems of authority. How does one become an authority? How does one ethically use an authoritative text? In this chapter I want to look at a closely allied phenomenon, trust. It too is also both practical and rational. Where authority seems to function hierarchically, as the rest of us defer to an authority, trust is a more democratic phenomenon. We trust each other. Trust uncovers a different dimension of rational friendship than authority.

When looking at authority I developed Aristotle's thesis that the *ethos* that should be most credible is the *ethos* produced by argument. I quoted Justice Douglas's remark that "confidence based on understanding is more enduring than confidence based on awe."[1] In this chapter I want to look at that normative dimension of *ethos* from the opposite point of view, not of the audience being persuaded but of the speaker trying to persuade someone. I will show that argumentative *ethos* is preferable for the speaker as well as the hearer. We will finally find a connection between *ethos* and ethics.

Why Do I Want to Be Trusted?

Why do I want to be trusted? It is obvious why I want and need to rely on others, but that by itself does not explain my desire for others to depend on me. Consequently, while trust has been a popular subject for analysis recently, it has been approached from the point of view of trusting, its costs and benefits. I want instead to look at the desires and risk of being trusted. The answer might seem simple: from trust comes power, and so the more I can get others to trust me, the better.[2]

It is easy to see why I need to trust others, although not easy to understand when and how I should. Figuring things out for oneself is often too expensive, so I have to believe others. If I had to rely on my own knowledge, I would be very constricted in what I could do. So I need to trust. The same instrumental account applies to my wanting to be trusted. I want you to do things that are to my advantage rather than yours, and so I have to persuade you to do something that serves my interest. Getting you to trust me is much cheaper than threatening sanctions if you don't go along with me, committing myself to be punished if I don't deliver, or spending all the time it might take to give a full proof that your interest necessarily entails the policy that I recommend. Being trusted has the same economic advantages that trusting others has.

But at least sometimes my desire that you believe me goes deeper than such instrumental advantage. I want to be trusted for more than what I get out of it. Rhetorical handbooks offer instructions in how to win an audience's trust, but sometimes I am not satisfied if I can trick someone into trusting me, but want the other person to have good reason to find me trustworthy. I want, sometimes, real trust, not a trust I have acquired through sinister manipulation. If a successful explanation means reducing a phenomenon to self-interest, the will to be believed looks absurd. Where does that desire come from?

Significant as the question why people should want to be trusted is, I think that my question has gone almost completely ignored. Others focus on why we trust others, and when we should, how community—scientific community, linguistic community, political community—is impossible without trust. How essential trust is to our lives is underlined by Aristotle's instructions to tyrants, which tell the tyrant to make sure that citizens don't trust each other.[3] Read "trust" for "charity" in the following lines of Davidson's, and we see why we cannot live in a community without trust: "Charity is forced on us: whether we like it or not, if we want to understand others, we must count them right in most matters."[4] We have no choice but to trust. We only have choices about whom to trust, how, when, and about what. Since we have to trust others, it is simply an adaptive preference that we believe them to be trustworthy. If I have to trust you, believing that you are trustworthy makes my trusting you easier.

But to explain what function trust serves is incomplete without showing what impels people to put themselves in a position to be trusted. But it could not serve these essential human functions if people did not, for reasons independent of those functions, want to be trusted. One cannot account for the desire in terms of the function it serves. That would be equivalent to saying that giraffes grow long necks so that they can reach higher branches, or that I like being praised because praise helps to keep all of us in line. The long necks of giraffes help them to reach higher branches, but that does not explain why giraffes have come to have long necks. And similarly for the pleasure I get in being praised. Its social function does not account for why I enjoy it. Functional explanations without motivational explanations are inadequate. Functions without motives don't function. No one understood that better than Adam Smith:

> The wheels of the watch are all admirably adjusted to the end for which it was made, the pointing of the hour. All their various motions conspire in the nicest manner to produce this effect. If they were endowed with a desire and intention to produce it, they could not do it better. Yet we never ascribe any such desire or intention to them, but to the watch-maker, and we know that they are put into motion by a spring, which intends the effect it produces as little as they do. But though, in accounting for the operations of bodies, we never fail to distinguish in this manner the efficient from the final cause, in accounting for those of the mind, we are very apt to confound these two different things with one another. . . . We are very apt . . . to imagine that to be the wisdom of man, which in reality is the wisdom of God.[5]

It may help to make sense of my question by two brief analogies. First, my initial formulation sounds like questions about justice in the *Republic:* I see why it is to my advantage for *you* to be just, but it certainly doesn't follow that I should myself want to be just. It is to my advantage to appear just, but not, it seems, to be just. Similarly, just because I want you to be trustworthy, it does not follow that I too want to be trustworthy. I can settle for simply being trusted. There is nothing automatic in the inference from admiring something in another to wanting to have it for oneself. I can want the reality in others and settle for the appearance in myself.

The similarity between trust and justice is only half the story, though. For trust, it's not enough for me to have a certain quality. I want others rightly to think that I do. To be trusted is to be *seen* as trustworthy. My desire to be trusted is only satisfied by both the appearance and the reality of being trustworthy.[6]

Now my second analogy. In *Civilization and Its Discontents*, Freud notes a similar transition concerning love. Just as the reasons I need to trust others are obvious, so too it is obvious why I want to be loved. Especially when young, I am dependent on other people for the gratification of my needs. I will not get what I want unless they have reason to give it to me. They have power and I don't, and so they need a strong reason. The more lovable I am the better. Hence infants' big eyes and button noses. But it does not follow that I have a need to love. Then I have to give rather than receive. What's in it for me? That is a transformation that needs to be explained, and Freud says that "only a small minority" of people are satisfied with loving rather than being loved. As with the analogy to the *Republic,* we need to take things one step further. Sometimes love is indeed not enough, and I want not just to be loved but to be lovable. I don't want you to be simply attracted by my good looks, but want to be loved for who I really am.[7] The same for trust. I want to be trusted for noninstrumental reasons. I want to be trusted because of my character, and not for other, adventitious traits. I want to be accurately seen as trustworthy.

The connection between trust and persuasion, two translations of *pistis,* is an intimate and fundamental one. The difference between strategic trust—trusting and being trusted reducible to interest—and being actually trustworthy is parallel to the difference we explored in chapter 2 between the sophistic aim of getting you to agree with my conclusion, for whatever reasons, and the Aristotelian end of your following my reasoning. Accepting an argument is much more demanding than accepting a conclusion. Why be more ambitious than instrumental reason demands? It is easy to see how democracy can involve different people agreeing on a conclusion for different reasons. That is the pragmatic picture of deliberation that aims at a modus vivendi. I assent to free exercise of religion because I find religious variety entertaining, you because of fear of persecution, and someone else because she thinks faith cannot be coerced. We agree on a conclusion for diverse reasons. But when I present an argument, I want you to accept my conclusion because of the argument. Part of the moral I drew from the South African Truth and Reconciliation Commission in chapter 1 was that sometimes the more ambitious desire to reason together, and not just agree on a conclusion, is ethically appropriate. Seeing why I should ever want you to accept my reasoning and not only my conclusion is the same as seeing why I want to be believed.

Trust and Adam Smith

I have found precisely one philosopher who addresses my question of why it is important to be trusted. Aristotle, unique among philosophers, forges an intimate connection between humans as rational animals and as political animals. Adam Smith comes in alongside Rousseau in second place. The connection between being rational and being political is pervasive in Smith, and leads him, alone among philosophers, to ask why I should want to be believed. He offers an explanation of the will to be believed in the final section of the final part of his *Theory of the Moral Sentiments*. Part VII is "of Systems of Moral Philosophy," and Section 4 is on "the Manner in which different Authors have treated of the practical Rules of Morality." It is there, when talking about the "rules of veracity" that Smith turns from credulity, which children have as an instinctive disposition, to the first-person case of being believed, rather than the third-person case of believing.

Smith's brief argument raises all the crucial questions about the desire to be trusted. First, to be believed is to be obeyed, and conversely. We esteem and respect those who lead and direct us. "The man whom we believe is necessarily . . . our leader and director, and we look up to him with a certain degree of esteem and respect." Obedience freely given is not only better from the point of view of the leader, but it feels better for the obedient. We like to think that those with power over us deserve it. We don't like to think of ourselves as coerced or manipulated, so we like to ascribe virtues to our leaders. Therefore obedience rarely stands alone, but usually becomes amplified into respect and trust.[8]

Next, from admiring people we come to wish to be admired ourselves. Therefore we wish to become leaders. This is the derivation of the natural will to power. "As from admiring other people we come to wish to be admired ourselves; so from being led and directed by other people we learn to wish to become ourselves leaders and directors." Given the innate disposition to believe others, plus the fact that we admire those whom we obey, it follows that we want to be admired, and therefore believed.

But Smith claims that this is not enough. "We cannot always be satisfied merely with being admired, unless we can . . . persuade ourselves that we are in some degree really worthy of admiration; so we cannot always be satisfied merely with being believed, unless we are at the same time conscious that we are really worthy of belief." Being believed is one of those conditions where we want the reality, not merely the appearance. Even if we had strategic or economic reasons for being believed, they couldn't be enough to give us reason to want to be really worthy of belief.

It is not just the existence of the desire to be trusted that needs explanation, but its power. Smith claims that this will to be believed is so strong that "it is always mortifying not to be believed, and it is doubly so when we suspect that it is because we are supposed to be unworthy of belief and capable of seriously and willfully deceiving." The will to be believed is a powerful and universally felt emotion, whose strength needs explanation.[9]

Smith's argument thus needs one more step. This "desire of being believed, the desire of persuading, or leading and directing other people, seems to be one of the strongest of all our natural desires," so strong that it may be the origin of the faculty of speech. "Great ambition, the desire of real superiority, of leading and directing, seems to be altogether peculiar to man, and speech is the great instrument of ambition." There is an intimate connection between belief and persuasion. I want to persuade you not only to get what I want in some particular situation but because I want you to believe me. I not only want to win, but to be a winner. Persuasion is the great instrument of belief.[10]

Smith's argument offers a great deal. The desire to be trusted is a powerful and specifically human emotion, the foundation of persuasion, language, and community. If this is right, then there is a pervasive motive to do something—talk, persuade, be trusted—for its own sake and not only for its rewards. There is a strong motive to have the reality, trustworthiness, and not just the appearance.[11]

Troubles with Smith's Analysis

I want to raise objections to Smith's argument as a way of pushing it further. First, the argument assumes that being believed and being disbelieved or distrusted are the only alternatives as though virtue and vice were the only possibilities. We need to trust others in order to overcome ignorance, vulnerability, and isolation. But there are other means of accomplishing those ends. Just as liberalism seemed, in the first chapter, to elaborate ways of living together that removed the need for friendship, so recent human progress is marked by the decline in the need for personal trust: effective centralized government, an economic marketplace, and depersonalized scientific institutions all gain in efficiency from a reduction in the amount we need to rely on trusting others, and can rely on facts of one sort or another instead.[12] Trust reduces complexity, but effective government does a better job of that reduction. This is the possibility I explored in chapters 3 and 4 that practical reason be replaced by theoretical reason, eliminating trust in favor of impersonal sorts of dependability. These are cases in which Smith's initial inference, from being led or directed to respecting the person I am obeying, fails.

For people who are just doing their job, I have neither trust nor suspicion. Such is the progress of modernity. Maybe my will to be believed is no longer functional.

Not only does modernity reduce the occasions when we have to trust others, substituting impersonal sources of reliability and predictability, but it would be wrong to think that I always want to be trusted. The will to be believed is not always appropriate or operative. I would rather be trusted than suspected. But I deny that I always want to be trusted. In "Confronting the Sophist" I argue that reasoning is an attractive possibility, not a categorical duty, and the same holds here. Sometimes I want to function in a relationship that depends on neither trust nor suspicion. "Don't take my word for it; evaluate my arguments for yourself."[13] My work as a teacher is as frustrated by students' trust as by their suspicions. As long as that trust, like the suspicion, is not founded in reasoning but in the simple fact that I have the power of the teacher, it is a barrier to an effective teaching relationship. Sometimes the rule of law is superior to the rule of men, even if that means preferring justice to friendship and rules by themselves to reason along with *ethos*.

The will to be believed is not a selfish desire for the benefits of being trusted. It is the desire to participate in a certain kind of community. In the minimal sense, we are all entitled to respect and to be regarded as moral agents. If someone does not accord me that much trust, but instead questions or ignores everything I say, then she is rejecting me from her community. We do not need to earn this sort of trust. Indeed, as individuals we cannot earn it. We can only create, and destroy, communities in which such trust is presupposed. If the will to be believed is a fundamental human desire, then we have discovered yet another facet of Aristotle's observation that humans are political animals.

But that sort of trust does not satisfy the will to be believed. You might rely on my words because you think I am surrounded by constraints and incentives that make it not worthwhile for me to cheat you, or because you think that your little case is not worth my bothering with. Lots of life is filled with transactions in which I trust a person to do something without thereby trusting the person. I trust an office or a uniform rather than a person; this is *ethos* that does not come from reason. When trust is not rational, none of Smith's inferences is valid. If this sort of impersonal trust counts as trust at all, it is surely distinct from trusting a person.[14] Such trust is equivalent to the shared understanding, explored in the first chapter, that we have to have even to disagree, the banal agreement on facts that Davidson posited as underlying his principle of charity, or that Hirsch developed as a common culture literacy. True trust is more demanding than that.

The will to be believed is a desire that the self be the object of belief. Since ascriptive trust is often less costly than my being trusted for who I am, we need to know why I should choose the more expensive alternative. The will to be believed is a desire that is not satisfied by reduction to belief *that* something is true, even something about me.[15] The question of the will to be believed is the question of the superiority of rational *ethos*. I believe what a credentialed—note the connection of credentials to credence to belief and trust—scientist says without trusting the scientist him- or herself. Commercial relations depend on trusting *that* we will get what we pay for without trusting any person. A society of strangers could not function otherwise, which is why we cannot live as the sophists in chapter 2 recommended. (In the final chapter, I will push this argument further. Here I simply claim that impersonal relations and scientific forms of knowledge cannot fully displace relations of trust and ethical forms of knowledge. In chapter 8 I will argue further that practical reason is the permanent underpinning of the rationality of the methodical and civilized replacements for practical reason.) Imagine what life would be like if we regarded everyone with the same suspicion with which we approach used car salesmen. We do not believe them. We use their words as the basis for inferences about their beliefs and desires, so we can negotiate the best price. Such inference is distinct from trust.[16]

Thus there are two ways in which Smith's argument fails. First, he fails to see the possibility of overcoming the need for trust altogether through achieving the same end by purely rational means without ethical implications. Second, he does not see that most of the time we only need nonsuspicion, not trust.

The next stage in Smith's argument has more problems. He claims that when I admire a quality in others, I then want to have it myself. As a generalization, that is evidently false. I marvel at this person's ability to multiply three digit numbers in her head, instead of needing a calculator, and at that person's ability to sing without having to breathe every two or three measures. One might even argue that it is a mark of the moral that it is only moral properties for which the inference from admiration to wanting the quality for oneself is licit. The inference from admiration to emulation is the ethical parallel to the universalizability of moral judgments.

And the further argument from being believed to being worth believing is equally troublesome if it depends on the false generalization that I want actually to have all the qualities I am thought to have. My Provost has the reputation of never losing a piece of paper and always acting quickly on whatever comes over his desk. While unmerited, the reputation by itself serves him quite as effectively as would the reality. So long as people believe him, whenever they themselves find that the Provost does not respond quickly, they discount it as anomalous or blame someone else. I would like such a reputation myself. I have no interest in possessing the reality. Maybe it is a mark of the moral that it is only for moral properties that the inference from wanting the appearance to wanting the reality is licit. The useful question to ask is when those two moves, from admiring a quality in others to wanting it for myself and from wanting others to think I have a quality to actually having it, are legitimate. Why should this pair of inferences be legitimate in the particular case of the will to be believed?

One final trouble with Smith's argument. I am certainly willing to grant that "great ambition, the desire of real superiority, of leading and directing," is "altogether peculiar to man." But while uniquely human, such ambition is also quite unevenly distributed. While everyone wants to be believed and trusted, that desire does not always exist in the superlative degree, just as Freud notes that few people accept loving as a substitute for being loved. Smith has found a human universal—the will to be believed—and connected it with a trait which varies from person to person. Everyone wants to be believed, but not everyone wants to be a leader. The connection between the universal will to be believed and any particular behavioral manifestations needs, consequently, to be clarified. In particular, what happens to the will to be believed when the need for personal trust recedes? Is trust no longer functional? Does progress consist in replacing *ethos* by logos, commitments by science?

Trust and Convention

I want to know when Smith's inferences are valid. The reasons he offers for the existence of the will to be believed are too general to be convincing. He offers a universal explanation basis for a changing phenomenon. So I would like to focus more on the circumstantial: When is "show me your evidence" an insult? When is "What sanctions are there if you're wrong" an insult? When should I rather rely on something other than trust, such as professional competence or the fear of sanctions? When should I want others to trust me, and when do I want them to obey me for other reasons, such as professional and impersonal competence or the fear of sanctions? When am I "mortified" when my trustworthiness is not taken for granted but when instead people want me to earn their trust? When am I mortified when the opposite happens, when people rely on my credentials rather than on my personal integrity? When is "I'll take your word for it" an insult? As Baier puts it, "It would be offensive to make a surprise visit to check up on the babysitter, but only sensible, with a new untried one, to arrange to phone during the evening and stick to that arrangement."[17]

My students, for example, sometimes interpret my demand that they supply evidence for their opinions as an expulsion from community and a humiliating lack of trust. They rightly take the demand for evidence as a moral demand, because it is a condition for the functioning of a certain sort of ethical community. They interpret my rejection of the ordinary norms of the communities they are used to in favor of the norms of truth and a community of inquiry as a denial of membership in community in general. Asking for and giving evidence are not always welcome or appropriate. My students don't need Nietzsche to teach them that I need reasons only when I don't trust you. The demand for reasons is a gesture of suspicion. Reason and trust, my students often think, are at odds. Ethical relations between people are at odds with purely rational relations among them. We have to choose between friendship and truth.

These students fail to see that giving and taking reasons creates friendship and trust of a novel and rational kind. Smith's analysis of the will to be believed needs that connection between reason and trust. The difference between earning trust and overcoming suspicion is a shifting, conventionally defined difference. The witness in court, the scientist writing for a journal, the student presenting arguments in class, they all earn trust in different ways. The place of trust in our lives is variable and contextual and easy to misunderstand.[18]

My initial analogy with love is to the point here again. Unless I am interested in love because of the pleasure or utility it might bring, I don't want you to love me for my money or my good looks, but for who I am. To say that I want to be loved for who I am is to say that I want to earn your love, because "who I really am" is not some property alongside my wealth and beauty. I don't want you to love me because you have surveyed my past lovers and decided that I am for all the right reasons quite a lovable character. That would reduce belief *in* me to beliefs *that* certain things are true about me. On the other hand, while I may not mind sweeping you off your feet with love at first sight, that initial passion had better develop into something deeper. If you love me without my persuading you to love me by showing you that I am lovable, that it isn't really love; at least it isn't the love mature adults should have for one another. This is the superiority of rational *ethos* to *ethos* that comes from other sources. Argumentative *ethos* is real *ethos*, not a verbal mask for a deeper reality.

When *ethos* is the most important source of belief, we believe what someone says largely because we trust the person making the assertions. The priority of character over pure rationality is the priority of believing *in* someone over believing *that* something is true. Luhmann sees this difference between ethical reliability or dependability and nonethical predictability at the heart of trust: "Trust is . . . something other than a reasonable assumption on which to decide correctly, and for this reason models for calculating correct decisions miss the point of the question of trust."[19]

The trust worth having is trust generated by reasoning. This is the truth in Aristotle's prescription that one not rely on preexistent reputation but earn the trust in the speech itself. My students are very willing to grant me trust because of my credentials. Student evaluations report, I am proud to say, that they find with near unanimity that I have knowledge of my subject-matter! But they are justifiably suspicious of anything that goes outside those qualifications. They trust me to know more than they do, but not to be honest about requirements or criteria for grading, since past teachers often have hidden agendas. I tell them that they are judged on the quality of argument, not whether their political opinions agree with mine. They are rightly suspicious.

Yet, the class cannot succeed unless I earn their trust. They have to join a rational community. They cannot acquire the skills of reasoning without acquiring the intellectual virtue of trusting in reason and in reasoners. The trust that they automatically give me because of my credentials blocks their being persuaded to trust me in ways that will lead to good teaching and learning. But in chapter 4 I contrasted a view of *ethos* that it acts as an entrance ticket— if I trust you because of your credentials, then I will pay attention to your argument—with *ethos* as inseparable from argument. While sometimes ascriptive *ethos* gains me a hearing, at other times it creates a relation between speaker and hearer incompatible with the ethical relations of trust and friendship that I want to establish. I want your confidence, not credulity. Ascriptive trust resembles deference to one's betters, the passive obedience to authority in the last chapter, and so is incompatible with the real trust which can only exist between equals, even when one of the equal citizens knows more than the others. When students and teachers trust each other to confine their judgments of each other to argument, they become equals. Both suspicion and ascriptive trust can destroy equality and community.[20]

However, although I want to earn your trust rather than acquire it, or be given it, in some other way, direct efforts to get you to trust me are usually as self-defeating as direct efforts to get you to love me. Attempts to persuade directly through an appeal to character are very prone to backfire, as in the notorious, "Trust me; I'm not a crook." Like love, trust must seem spontaneous, not forced, not the direct object of one's efforts. In contrast to love, the spontaneity of trust means that *ethos* must come from argument and therefore cannot itself be the direct object of our efforts. That is why we resent having to prove that we are trustworthy, even though we want to prove that same thing. *Ethos* is the most powerful source of trust, but we can achieve our *ethos* only through reasoning, not through appearing ethical. The examples and maxims of the last chapter were argumentative ways of creating an *ethos*.

Let me try a live example about trust that makes the same point as I tried to make with the analogy about love. As I write this chapter, I am also preparing an application to NEH to direct a Summer Seminar. Government grants are increasingly governed by accountability, not trust. Although I have directed six such seminars in the past, with great success, I am now asked to provide a detailed daily schedule for the seminar. I feel that I am being scrutinized where before I was trusted. The need for accountability leaves less room for my judgment in designing and running the Seminar. Taken to its limit, instead of a grant, I will have a contract that spells out the services I must render in exchange for a fee. The loss of *ethos* is a personal loss to me and, I believe, reduces the effectiveness of the seminar.

However, I have also been on the other side, as a referee for such applications. In that seat I have been periodically offended at those who think that the ascriptive marks of trust should be enough and that they should not have to prove that they are trustworthy—What's a degree from Harvard for if not to make it unnecessary to prove oneself? Thus the delicacy of trust, and the apparent paradox I asserted above, that at the same time that I want to deserve your trust, I do not want to be told that I have to earn it. I want you to persuade me that you are trustworthy, but if you try to do so directly, I will not trust you.[21] Authoritative *ethos* must come from reason alone.

Trust, Appearance, and Reality

The paradox that trust should be earned but not demanded and tested comes from trust's peculiar relation of appearance and reality. For Socrates in the *Republic*, the truly just person shows his purity of heart by an indifference to appearances. The truly just person will therefore often appear unjust to others. The truly trustworthy person, though, must want to appear trustworthy and so be trusted.[22] There is a pervasive motive to have not only the reality but also the recognition in others of the reality for trustworthiness, along the anti-Platonic lines of Rousseau's *amour-propre*, Hegel's recognition, and Aristotle's citizen virtue, which needs the sphere of the political in which to manifest itself. These are variants on Smith's will to be believed.

When I want to be believed I want not only to possess inner worth. I want others to recognize my inner worth. Trustworthiness is one of those things in which some inner reality is not enough, but in which we need recognition by others for the reality truly to exist. I want to be thought of a having an insides, but an insides of a particularly visible sort. "Disclosure, absence of deception, almost defines what it means to be *inside* rather than *outside* an entity."[23] I cannot be a friend to someone who doesn't think I have an insides, but am only a thing to be manipulated, and I cannot befriend someone without thinking of her as someone with whom I can reason. As Smith puts it in the section I quoted above, "Frankness and openness conciliate confidence. We trust the man who seems willing to trust us."

A purely logical argument can produce consent, obedience, and action, if I show you that it is in your interest to act in a certain way. A purely logical argument can make me into an authority. But it doesn't produce trust, because I have not exposed my character in persuading you. I have persuaded you that something is true, or that something is a good thing to do, but I have not persuaded you of anything about myself. You might even feel defeated: I have produced a decisive argument, so you must reluctantly go along with it. Without *ethos* and trust, you don't join me in a community in the way that more successful arguments from authority in the last chapter work. And, in matters where it is hard to see where the truth lies, belief goes more to the trustworthy speaker than to the better argument (*Rhetoric* I.2.1356a5–13). Audiences trust speakers who stake their character on what they say, take responsibility for it.

Reputation, *ethos* separated from reason, and pure reason distinct from *ethos* are the default positions. They are easy to come by. Rational *ethos* is a difficult and praiseworthy achievement. Earned trust, or artful *ethos,* is superior both to trust that does not depend on reasoning and to reason by itself. The ethical speaker takes responsibility for what he says, instead of claiming that nature and necessity dictate the truth. But for that reason, the ethical speaker is not only more persuasive but in fact more trustworthy. When I want to be believed, I want the correlation between is and ought that I showed only possible on a rhetoric centering on argument and *ethos*.

A rhetorical handbook on how to get people to believe and obey you need not have anything to do with who should be trusted. It might, e.g., extol the powerful techniques of hidden persuaders. "Put your best arguments first." (Or is it last?) If how to secure belief and how to be worth believing had nothing to do with each other, then rhetorical instructions on how to become credible would have nothing to do with the desire to be believed. Only if how to be believed and how to be worthy of belief come together can rhetoric produce a sort of belief in audiences that satisfies the will to be believed.

Instrumental reasons and values track intrinsic reasons and values, as a series of effects tracks a corresponding series of causes. Reputation is persuasive because it is a sign of *ethos*. That is what it means for the art of the sophist to be parasitic on the art of rhetoric. Appearances are appearances, true or not, of a reality. We saw in chapter 2 that even the most manipulative rhetorician must appear rational to be effective. Sometimes this tracking masks the operations of intrinsic value at work, which is how practical wisdom and rhetorical persuasiveness can fall apart. Getting you to trust me is efficacious because trustworthiness is desirable for its own sake. This is the solution to the initial problem of the relation between trust's motives and purposes. Trust serves important personal and social functions because people value it for its own sake.

Without an intrinsic connection between *ethos* and persuasion, between trustworthiness and being trusted, the instrumental relations on which the rhetorician depends, and on which all social life depends, would be impossible. If I trust someone only because of reputation, I must think that I am trusting character, not reputation. Reputation cannot be the object of trust, but only a cause or sign. When I rely on reputation, I have to think that I am relying on character.[24] I cannot be moved by your praising me unless I believe that you are praising me, and not simply using language as a positive reinforcement. If I believe that you are simply encouraging me, rather than praising me, I won't be encouraged. Hence the functions that trust serves are ultimately explained by the will to be believed.

The will to be believed causes trust in a more direct way. We trust people who manifest their desire to be trusted by assuming responsibility. We trust people who want to be trusted, rather than those who avoid responsibility by appealing at every turn to natural necessity. The person who takes responsibility for what he advocates wants to be trusted. Someone who takes responsibility will of course get credit for good things that happen, since they seem to come from him rather than from necessity. But the leader will earn trust even when things turn out badly, by taking responsibility for them. (Naturally, like any rhetorical tactic, taking responsibility can be faked, as many successful politicians have shown. But once again, the success of such a deceptive tactic depends on the fact that we trust people who take responsibility for their actions.) We trust people who want to be trusted because they seem to trust themselves, as we comfortably rely on people who are self-reliant.[25] Smith was right after all, then, in asserting a connection between the will to be believed and the desire for leadership. We believe those who want to be trusted and who trust themselves.[26]

Because instrumental reasons and values track intrinsic reasons and values, there is harmony between the rhetorician's most successful devices for securing trust and the things that make someone trustworthy. In rational, as opposed to sophistic, rhetoric, is and ought come together. Before I noted that because of the will to be believed I not only want to possess inner worth but desire recognition by others of my inner worth. Fortunately that desire is matched by the way audiences respond. We trust those who show that they want to be trusted.

We trust people who trust themselves, and who are thus willing to be trusted by others. People who trust themselves are self-confident. One mark of the trustworthy person is the desire to be trusted. The analogy to love and friendship is apposite again. Aristotle's argument that self-love is the basis for friendship and love of others is not an expression of egoism. Along similar lines, trustworthiness is rooted in trusting oneself. Those who love themselves are lovable and therefore can be loved by others. Similarly, those who trust themselves are trustworthy and so can allow themselves to be trusted by others.[27] We trust those who trust themselves, and have to work at distinguishing such trust from bluff and bravado as much as we distinguish self-love from egoism. People who trust themselves are the people likely to trust us. We trust people who appear to trust us. Like friendship, trust is naturally reciprocal.

Minimal and Maximal Trust

Being trustworthy has two forms. On the one hand I want to be trusted in order to be a member of a community. Not to be trusted is to be suspected and expelled from full membership in the community. I don't want the hermeneutics of suspicion applied to me. This is a form of trust I always want and sometimes can appropriately demand. On the other I have a distinct desire to be trusted in a fuller sense when I want to earn your trust. In that case I not only want to be part of a community but an active member of it, a ruler rather than someone ruled. No one has a right to this form of trust. I must earn, rather than simply demand, it. The two desires and the two forms of trust are distinct.[28]

These two forms of trustworthiness find an analogy in Kant's conception of morality. On the one hand, everyone is worthy of respect, can demand it simply as a member of the human community. All rational beings are moral beings. On the other hand, some people are more moral than others, and are worth more admiration and respect. Just so for trust. Simply to be a member of a community is to be assumed to be trustworthy, yet some people earn our trust in a way others do not.[29]

There is, then, that much similarity between the will to be believed and James's will to believe. Rhetoric consists of those speech acts in which what we say makes things come true, and yet saying doesn't make it so. Both the will to be believed and James's will to believe fall under that description. If I want to be trusted, the best strategy for fulfilling that desire is to trust myself. The best way to trust myself is to make myself trustworthy. There is a true, nonvicious, Jamesian circularity between self-trust and being reliable and dependable.[30] Both are self-fulfilling, but not in a trivial way. Both the will to believe and the will to be believed take hard work, not wishful thinking. I might be able to trust others who are not trustworthy, but I can only trust myself if I regard myself as trustworthy.

Three Sources of Trust: Friendliness, Competence, and Virtue

Aristotle has something to say about the virtues we look for in trusting a person. In the *Rhetoric,* he tells us that independent of demonstration, there are three qualities in the speaker that cause belief: practical wisdom or prudence (*phronēsis*), virtue (*aretē*), and good will (*eunoia*) (II.1.1378a6–9).[31] There is a similar but more useful discussion in the *Politics.* There Aristotle is not talking about what works in persuasion but explicitly about how we *should* make these judgments. The *Rhetoric* asks the question of trust and *ethos* from the point of view of the rhetorician seeking to persuade; the *Politics* asks the same question from the point of view of the citizen deciding whom to trust. How to become trusted tracks, as it should, who ought to be trusted:

> Those who are going to rule in the authoritative offices ought to have three things: first, affection (*philia*) for the established regime, next, a very great ability (*dynamis*) for the work involved in rule; third, virtue and justice. . . . When all of these things do not occur in the same person, the question arises how one ought to make a choice. If, for example, someone were an expert general, but a vicious person and not friendly to the regime, and another were just and friendly, how should one make the choice? It would seem that one should look to two things: which [of these] do all have to a greater extent, and which to a lesser? In the case of generalship, then, one should look to experience rather than virtue, as all share in generalship to a lesser extent, in respectability to a greater extent. For a guardian [of property] or a treasurer, however, the opposite is the case: this requires more virtue than the many possess, but the knowledge is common to all. (*Politics* V.9.1309a33–38)[32]

What Aristotle calls *eunoia* or good will in the *Rhetoric* here becomes *philia* or friendship, while *phronēsis* or practical wisdom is replaced by ability or competence. I prefer to translate Aristotle's *philia* not so much as affection, as in Lord's translation I used above, but as being on one's side, caring about the other people and their ends. I will trust a leader if I think he is on my side. I don't really care whether he likes me, as the term "affection" suggests.[33] Trust is an ethical, not an emotional, phenomenon. These lines about authority and leadership make the connection Smith asserts between trust, persuasion, and leadership. If the will to be believed is a desire to be worth believing, then that desire should be connected to this trio of qualities, affection, ability, and virtue and justice, as well as the rhetorical trio of goodwill, virtue, and practical wisdom.

This new trio is worth keeping in mind because trust extends more widely than the more narrowly rhetorical occasions where we have no certain knowledge. Sometimes we *do* have secure expertise and capability, but need trust as well. Sometimes professional ability is a source of trust, as well as a substitute for it. If I am your doctor, the fact that I know what is best for you does not mean that I do not need you to trust me. I think the question of how competence and expert knowledge can be grounds for trust rather than a replacement of it is a serious practical problem, particularly urgent in the kind of world of knowledge and specialization we live in. Sometimes expertise can produce personal and ethical trust. According to *Politics* V, expertise is as much a source of leadership and credibility as loyalty and virtue are. Moreover, which of those three is paramount varies with circumstances.

If loyalty, competence, and virtue all contribute to trust, each, and especially expertise and ability can cut both ways, can enhance or destroy trust. There is a difference between standing behind one's expertise and hiding behind it, just as there is a difference between appealing to tradition and authority as arguments and as things that make argument unnecessary.[34] But the appeal and power of expertise raises the question of self-sufficiency. Why isn't skill and expertise enough? Why do I have to trust my doctor, and not simply defer to her knowledge?

have a story that I think illustrates the need that trust has for *eunoia* and *philia*, and therefore why trust is an irreducibly ethical, rather than logical, phenomenon. Some years ago I led a group of students for a semester in Athens and Rome. They had predictable problems, and it was my job to clean up after them. I did. I answered their questions, got them out of trouble, explained how their expectations and norms were different from what was possible, and desirable, in Greece and Italy. I manifested competence and a sense of virtue and justice. But I displayed no sympathy for their problems, most of which I found tiresome. I accepted their goals, and helped them to meet them, but I did not share their ends, and did not appear to. I completely lacked Aristotle's *eunoia* and *philia*. Therefore, while I solved all their problems, I got no credit for it, because the students did not trust me. They relied on me, since I predictably did what they needed, and they continued to come to me with their problems. They had beliefs that certain facts were true, including facts about my competence and dependability, but no belief in me. They depended on me, but they didn't trust me. Through lack of *eunoia* I became a technician, solving problems put before me but taking no interest in them.[35]

What about Aristotle's other requirement for trustworthiness, virtue and justice? There is an obvious answer: we trust good people. But I think that there is a more penetrating answer. To be virtuous is to engage in action which is its own end. To do something for its own sake is to take responsibility for what one does, to be willing to be held accountable, rather than putting responsibility off onto some goal, outside the action, for the sake of which one acted. That is the connection between being virtuous and being trustworthy. The virtuous person does things for their own sake. To perform an action which is its own end is to do something because of one's character, because that is the kind of person one is. I trust people who display, and risk, their character in their words and deeds.

There is a further connection with virtue and justice. Those who want to be trusted want to be trusted by earning trust, not just having trustworthiness ascribed to them. The person who wants to be trusted wants others to be persuaded not by his reasonings alone but by his character. I want to be regarded as doing things through choice and not as compelled by the nature of things, even when the nature of things is broad enough to include one's own feelings, desires, and thoughts.[36] If I persuade you through reason alone, you might obey me but you do not trust me. If I want to be trusted, that sort of obedience is quite unsatisfying. Trust, like *philia* and *eunoia,* must be reciprocal and involve mutual recognition. Even if I could be virtuous in a society of devils, I cannot be trustworthy in a community of suspicion. Virtuous action is action that is its own end; friendship between good people is a relationship of trust that we engage in not because of its results but for its own sake.

Being responsible for one's words and deeds, for how one persuades another and presents himself to another, is what it is to have an insides. One might think otherwise. Consider people who display their insides with the idiotic "I happen to believe . . ." or "happen to like . . ." or "happen to feel . . ." Aren't those beliefs, likings, or feelings inside? On my analysis they are not. These locutions are a disavowal of responsibility. To have an insides is to take responsibility for those beliefs, likings, and feelings.[37]

Trust in a Democratic, Technological, Bureaucratic World

The contemporary problem of trust, then, is how this powerful and universal desire to be trusted can be satisfied appropriately in a world which has displaced personal trust from so much of our intercourse, legal, scientific, economic, and social. The will to be believed persists while the need to trust others diminishes in importance as it is replaced by more predictable relations among people.

The contrast between ancient praxis and modern technique is a familiar topos. It makes into a historical narrative the difference between theoretical and practical rationality that we've been looking at all along. The problem is always to take the contrast between ancient praxis and modern technique as something other than the occasion for nostalgia. My distinction of trust and expertise is similar to the one Rorty draws between solidarity and objectivity, as well as the theme of the rational as civilized threatened by the rational as methodical. Predictability has its uses. There is no practical or ethical implication in either direction: we have no duties to expand either the realm of character or that of knowledge. Where there is science, or the rule of law, or the efficiency of a market economy, to protest in the name of dehumanization is futile.[38]

Today, it is arguable that the desire to be believed persists while becoming harder to satisfy. The nostalgic response to this lack of fit between psyche and society is to lament how alienated we are from the world we live in, and to call, with Rorty for edification to replace science, or to give a Romantic interpretation to my argument and see it as a plea for lost personal relationships instead of lost ethical relationships. I prefer instead to see the same lack of fit as reason to hope that the roots of human excellence can persist even when political structures range against them.

The the role and reach of *ethos* and personal trust reduced with the progress of science and bureaucracy is to view ethics as a residual phenomenon. Throughout the book I have tried to show how *ethos* and rhetoric are constitutive of political life, and not activities we have to practice until real knowledge comes along. It is wrong to infer that character is what is left when reason is exhausted, making *ethos* interstitial in rhetoric and, even worse, morality interstitial in life. Directing attention to our will to be believed as well as the shifting need to trust others is a another way to counter this common interstitial reading. Showing how rational *ethos* can go beyond argument itself is a rebuttal to that interpretation of *ethos* and ethics as shrinking with the progress of knowledge.

Aristotle versus Smith

Aristotle and Smith are among the only great philosophers who take friendship seriously and who think that human practical rationality comes from the fact that we are political animals. I have derived from Smith a facet of *ethos* that could not be visible from within Aristotle's *Rhetoric,* or indeed his *Ethics* either, namely the connection between trust as a bond of community and the will to be believed. But there is also a useful contrast between Aristotle's vision of rhetoric and Smith's that sharpens our picture of the role of *ethos* within practical reason. For Smith, the capacity to influence and persuade one another is rooted in the human emotion of sympathy. We can feel pleasure and pain because others feel those emotions. When we feel pleasure, we want others to share it. Therefore we can communicate not only our thoughts but our emotions.

While Aristotle explores a set of particular emotions that depend on our emotional reactions to the feelings of others—in the *Rhetoric* he lists pity, indignation, envy, and zeal—our ability to persuade others, and so our ability to get others to trust us, does not depend on any such emotions, nor, as I argued in the first chapter, on sympathy, but on interest. There is therefore a significant reversal in the relation between thought and emotion in Aristotle and Smith. Smith takes our ability to communicate opinions and ideas as a given. The ability to communicate emotions requires us posit the specifically human emotion of sympathy. For Aristotle, animals can communicate pleasure and pain by voice (*phonē*). Only humans have language, *logos,* and therefore can communicate interest and harm, and therefore justice and injustice (*Politics* I.2.1253a7–11). In this context pity, indignation, envy, and zeal become specifically moral and political emotions, and not passions of a prepolitical human nature.

At the beginning I said that most current studies of trust ask whether trust is cognitive or emotive. I also suggested that Aristotle's rhetorical psychology of logos, pathos, and *ethos* would locate trust as an ethical rather than either logical or emotive phenomenon, and that rational *ethos* enriches both logos and pathos. Warren's statement about *Brown,* that the opinion should be "unemotional," means something very different when the only alternative to emotion is reason and when the opinion is unemotional by being ethical. Just as Aristotle's barring irrelevant emotions from the art of rhetoric at the start of the *Rhetoric* makes possible the specifically ethical consideration of the emotions in Book II, so an unemotional judicial opinion creates and legitimizes a new set of emotions in *Brown.*

Smith's will to be believed is a human universal. Its manifestations in human history must be so variable that any universal grounding must be questionable. By contrast, Aristotle's will to be believed is, like *ethos,* unique to those communities that can be called political. These are communities in which we talk about the useful and the just together. These are communities, then, in which we have ethical and friendly relations to one another. They are communities in which the will to be believed is engendered and realized.

CHAPTER 7

Taking Reasoning Seriously

RHETORIC, HERMENEUTICS, AND PRACTICAL

REASON IN THE INTERPRETATION

OF THE CONSTITUTION

Law is so important in the modern period not simply because it promises order, but because it expresses an understanding of the political order as a community of equals that freely creates itself on the basis of deliberation and choice.[1]

Practical reason lives in a space contested by theoretical and scientific reason on the one hand and by the dismissal of reason in the name of passion and force on the other. The autonomy and integrity of practical reason depend on the three theses that I derive from Aristotle's *Rhetoric,* that reason is the body of persuasion and conviction, that *ethos* is the most powerful source of such conviction, and that the *ethos* that is and ought to be most authoritative comes from reasoning itself. While these three theses are abstract enough to fit any rhetorical situation, I have also tried to show how they are reconfigured in contemporary circumstances. In the first chapter I pointed to the restricted yet crucial role of rhetorical friendship in liberal democracy. The perennial confrontation between Aristotelian and sophistic rhetoric takes on a new practical dimension in circumstances where the power of reason seems so questionable. The ampliative nature of ethical reasoning has been transformed by the invention of the written constitution and attendant practices of judicial review. Finally, authority and trust are manifestations of *ethos* that face novel problems in a world dominated by democracy, bureaucracy, and technology. In this chapter I want to move beyond my three Aristotelian theses to a new dimension, implicit so far, of practical reason unique to modern democratic circumstances—the dimension of pluralism, plural ways of reasoning practically, and plural ultimate goods that we reason toward.

Practical Reasoning between Philosophy and Rhetoric

Recently I have been listening to the Minnesota legislature debate whether to extend protection against discrimination to homosexuals. Much of the public debate turns on whether homosexuality is a matter of choice or destiny. Politicians, it appears, must think that law is subordinate to metaphysics, that practical reason must defer to science. In Rorty's terms that I used in the Introduction, we become civilized by becoming methodical. Former Justice Blackmun was criticized for maintaining that the Supreme Court need not decide the metaphysical question of when human life begins. But if he had tried, wouldn't he have been doomed to sounding as stupid as my politicians? Isn't there something seriously wrong when questions of law and justice depend on metaphysics?

As a practical argument gets more philosophical, technical, or precise, it gets worse. Aristotle advises the rhetorician: "Do not seek enthymemes about everything; otherwise you do what some of the philosophers do whose syllogisms draw better known and more plausible conclusions than their premises" (*Rhetoric* III.17.1418a10). "The easy use of words and phrases and the avoidance of strict precision is in general a sign of good breeding; indeed, the opposite is hardly worthy of a gentleman" (*Theaetetus* 184c). Should we lower our expectations and become antiphilosophical rhetoricians and sophists?—"Let's be realistic and admit that the law is all power and irrational desire anyway. We've got to protect our way of life against these degenerates." Should we, instead, think that the cure for such bad philosophy is better philosophy and more exact scientific determination of the beginning and end of life, or the genetic basis for homosexuality?

The question of how to respond to the way a practical argument gets worse the more it becomes philosophical or scientific recalls the ancient battle between philosophy and rhetoric over which of them gets to possess practical wisdom, the battle I joined in chapter 2. Sometimes philosophy and science seem unnecessary because rhetoric in the minimal sense of argument on both sides of a question produces satisfactory results. The marketplace of ideas supplies people with what they want. We aim at agreement and so the most persuasive appeal wins, with no further standard of appeal. At other times, such rhetorical practice is challenged, and so seems to require a theory to back it up. Philosophy supplants rhetoric and gives practical argument a sure foundation. Dissatisfaction with rhetoric moves people to philosophy, and disappointment at what they find there moves people back to rhetoric.

Legal "realism" repeats sophistical rhetoric's suspicion of ideas and claims that there is nothing beyond argument and beyond winning an argument. The philosophic "realism" of natural law continues the philosophical project of judging reasoning in terms of how well it represents some truth independent of that reasoning. The trouble is not that metaphysics is irrelevant but that its comforts sometimes make people think that they no longer need to do the work of deliberation. Slogans such as "justice: political, not metaphysical," the priority of democracy to philosophy, "antifoundationalism," and "the end of philosophy" are rediscoveries of the revenge rhetoric periodically takes on philosophy. Truth is reduced to agreement and method abandoned in favor of civility.[2]

Rhetoric's victories over philosophy are often as short-lived as philosophy's defeats of rhetoric, making the struggle seem interminable. People want their opinions to have the strongest possible backing, and won't be talked out of such a desire. Once people have tasted the waters of philosophy, no matter how diluted or recycled, innocence is hard to regain. If I am eager to discriminate against homosexuals and know that my feelings of revulsion cannot be shown in public, I have to look for reasons, like the distinction between nature and choice, to stand behind my desires. Whether Kant was right that theoretical reason contains a drive for system which makes reason's reach exceed its grasp, *practical* reason seems inevitably to get ahead of itself, and claim accomplishments beyond its capacities.

In spite of how common such philosophical ambitions and rhetorical responses are, practical wisdom does not have to be a prize over which philosophy and rhetoric contend. It evades that fight and becomes its own master when the internal values of the practice of argument and the forms of practical argument themselves are the best way of embodying our ethical aspirations. Rhetoric argues both sides of a question. Nature and choice can each be a reason both for and against extending protection against discrimination to homosexuals. As Michael McConnell says, "it used to be thought that sexuality was entitled to constitutional protection because each person should be free to choose the objects of his or her affection. Now it is more often argued that sexuality is entitled to constitutional protection because it is *not* a choice, but something inherent in the person's nature, which cannot be changed."[3]

Argument by itself is consequently incomplete. Philosophy's replacement of practical by theoretical reasoning urges us to keep looking until we find a decisive argument. Sophistic draws the moral that reason can only be used to help us get we want anyway, and not to figure out what to want. But recognizing that argument by itself is incomplete can also be an ethical opportunity. The recognition that there are alternative reasonable solutions, conclusions, and judgments is an ethical advance over thinking that anyone who disagrees and reaches a different conclusion must be dishonest or stupid, an advance in the rational as civilized to which rhetoric makes a fundamental contribution. Seeing practical wisdom as an ethical alternative to both philosophy and rhetoric gives slogans like "justice: political, not metaphysical" and the others an ethical rather than simply an antiphilosophical meaning.

To practical reason, the existence of choice and responsibility shows we are being true to praxis, while to antirhetorical philosophy and antiphilosophical rhetoric, choice signifies incompleteness and failure. The battle between rhetoric and philosophy comes from and flourishes in the absence of the ethical. Both philosophy and rhetoric engender desires for an absence of the ethical, the hope that philosophical wisdom will substitute for prudence and then the hope that rhetorical power by itself suffices. Both seek to eliminate judgment, philosophy by algorithmic methods and the quest for certainty and rhetorical *technē* by substituting craft values of ingenuity and virtuosity for virtue. The tradition that follows Hobbes in ending debate by scientific principles goes in the one direction; following Machiavelli by relying on the self-sufficiency of coercion and seduction goes in the other. Philosophy and rhetoric are methods of suspicion and justice—either aiming at truth or agreement—while practical reason is a method of trust and friendship.

Since political questions become subjects for litigation in America, these perennial questions about practical wisdom, philosophy, and rhetoric have become questions about legal and hermeneutic argument. Popular polemics about constitutional interpretation replicate old struggles between rhetoric and philosophy about where to locate practical wisdom. These revivals quickly become rituals, though, which makes the polemics between people like Stanley Fish or Robert Bork and their opponents often look as though all the parties are sleepwalking through arguments we have all heard before. We can do better.

Hermeneutics is the attitude we adopt toward texts when we put two distinct demands on them. We want our interpretations to be faithful to the text, and we want the result of the interpretation to achieve further values, such as justice. We encountered this pair of demands when talking about authority. The Constitution, or a Supreme Court ruling, is authoritative if it is duly authorized and embodies rational aspirations to justice. Our

Constitution is like scripture in placing both requirements on the reader. Hermeneutics is an attitude toward a text which we hope will not only be binding on us but *rationally* binding.[4] The law not only forces us to obey, but is an authority. It combines logos and *ethos*. Hermeneutics in this regard is part of the general rhetorical situation I discussed in the last chapter: I want my decisions to be the best decisions I can make, and I want them to be my decisions. In hermeneutics, I want to uncover truth by being faithful to a text.

The separation of legitimacy from justice locates constitutional argument and interpretation between rhetoric and philosophy in the practical and the ethical. I want to *do* justice, and I also want it to be *justice* that I do. Aristotle says that "there are two things which most of all make men care and love, one's own and the lovable" (*Politics* II.1.1262b22–23), but we don't want those to be two separate sources of value. These are the two demands of rational fidelity. I want to be teaching my son, not just that my son learn something regardless of the source. But I also want what I do with him to be *teaching*, and not something else I mistake for teaching. We want the things that we determine to be just actually to be just, and not merely what we like and have the power to impose on others. We want to achieve justice, but to achieve it in a way that has an intrinsic relation to those just accomplishments. We want our community to be just, but we want it to be just through our efforts.[5]

The idea of rational fidelity has, under different guises, been developed as a central problem for constitutional hermeneutics by several recent thinkers. I've already appealed to Joseph Vining's distinction between the authoritative and the authoritarian. Sanford Levinson calls the object of his inquiry "constitutional faith." Paul Kahn asks whether reason and will, or reason and history, can coexist in constitutional interpretation. Rational faith, constitutional faith, and the authoritative are different ways of framing the problem of constitutional hermeneutics and hence of practical reason today. They are variations on the theme of the hermeneutic circle.[6]

Determining the meaning of a contract is easier than the hermeneutics of the Constitution, because we have lower expectations for contracts. The meaning of a contract has to be only minimally rational. We ask what it meant for the parties, not what it means for us. A contract satisfies the wishes of its parties, but a constitution is binding on people other than the ratifying parties, and so obligation and fidelity have to come from reason. The meaning of a contract must be something its parties can agree to, but the meaning of a constitution must go beyond legality to justice and friendship. Aristotle explicitly draws the connection between contract and constitution as the difference between justice and friendship when he says that "any state that is properly so called . . . must pay attention to virtue; for otherwise the community becomes merely an alliance, . . . a guarantee of men's just claims on one another, not designed to make the citizens virtuous and just" (*Politics* III.5.1280a5–12). Constitutional hermeneutics makes it possible for the U.S. Constitution to be a constitution in Aristotle's sense, in spite of the vast differences between his world and ours. Constitutional hermeneutics lets us seek rational allegiance to an old document that governs us as citizens. A written constitution allows for new virtues of political friendship.

A robust sense of hermeneutics as reading a constitution rather than a contract develops alongside a conception of argument and rhetoric as a practice with its own standards, not just a technique for getting what you want anyway. The point of a contract is to have limited purposes which therefore leave the parties unchanged, while constitutions embody concern for the parties' moral education and virtue: "In contracts for the exchange of commodities and military alliances . . . [the parties] associate on the same footing when the came together as they did when they were apart. . . . Political fellowship exists for the sake of noble actions, not merely for living in common" (*Politics* III.5.1280b25–81a4). To seek justice through constitutional hermeneutical argument is to reenact the ratification of the Constitution. As I showed in the discussion of authority in chapter 5, we have rational fidelity to the document by becoming parties to it, which is clearly impossible for contracts. If citizenship could be reduced to a contract, then practical reason could be replaced by purely instrumental rhetoric. When society *is* reduced to a contract, practical reason is replaced by purely instrumental rhetoric.[7]

The ideal of justice under law differs from either justice or law by themselves in precisely this way, mediating, once again, between truth and agreement by putting argument prior to both. If we could ignore the Constitution in favor of the simple command, "Do justice," or follow the law without thinking about its purposes, what is sometimes called legalism, then pluralism would have to be suppressed in favor of uniformity. We wouldn't have to think in order to do the right thing.

For example, legalism is exactly what happened when slavery became a more and more practically unavoidable issue. In the early political life of the United States, slavery was considered a peripheral legal issue, and its presence in the Constitution a political compromise that did not affect the devotion that all owed to it. Later, slavery and its expansion become such a central issue that its presence in the Constitution was more than an embarrassment; it made rational fidelity to the national government questionable. Ethical argument could not be used in the interpretation of a document whose commitment to justice, as opposed to compromise and agreement, was not evident. As long as slavery was legal, legal argument could not be about justice.[8] Lincoln's strategy of making the Declaration of Independence controlling over the Constitution was his way of making the document something that commanded ethical allegiance and not merely the obedience demanded by a contract. He could then ethically rebut the abolition claim that the Constitution was "a covenant with death" and an "agreement with Hell" without denying the presence of slavery in it.[9]

In what follows, I want to show how three aspects of practical reason emerge from the rhetoric and hermeneutics of contemporary jurisprudence. The three features of contemporary practical reason are (1) pluralism, (2) the distinction between legitimacy and justice, and (3) the rediscovery of the ethical. All have roots in classical rhetoric and by this point in the book they should look familiar. The best contemporary jurisprudential theory and practice articulate them in characteristically modern ways, so this activity illustrates both the continuities between past and present and the peculiar demands that practical reason faces today.

Pluralism

Pluralism has been the great twentieth-century American, democratic development in practical reasoning. Pluralism pushes practical reason toward rhetoric and away from philosophy. It makes practical wisdom more rhetorical. Rhetoric as a faculty of proving both sides of a question is at home with interest-group pluralism. This is the pluralism of a modus vivendi in which might makes right. But when rhetoric and interpretation become subject to reflection, pluralism becomes a way of life, from contract to constitution, and rhetoric develops from antiphilosophic instrumental reasoning to ethical and prudent philosophy. This is the movement we earlier saw in the TRC and in *Brown*.

Pluralism has been present in American politics from the beginning. The *Federalist Papers* argued against the idea that homogeneity is necessary for successful democracy and freedom, and claimed instead that diversity and conflict are the guardians of freedom. The battle between Federalists and Anti-Federalists over heterogeneity and homogeneity continues today in fights between "liberal" advocates of a neutral state that accommodates differences and "conservatives" who argue for homogeneity either of the nation or of the local moral communities who manifest their philosophic wisdom in racial, religious, or sexual discrimination. The Federalists aimed at agreement, the Anti-Federalists at truth. The American founders responded to the pluralism of interests and factions by developing the institutional pluralism of separation of powers and a federal system.[10]

The Federalists won the battle between agreement and truth by transforming conflict, and plurality, from external givens that set the problem for government into internal features of political and constitutional practice. Argument on both sides is not instrumental but constitutive of the American political *ethos*. As I argued in the first chapter, Lincoln and Douglas reenacted this dispute about pluralism and plural truths concerning slavery. Douglas thought that government should aim at agreement, Lincoln at truth. Lincoln won by finding unity in common atonement, and ultimately, as in South Africa, in "a new nation."

That same battle between rhetoric and philosophy, between Federalist and Anti-Federalist, between Douglas and Lincoln, is played out today in disputes about whether there must be a single preferred method for interpreting the Constitution or whether pluralism has a place here too. That constitutional interpretation in fact employs a variety of kinds of argument is as undeniable as the pluralism of interests and beliefs that characterized America from the beginning. At issue is whether that variety should be replaced by a single correct method, or whether the variety itself is essential to rational fidelity and modern practical reason. Just as the Federalist converted factions and disagreement from an external given to be controlled by the government into a constitutive part of politics, the pluralism of modes of argument develops rhetoric from an instrument of power to be used for purposes prior to rhetoric into a rhetorical culture of argument.[11]

Accounting for plural modes of interpretation has become a difficult and important theoretical task only since, and because of, *Brown*. *Brown* caused an epistemological crisis.[12] It is practically impossible to question the rightness of the result in *Brown*, yet that result does not easily follow from constitutional text, original meaning, original intent, or subsequent history of doctrine and interpretation.[13] The need to justify *Brown* created a new practice, the theoretical activity of understanding plural modes of constitutional interpretation. When the expansion of slavery became an urgent political issue, constitutional interpretation faced one crisis, to which it did not respond successfully. When segregation became incompatible with the American *ethos,* constitutional interpretation faced a new crisis.

Philip Bobbitt's *Constitutional Interpretation* and his earlier *Constitutional Fate* are perfect places to look at the relations between philosophy and rhetoric as they both encounter the twentieth-century fact of pluralism, and the specifically American phenomenon of political questions becoming legal questions and legal questions ultimately turning on textual interpretation.[14] The three features of contemporary practical wisdom—pluralism, the distinction between legitimacy and justice, and the rediscovery of the ethical— are all prominent in his account. Pluralism emerges through a "grammar" of six different modes of constitutional argument, "a system that specified six forms of constitutional argument that permitted one to map any constitutional proposition onto a field of legitimacy" (*CI*, x). Bobbitt's grammar, like Burke's *Grammar of Motives,* qualifies as a rhetoric, since it not only shows how to distinguish well-formed from deficient statements, but ties those modes of argument to purposes for which they are appropriate. By showing how each mode is purposive, he shows how arguments are legitimating, and not merely rule-following, as a narrower form of grammar might.

In *Constitutional Interpretation,* the six modes generate six distinct arguments concerning the constitutionality of using private money to fund secret policies such as aid to the Nicaraguan Contras, and that example is enough to clarify the meaning of the six modes for our purposes. In good rhetorical fashion, any or all of the six modes could be used to argue both for and against a given policy or law, although in this case the more obvious and straightforward arguments are mostly against secret funding. One can, first, argue *historically* that Article I of the Constitution "provides the link between government operations and the democratic mandate by requiring that all funding take place by statute, that is, by the actions of persons who can be turned out by the voters every biennium. . . . To circumvent Article I by relying on non-appropriated funds . . . is to strike at the heart of this idea" (*CI*, 72). History gives life to the clause of Article I that demands that all funding come from Congress. *Structural* argument begins from the fact that "the people and not the state are sovereign" (73). Secret policies make it impossible for the people to be sovereign. Moreover, the constitutional separation of powers requires cooperation, not unilateral action, and "that cooperation makes the difference between power and law" (75). The Constitutional structure of divided government, checks and balances, coordinating and conflicting powers, provides an argument against secret funding of the Contras.

A *textual* argument can be made for "quasi-private entities to conduct paramilitary operations," since Congress can grant letters of marque and reprisal. But the text is "equally clear" on forbidding "off-budget funding" (75). There are *prudential* arguments, perhaps easier for us nonlawyers to generate, why "the Enterprise" was an irresponsible idea. It just doesn't look good when exposed. *Doctrinal* argument invites us to look for relevant precedents and analogies. Is using private funding for the Contras like a city taking private donations instead of taxes to run an art museum, or is it like the city allowing a privately funded and operated police force to aid in the public purpose of reducing crime?[15]

Finally, there are *ethical* arguments against such a policy. The "patriotic and highly intelligent men and women [who carried out Reagan's policies] replaced their country's vision of itself, as expressed in law, with their own vision for it. . . . The Enterprise did not reflect a commitment to serve the nation's policies whatever they might be" (81). Just as conservatives like to polemicize against "activist judges," so here it is unethical to substitute private judgment for the *ethos* of the community.

Readers interested in the rich details of such an analysis need to turn to Bobbitt's work itself. My concern here is with placing pluralism and practical reason in relation to rhetoric and philosophy. There are two ways of understanding the methods of constitutional interpretation. One claims that any legitimate method of interpretation must be justified by a theory of politics, of interpretation, of history, or of democratic values.[16] That line of argument makes metaphysics prior to rhetoric and prudence, subordinating hermeneutics to epistemology. The other way makes these modes of argument themselves ultimate, needing no such foundation. They aren't ultimate premises but ultimate modes of reasoning. This is the priority of politics to epistemology, of rhetoric to philosophy.

But if we take that line, we then have to see how such rhetoric does not degenerate into sophistic. Does argument without foundations mean that might makes right, or that there are practices of reason that are self-legitimating? Bobbitt's distinction between justice and legitimacy, which I will examine next, will be his way of advancing a constitutive or ethical rather than instrumental conception of the autonomy of practical reason.

Rather than reenact the arguments between ethical and sophistic rhetoric from my second chapter, here I want to show what ethical self-legitimation looks like. The pluralism of modes of argument shifts the center of attention and the locus of valuation from underlying philosophical principles to argument as an activity. The practical and rhetorical concentration on forms of argument, instead of substantive principles or ideologies, allows fidelity to the Constitution itself, rather than the subordination of the Constitution to a theory or favored object of belief. Rational fidelity demands allegiance to the written Constitution, but it turns out that the identity, meaning, rationality, and justice of "the Constitution" are located by these modes of argument, rather than by the methods we use to denote an extra-argumentative object.

Since the forms of argument are not premises, as in philosophical anti-rhetoric, they are not themselves the objects of argument and dispute. They are powers for generating such objects. Aristotle defined the art of rhetoric as a power, and not as a set of beliefs, and in chapter 2 I tried to show how there can be rational judgment between incommensurable values and ideas when those incommensurables are conceived as powers. Such powerful forms of argument as Bobbitt outlines can be themselves fundamental to a rhetorical culture of argument and justice that needs no further backing.

The six modes of interpretation that Bobbitt offers are not generated by some theory of either justice or hermeneutics. They emerge from the developing practice of constitutional argument and interpretation itself. They are six distinct ways of fleshing out the idea of popular sovereignty and a written constitution. The demarcation between legitimate and illegitimate modes of argument, like the boundary between the rational and the irrational, is always subject to rhetorical negotiation. They would not be appropriate or rational in all circumstances. They are inconceivable apart from popular sovereignty and a written constitution. Several of them are just what the Enlightenment rejected as irrational—fidelity to a text, deference to precedent, a prudence and an *ethos* that seemed to take as natural and necessary what are in fact merely local traditions. These modes fail to measure up to the standards of theoretical reason. Doctrinal interpretation valorizes an economizing of decision-making by providing a shortcut to judgment. Structural interpretation assumes that role morality and the separation of powers have ethical value, as opposed to the anarchic omnicompetence of philosophic reason. Each mode is a variety of authority. Each is functional, and rational, only in appropriate conditions. Each might be external criticism in some circumstances but becomes internal to contemporary constitutional argument.

Constitutional argument has to be centered on the plural modes rather than derived from principles superior to the Constitution itself. There is no textual argument for textualism, no ethical argument for ethical argument.[17] Otherwise some theory or principle will be superior to the Constitution itself. A theory of contracts, for example, that would justify an ideology of original intent would then become authoritative over the Constitution. The ideologies erected in defense of original intent or consideration of consequences are bad philosophy trying to justify good practices. Instead, the constitutional idea of justice under law itself implies both the focus on modes of argument and a system of multiple modes of argument:

> The principles of constitutional law are patterns of choice between kinds of constitutional argument. From each of these patterns one may derive a particular justification for judicial review. It is an error virtually endemic to most constitutional commentary, however, to do this in reverse, deciding first on what seems to be a convincing basis for judicial review and thereafter being persuaded by those arguments appropriate to that particular judicial role. This is a profound error, because it assumes that the commentator comes to the question of judicial review from a fresh perspective, one outside, as it were, the process of legal argument. (*CF*, 123)[18]

Plural modes of judicial argument, therefore, are a constitutional requirement. The need for plural argument comes from rational fidelity to the written text within the circumstances of democracy and friendship. Pluralism is then not a datum from which one begins, Rawls's "fact of pluralism." Plural modes of argument follow from the idea of justice under law. The constitutional rule of law supposedly emerged as a remedy to civil war created by the lethal competition among branches of Christianity. Historically, plurality might lead to the rule of law, limited government, and a written constitution, but my argument suggests the opposite: a conception of justice that ties it to these legal institutions makes pluralism inevitable.

Limited government and a written constitution are solutions to the problems of plural interests and competing sects, but limited government and a written constitution themselves in turn require this more robust, intellectual, form of pluralism. Rhetorical, argumentative pluralism prevents interest-group pluralism from being reduced to instrumental reason satisfying preferences, which would be the victory of rhetoric over philosophy.[19] Justice through law and rational fidelity require argumentative pluralism. From pluralism being a fact of life we must grudgingly accept, it becomes an opportunity for the development of new facets of practical reason.

Justice and Legitimacy

Bobbitt's pluralism shows what practical reasoning looks like in the face of contemporary rhetorical and hermeneutic problems. It is, first, a purposive pluralism of modes of argument, requiring, second, the distinction between legitimacy and justice, and issuing, finally, in the double senses of the ethical, a narrow one where the ethical is a mode of argument in its own right, and a wide one characterizing the whole field of constitutional interpretation. I now want to turn from pluralism to the second feature, the distinction between legitimacy and justice.

The distinction between legitimacy and justice is a fundamental contribution rhetoric and hermeneutics make to practical reason. I already used it in chapter 4 to make sense of rational authority. There I showed the rational nature of the ethical by showing how rationality alone could lead to legitimacy, but we need *ethos* to reach decisive conclusions and practical choices. But to reach justice, we needed an *ethos* generated by nothing but the arguments for legitimacy, reenacting Aristotle's third thesis that the most authoritative *ethos* is produced by argument. Here the dependence of *ethos* on legitimate argument shows itself in the denial of foundational theory for interpretation and judgment. *Ethos* simply is the self-justifying nature of legitimate argument.

Separating legitimacy from justice directs attention to judicial argument, the locus of legitimacy, and away from the motives and results of arguments, that might be home for a justice defined as something other than justice under law. Focusing on legitimacy has large advantages. It lets losers have something—legitimacy—and lets them see themselves and be seen by others as part of a community, and so makes pluralism look like a good thing even to those whose inclinations are more sophistical or philosophical. Separating legitimacy from justice is an act of friendship centering on a common activity instead of common ends or beliefs. As Bobbitt puts it, "The multiplicity of incommensurate modalities . . . allows different groups in America to claim the Constitution as their own in the face of reasoned but adverse interpretations." Plural modes of argument "allow changes to come without requiring that the Constitution be repudiated, when a precedent has been rightly decided within a particular mode, but has come to mean something unacceptable in the world within which it must operate" (*CI*, 158). The more difficult it is to amend the Constitution, the more its meaning becomes disputed and changed. Laws allowing and requiring racial segregation were once constitutional, but we don't need to amend the Constitution to change the constitutionality of those laws. We can simply supply better arguments. Making legitimate modes of argument central expands the range of community. It can be an act of friendship to continue an argument as much as to come to agreement.

But separating legitimacy from justice should be troublesome as well as attractive. The judicial autonomy that results from focus on argument insulates judicial arguments and decisions from motives and results. That is what it means for practical argument to have its own standards, and in that sense to be self-justifying. But those intentions and purposes give legal reasoning its point. Without them, logical argument looks like a game. When argument becomes a game with its own rules, who would want to play? Autonomy seems to mean pointlessness. By directing attention to the plural modes, aren't we directing attention *away from justice* and driving a separation between the lawful or legitimate and the just?

The danger of autonomy becoming insularity and pointlessness has been present from the beginning of rhetoric. When Aristotle defines rhetoric as the art of finding in each case the available means of persuasion, he distinguishes such argumentative activity and achievement from another kind of success, that of actually persuading some audience, and so distinguishes the internal ends of a practice from the external ends that motivated it in the first place. He draws an analogy to medicine: a doctor can do everything medically possible to heal a patient, and yet the patient can die (*Rhetoric* I.1.1355b10–13). The operation was a success measured by its own internal standards of art and so the doctor is beyond censure, and beyond malpractice suits. But that is hardly consolation to the patient or his family. Should we follow Aristotle in constructing a rationale for protecting a profession from external, lay criticism? The legitimacy/justice distinction protects constitutional interpretation from criticism in the name of justice by turning attention to process values or craft values. An advocate or a judge who demonstrates the legitimacy of an argument or a decision by claiming that it relied on a structural argument is not only evading the question of justice but denying our right to raise such a question. Meaning is walled off within a hermeneutic circle. Outsiders have no place to criticize judicial argument and decision. Vining raises this worry eloquently:

> Lawyers, being so aware of processes, are prone to making the mistake of thinking that since outcomes are contingent there is only process left to hold onto, and that commitment to law is commitment to process, or, as it is called in law, procedure. Law *is* procedure, it is sometimes said. But since there can be no real commitment to process— when one embraces one's child, husband, wife, or lover, one does not fold one's arms around a process—the result is that there is no real commitment to law. Lawyers' mistake in thinking contributes greatly to the relativism and emptiness they so often espouse and suffer so needlessly. Process is not all that is left when particular outcomes are seen to be contingent.[20]

How does autonomy differ from insularity? Legal argument is legalistic and merely procedural unless it aims at justice, but it aims at justice by supplying arguments about what justice means. Legal argument is not a means to justice in the way that playing tennis well can be the means to winning a bet. The practical relation between an activity and its purposes is not the instrumental relation of means to end.

Antiphilosophic rhetoric can only conceive of only external relations between constitutional reasoning and justice. Even when constitutional arguments are supposed in the long run to result in justice, because of the invisible hand of the adversary system, there is no intrinsic connection between a clever argument and a just result. In sophistic we try anything, because winning is the only thing. There is no difference between reasoning and rationalizing in a state of nature. Successful argument determines the lawful. If you want justice, you need to look elsewhere. We reason as best we can, and then hope for the best.

In a philosophy without room for practical reason, on the other hand, argument and justice are so tightly connected that argument's results are beyond criticism, just because the legitimacy/justice distinction has no place. With the right method, hooked up to the right principles, justice follows necessarily. If I follow the rules of deductive argument, I have constructed a valid argument. Following legitimate procedures authorizes their conclusions and so places them beyond criticism. Someone who admits that an argument is valid and yet criticizes it because he doesn't like the result misunderstands the nature of such an argument. It would be like following and accepting a proof in Euclid and then going out to check if two given triangles really were equal. Because it is monological, the philosophical impulse to reduce argument to logic, like the sophistic debunking of argument, destroys community.

In practical reasoning, as opposed to both sophistical rhetoric and foundational philosophy, constitutional interpretation and arguments have the autonomous value of legitimacy, but this autonomy will not mean a protection from criticism or a substitution of craft values for substantive ones. The intrinsic, practical relation between argument and justice *is* the Constitution. The Constitution is a practice, a form of praxis. As Dewey puts it,

> Society not only continues to exist *by* transmission, *by* communication, but it may fairly be said to exist *in* transmission, *in* communication. There is more than a verbal tie between the words, common, community, and communication. Men live in a community in virtue of the things which they have in common; and communication is the way in which they come to possess things in common. . . .
>
> A democracy is more than a form of government; it is primarily a mode of associated living, of conjoint communicated experience.[21]

Any mode of interpretation can be used to constitute a legitimate argument. Any mode can equally be used instrumentally to rationalize a favored cause. There is no method of interpretation or argument that cannot be abused by being used instrumentally. As we saw in chapter 2, the difference between reasoning and using reason is always potentially contested. The different modes of interpretation function as elaborated versions of Aristotle's maxims which I explored when discussing the *Brown* decision earlier. "The Constitution is a living document." "The rule of law means that we are controlled by the intentions of the founders." These are maxims that guide interpretation. Maxims and modes of interpretation embody the wisdom of public, democratic knowledge. They can be used as clichés which substitute for thought, or can help thought develop itself. Maxims and modes can both be used in reasoning or exploited in rationalizing.

As we've seen, Aristotle says that the use of maxims "make the speech 'ethical.' . . . Speeches have character insofar as deliberative choice is clear, and maxims accomplish this because one speaking a maxim makes a general statement about preferences, so that if the maxims are morally good, they make the speaker seem to have a good character" (*Rhetoric* II.21.1395b13–

17). The pluralism of modes of constitutional reasoning allows us to advance beyond the *Rhetoric*. Each mode of interpretation embodies its own *ethos*. Fidelity to text, the self-limiting role morality of structural interpretation, the obligation to formulate clear instructions to lower courts by doctrine, the prudent calculation of consequences: all these are *ethē*, distinct sorts of character and of intellectual virtue. Each, too, is an argumentative *ethos* and not an *ethos* rooted in something outside argument itself. Each can degenerate into ideology, special pleading, and idolatry. Unlike scientific theories, maxims and modes of interpretation are universally accessible, a part of democratic knowledge and the rational as civilized. Yet the modes, like maxims, can be used with greater or less effectiveness. They are universally available, but not universally appropriate.

Practical reason then offers a different understanding of the relation between legitimacy and justice than either sophistical rhetoric or foundational philosophy. If my preferred method always resulted in justice, that would be a philosophical proof that my method is the right one. But looking at the matter ethically, the coincidence between my conception of justice and the results of my argument are grounds for accusing me of special pleading and rationalizing. That's what it means for philosophic argument to be too strong for praxis. On the other hand, if my preferred method consistently generated manifestly unjust results, then it is no defense to say that they may be unjust, but they are legitimate, and I've done my job. I could no longer have rational faith in the Constitution. I would be living under a regime in which hermeneutics and practical reason would be impossible, as many people prior to the Civil War thought about the Constitution. A Constitution that legitimated slavery could not be read ethically. As Sunstein puts it,

> Any system of interpretation that disregards the constitutional text cannot deserve support. This is not merely an axiom. It depends on some substantive political arguments. . . . Part of the argument for textualism in American constitutional law is that our constitutional text, generally speaking and properly interpreted, does indeed promote human liberty. A text that guaranteed general slavery or allowed frequent torture need not be taken as binding.[22]

The ends of ethical methods are partly, but only partly, defined by their methods, just as the successful use of the methods is partly, but only partly, defined by success at reaching the external end. Bobbitt expresses the hermeneutic circle perfectly:

Our values do not necessarily precede our choices; rather, making decisions actualizes and in some cases even precipitates our values. Before all choices, there are no values, only vague attractions, repulsions, attitudes. . . . It is not that values are a pre-condition for making choices, but rather the other way around. (*CI*, 166)

Recall my earlier example of the Lincoln-Douglas debates, in which Douglas takes the *ethos* of the community as a given, while Lincoln sees it emerging from our practical confrontation with our ideals. The practical and ethical relation between internal and external ends, between finding the available means of persuasion and persuading, between acting generously and actually benefiting someone, is more complicated than either sophistic or philosophy would have it.

The distinction between legitimacy and justice points to a further ramification of the position of practical reason between rhetoric and philosophy. Practical argument is autonomous. The modes of argument are self-justifying, and attempts to justify them by reference to something outside themselves fail. The autonomy of practical reasoning is a theme that has run through this book from its beginning, starting with the idea of common, democratic knowledge in the first chapter. The autonomy of practical reasoning was in the first place the autonomy of common opinion, which Aristotle says is that from which rhetorical argument draws its premises and which such argument is then about. Within the autonomy of practical reasoning, the fact that advocates are trying to win a case is an advantage, not a pollution of a purer form of argument. The more partial goals that seem extraneous to the pursuit of truth and agreement by purely logical standards are a help to self-criticism, self-correction, and self-reliance. Without it, the autonomy of practical reasoning would be self-indulgent.

With the distinction between legitimacy and justice in hand, let me return briefly to the opening arguments about whether to extend protection against discrimination to homosexuals. There are no legitimate constitutional arguments about "nature" or "choice" because neither nature nor choice is by itself a constitutionally protected value. "The decision has a legal grammar, a grammar surprisingly like that of 'reasonable care,' 'malice aforethought,' 'notice,' 'unconscionability,' and not at all like that of 'pro-choice' or 'right-to-life'" (*CI*, 178). While that claim can look like protecting professional expertise against concerned citizens, we can now see it as a way of changing our understanding of justice from something that exists prior to argument, and indeed to the Constitution, to justice as an activity constituted in part by the activity of constitutional hermeneutics. Forcing us to abandon the language of nature and choice and adopt the language of due process and equal protection forces us into an argumentative community. Because our community becomes more rational, this is ethical progress.

The Discovery of the Ethical

Ethos plays a double role in the *Rhetoric.* The ethical is one of the three sources of proof, alongside the rational and the emotional. At the same time all persuasion that falls within the art of rhetoric is ethical. Similarly, Bobbitt sees the ethical as one among the six modes, and at the same time all interpretation is ethical.

Bobbitt introduces the ethical in the sense in which all fully practical reason is ethical by contrasting the hermeneutics of the "businessman, who is anxious to get from point 'a' to point 'b,' and who has a very clear idea of where 'b' is located, [for whom] the law is simply a set of rules that imposes certain costs on doing business," with the public official for whom "law is a map, a set of directions in a contentious democracy where there are many different views of where 'b' lies, or even what it is" (*CI,* 80). Bobbitt's businessman, reducing law to contract, has to obey the laws, but the public official has to execute them faithfully. When argument is ethical, the rhetoric available to serve any master is replaced by practical argument which is its own master. Any mode of argument can either be used the way the "businessman" uses law or the way the public official, with something that could accurately be called *civic virtue,* interprets it. This is the ethical difference between justice and friendship, between reasoning and merely using reasoning.

I want to explore four parallels between *ethos* as a mode of proof in Aristotle's *Rhetoric* and Bobbitt's presentation of the ethical as one of his six modes of constitutional argument. Each shows how hermeneutic and persuasive activity in modern constitutional democracies advances beyond what Aristotle has to offer. First, Aristotle stresses that the *ethos* which is the most persuasive kind of proof is internal to the speech itself, not the reputation of the speaker. Bobbitt similarly restricts the ethical to constitutional ethos, not to the values held by judges or by the community that can be identified in some other way. Second, in both cases, the ethical emerges only as one source of proof or mode of argument among others. Other methods might exist without the ethical, but the ethical cannot exist without them. Third—in a way that follows from the second—ethical argument as a distinct mode of argument will be relatively rare, and dangerous. Usually argument will be ethical simply by being argumentative and aiming at its internal end. When reasoning is constitutive rather than instrumental, it is ethical. Persuasion and interpretation that is ethical as opposed to logical and emotional, in Aristotle's case, or opposed to the other modes of interpretation, in Bobbitt's, will be rare. Finally, to argue ethically is to argue trying to achieve the internal end of argument, making a legitimate case, while to argue unethically is to aim directly at the external end of winning the case. The more ethical legal argument becomes, the less worry there needs to be about morality being reduced to legality.

1. Aristotle distinguishes between *ethos* produced by the argument and *ethos* as a preexistent property hearers impute to speakers. Even though such reputation may well be far more persuasive, it is not part of the art of rhetoric. When applied to constitutional interpretation, the distinction between internal and external *ethos* clearly becomes a substantive and important distinction backed by a moral rationale and not just moralizing. Bobbitt distinguishes between constitutional *ethos* and other ethical values that judges might hold:

> The principal error one can make regarding ethical argument is to assume that any statue or executive act is unconstitutional if it causes effects that are incompatible with the American cultural ethos. This equates ethical argument, a constitutional form, with moral argument generally. . . . The "morality" of the American constitutional system is, broadly speaking, that of the values of limited government, forbearance and pluralism. (*CI*, 20–21)

There is all the difference in the world between arguing about discrimination against homosexuals in terms of a private preference for privacy, or upholding such discrimination in terms of "the American cultural ethos," meaning the traditions and preferences of a majority, and a constitutional argument about the limits of government, which is truly an issue about *constitutional ethos*.[23]

2. In both the *Rhetoric* and contemporary constitutional hermeneutics, the ethical emerges only as one source of proof or mode of argument among others. The *ethos* internal to the practices of constitutional argument is a spirit committed to reading the Constitution as a constitution, not as the

businessman reads a contract. If I read the Constitution ethically, then I am committed to recognizing the other forms of argument as well. That commitment is a powerful new form of political friendship. We therefore have the non-Aristotelian result that to argue ethically is necessarily to be a pluralist with regard to argument. The constitutional interpreter who argues historically, textually, or prudentially may or may not be a pluralist, but the one who argues ethically must be.[24]

Because of this implicit commitment to plural legitimate argument, the ethical—whether in Aristotle's *ethos* versus logos and pathos or in contemporary constitutional hermeneutics—is difficult to isolate as a distinct mode of proof because its operation is so often tacit, negative, and regulative. The textualist, for example, denies that a right to privacy can be found in the Constitution, since it contains no words about privacy. The argument from *ethos* claims that the right to privacy is to be found in the constitutional ethos of limited government itself. The argument could go like this: No one would even suggest that the government may order women to have more children or that some people, chosen by lot, must spend their lives in military service. Therefore the idea of limited government implies a right to privacy. Ethical arguments reject possibilities, here forms of coercion, before they are even raised, which makes ethical argument often hard to see. Of course such a right to privacy based in limited government does not by itself establish the rights of homosexuals to live without discrimination, but it is the beginning of an argument.

3. We can offer an even stronger conclusion. The *Rhetoric* shows how direct ethical arguments are especially prone to backfire. As I mentioned in the discussion of trust, "Trust me; I'm not a crook" is rarely successful; politicians who declare that they are acting as their conscience dictates, and not for the sake of popularity, are almost always rightly suspected of insincerity. We trust those who accept responsibility and trust themselves, but saying "I accept responsibility" doesn't make it so. Ethical self-advertising *should* be self-defeating. Argument is for the most part ethical by being argumentative, that is, by aiming at its internal end of finding and presenting the best argument in the situation. Direct ethical appeal is not tied to argument and so not rational. It is a peculiarity of ethical argument that it works best when modifying, restraining, and regulating the other modes. The textualist who recognizes the legitimacy of other modes of interpretation is reasoning ethically.

We argue ethically in order to do justice, in order that justice result from our argumentative activities. The activity of constitutional fidelity constitutes, as all practices do, a community and culture, in this case a community and culture of argument. Unlike philosophy and rhetoric when they define themselves as polemical opposites, practical argument requires ethical as well as intellectual virtues. The internal values of legitimate argument bar totalitarian ambitions and legislate civility, making possible a community of disagreement. To argue ethically is to be part of a community. The greatest power of ethical argument comes then not in its direct manifestation but in what happens to the other modes of argument when they become one among many. Historical argument is different when it is historical argument as opposed to legitimate alternatives. Argument from precedent and doctrine becomes ethical through its opposition to prudential argument about consequences.

4. The ethical does double duty. It is one mode of argument among others, and yet at the same time all legitimate argument is ethical. The difference between legitimate and illegitimate arguments in any of the modes is the ethical difference between argument as constitutive and argument as a means. Someone whose methods of argument always lead to conclusions which coincided with a political platform is arguing as unethically as someone who is indifferent to whether the results of argument were just or not.

This vision of constitutional hermeneutics, rhetoric, and practical wisdom, in which pluralism, the internal ends of argument, and the ethical dimensions of argument develop together, is ethically superior to the more popular sophistical and philosophical constructions of constitutional interpretation. The latter two pretend that the superiority of their position is metaphysical, not ethical. The ethical only enters their accounts as alarms concerning external ends: strict constructionists are racists and their opponents want to impose antireligious equality on us.

While rhetoric begins as a neutral power equally available in the service of any purpose external to itself, ethical rhetoric is not that same rhetoric oriented to good ends, but a rhetoric which locates its value in the forms of arguments themselves, aiming at a justice that they only partly define. Ethical argument satisfies both the desire for stability that motivates philosophy's quest for certainty and the desire for autonomy that motivates rhetoric's desire for self-assertion. Constitutional hermeneutics, rhetoric, and practical wisdom develop and exercise the intellectual, emotional, and ethical abilities most likely to advance justice.

CHAPTER 8

Rhetoric and the Unity of Practical Reason

Rhetoric has been my guide to understanding practical reason. No matter how much we can learn about practical wisdom from looking at rhetorical activity, we still must wonder about the relation between the two. Is education and practice in rhetorical excellence the route to the acquisition of practical wisdom? Could someone exercise practical wisdom without being an effective persuader? Both the art of rhetoric and the virtue of practical wisdom concern deliberation. Both are about particulars beyond the reach of art, and involve a rationality beyond rules. Either they are competitors or they somehow reinforce each other. Which is it?

The best answer to that question is a contingent one, revolving around the circumstances of friendship. There are, to recall one of the problems from the second chapter, circumstances with a difference between reasoning and rationalizing, and other cases in which all reasoning is rationalization. Sophistic makes values, such as commitment, authority, and trust, incoherent. With a difference between reasoning and rationalizing, rational rhetoric, practical wisdom, and political friendship can all flourish.

The more we take disagreement to be a permanent part of the situation of practical reasoning, and not something soon to be overcome by appropriate theory or universal enlightenment, the more rhetorical facility becomes a central part of practical reason. The more pluralistic practical reason appears, the more urgently do we need to defend it against accusations of relativism and irrationality. I've talked about those accusations before, but now I want to look at them more practically and directly. Practical wisdom and rhetoric both need to worry that the abilities of which they are composed are not necessarily unified, and not necessarily respectable. Some people have skills and abilities that let them deliberate successfully, to persuade others of their point of view, to defend themselves against the accusations of others, to appropriate the symbolic resources of a community to their own advantage. Why should these skills be dignified by being called an art of rhetoric or honored as the intellectual virtue of practical wisdom?

The spirit of compromise essential to politics might be morally reprehensible. The single-mindedness necessary for effective practical action might conflict with the open-mindedness needed for progress. The zeal of the advocate has nothing in common with the restraint and moderation of a judicial temperament. The ability to frame and celebrate symbolic issues might be at odds with the power to solve concrete problems. There is no more reason to expect interconnectedness here than in the diverse skills exhibited by different basketball players who maximize some abilities at the cost of others.[1]

These questions are variations on the old Socratic problem of the unity of the virtues. If the virtues are not related to each other, then they are not virtues, but only a disparate set of skills or talents. Some people are courageous, others generous. When those abilities are called for, such people are welcome. But when my house needs painting, I'm glad to have a house painter around too. Only when courage and generosity seem connected to each other, and to what it is to be human, is courage more valuable than house painting. If inspiring and unifying a nation, formulating and executing productive policies, and making sensible judgments about people and actions are just a series of useful talents, then there is no reason to think that they go together. We should specify those powers, and hire professionals when we need those functions performed.

The Unity and Plurality of Practical Reason

The problem of the unity of practical reason is as old as practical thought itself. Americans expect and demand that their presidents be adept at a variety of difficult activities, and discover—after the fact, every time—that facility at one has no correlation with the others. A president has to inspire and unify a nation, must reward friends and punish enemies, and must deliberate and formulate policies that lead to security and prosperity. Examples of these abilities going together are rare. Why do we have such expectations, and why don't we learn from experience?

This isn't a problem in the way we choose presidents. It cannot be solved by campaign finance reform or changing to a ministerial form of government. It cuts deeper. The activities we expect from presidents are manifestations of the classical three kinds of rhetoric—the epideictic ability to honor and praise the noble, the forensic power to determine justice and assess rights and punishments, and the deliberative ability which calculates effective means to desired ends. When laid out this way, it is difficult to see why the methods of rationality appropriate to the three kinds of rhetoric should be rooted in a single faculty of practical reason or a single art of rhetoric. As abilities they seem independent. As activities they often conflict with each other. Someone displaying all three abilities seems to be a rare instance of superhuman or heroic virtue, rooted in something other than reason. It looks like there is no such thing as practical reason, just a series of unrelated skills.

Everyone can supply further examples of the diversity and conflict among the varieties of practical wisdom for themselves. But people frequently, in the teeth of such evidence, deny the diversity and conflict. Anyone who asserts a necessary connection between democracy and the free market in goods, or among the marketplace of ideas, the marketplace in commodities, and the rationality of science, posits a unity of practical reason. Is this wishful thinking or something more?

I want to attack this problem by looking at Rorty's article, "Rationality and Cultural Difference."[2] He articulates the prima facie implausibility of the unity of practical reason, raises all the important issues, and gets them all wrong, and so I want to use his work as a way of articulating the unity of practical reasoning. In my Introduction I pointed to Rorty's distinction of two kinds of rationality, the methodical and the civilized. Here he adds a third, to show that we can live without it. His three meanings of rationality coincide with the three genres of rhetoric. Corresponding to deliberative rhetoric is Rorty's technical reason, methodical means/end reasoning, reasoning that enables people to get what they want. While a useful skill, technical rationality would not be counted a virtue, but is open to criticism as mere cunning and cleverness. A life organized around technical rationality cannot be satisfying, although many people devote their lives to gathering and spending. The accumulation of means without regard for their ends is both irrational and unsatisfying.[3]

Rorty's second form of rationality is tolerance, "the ability not to be overly disconcerted by differences from oneself, not to respond aggressively to such differences" (186). With its emphasis on rights, it corresponds to judicial rhetoric. When we say that someone acts *reasonably*, we mean reason and rationality in this sense, interpreting being rational as being civilized. The reasonable person does not stand on principle but compromises and tolerates others, does not have principles but only preferences. We should aim at agreement and stop promoting the uncivil dogmatism that comes from raising the stakes by insisting that there's some sort of truth beyond agreement.

Liberal societies are organized around reasonableness and judicial rhetoric as much as technical reason and deliberative rhetoric organizes bureaucracies and market economies. Like technical reason, tolerance is a fine thing, but organizing a life around tolerance and reasonableness seems as unsatisfying as organizing one around technical reason. Tolerance allows me to worship my own gods, but tolerance itself cannot become a popular object of worship. In modern societies, the supposed separation of the right from the good produces a rhetorical division of labor: individuals engage in deliberative reasoning about the good, while the judgment of rights keeps us from killing each other, which is what it means today to be civilized. The joint power and success of deliberative and judicial rationality constitute modernity.

Rorty identifies a third kind of rationality, one which "establishes an evaluative hierarchy, rather than simply adjusting the means to taken-for-granted ends" (186). Epideictic rhetoric uses the language of nobility to affirm values and articulate new vocabularies rather than to reason in the narrower and more orderly sense associated with technical reason and deliberation or the legalisms of forensic rhetoric. Epideictic rationality, the most impractical-looking of the kinds of practical reason, moves comfortably back and forth between fact and fiction. It seems so rarefied that Rorty claims we would not notice if it disappeared. He thinks that this form of rationality "is the name for an extra added ingredient that human beings have and brutes do not" (186), and is therefore always a pretext for invidious distinctions between Us and Them. He proposes to substitute poetry and irony for philosophy.

When the three kinds of rhetoric and practical reason fall apart, we have that much less cause to take rhetoric or practical reason seriously as embodiments of human rationality or of political excellence. Technical rationality can be routinized into bureaucratic rationality and simple rule-following. Reasonableness can become moderation and politeness. If the activities of practical intelligence can be fully separated from each other, we will have no right, and no reason, to use terms like "rationality as such." There are just some talents that we find useful in presidents, legislators, judges, and citizens. We should now be mature enough to value these powers for what they are, and not have to glorify them by calling them virtues.

Technical rationality and tolerance are obviously good things. We live in a world in which prayer and magic are not reliable and in which we have to do something to get what we want. Given a world in which people do not all agree, tolerance is better than fighting. But those rationales aren't good enough; by themselves these modes of rationality cease being rational because I cannot live a life of calculation or toleration. The ethical desire for the unity of practical reason is a desire to keep the modes of rationality rational.[4]

Rorty thinks that the relation between instrumental rationality and tolerance is worth worrying about because there is no necessary connection between them. We can hope that the other two kinds of rationality will coincide, but can have no reasonable expectations that progress in one will do anything for progress in another. We were lucky in the past that market economies and tolerant societies grew together. We will be lucky if things stay that way in the future. Any connection between the increased technical rationality embodied in the spirit of capitalism and the increased tolerance of differences depends on historical factors, and has nothing to do with the nature of these kinds of rationality. It is fortunate, and fortuitous, that the nationalizing interpretations of the U.S. Supreme Court fostered first the development of industrial capitalism and then the expansion of individual rights, both against the tyranny of local majorities.[5]

While there are no necessary relations among the kinds of rationality, increases in technical rationality and tolerance have gone together in the past, and their combination accounts for much of the power of Western civilization to offer something that other cultures want, on terms that other cultures find easy to accept. Rorty too sees this, and attributes the insight to Dewey:

> For Dewey, there was a connection, but not a necessary or unbreakable one, between the increase[s] in . . . efficiency and tolerance. As we became more and more emancipated from custom—more and more willing to do things differently than our ancestors did for the sake of coping with our environment more efficiency and successfully—we became more and more receptive to the idea that good ideas might come from anywhere, that they are not the prerogative of an élite, and not associated with any particular locus of authority. (192)

When nothing is sacred, it is easier to experiment and find new methods for satisfying needs, and it is also easier to tolerate others who have allegiance to different gods. Rorty thinks it an open question for the future whether increased tolerance will come from additional technical rationality or from more resistance to technical rationality on behalf of traditional cultures and noneconomic values. "Obviously, increasing flexibility and efficiency can as easily be used to oppress as to free—to increase suffering as to decrease it, to decrease [tolerance] as to increase it. So there is nothing *intrinsically* emancipatory about a greater degree of instrumental rationality" (193). While that may be an open question, he also claims that increased technical rationality and increased tolerance came along with, and will continue to be correlated with a *decrease* in, the other form of rationality, the kind that makes a life of reason its own end. "Liberals who are also pragmatists [should] . . . just drop the whole idea of" the epideictic form of rationality (188).[6] Far from needing reason as its own end, the beneficial forms of reasoning evolved by getting rid of more substantive forms of rationality that retarded scientific progress and the growth of tolerance. The Enlightenment was essentially a battle against religion, and Rorty would continue that project by destroying philosophy too.

Pragmatism, Unity, and Pluralism

I want to quarrel with Rorty on two points. First, he makes the fatal, and decidedly unpragmatic, inference that because the associations among the kinds of rationality, and in particular that between instrumental rationality and tolerance, are historically contingent rather than eternal, it follows that their continued alliance is a matter for hope rather than for planning. He thinks that the relation between instrumental rationality and reasonableness or tolerance is not necessary, therefore contingent, and that therefore a matter of chance. Here is a place to see how *ethos* can exceed rationality without becoming irrational.

Unlike Rorty, Dewey thinks that how to strengthen the relation between further increases in instrumental reasoning, or science, and in tolerance, or democracy, is a critical subject for deliberation and practical reason:

> By proper selection and arrangement, we can even make out a case of the idea that all past history has been a movement, at first unconscious and then conscious, to attain freedom. A more sober view of history discloses that it took a very fortunate conjunction of events to bring about the rapid and seemingly complete victory of democracy in the nineteenth century. The conclusion to be drawn is not the depressing one that it is now in danger of destruction because of an unfavorable

conjunction of events. The conclusion is that what was won in a more or less external and accidental manner must now be achieved and sustained by deliberate and intelligent endeavor.[7]

The *Federalist* opened by saying that until now good governments were happy accidents, and that now for the first time we can create one through deliberation. I want to claim something parallel. Technical reason and tolerance in the past grew together through good fortune. They were political allies against common enemies. We now are, for the first time in human history, in a position to make their continuing development subject to deliberation. The rational activity of thinking about ends can replace more arbitrary orientations to our ends.

My second criticism of Rorty shows the benefits of thinking about practical reason rhetorically. He makes the categorical claim that what I have been calling epideictic rationality is not functional and should wither away. Philosophy is a successor subject to religion and should follow religion into the museum of past curiosities to be understood but not practiced. We are now sophisticated enough to be able to live with irony and poetry instead of philosophy. The quest for certainty is over.[8] Since the right is prior to the good, the good becomes private, and there is no need for and no possibility of a theory of the good. Negative liberty is enough. Not only can philosophy wither away, but its public parallels, cultural and symbolic politics and civil religion, are similarly irrational survivals not necessary to anyone sophisticated enough to distinguish public decency from private speculations and enjoyments.

I want to argue, instead, that the continued productive association between instrumental rationality and tolerance depends on the flourishing of reasoning as an activity that is its own end. We need the life of reason to make the other two into modes of *rationality*, and not just kinds of action that some might like, others not. Discourses about the useful and the just become incoherent without reference to the noble. The methodical and the civilized become useful skills instead of virtues and necessary features of living well unless they are dignified and rationalized by connection to the third kind of practical reason, reason as its own end.

If pragmatism has a lasting contribution to make to the world, it surely is its pluralism, its confident assertion that there are plural sources of value, plural ultimate values, and plural methods of achieving ultimate values. Pragmatism seems to me a successor project to Aristotle's, one which, for all Dewey's, and Peirce's, talk about communication, neglected the rhetorical dimension of practical wisdom.

How can the life of reason forge strong bonds between the other two, more practical looking, forms of rationality? Am I arguing, with Strauss and Bloom, that the Great Books will make us free? What of Rorty's contrary point that the great Western European breakthrough in both methodical and civilized rationality came from desacralization and so from abandoning reasoning as something more substantive than the methodical and the civilized?

Rorty prevents us from assuming a natural harmony between science and democracy, and between the free market and intellectual freedom. The methodical and civilized modes of rationality commonly assume that some single form is uniquely designed to be the embodiment of reason, as in those who make a fetish of the scientific method, two-party democracy, or the free market. Sometimes these may be good bets to promote rationality, but they become irrational when their connections to reason are made absolute. The life of reason makes practical reason a unity by preventing the natural tendency toward uniformity—and eventually, to irrationality—in the other modes of rationality.

There is, then, a very common fallacy of mistaking some historically contingent connections for absolute necessities. Along with that fallacy is the tendency for both the methodical and the civilized to define rationality in their own image. Some worry about the characteristically modern tendency of instrumental reason to define rationality with dehumanizing consequences. Others claim that toleration and reasonableness, when they become central ethical values, undermine themselves, producing a naked and therefore vulnerable public square of tolerance without faith. As we will see, Dewey thought a crucial contribution of philosophy to practical intelligence was that it resisted those reductions of unity to uniformity. Rorty's skepticism is itself a moment in that resistance.[9]

My thesis is that without the unity of practical reason, the rationality of the methodical and civilized modes of practical reason disappears. Rorty too argues against uniformity, but his argument turns against rationality too. A true pragmatist would realize that once we acknowledge that false unities and imposed uniformities won't do, we can now go on to talk about the real and practical unity of practical reason. Dewey's search for a public, as opposed to a society taken as given, is a search for unity. Once we know that practical reason cannot be reduced to scientific reason, what then can we say about practical reason and about suitable forms of unity and rationality? In the last chapter we saw again that friendship meant a common activity, not doctrinal agreement. Any useful and responsible unity of practical reason has to allow for the flourishing of conflict as well as agreement.[10]

Why should anyone think that the three kinds of rationality and rhetoric should be integrated? It would be nice if increasing the technical rationality of capitalism—getting to work on time, and working as part of a team, matching production to the desires of consumers—led to increased rationality of tolerance and democracy, and even led to people valuing the pursuit of rationality in their leisure time. But enough counter-examples exist to declare such millenarian hopes one of the more antiquated facets of the Enlightenment. According to theoretical reason, connections must either be necessary and universal or simply accidental. Practical reason, as we've seen before, can do better by finding reliable connections. We can deliberate about how to fortify the relations between the methodical and the civilized instead of claiming that they are necessarily related, or being disappointed and thinking it's all a matter of luck and hope instead. As Dewey says,

> To represent naturalistic morals as if they involved denial of the existence and the legitimacy of any sort of regulative end and standard is but another case of translation of a position into the terms of the position of its opponents. The idea that unless standards and rules are eternal and immutable they are not rules and criteria at all is childish.[11]

The association between science and democracy, between instrumental rationality and tolerant reasonableness, is less than a necessary connection but more than a contingent one. It is an *ethical* connection, fortified and made more than coincidental by making reason into its own end. The methodical and the civilized will reinforce each other when the people who engage in them also make reasoning into its own end.

What Makes Instrumental Rationality and Tolerance Rational?

We can get beyond unfruitful debates about whether the free market is good for democracy or whether democracy causes science to flourish or the other way around by looking at the question more pragmatically. The crucial practical question for the unity of practical reason is how it can be a self-sustaining enterprise—self-replicating, self-correcting, self-generating and self-supporting. If it is, then it has its own values and autonomy. It will be valued for its own sake, and not only for its rewards.

For example, some have argued that technical rationality cannot be self-sustaining, because it depends on customs of reasonableness and trust that it cannot itself engender and which it may in fact endanger. Development economics explores the conditions in which instrumental rationality can sustain itself.[12] More "advanced" societies face the opposite problem of how to prevent technical rationality from degenerating into something so technical it becomes irrational. Instrumental rationality can be routinized into professions that are no longer rational. MacIntyre's *After Virtue* offers an account of what happens to technical reason when separated from other modes of practical wisdom, the problem of the mindlessness and irrationality of bureaucratic and instrumental reason. While people in poor countries worry about how to institutionalize technical rationality, those in rich countries worry about how to escape from its domination.

Similarly, tolerance doesn't emerge out of a desire for tolerance, but out of a desire not to be persecuted, and it often seems to become much less powerful once that initial desire leaves. Tolerance can be an irrational "value" to be respected, and adhered to, without itself embodying reason. Recent complaints about "rights talk" reduce rights to claims that are especially difficult to refute or especially strongly felt, without connection to other modes of argument.[13] My South African example showed how tolerance and civilized rationality can be repressive as well as liberating. Separated from the rest of practical rationality and other human values, the reasonableness that lets the guilty go free rather than punish the innocent and the tolerance that tolerates the intolerant and intolerable are as irrational as holding to a hypothesis against the evidence or pursuing efficiency for its own sake.[14] The judicial rationality of tolerance and reasonableness is always in danger of degenerating from the law as reason without passion to the law as mindless legalism in which might makes right, for example in "original intent" and the reduction of property to first possession.

In another context, Rorty sees philosophy as exactly what prevents toleration and judicial rhetoric from becoming legalistic:

> "Philosophy" is precisely what a culture becomes capable of when it ceases to define itself in terms of explicit rules, and becomes sufficiently leisured and civilized to rely on inarticulate know-how, to substitute

phronēsis for codification, and conversation with foreigners to conquest of them.[15]

Philosophy in this sense is epideictic rationality, irreducible to the other two, yet keeping them rational. I differ from Rorty, though, in doubting the value of leisure as a factor in the flourishing of this kind of practical rationality. My examples of the TRC and *Brown* suggest on the contrary that philosophy, as a reflective affirmation of the circumstances of friendship, emerges as much from a crisis as from leisure. The substitution of *phronēsis* for codification is the evolution of justice into friendship. In this sense, philosophy means not the replacement of practical by theoretical reason, as it did in the pejorative sense in the last chapter and in Rorty's death wish for it; philosophy is simply practical reason reflecting on itself. Being "sufficiently leisured and civilized" is both cause and effect of philosophy and the ability to make reason into its own end, reenacting the circularity between logos and *ethos*, thought and character, I have been examining throughout. Philosophy in that sense is one of the circumstances of friendship.

Rorty regards philosophy simply as the name for this happy result of the maturity of a culture. I think we can give more specificity to philosophy as an activity by seeing how it emerges out of the common activities of deliberation and judgment. In the conditions that liberal democracies face, philosophy is the name for a solution to the problems posed by the rule of law and the powers of scientific methods. Both rule of law and the regime of science can be oppressive as they become mindless and irrational. The remedy is for them to become more transparently rational by becoming ethical.

The problem to which *ethos* is a solution is how practical rationality can be self-sustaining and fully rational. Tolerance seems to be an unstable form of rationality because it can generate breathing space for the development of intolerance. Deliberative rationality can lead to free riders. Since people engage in instrumental rationality only for its rewards, people will try to get the rewards without working. Therefore, neither technical rationality nor toleration and reasonableness is self-engendering or self-sustaining. The practical project to which reasoning as its own end is the solution is to find the conditions under which these forms of practical rationality can sustain themselves.

Rorty seems to think that technical rationality can probably take care of itself, at least in postmodern bourgeois liberal societies. Science will spread throughout the world. Democracy is not so secure. The rationality of reasonableness and tolerance needs all the support—hortatory, social, and material—it can get. Reasonableness and tolerance need support especially because their link to technical rationality can no longer be assumed. I believe that that warning must be taken seriously, much as I want to fight with his remedy:

> There is a moral purpose behind this light-mindedness. The encouragement of light-mindedness about traditional philosophical topics serves the same purposes as does the encouragement of light-mindedness about traditional theological topics. Like the rise of large market economies, the increase in literacy, the proliferation of artistic genres and the insouciant pluralism of contemporary culture, such philosophical superficiality and light-mindedness helps along the disenchantment of the world. It helps make the world's inhabitants more pragmatic, more tolerant, more liberal, more receptive to the appeal of instrumental rationality.[16]

Rorty goes wrong in thinking that the disenchantment of the world is always a useful project. Disenchantment leads us to aim at agreement rather than truth. As we saw in the first chapter with the example of the man who believed that English originated in central Africa, "light-mindedness" does not necessarily lead to tolerance. For example, in Supreme Court jurisprudence, to treat religious beliefs and practices such as smoking peyote or wearing a yarmulke as preferences means not taking them seriously.[17] Tolerance becomes condescension. Rorty ignores the difference between being light-minded toward one's own beliefs and toward others. I can be more tolerant by adopting more moderate attitudes toward my own beliefs, but when I adopt the same attitude toward others, I become patronizing. The disenchantment of the world is distinct from the disenchantment of other people.[18]

Philosophy might sometimes take the form of Rortean irony, but there are other useful roles that reasoning as its own end can play. Sometimes the only way to be friends with someone radically different from ourselves—people who accept the biblically mandated separation of the races, who believe that English originated in central Africa, or who encounter the divine through smoking hallucinogenic drugs—is to bracket the truth-claims of their beliefs and values, but sometimes confrontation and disagreement, and sometimes through the intermediate propositional attitudes I explored in chapters 3 and 4, create friendship.

The Need for the Life of Reason

I had two disagreements with Rorty. First, the contingency of the relation between technical rationality and tolerance poses a problem for deliberation and practical reasoning, not just a subject for private hope. Rorty has been beaten up on that ground before. But in addition, I maintain that the conditions under which technical rationality and tolerance support each other are not simply material and social conditions but intellectual conditions. In particular, technical rationality and tolerance support each other when the life of reason flourishes and unifies practical reason.

Since that must sound wildly abstract, I need eventually to argue for a third conclusion, that the flourishing of the life of reason does not mean increased funding for philosophy departments, but just the kind of ethical persuasive activity I have identified throughout this book. Philosophy is what happens when people regard each other as rational agents, and so is a highly moral activity. Dewey recognized the intellectual dimensions of the problem, in addition to the material ones, when he said, speaking of *The Public and Its Problems,* that "there are too many publics and too much of public concern for our existing resources to cope with. The problem of a democratically organized public is primarily and essentially an intellectual problem, in a degree to which the political affairs of prior ages offer no parallel" (126).

William James offers a similar diagnosis, showing how deliberative rationality must not degenerate into purely instrumental rationality:

> Ideality often clings to things only when they are thus taken abstractly. "Causes," as anti-slavery, democracy, etc., dwindle when realized in their sordid particulars. Abstractions will touch us when we are callous to the concrete instances in which they lie embodied. Loyal in our measure to particular ideals, we soon set up abstract loyalty as something of a superior sort, to be infinitely loyal to; and truth at large becomes a "momentous issue" compared with which truths in detail are "poor scraps, mere crumbling successes." [19]

Surely one of the major problems facing the public uses of practical reason in America today is that abilities to deal with abstractions and with concrete problems are not often found together. Freedom becomes an abstract cause, which allows powerful economic interests to persuade the public that the freedom of thought and of ethical autonomy is reducible to the freedom of the market. Practical reason suffers, and becomes irrational, when our thinking about the abstract and the concrete diverge. The difference, in my first chapter, between what each knows and what everybody knows can become a difference between our judgments about abstractions and about particulars. Someone can sincerely assert that some of his best friends are blacks, yet hold to abstract stereotypes at odds with his behavior toward individuals, and politicians have become adroit at exploiting the contradictions. The ethical success of the TRC and of the *Brown* decision came from their holding together the abstract and the concrete.

Reasoning as its own end, and not some more practical-looking political, social, or economic reform, is the most important condition for the self-maintenance of the other modes of rationality. It allows us to integrate the intellectual virtues of dealing with past and with future, the ability to solve concrete problems, and the ability to manipulate powerful symbols. Aristotle offers a similar argument when he says that the justice that distinguishes mine and thine depends on concord where friends have all things in common, and not on legal arrangements that destroy private property. Judicial rationality alone cannot support itself but requires another form of practical rationality, being of one mind. Communities need friendship in addition to justice in exactly the way that practical rationality needs the life of reason as well as judicial and technical reason. Such concord offers an answer to the question of how the life of reason can be embodied in the activities of a community, and not in philosophy departments. Civic education will embody the life of reason for a community. Unlike the other modes of practical rationality, the life of reason is a rational relation of people to their ends. In Aristotle's *Politics* the life of reason is not the contemplative life of the ending of the *Ethics* but a civic education centered on the development of proper character. It is that conception of philosophy that I want to follow out here.

The three kinds of rhetoric have three distinct ends: deliberative rhetoric talks about the useful, judicial rhetoric about the just, and epideictic rhetoric about the noble (*Rhetoric* I.3.1358a36–b21). Questions about the practical necessity for reasoning as its own end ask what practical function is served by a concept of the noble, not reducible to the useful and the just. It is easy to see why practical reason needs concepts of utility and justice, but not so obvious why those two are not jointly sufficient. Contemporary contrasts between the right and the good certainly act as though they are enough. A vision of politics in which the public sphere is the domain of rights, and the private sphere lies beyond good and evil in a regime of pleasure and pain, is a world of tolerance and instrumental rationality. Is anything missing from that paradise?

Deliberative and judicial rhetoric are so central to our lives that they are housed in specific political bodies, deliberative assemblies that employ deliberative rhetoric to deliberate on and agree on policies, and judicial forums that use judicial rhetoric to make judgments of guilt and punishment. We legitimately complain when Congress makes constitutional pronouncements or when the Supreme Court legislates. There are no epideictic institutions. Examples of epideictic rationality can appear anywhere: presidential actions and discourse can unify and rationalize technical and judicial rationality, as Lincoln did, but so can deliberative bodies, as the Reconstruction Congress did. So can judicial bodies, such as the Warren Supreme Court. So, finally, can extralegal political movements and ad hoc institutions, such as the South African Truth and Reconciliation Commission, which had a mixture of deliberative, judicial, and epideictic responsibilities. All these produced rational discourse about ends.[20] Reasoning as its own end occurs anytime when deliberative or judicial rationality moves beyond fitting rules to cases to reflect about its ends. Rorty says that "'philosophy' is precisely what a culture becomes capable of when it ceases to define itself in terms of explicit rules, and becomes sufficiently leisured and civilized to rely on inarticulate know-how, to substitute *phronēsis* for codification." I would rewrite this statement this way: Reasoning as its own end is precisely what a culture does when it ceases to define itself in terms of explicit rules, and becomes sufficiently self-confident to rely on reflection and reasoning about ends, to substitute *phronēsis* for codification.

It may be hard to see why practical reason needs its epideictic form as well as instrumental rationality and tolerant reasonableness. It is easier to understand on the substantive side. The useful and the just are incomplete forms of value unless there are also goods that are their own end. Unless there are some ethical activities worth doing for their own sake, no action can be truly useful or just. And yet the useful and just are never reducible to activities done for their own sake. Instead action that is its own end is the perfection of instrumental and just actions, not a separate category of acts. To try to make the rationality of reasoning about ends into a method, or to offer it an institutional home, is like trying to devise a method for creativity or for friendship. Yet engaging in reasoning as its own end is exactly the method of communication Dewey pointed toward but never developed himself.[21]

Practical Rationality and Human Nature

We can develop this third sense of rationality further by noting another difference between Rorty and Dewey. Rorty claims that the idea of a fixed human essence, Philosophy with a capital P, and rationality in the sense of the life of reason all stand and fall together. All these are our legacy of the Enlightenment (or, sometimes Plato or Descartes). Current attacks on objectivity, on "Truth with a capital T" are a continuation of atheism by other means. Dewey has a more challenging idea. Far from the life of reason becoming impossible without an eternal human essence, Dewey argues that *only* when we discard the idea of an eternal human essence that a life of reason can go on. Fixed human nature is tied to fixed human ends. Dewey, here the better historian than Rorty, sees the idea of human nature as historically conditioned, not a perennial idea that we can only now overcome.

Aware of the dangers and opportunities of pluralism, Dewey reenacts Aristotle's discovery of politics as shared activity. Common activities do not require unanimity concerning ultimate beliefs. Dewey goes further than Aristotle by rejecting the idea that a good polis requires its citizens all to have the same right ends, the pursuit of a life of happiness defined as activity in accordance with virtue. For Aristotle, we deliberate about means, not ends. Modern democracy makes possible reasoning about ends. As Claude Lefort puts it, "Modern democracy invites us to replace the notion of a regime founded upon laws, of a legitimate power, by a notion of a regime founded upon the *legitimacy of a debate as to what is legitimate and what is illegitimate*—a debate which is necessarily without any guarantor and without any end."[22] We can fully deliberate and reason intelligently about ends only when we abandon the idea of a fixed human essence.[23] I draw the opposite implications from Dewey that Rorty draws. Only now in a democracy—where human nature can be subject to deliberation—can the life of reason take a fully public, not private, form:[24]

> If human nature is unchangeable, then there is no such thing as education and all our efforts to educate are doomed to failure. For the very meaning of education is modification of native human nature in formation of those new ways of thinking, of feeling, of desiring and of believing that are foreign to raw human nature. If the latter were unalterable, we might have training but not education. For training, as distinct from education, means simply the acquisition of certain skills.

Native gifts can be trained to a point of higher efficiency without that development of new attitudes and dispositions which is the goal of education. But the result is mechanical. It is like supposing that while a musician may acquire by practice greater technical ability, he cannot rise from one plane of musical appreciation and creation to another.[25]

If humanity has a fixed essence, then that essence might be an object for theoretical study, but it could not be a subject for practical deliberation. A fixed human nature destroys the autonomy of practical reason. When we abandon the idea of a fixed human nature, the relation between theory and practice can be democratically transformed.

Dewey's insight that the lack of a determinate human nature allows rationality to be its own end in a new and more complete way is not just a parochial philosophical point about whether humanity has an essence. In chapter 7 I tried to show how such tired philosophical debates about relativism, incommensurability, and foundationalism became live practical issues in the right circumstance. Similarly, here we face a consequential question about whether we should abandon claims about a fixed human nature. Rorty maintains that only with fixed human essences and transcendental sources of reason and value can reason be an end; many others have claimed that community, with true justice and friendship, is possible only with homogeneity, whether of creed, of tradition, or of blood. In the first chapter I pointed to Hirsch's project of identifying what every American needs to know as a recent and innocent-looking example of this perennial project of making community depend on homogeneity. The democratic unity of practical reason makes these more irrational sources of unity unnecessary.

Only when we democratically abandon a fixed human essence is the life of reason fully possible because the function of the life of reason is to think rationally and publicly about ends.[26] Only if reason is an end can our ends be the objects of reason. To think rationally about ends is to make reason into a practical end, an end of life. I want to invoke Peirce rather than Dewey at this point to make the point clear that rationality, paradoxically, is the only ultimate end of action:

I do not see how one can have a more satisfying ideal of the admirable than the development of Reason. . . . The one thing whose admirableness is not due to an ulterior reason is Reason itself comprehended in all its fullness, so far as we can comprehend it. Under this conception, the ideal of conduct will be to execute our little function in the operation of the creation by giving a hand toward rendering the world more reasonable whenever, as the slang is, it is "up to us" to do so.

I seem to have been inclined to subordinate the *conception* to the act, knowing to doing. Subsequent experience of life has taught me that the only thing that is really desirable without a reason for being so, is to render ideas and things reasonable.[27]

The function of the life of reason is to reason about ends. Reasoning about ends sometimes sounds mystical, like making a radical choice between good and evil, or between incommensurable forms of goodness, a choice that must be irrational and a matter of free will, or grace, not intelligence. That way lies romanticism.[28] Others assimilate reasoning about ends to reasoning about the means toward some more ultimate end which cannot itself be determined by reason—the route of utilitarianism. Both romanticism and utilitarianism emerge out of the denial of a fixed human nature, and they consequently lie at the beginning of the possibility of reasoning over ends. Once we see that to reason about ends makes reason into an end such thinking becomes more intelligible than its irrational alternatives. Reasoning about ends, as Dewey points out, battles against false absolutisms and false uniformities, such as the substitution of law for justice or method for thinking. Such reasoning about ends, then, is not necessarily an intellectual life or a search for theoretical wisdom. Throughout I have appealed to examples like the TRC and the *Brown* decision to avoid the misunderstanding that an argument like Peirce's leads to the conclusion that we should all become philosophers. Reasoning about ends includes reasoning about the connection between the varieties of practical reason, the construction of practical connections between being methodical and being civilized.

Consequently, just as Dewey says that democracy is aristocracy made universal, so democracy is the life of reason made universal, and so free from external limitations. The life of reason, unlike the other two dimensions of practical reason, seems an elitist luxury. Only in a democracy can a life of reason not be an imposed unity of culture like the Great Books curriculum, but a common, yet individualized, inquiry and search for wisdom.

Philosophy and Democracy

Philosophy and reason as its own end keep the other modes of practical rationality vital and rational. The question of the place of philosophy in a democracy is: What can we do to insure that practical rationality be self-sustaining and self-supporting? I want to approach that question by returning to an aspect of Deweyan pragmatism that is to Rorty the most dated and eliminable: science as a model for democracy. Throughout this book my emphasis on legal reasoning has shown how reasoning as its own end and political friendship emerge out of judicial rhetoric at its best. Here I want briefly to see how instrumental rationality and scientific reasoning too can engender reasoning about ends. I have shown that we can say about legal reasoning what Dewey said about science:

> Take science (including its application to the machine) for what it is, and we shall begin to envisage it as a potential creator of new values and ends. We shall have an intimation, on a wide and generous scale, of the release, the increased initiative, independence, and inventiveness, which science now brings in its own specialized fields to the individual scientist. It will be seen as a means of originality and variation.[29]

Holding democracy up to the model of science is, *pace* Rorty, very different from imposing the model of instrumental reasoning on democracy, from reducing the rationality of being civilized to the rationality of being methodical, thinking that if we could only reason more scientifically, practical reason would lead to consensus instead of diversity of opinion. As Dewey puts it in *The Problems of Men*:

> The chief influence in retarding and preventing the conscious realization that will give unity and steadiness to the democratic movement is precisely the philosophy of dogmatic rigidity and uniformity. In consequence, the chief opportunity and chief responsibility of those who call themselves philosophers are to make clear the intrinsic kinship of democracy with the methods of directing changes that have revolutionized science.[30]

Of course holding science up as a model for democracy is part of what Rorty likes to call the bad Dewey, who obstinately keeps saying what Rorty wishes he wouldn't. But it's worth keeping the argument straight here. I invoke science to make reasoning into an end, not to assert an identity between instrumental rationality and democratic tolerance. Science helps make reasoning into an end because it combats "dogmatic rigidity and uniformity." "Every discovery in physical knowledge signifies . . . a change in the processes of production . . . [but] there is next to nothing of the same sort with respect to knowledge of man and human affairs."[31] Moral knowledge is not as strongly connected to action as scientific knowledge, a neat reversal of "internalist" conceptions of practical reason that claim that practical reason, unlike scientific reasoning, is inherently motivating and action-guiding. Dewey sees that the problem with moral knowledge is its lack of connection to action, the problem manifested in the trouble with contemporary democratic politics that the ability to frame and celebrate symbolic issues is at odds with the power to solve concrete problems, a serious disunity to practical reason:

> If it were treated as what it is, the method of intelligence itself in action, then the method of science would be incarnate in every branch of study and every detail of learning. Thought would be connected with the possibility of action, and every mode of action would be reviewed to see its bearing upon the habits and ideas from which it sprang.[32]

Science is a model for democracy because of its ability to demonstrate the importance of rational *ethos*. I chose Aristotle rather than Plato to battle the sophists because, in rhetoric and in ethics, good action, action that is chosen for its own sake, need not be disinterested. The fact that I stand to gain if my argument succeeds does not mean that it's not the best argument. Aristotelian virtue does not rely on purity of motive. I can choose to act liberally as its own end while still aiming at helping my friends financially.

The same is equally true for Aristotelian politics:

> The many, none of whom is a good man, may nevertheless be better than the few good men when they get together. Not that each by himself will be better but that as a whole they will be, as meals to which many have contributed are better than those provided by one outlay. For each of these many may possess some part of goodness and wisdom; and when they get together, as the mass may be a single man with many feet and many hands and many senses, so it may be with their character and thought. That is why the many are better judges of works of music and poetry; some judge one part, some another, and altogether they judge it well. (*Politics* III.11.1281b3–10)

There is nothing automatic about adding partial truths into a higher wisdom. Politics needs institutions that make such addition possible. Those institutions are the circumstances of friendship. Scientific institutions can point the way.

Scientists are not morally superior to other citizens. They have ambitions, rivalries, and the same set of low desires that characterizes the rest of us. However, science as an institution has figured out to make those aspects of character irrelevant, so that the scientific *ethos* is constituted by honest consideration of evidence and the other required intellectual virtues instead of the personal predilections of individual scientists. Experimental science as an institution developed by creating circumstances in which people could trust each other, could take language as referring to an external world instead of as a device for manipulation that had to be seen through to the speaker's motives.[33] When the institutions of science function properly, we have no trouble separating the "real" *ethos* of the scientist from the rational *ethos* of the scientist as participant in the activity of science. It is that rational *ethos* that counts. A community in which people relate to each other through their rational *ethē* is ethically superior to a community of virtue. Current American democracy that ignores argument in favor of personality could learn something from scientific practices that are able to do the opposite.

Taking rhetoric seriously can help here. For all their talk of communication, neither pragmatists nor contemporary communitarians attend to rhetorical argument, which they should hold central. While rhetoric may have been allied with ancient democracy, modern egalitarian democracy includes a suspicion of eloquence that equates excellence in speaking not with practical wisdom but with social class. To be persuaded by someone because he or she speaks well is as undemocratic as being persuaded because someone is rich. As I mentioned in chapter 5, instead of an art of persuasion, we mostly try to develop arts of not being persuaded, the rational equivalent of defensive driving. There is a strong correlation between the triumph of democracy and the decline in the study of rhetoric.

Democracy likes to level people by exposing hidden motives that let us discount what people actually say. We would be better off doing the opposite, to ignore persons in favor of the logic and *ethos* of argument. Seeing how the institutions of science succeed, and sometimes fail, to make this separation and this shift of attention can, as Dewey hoped, connect knowledge and action. A community in which people relate to each other through their rational *ethē* has more democratic potential than less rational forms of community.

Self-regulation is more complicated, and takes more deliberation, in practical reasoning than in science. As we've seen from chapter 2 on, there is no automatic harmony between partisanship and impersonal goals. Instead we find permanent paradoxes about unity and diversity. These paradoxes, which go the heart of what it means for a community democratically to think about its ends, naturally center on public education. Most people who want diversity with respect to science, such as the advocates of creationism or supply-side economics, want unity concerning "values," American or "Judeo-Christian," while most who insist on uniformity in science teaching also advocate, or tolerate, diversity in values. Rorty himself argues wisely for diversity in higher education alongside uniformity in the socializing functions of elementary and secondary schools.[34] Those who want unity in higher education—the "Great Books"—seek diversity in lower education, with public subsidies for religious schools and exemptions for parents to indoctrinate their own children. Those paradoxes, and the attendant permanent possibilities for hypocrisy, are part of the problem of practical rationality today. As science gives us resources for "resisting dogmatic rigidity and uniformity" and allowing "unity and steadiness to the democratic movement" instead, in practical reason we achieve the equivalent sort of autonomy by substituting *ethos* for reason, political friendship for the rule of law.

Democracy and practical reason can learn from science here. The autonomy of science doesn't mean insularity. It means protecting scientific inquiry from premature applications to nature and premature falsification, from discounting internal ends in favor of external ones. There can be a conflict between a scientific determination of whether I'm ill and how I feel. Neither science nor my own opinion has automatic priority. In the long run, but only in the long run, scientific conceptions of health have to correspond with popular judgment. Rational rhetoric lets us think in a similar way about communication. All persuasion was done to persuade someone, but we shouldn't judge the value of any particular instance of persuading by whether it succeeds. Scientific methods are designed to lead to truth, but they redefine the marks of truth for us in the process. Similarly, the art of rhetoric is designed to persuade, but redefines what counts as successful persuasion. Legal methods are supposed to secure justice, and they sometimes redefine the justice they aim at. Those redefinitions are moments when we reason about ends.

Science is a model for democracy, but not because scientific inquiry is natural and scientific method simply the refined codification of successful methods for practical satisfaction, but just because its modes of rationality run counter to ordinary habits, as the internal ends of practices can correct given, external ends. The debates about the autonomy of science, whether it is an instrument to further antecedent ends or sets its own agenda, maintain the tension between internal and external ends. Here too lies a lesson for rhetoric. The intellectual virtues of reflection are not habits in the sense that they make habitual, routine, and mindless the ways we already have of coping with the world. The intellectual virtues of reflection can be as critical as they can be complacent. Practical reason can be self-sustaining because it sets its own standards. Because scientific and legal rationality can be at odds with ordinary rationality, I need to distinguish the pragmatist's modeling democracy on science from the popular idea that democratic debate is the model for scientific methods. On that distinction Peirce has the last word:

> Some people fancy that bias and counter-bias are favorable to the extraction of truth—that hot and cold partisan debate is the way to investigate. This is the theory of our atrocious legal procedure. But logic puts its heel upon this suggestion. It irrefragably demonstrates that knowledge can only be furthered by the real desire for it, and that the methods of obstinacy, of authority, and every mode of trying to reach a foregone conclusion, are absolutely of no value.[35]

Democracy cannot be a model for science—the judicial trial is no model for how scientific truth emerges. If only Holmes had listened to Peirce instead of coining the phrase "marketplace of ideas" that eliminates truth in favor of satisfying preferences. Science as the model for democracy doesn't mean social engineering, quantifying methods, as it would if both were conceived as modes of technical rationality. Instead, science is the model for democracy by teaching us how to reason about ends.

We see epideictic rhetoric and reasoning about ends at work most today in cultural and symbolic politics, the side of politics most challenging for pragmatism because its relation to practice is most unclear. It has no evident "cash value." Such rhetoric more often looks like an obstacle to inquiry than an engendering condition of reasoning about ends: the attitude that school prayer will reduce crime is a barrier to deliberating seriously about crime. Celebration of abstract ends prevents us from deliberating toward what Dewey calls "ends in view." Reflection about ends has its own form of abuse, which is a celebration of values and ends disconnected from action. That perverted form is exactly the side of epideictic rationality Rorty celebrates when he wants to substitute poetry for philosophy. The other modes of rationality are generated by nonrational exigencies—the need to plan how to get what we want and the need to live together—while epideictic rhetoric and the life of reason come from the demands of reason itself.

Aristotle says that epideictic and deliberative rhetoric are related by a change of phrase (I.9.1367b37–1368a10), but we need to turn attention, as Aristotle does not, to the conditions under which that can be the case, the conditions under which deliberating toward a concrete end and celebrating ultimate ends are part of a single activity. Practical reason will not be as rational as science until it is as connected to action as scientific knowledge is.

Reasoning about ends makes the diverse modes of practical reason into a unity and keeps the others rational. It cannot do so by *proving* that utility and justice are not really at odds but are harmonized by the good and the noble. Instead, it develops rational ethical *desires* for achieving that harmony. The life of reason requires the development of rational sentiments and intellectual virtues. Like science itself, practical rationality requires appropriate emotions. Dewey observes that the scientific

> interest has developed a morale having its own distinctive features. Some of its obvious elements are willingness to hold belief in suspense; ability to doubt until evidence is obtained; willingness to go where evidence points instead of putting first a personally preferred conclusion; ability to hold ideas in solution and use them as hypotheses to be tested instead of as dogmas to be asserted; and (possibly the most distinctive of all) enjoyment of new fields for inquiry and of new problems.[36]

Practical reason has to be sustained by intellectual virtues which keep instrumental reasoning and civility from becoming irrational routines. In practice, reason without *ethos* is self-defeating. The ampliative nature of practical reason, in its instrumental and judicial varieties, makes reasoning about ends possible.

The Autonomy of Practical Reason

Associating the dimensions of practical reasoning with the kinds of rhetoric reconfigures practical reasoning as a set of *powers* rather than a set of beliefs, as language becomes a set of tools instead of a mirror of nature. As Peirce taught, beliefs are habits of action. We saw this transformation when Bobbitt redefined theories of constitutional interpretation as modes of reasoning rather than sets of belief. Beliefs can be refuted, and they can become unintelligible and so ignored or transcended. But powers either are realized or they are not. They are either appropriate to circumstances or they are not. As we saw in chapter 2, a different set of criteria comes into play for powers than for beliefs, and the whole idea of "foundations" is inapplicable to powers. Worries about the connection between being methodical and being civilized are reformulated when we think of the different kinds of practical reason as powers rather than beliefs.

Throughout, conceiving of practical reason as a set of powers has let us think about the unity between the methodical, the civil, and philosophical, the three dimensions of practical rationality. In the first two chapters I showed how theoretical approaches to incommensurability made incommensurable modes of rhetoric and philosophy into sets of beliefs, and so made problems of incommensurability intractable, while ethical approaches treated philosophy and rhetoric as sets of powers that could be compared ethically. In the South African Truth and Reconciliation Commission, we saw how democratic friendship allowed practical reasoning to be more expansive and ambitious than liberal rules of self-denial would permit. The third and fourth chapters looked at the ethical surplus provided by ampliative ethical reasoning, a facet of rhetorical and ethical practical reason that demonstrates its power but which makes no sense if practical reason is grounded in a series of theses rather than a power. The Supreme Court's decision in *Brown v. Board of Education* showed how ethical reasoning could exceed the purely logical while never ceasing to be logical. In considering authority in chapter 5, I showed how modes of argument were practices that justify themselves and do not stand in need of outside justification. The Court's successful construction of *Brown* as an authority demonstrated the superiority of reasoning to other means of effecting practical ends such as securing obedience. Similarly, in chapter 7, the modes of constitutional interpretation did not require justification as beliefs do, because they are activities and practices. The legitimacy of these activities exemplified the autonomy of practical reason in the face of the contemporary demands of pluralism.

My use of the kinds of rhetoric to discuss the modes of practical rationality conceives of practical reason as a series of purposeful ways of thinking. Technical rationality is not grounded in metaphysical theses about the uniformity of nature, but is a collection of ethical abilities to achieve goals by intelligently manipulating resources. Judicial rationality, or reasonableness, is not based on the equality of man or the sanctity of human life, but on the abilities, cognitive, affective, and practical, to be one among many. Epideictic rationality or reason as its own end, finally, is not based on metaphysical beliefs in transcendental truths but in the ability—cognitive, affective, and practical—to determine one's own life and one's own ends.

Like the autonomy of science, the autonomy of practical reason is always in danger of becoming self-isolation. The identity I have relied on, between *pistis* as referring to a trustworthy speaker, a cogent argument, and a convinced audience, depends on the autonomy of practical reason. In the first chapter, the autonomy of practical reason faced the problem of the autonomy of common opinion, democratic knowledge, what everybody knows. Rhetoric takes its premises from common opinion, takes those opinions as its subject-matter, and aims at a persuasion that depends on those same opinions. Rhetorical argument can only persuade someone of something that the audience is able and willing to hear. An example like the South African Truth and Reconciliation Commission shows the dangers of autonomy and insularity. Yet the same example shows how the autonomy of the power of practical reason can overcome the dangers of isolation.

The autonomy of practical reason took a second form in the next chapter. We had to wonder whether the activity of persuasion was not itself corrupting. By aiming at victory, at persuading an audience, were we not sacrificing rationality and its orientation to truth? Here I think is the great advantage of Aristotle's association of rationality with living in political communities. "Speech is for making clear what is beneficial or harmful, and hence also what is just or unjust." The just does not exist and cannot be known apart from the useful and the harmful. Justice is not a set of concerns different in kind from the useful, and the true is not set off in a realm distinct from the strategic. Aristotle differs from Plato in thinking that we can aim at effectiveness and at rightness together. Practical reason can be corrupted by aiming at effectiveness alone, but it can equally be corrupted by aiming only at justice and ignoring consequences. The sophists interpreted the autonomy of practical reason as meaning that the verdict of pervasive excellence belongs with the audience. Rational rhetoric takes it to mean that deliberation and persuasion have their own internal standards of excellence.

The autonomy of practical reason faced a different kind of problem in the third and fourth chapters. Practical reasoning is ampliative. It affirms conclusions that are stronger than the premises that led to them, and affirms them with greater security than it holds the evidence that leads to them. This creative side of practical reasoning is potentially irresponsible. Only the *ethos* of the community and the judgments of the audience keep it in check. Speakers, and thinkers, need the judgment of the audience to keep their autonomy from becoming license.

In the next pair of chapters, the autonomy of practical reason took the form of authority and trust, two further translations of *pistis*. In looking at authority, I did not ask the more usual question of how authority can cause or justify obedience, but wondered how authority can be created, transmitted, and destroyed. My examination of trust then asked not for the conditions under which someone should trust someone else, but why someone would want to be trusted. In both cases, people exercise practical reason not solely for its results but in order to be part of a certain kind of community, showing us a new dimension of the autonomy of practical reason.

Finally, the contemporary fact of pluralism creates new opportunities and dangers for the autonomy of practical reason. The existence of competing arguments and incommensurable values reminds us that rhetorical arguments lack the kind of necessity that purely logical arguments sometimes have. The lack of conclusiveness seems to open up the possibilities of arbitrariness, of determination by something other than argument, and so leads back to my earlier questions about whether there was really any difference between reasoning and rationalizing. We can only make such a distinction to the extent that we engage in practical reasoning for its own sake and not solely for the results it may bring. If we model practical reasoning on science and theoretical reasoning, conflict is a sign of failure. If practical reasoning is autonomous, then rationality can lead to conflict as easily and as rationally as to consensus.

This brief summary of the dimensions of the autonomy of practical reason lets me end by saying something very brief about the practical contribution of this study. I have not tried to offer a conclusive demonstration of why anyone should be rational. I haven't tried to uncover a universal obligation to engage in practical reason, rather than the perennially tempting alternatives of rationalizing and manipulating others or appealing to impersonal standards of theoretical reason. There is no such universal obligation. From the inside, acting rationally and speaking rationally to others are attractive. From the outside, they seem inefficient, impractical, and sometimes even unintelligible.

The examples I have explored are not models to be imitated. The achievements of the TRC, of Lincoln, of Earl Warren in the *Brown* decision, are irreversible within their respective local political histories. It is impossible, for example, to think about race, or equality, or the role of different parts of government, or the relation between society and state, in the United States without arguing over *Brown*. Each of them, though, resists generalization, and instead becomes a permanently contested example for the future. It is wrong to take the example of *Brown* and generalize by talking about the Supreme Court as *the* "forum of principle," or "The Supreme Court as Exemplar of Public Reason."[37] It is rarely even *a* forum of principle. (Similarly, my pragmatic use of science as a model for democracy is not cheerleading for science as a solution to all our practical problems.) These examples, instead, are aids to reflection on the crucial question of the conditions under which practical rationality can sustain itself, can flourish and not be driven out by what I called the default possibilities of reasoning without character and character without reason. The ampliative and friendly nature of these examples prevents generalization into rules. Instead I have shown how the internal point of view from which practical reason is intelligible and desirable is in fact a point of view available to all. It is not available, let alone desirable, to all, in all circumstances.

But we all should be able to reason from the place of rational persuasion in the Truth and Reconciliation Commission or Lincoln's Second Inaugural or the *Brown* decision to the place of rational persuasion in our own lives and communities. The conditions under which practical rationality in general can flourish are the conditions in which rational discourse about the ends of action is understood as a part of practical reasoning. Practical reason flourishes when a community recognizes that impractical-looking forms of discourse such as philosophy, epideictic rhetoric, and the celebration of common symbols are indeed practical. Instead of complaining about the demagogic exploitation of symbolic resources, we should learn to make connections, as speakers and as citizens listening to political rhetoric, between the symbolic and the more directly practical. Then we will be able to keep the instrumental rationality and the tolerant reasonableness that together rightly dominate our practical lives from becoming routinized and irrational.

NOTES

INTRODUCTION

1. The possible bibliography here is overwhelming. Seminal is Max Horkheimer and Theodor W. Adorno, *Dialectic of Enlightenment* (New York: Herder and Herder, 1972) and Jürgen Habermas, "Technology and Science as 'Ideology,'" *Toward a Rational Society* (Boston: Beacon Press, 1970).

2. Anthony Kronman, "Rhetoric," *University of Cincinnati Law Review* 67 (1999): 693.

3. The details of my reading of the *Rhetoric* itself are available in *Aristotle's Rhetoric: An Art of Character* (Chicago: University of Chicago Press, 1994).

4. Richard Rorty, "Science as Solidarity," reprinted in *Objectivity, Relativism and Truth: Philosophical Papers*, vol. 1 (Cambridge: Cambridge University Press, 1991), 35–45. The quotations are from pages 36 and 37. See too Stephen Toulmin, *Return to Reason* (Cambridge, Mass.: Harvard University Press, 2001), 94: "From the Judgment of Solomon on, literature and scripture have preserved stories showing how hard it is to treat situations 'rationally' (without distortion) and also 'reasonably' (without injustice)." For an early contribution of Habermas to the same issue, see "Technology and Science as 'Ideology,'" in *Toward a Rational Society: Student Protest, Science and Politics*, trans. Jeremy Shapiro (Boston: Beacon Press, 1970).

5. John Henry Newman, *An Essay in Aid of a Grammar of Assent* (Garden City, N.Y.: Doubleday, 1955), 240. First italics added.

6. David Hume, *Treatise of Human Nature*, ed. L. A. Selby-Bigge (London: Oxford University Press, 1888), Book III, Pt. II, Section 2. John Rawls, *A Theory of Justice* (Cambridge, Mass.: Harvard University Press, 1971), 126–30. See too "the circumstances of politics" in Jeremy Waldron, "Deliberation, Disagreement, and Voting," in *Deliberative Democracy and Human Rights*, ed. Harold Hongju Koh and Ronald C. Slye (New Haven: Yale University Press, 1999), 210–26, as well as his "The Circumstances of Integrity," *Legal Theory* 3 (1997): 1–22.

7. Charles Taylor, "Social Theory as Practice," in *Philosophy and the Human Sciences: Philosophical Papers*, vol. 2 (Cambridge: Cambridge University Press, 1985), 91–115, at 104.

CHAPTER ONE

1. *The English Works of Thomas Hobbes*, ed. Sir William Molesworth (London, 1839–45), 5:193. See also page 194: "Because neither mine nor the Bishop's reason is right reason fit to be a rule of our moral actions, we have therefore set up over ourselves a sovereign governor, and agreed that his laws shall be unto us, whatsoever they be, in the place of right reason, to dictate to us what is really good." Both quoted in David Gauthier, "Constituting Democracy," in *The Idea of Democracy*, ed. David Copp, Jean Hampton, and John Roemer (Cambridge: Cambridge University Press, 1993), 326.

2. John Rawls, *Political Liberalism* (New York: Columbia University Press, 1993), 50. See too Rawls, "Justice as Fairness: Political Not Metaphysical," *Philosophy and Public Affairs* 14 (1985): 223–51, at 230: "The aim of justice as fairness as a political conception is practical, and not metaphysical or epistemological. That is, it presents itself not as a conception of justice that is true, but one that can serve as a basis of informed and willing political agreement between citizens viewed as free and equal persons."

3. Richard Rorty, "The Ambiguity of 'Rationality,'" *Constellations* 3 (1996): 74–82. I will explore the unpragmatic nature of Rorty's arguments in more detail in the final chapter. Here it is enough to note that "blurring" the distinction imposes a monism of value. The TRC was more reflective, as well as more pragmatic, by constantly facing the question of whether the truth makes us free.

4. Richard Rorty, "Religion as Conversation-Stopper," *Common Knowledge* 3 (1994): 5. Also Bruce Ackerman, "Why Dialogue," *Journal of Philosophy* 86 (1989): 5–22, at 10: "It is precisely because the liberal state does not aim for moral truth that its citizens must recognize themselves under such peremptory dialogic obligations." And Seyla Benhabib, "Liberal Dialogue vs. A Critical Theory of Discursive Legitimation," in *Liberalism and the Moral Life*, ed. Nancy Rosenblum (Cambridge, Mass.: Harvard University Press, 1989), 146–47: "If 'peace' is not the supreme moral good, then there is no reason to engage in such a public conversation [according to liberal standards of fairness and neutrality]; one's vision of the good may in effect dictate that the disruption of seeming tranquility and civility of this order is the supreme good."

It is important therefore to contrast my analysis with that of Mark J. Osiel, for whom it is liberals who aim at truth, as opposed to "communitarians" who don't care whether their myths are true or not. See Osiel, *Mass Atrocity, Collective Memory, and the Law* (New Brunswick, N.J.: Transaction, 1987), 178–79: "Those seeking to construct a liberal mythology for their society necessarily labor under a special burden: *their* myth must be truthful, not merely pleasant. . . . Truthful stories about the origins of most nation-states cannot be entirely flattering, and so are unlikely to be solidarity-enhancing. . . . Simply ignoring discomforting truths about our past will not be useful to liberalism, even if usefulness is to be our guiding star. A national story that left out key facts concerning the enormous harm that the nation had done to others would not encourage the kind of moral self-scrutiny (in light of liberal principles of respect for persons) that is most needed, especially in the aftermath of administrative massacre." Politically, there is no reason to expect people to be consistent. Those for whom triumphalist and emotionally satisfying myths about American history are preferable to more ethically complex truth are often insistent on truth rather than agreement on current moral issues.

5. Jeffrey Stout, *Ethics after Babel: The Languages of Morals and Their Discontents* (Boston: Beacon Press, 1988), 212: "What made the creation of liberal institutions necessary, in large part, was the manifest failure of religious groups of various sorts to establish rational agreement on their competing detailed visions of the good. It was partly because people recognized putting an end to religious warfare and intolerance as morally good—as rationally preferable to continued attempts at imposing a more nearly complete vision of the good by force—that liberal institutions have been able to get a foothold here and there around the globe.

"In other words, certain features of our society can be seen as justified by a self-limiting consensus on the good—an agreement consisting partly in the realization that it would be a bad thing, that it would make life worse for us all, to press too hard or too far for agreement on all details in a given vision of the good."

6. Cass R. Sunstein, "Incompletely Theorized Agreements," *Harvard Law Review* 108 (1975): 1733–72, at 1733, 1735, 1736 n. 8.

7. For one observation of the difference in practical reason that aims at agreement and that which aims at truth, David Strauss argues that formalistic legal reasoning has its place when agreement is the goal: "Issues of equality and reproductive freedom . . . elicit strong reactions. In these contexts, people are less likely to accept a solution just for the sake of having the matter resolved with minimal friction. They are willing to live with controversy as the price of trying to resolve the issue in the way they think is right. They are therefore much more likely to force the issue by directly addressing the moral rights and wrongs. But in dealing with separation of powers issues it is more important that the issue be settled than that it be settled just right—so that we know which acts are valid, which political actor must make which decision, and so on. Consequently our practices are more formalistic. That is what conventionalism predicts, and that is our practice. The more important the provision, the less formalistic its interpretation." David A. Strauss, "Common Law Constitutional Interpretation," *University of Chicago Law Review* 63 (1996): 918.

8. Martin Luther King Jr., "Letter from Birmingham Jail," in *Why We Can't Wait* (New York: Harper and Row, 1964), 87. David Luban usefully makes the contrast between aiming at agreement and at truth this way: "Our language itself registers the ambivalence we feel between the need for peace and the claims of justice: disputants compromise; ideals are compromised." David Luban, "Some Greek Trials: Order and Justice in Homer, Hesiod, Aeschylus and Plato," *Tennessee Law Review* 54 (1987): 279–325, reprinted in David Luban, *Legal Modernism* (Ann Arbor: University of Michigan Press, 1994), 283–334.

9. "In places like Yugoslavia where the parties have murdered and tortured each other for years, the prospects for truth, reconciliation and justice are much bleaker [than in South Africa]. These contexts, however bleak, are instructive because they illustrate everything that is problematic in the relation between truth and reconciliation. The idea that reconciliation depends on shared truth presumes that shared truth about the past is possible. But truth is related to identity. What to believe to be true depends on some measure, on who you believe yourself to be. And who you believe yourself to be is mostly defined in terms of who you are not." Michael Ignatieff, "Articles of Faith," *Index on Censorship* 5 (1996): 113–14. For comparisons among the truth commissions and transitional arrangements around the world, see Neil J. Kritz, ed., *Transitional Justice: How Emerging Democracies Reckon With Former Regimes* (Washington, D.C.: United States Institute of Peace Press, 1995), and A. James McAdams, ed., *Transitional Justice and the Rule of Law in Democracies* (Notre Dame, Ind.: University of Notre Dame Press, 1997).

10. I will return to this point in more detail in chapter 5, but that inequality was part of the American *ethos* can be seen from Harlan's famous dissent in *Plessy v. Ferguson*, which contained the often-quoted statement that the law is color-blind.

11. Truth and Reconciliation Commission, *Truth and Reconciliation Commission Report* (Cape Town: The Commission, 1999; distributed New York: Macmillan Reference and Grove's Dictionaries), 1:6. Compare Kenneth Roth's account of Haiti: "Haiti illustrates the dangers of ignoring accountability for past violent abuse in the haste to secure a 'transition to democracy.' Each time a supposedly reformist regime took power, Haitians were asked to forget the past, to look forward to a new era. Sooner or later, this impunity emboldened reactionary forces to resume the killing." Kenneth Roth, "Human Rights in the Haitian Transition to Democracy," in *Human Rights in Political Transitions: Gettysburg to Bosnia,* ed. Carla Hesse and Robert Post (New York: Zone Books, 1999), 126.

12. "The victims, as witnesses, appeal not only to the judges but implicitly to the community at large. Each victim, finally rescued from oblivion, seeks recognition of the essential humanity that was denied him. For this reason, the trial, as an event in the life of the entire community, not only furthers legal justice but also, at the same time, helps to reconstruct the nation's ethical foundations." Huge Vezzetti, "El Juicio: Un Ritual de la Memoria Colectiva," *Punto de vista* 3, no. 5 (1985): 7, cited and translated in Mark J. Osiel, *Mass Atrocity, Collective Memory, and the Law,* 30.

13. Locke defines this sort of civility as "that general goodwill and regard for all people, which makes anyone have a care not to show . . . contempt, . . . but to express a respect and value for them according to their rank and condition. It is a disposition of the mind that shows itself in the carriage, whereby a man avoids making anyone uneasy in conversation." John Locke, "Some Thoughts on Education," in *John Locke on Education,* ed. Peter Gay (New York: Teachers' College, Columbia University, 1964), 104.

14. Quoted in Anthea Jeffrey, *The Truth About the Truth Commission* (Johannesburg: South African Institute of Race Relations, 1999), 10. See too Michael Ignatieff, "Articles of Faith," *Index on Censorship* 5 (1996): 113: Truth Commissions "cannot bring [society's arguments with itself] to conclusion. Critics of truth commissions argue as if the past were a sacred text which had been stolen and vandalized by evil men and which can be recovered to a well-lit glass case in some grand public rotunda like the U.S. Constitution or the Bill of Rights. But the past has none of the fixed and stable identity of a document. The past is an argument and the function of truth commissions is simply to purify the argument, to narrow the range of permissible lies." I agree with Margalit that using terms such as "healing truth" and "narrative truth" "made truth, real truth, look like a very soft notion" and that there are better ways of making the point that, in his words, "there is more to the apartheid experience than just telling the facts." Avishai Margalit, *The Ethics of Memory* (Cambridge, Mass.: Harvard University Press, 2002), 170. For a range of possibilities for thinking about truth, from the "disquotational theory" in which to call a proposition true is to say that what it says is the case, all the way up to truth as a transcendental, coextensive with being and the good, see Lenn Goodman, *In Defense of Truth: A Pluralistic Approach* (Amherst, N.Y.: Humanity Books, 2001).

15. Antjie Krog, *Country of My Skull: Guilt, Sorrow, and the Limits of Forgiveness in the New South Africa* (Parktown, S.A., 1998; New York: Times Books, 1999), 68. Page citations from the South African edition.

16. Ibid., 328.

17. Ibid., 22–23.

18. There are also evident dangers to treating such fantasies as true. The "recovered memory" movement in the United States in the 1990s, in which many people came to believed that they had been abused as children, shows some of the ethical dangers of treating strongly held beliefs as true.

19. Ariel Dorfman, *Death and the Maiden* (New York: Penguin, 1991), 24.

20. See also Carlo Ginzburg, *History, Rhetoric, and Proof* (Hanover: University Press of New England, 1999): "The most elementary communication presupposes a shared, obvious, and thus unstated knowledge. . . . The tacit knowledge evoked by Aristotle is tied to one's belonging to Hellas; the 'everyone' is 'all the Greeks,' and, in fact, Persians are excluded from that knowledge. We know that Greek civilization established itself by standing up to the Persians, and, more generally, against the barbarians. But Aristotle also tells us something else, that the discourses analyzed by rhetoric—those spoken in the public squares and in courtrooms—refer to a specific community, not to men as rational animals. Rhetoric moves in the realm of the probable, not in that of scientific truth, and in a circumscribed perspective, far removed from innocent ethnocentrism" (22). And: "In saying that in the enthymeme a well-known premise does not need to be mentioned, Aristotle places himself, as we would say today, in an anthropological, not a logical perspective—or more precisely, in the perspective of rhetoric, which always refers to a concrete, and therefore circumscribed community. Admittedly, although the unspoken premise of his enthymeme, the fact 'that the prize at the Olympic games is a crown,' does not need to be mentioned 'for everybody knows it,' (*gignōskousi gar pantes*), here 'everybody' actually means every Greek, not every rational being" (41–42).

21. The first of many was E. D. Hirsch, *Cultural Literacy: What Every American Needs to Know* (Boston: Houghton Mifflin, 1987). See also Donald Davidson, *Inquiries into Truth and Interpretation* (Oxford: Clarendon Press, 1984). I appeal to Hirsch's proposals precisely because they seem to me to parallel Davidson's denial of incommensurability, which bases our mutual understanding on the most banal sort of shared knowledge.

22. Richard Rorty, "The Priority of Democracy to Philosophy," in *The Virginia Statute of Religious Freedom*, ed. Merrill Peterson and Robert Vaughan (Cambridge: Cambridge University Press, 1988), reprinted in *Reading Rorty*, ed. Alan R. Machalowski (Oxford: Blackwell, 1989), 293: "Moral commitment, after all, does not require taking seriously all the matters which are, for moral reasons, taken seriously by one's fellow citizens. It may require just the opposite. It may require to josh them out of the habit of taking topics so seriously. There may be serious reasons for so joshing them. More generally, we should not assume the aesthetic is always the enemy of the moral. I should argue that in the recent history of liberal societies, the willingness to view matters aesthetically . . . to be content to indulge in what Schiller called 'play' and to discard what Nietzsche called 'the spirit of seriousness' has been an important vehicle of moral progress."

23. Alasdair MacIntyre, "Epistemological Crises, Dramatic Narrative and the Philosophy of Science," *Monist* 60 (1977): 453–72. Richard Rorty, *Philosophy and the Mirror of Nature* (Princeton, N.J.: Princeton University Press, 1979), 320: "Normal discourse is that which is conducted within an agreed-upon set of conventions about what counts as a relevant contribution, what counts as answering a question, what counts as having a good argument for that answer or a good criticism of it. Abnormal discourse is what

happens when someone joins in the discourse who is ignorant of these conventions or who sets them aside."

24. Ernest Gellner, *Plough, Sword, and Book: The Structure of Human History* (Chicago: University of Chicago Press, 1988), 194: "*Fundamental changes transform identities.* Yet without a single persisting and somehow authoritative identity, there is no one available to give his full consent to a radical transformation. No one is available to confer the democratic sacrament, blessing and vindication on it. . . . When applied to the making or validating of fundamental and radical choices, the idea of consent quite literally has no meaning. Critics of actual democratic systems like to say that they only work where their basic organizational assumptions are not challenged. The charge can be strengthened: it is only then that the idea of democracy has any meaning. When truly radical options are faced, there simply is no one available to give that overall consent. You cannot consent to a change of identity. There is no 'you.' The very notion of a change of identity precludes it. The pre-metamorphosis self is no longer, and the post-metamorphosis self is not yet."

25. Charles Taylor, "Social Theory as Practice," in *Philosophy and the Human Sciences: Philosophical Papers,* vol. 2 (Cambridge: Cambridge University Press, 1985), 91–115, at 104. See too Bernard Williams, *Ethics and the Limits of Philosophy* (Cambridge, Mass.: Harvard University Press, 1985), 101: Rationalism "is the aspiration that society should be transparent, in the sense that the working of its ethical institutions should not depend on members of the community misunderstanding how they work." Williams usefully qualifies this at p. 102. "It is one aspiration, that social and ethical relations should not essentially rest on ignorance and misunderstanding of what they are, and quite another that all the beliefs and principles involved in them should be explicitly stated. That these are two different things is obvious with personal relations, where to hope that they do not rest on deceit and error is merely decent, but to think that their basis can be made totally explicit is idiocy." For the connection between transparency and my distinction between aiming at truth and at agreement, see David Estlund, "Making Truth Safe for Democracy," in *The Idea of Democracy,* ed. David Copp, Jean Hampton, and John Roemer (Cambridge: Cambridge University Press, 1993), 78: "Why not call the principles that are derived from the overlapping consensus 'true'? The reason seems to be that there is no collective comprehensive conception of which they are a part. Since something is true only as a part of a comprehensive conception, there is no collective standpoint from which the principles could be held to be true. They are accepted by *each* individual as true (or reasonably close), but this cannot be the basis on which they are accepted by *all,* since not all believe them for the same reasons."

26. Kader Asmal et al., *Reconciliation Through Truth: A Reckoning of Apartheid Criminal Governance* (Cape Town: Philips, 1996), 9–10.

27. "Too often . . . political programs of self-restraint have the force of denying voice to the oppressed. When there is a situation of unequal political power, especially, the demand for civility may seem just another strategy of ideological continuance. As long as we can force subordinate groups to adopt the nostrums of 'proper behavior,' perhaps even making them complicit in adopting perversities like 'good girl' or 'good nigger' roles, the perpetuation of our system of dominance is assured. Armed with a theory of

justice turning on propriety, we can always . . . indulge the luxury of labeling threatening political behavior 'uppity.' . . . The arguments for restraint act both to maintain the status quo and to disguise the fact that the status quo is oppressive." Mark Kingwell, *A Civil Tongue: Justice, Dialogue and the Politics of Pluralism* (University Park: Pennsylvania State University Press, 1995), 231–32. See also John Stuart Mill, *On Liberty,* in the *Collected Works of John Stuart Mill,* vol. 18: *Essays on Politics and Society,* ed. J. M. Robinson (Toronto and Buffalo: University of Toronto Press, 258: "It is fit to take some notice of those who say, that the free expression of all opinions should be permitted, on condition that the manner be temperate, and do not pass the bounds of fair discussion. Much might be said on the impossibility of fixing where these supposed bounds are to be placed; for if the test be offence to those whose opinion is attacked, I think experience testifies that this offence is given whenever the attack is telling and powerful, and that every opponent who pushes them hard, and whom they find it difficult to answer, appears to them, if he shows any strong feeling on the subject, an intemperate opponent. But this though an important consideration in a practical point of view, merges in a more fundamental objection. Undoubtedly the manner of asserting an opinion, even though it may be a true one, may be very objectionable, and may justly incur severe censure. But the principal offences of the kind are such as it is mostly impossible, unless by accidental self-betrayal, to bring home to conviction. The gravest of them, is to argue sophistically, to suppress facts or arguments, to misstate the elements of the case, or misrepresent the opposite opinion. But all this, even to the most aggravated degree, is so continually done in perfect good faith, by persons who are not considered, and in many other respects do not deserve to be considered, ignorant or incompetent, that it is rarely possible on adequate grounds conscientiously to stamp the misrepresentation as morally culpable; and still less could law presume to interfere with this kind of controversial misconduct."

28. Strauss, "Common Law Constitutional Interpretation," 924: "When a nation does not have well established traditions, the words of its constitution are correspondingly more important in providing something on which people can agree. When a nation is just starting, it is important for political actors to be able to point to the text of the constitution to justify their actions. Creative interpretations of that text will breed distrust and make it more likely that whatever consensus exists will dissipate. Once people think that their political opponents are playing fast and loose with the text, all consensus is more likely to break down because there is so little to fall back on. Only by staying very close to the text—being as formalistic as possible—can political actors in an immature regime convince others that they are acting in good faith. By contrast, once a society develops political traditions, political actors can be more confident that their opponents, even if arguably departing from the text, will operate within the traditions, or will be reined in by other forces in society if they do not do so."

29. Richard Rorty, "Religion as Conversation-Stopper," 4: "Moral decisions that are to be enforced by a pluralistic and democratic state's monopoly in violence are best made by public discussion in which voices claiming to be God's, or reason's, or science's, are put on a par with everybody else's." Kent Greenawalt, *Private Consciences and Public Reasons* (New York and Oxford: Oxford University Press, 1995), 157: "At least for many

religious arguments, the speaker seems to put himself or herself in a kind of privileged position, as the holder of a *basic* truth that many others lack. This assertion of privileged knowledge may appear to imply inequality of status that is in serious tension with the fundamental idea of equality of citizens within liberal democracies." See also Stephen Holmes, "Gag-Rules or the Politics of Omission," *Passions and Constraint: On the Theory of Liberal Democracy* (Chicago: University of Chicago Press, 1995).

30. Jonathan Shay, *Achilles in Vietnam: Combat Trauma and the Undoing of Character* (New York: Atheneum, 1994), 180–81. Shay's comment that "the customary meanings of words are exchanged for new ones" is reminiscent of Thucydides' observation that in the madness of war "words lose their meaning." See further James B. White, *When Words Lose Their Meaning* (Chicago: University of Chicago Press, 1984). See also Lee C. Bollinger, *The Tolerant Society: Freedom of Speech and Extremist Speech in America* (Oxford and New York: Oxford University Press, 1986), 117: "A willingness to compromise and even to accept total defeat are essential components of the democratic personality. Democracy, like literature . . . requires a kind of suspension of disbelief. At the norm-setting level, as well as at the enforcement level, a capacity to inform one's beliefs in the interest of maintaining a continuing community is critical. The problem of deciding on the nature of the commitment to one's belief is one of exquisite complexity."

I must note that Shay's purpose and manner of learning from the ancients is quite different from mine. He holds that unless maimed, people will develop the crucial capacities of love and trust, *ethos, philia,* and *thumos,* and consequently learned from Homer and the tragedians why and how to avoid destroying the otherwise normal development of human character. I believe, on the contrary, that the full development of good human character depends on the very specialized context that Aristotle outlines, without which all of us are maimed, not in the terrifying way Shay describes, but in ways that prevent us fully from engaging in friendship and trust and the reciprocal political relations that are central to Aristotle's good life.

31. Lenn Goodman, *God of Abraham* (New York and Oxford: Oxford University Press, 1996), 101. For another Jewish example, we are told that God preferred Hillel's interpretations to Shammai's because his "teaching was more 'kingly and humble,' and because Hillel's school taught the other school's interpretation. Tolerance of other views, as a self-corrective ideal, created greater access to truth." Theodore Y. Blumoff, "The New Religionists' Newest Social Gospel: On the Rhetoric and Reality of Religions' 'Marginalization' in Public Life," *University of Miami Law Review* 51 (1996): 1–56, at 30.

32. James Bohman, "Deliberative Democracy and Effective Social Freedom: Capabilities, Resources, and Opportunities," in *Deliberative Democracy: Essays on Reason and Politics,* ed. James Bohman and William Rehg (Cambridge, Mass.: MIT Press, 1997), p. 332: "Deliberative democracy should not reward those groups who simply are better situated to get what they want by public and discursive means; its standard of political equality cannot endorse any kind of cognitive elitism." See also Ernest Gellner, *Words and Things,* repr. in Beryl Lang, *Philosophy and the Art of Writing: Studies in Philosophy and Literary Style* (Lewisburg, Penn.: Bucknell University Press, 1983), 441: "To *justify* is to put in doubt, to make dependent a basic position on cleverness—that is, plainly, ungentlemanly. Goethe, a not unsympathetic expert on snobbery as on so many other

matters, remarked somewhere that the nobility lies in being, not knowing or doing. ('Never explain!') Philosophy has always been the ignoble attempt to root or justify or confirm *being* in *knowing*."

33. William Brennan, "Reason, Passion, and 'The Progress of the Law,'" *Cardozo Law Review* 10 (1988): 17. Similarly, just as *ethos,* logos, and pathos can all be used to advance progressive or retrograde causes, there is nothing inherently superior about narrative rather than argument. For this see chapter 5.

34. Philip Selznick, "The Idea of Communitarian Morality," *California Law Review* 75 (1987): 460–61: "From the standpoint of critical morality . . . parochial experience may not be taken as final or treated as an unqualified end in itself. There must be a corollary commitment to press the particular into the service of the general, that is, to draw from one's special history a universal message. To do so is, inevitably, to create a basis for criticizing one's own heritage, not only from within but also from the standpoint of others' experiences and more comprehensive interests." I think there are other ways of moving from experience to rational *ethos* than as a "universal message," but apart from that Selznick's formulation captures Aristotle's idea of *ethos* as a function of argument. I have explored problems of how to listen in "Rhetoric, Religious Argument and Democratic Deliberation: Why Should Anyone Listen?" *Wake Forest University Law Review* (2001), and "How Can a Liberal Listen to a Religious Argument?" *Talking About Religion in the Disciplines,* ed. J. B. White (Notre Dame, Ind.: University of Notre Dame Press, forthcoming).

35. "Acts, like public acknowledgments, having this kind of symbolic sacramental value can become indelibly etched in the moral slate of the society and have a long-term effect. That is why, for example, it was so important that the Chilean Truth Commission's report be presented in a sacramental manner, so that it entered into the annals of the nation and onto that slate of values." José Zalaquett in Naomi Roht-Arriaza, "The Need for Moral Reconstruction in the Wake of Past Human Rights Violations: An Interview with José Zalaquett," in *Human Rights in Political Transitions: Gettysburg to Bosnia,* ed. Carla Hesse and Robert Post (New York: Zone Books, 1999), 209. The TRC, like the example of *Brown* to follow, rebuts Arendt's claim that "the purpose of a trial is to render justice, and nothing else; even the noblest of ulterior purposes . . . can only detract from the law's main business: to weigh the charges brought against the accused, to render judgment, and to mete out due punishment." Hannah Arendt, *Eichmann in Jerusalem* (New York: Viking Press, 1963), 204.

36. That *homonoia* is a shared activity rather than a common creed or set of values is argued by Bernard Crick, *In Defense of Politics* (Chicago: University of Chicago Press, 1972), 24: "It is often thought that for [politics] to function, there must already be in existence some shared idea of a 'common good,' some 'consensus' or *consensus juris.* But this common good is itself the process of practical reconciliation of the interests of the various . . . groups which compose a state; it is not some external and intangible spiritual adhesive. . . . Diverse groups hold together because they practice politics—not because they agree about 'fundamentals,' or some such concept too vague, too personal, or too divine ever to do the job of politics for it. The moral consensus of a free state is not something mysteriously prior to or above politics; it is the activity (the civilizing

activity) of politics itself." See also Cass R. Sunstein, *The Partial Constitution* (Cambridge, Mass.: Harvard University Press, 1993), 23–24: "The framer's belief in deliberative democracy drew from traditional republican thought, and . . . departed from the tradition in the insistence that a large republic would be better than a smaller one. It departed even more dramatically in its striking and novel rejection of the traditional republican idea that heterogeneity and difference were destructive to the deliberative process. For the framers, heterogeneity was beneficial, indeed indispensable; discussion must take place among people who were different. It was on this score that the framers responded to the antifederalist insistence that homogeneity was necessary to a republic."

37. "While having much to say about character and authority, Cicero ignores the Aristotelian notion of a 'rational ethos' or 'ethos of trustworthiness' and, in its place, emphasizes *conciliare* or an ethos of sympathy. Rather than serve as a projection of truthfulness and trustworthiness, Ciceronian *ethos* resembles a milder form of pathos." James S. Baumlin, "*Ethos,*" in *Encyclopedia of Rhetoric,* ed. Thomas O. Sloane (Oxford: Oxford University Press, 2001), 269.

38. The elevation of sympathy is often another instance of the deep reflex that makes reason and emotion the only alternatives. See, for example, Richard Rorty, "Human Rights, Rationality, and Sentimentality," *Truth and Progress* (Cambridge: Cambridge University Press, 1998), 167–86, esp. 170, 176. Rorty writes (180): "Foundationalists think of these people [e.g., people who want to kill Salman Rushdie or otherwise show contempt for human rights] as deprived of truth, of moral knowledge. But it would be better—more concrete, more specific, more suggestive of possible remedies—to think of them as deprived of two more concrete things: security and sympathy. By 'security' I mean conditions of life sufficiently risk-free as to make one's difference from others inessential to one's self-respect, one's sense of worth. . . . Security and sympathy go together, for the same reasons that peace and economic productivity go together. The tougher things are, the more you have to be afraid of, the more dangerous your situation, the less you can afford the time or effort to think about what things might be like for people with whom you do not immediately identify. Sentimental education works only on people who can relax long enough to listen." I think there's quite a bit more to be said about the connection between security and sympathy, and will return to this question in the final chapter.

39. "People constitute a community, a *we,* by virtue of thinking of each other as *one of us,* and by willing the common good *not under the species of benevolence*—but by willing it as one of us, or from a moral point of view." Richard Rorty, quoting Wilfred Sellars in *Contingency, Irony, and Solidarity* (Cambridge: Cambridge University Press, 1989), 190.

40. Stephen Holmes, "Constitutionalism, Democracy, and State Decay," in *Deliberative Democracy and Human Rights,* ed. Harold Hongju Koh and Ronald C. Slye (New Haven: Yale University Press, 1999), 129–130: "A minimal constitution . . . lays down a publicly known set of rules to settle conflicts without violence. To be realistic, this formula refers exclusively to conflicts between *important* social actors. Members of society with nothing to offer and no ability to threaten—those who, for whatever reason, lack the organizational capacity effectively to pursue their interests—are excluded from the minimal constitutional pact. According to this model, democratization is the process of

inclusion whereby out-groups gradually become in-groups, dealing themselves into the constitutional bargain, extracting concessions (rights) in exchange for their useful cooperation. As the process of democratization advances . . . certain members of the inner circle try to enhance their relative bargaining position by using the democratic formula of elections. To gain votes, in turn, they grant concessions not just to powerful lobbies, but to broad swaths of the electorate. In this way the citizenry at large gains not a fair share but at least a small share of the public resources extracted (from them) by the state." See also Milner S. Ball, "Reparations and Repentance," *George Washington Law Review* 68 (2000): 1017–18: "When I respond to victims because I feel their pain, I, not they, become the point. I colonize their suffering. I consume it to feed my need for self-exhibition. And when I come to think that they are undeserving of me and my charity—that they do not satisfy my criteria for what a victim should be—then their condition begins to look to me like their own doing. They are at fault. They become blameworthy in my eyes, and I turn on them. That is what they deserve. I continue to feel good about myself and angry at the victims who were unresponsive to my efforts to help."

41. Condorcet, *Réflections*, in *Oeuvres de Condorcet*, ed., A. Condorcet O'Connor and M. F. Arago (Paris: Firmin Didot, 1847–49, 3:243–44. Quoted in Emma Rothschild, *Economic Sentiments: Adam Smith, Condorcet, and the Enlightenment* (Cambridge, Mass.: Harvard University Press, 2001).

42. Wendy Brown, *States of Injury, Power and Freedom in Late Modernity* (Princeton, N.J.: Princeton University Press, 1995), 27.

43. See, for example, John D. Schaeffer, "Vico's Rhetorical Model of the Mind: *Sensus Communis* in the *de nostri temporis studiorum ratione*," *Philosophy and Rhetoric* 14 (1981): 152–67.

44. John Dewey, *The Public and Its Problems* (Chicago: Gateway Books, 1946; first published, Henry Holt, 1927), 77. See too Benjamin Barber, *Strong Democracy: Participatory Politics for a New Age* (Berkeley: University of California Press, 1984), 190: "The *I* of private self-interest can be reconceptualized and reconstituted as a *we* that makes possible civility and common political action."

45. My distinction between what each knows and what everybody knows is parallel to the distinction Margalit develops between "shared memory" and "common memory." Avishai Margalit, *The Ethics of Memory*, esp. 50–52. See also Hannah Arendt, "Truth in Politics," *Between Past and Future* (New York: Viking Press, 1961), 227–64, at 236: "The same public that know [some facts] can successfully, and often spontaneously, taboo their public discussion, and treat them as though they were what they are not—secrets." Also Lawrence Weschler, *A Miracle, A Universe: Settling Accounts with Torturers* (New York: Pantheon, 1990), 4: "Fragile, tentative democracies time and again hurl themselves toward an abyss, struggling over this issue of truth. It's a mysteriously powerful, almost magical notion, because often everyone already knows the truth—everyone knows who the torturers were and what they did, the torturers know that everyone knows, and everyone knows that they know. Why, then, the need to risk everything to render that knowledge explicit?

"The participants at the Aspen Institute conference worried this question around the table several times . . . until Thomas Nagel, a professor of philosophy and law at New

York University, almost stumbled upon an answer. 'It's the difference,' Nagel said halt-ingly, 'between knowledge and acknowledgement. It's what happens and can only hap-pen to knowledge when it becomes officially sanctioned, when it is made part of the public cognitive scene.' Yes, several of the panelists agreed. And that transformation, offered another participant, is sacramental."

46. Robert Meister, "Forgiving and Forgetting: Lincoln and the Politics of National Recovery," in *Human Rights in Political Transitions: Gettysburg to Bosnia,* ed. Carla Hesse and Robert Post (New York: Zone Books, 1999), 135–76, at 159. Meister's entire article parallels my concerns since he too ties Lincoln, the American civil rights movement, and the South African TRC together.

47. Lenn Goodman, *In Defense of Truth,* 313: "Respectable Germans rode the trains and subways of the Third Reich for years, passing right by the death camps without seeing or smelling the horror within. How much of what we see depends on what we or those around us are willing to see? And how much of what we speak depends on what is deemed acceptable to speak? How long was it before the Holocaust was widely spoken in the West? And how long will it be before it is widely denied? It may trouble us that it took a poet's pain, the nightmare writing of Elie Wiesel, to bring the Holocaust to daylight. But in America there was little but denial and the rosy image of a musical comedy war before Elie Wiesel wrote."

See my "Saying What Goes Without Saying: Bacon's *Essays* on Speech, Intelligence and Morality," in *Essays in Honor of Wayne Booth,* ed. Fred Antczak (Columbus: Ohio State University Press, 1994). For some of the obstacles that prevent what each knows from immediately becoming what everyone knows, see Eric A. Posner, *Law and Social Norms* (Cambridge, Mass.: Harvard University Press, 2000).

48. Statement by Wynand Malan to the TRC, May 16, 1997. Quoted in Meister, "For-giving and Forgetting," 157.

49. For an example of the costs of repressing and admitting truths about racial differ-ences in education, see Randall Kennedy, "Facing the Dilemmas of Difference: Com-ments on the Essay by Mamphela Ramphele," in *Promise and Dilemma: Perspectives on Racial Diversity and Higher Education,* ed. Eugene Y. Lowe Jr. (Princeton, N.J.: Princeton University Press, 1999), 162–68. Kent Greenawalt, "'Truth' or Consequences," *Theory and Practice: Nomos 37,* ed. Judith Wagner Decew and Ian Shapiro (New York: New York University Press, 1995), 386–400, raises the analogous question about the ethical dangers of supposing, for the sake of argument, that race is a reliable indicator of signifi-cant differences in intelligence. In law, this is often called the exclusionary theory. Law tells us that there are certain reasons which we must exclude from our deliberations. See Joseph Raz, *The Authority of Law: Essays on Law and Morality* (New York: Oxford University Press, 1979), and Frederick Schauer, *Playing By the Rules: A Philosophical Examination of Rule-Based Decision-Making in Law and in Life* (New York: Oxford Uni-versity Press, 1991). I will return to this idea of exclusionary reasons in chapter 5.

50. Krog, *Country of My Skull,* 125. For the analogy to American Congressional investi-gations, see Sanford Levinson, "Trials, Commissions, and Investigating Committees: The Elusive Search for Norm of Due Process," in *Truth v. Justice: The Morality of Truth Commissions,* ed. Robert I. Rotberg and Dennis Thompson (Princeton, N.J.: Princeton

University Press, 2000), 211–34. There are other grounds for the inadmissibility of truth in law. One of the most interesting for our purposes is privilege. I cannot be forced to offer true evidence, and in some cases may not offer it even if I want to, if I came to know something in a manner whose confidentiality prevents disclosure. See Stephen Holmes, "Gag-Rules or the Politics of Omission," *Passions and Constraint: On the Theory of Liberal Democracy* (Chicago: University of Chicago Press, 1995). See also Stephen Carter, *God's Name in Vain: The Wrongs and Rights of Religion in Politics* (New York: Basic Books, 2000), 61: "In a liberal democracy, we often deny ourselves access to useful information in order to preserve important values."

51. John Dewey, *The Quest for Certainty* (New York: Capricorn Books, 1929), 260. See also Hannah Fenichel Pitkin, "Justice: On Relating Public to Private," *Political Theory* 9 (1981): 261–88: "Drawn into public life by personal need, fear, ambition, and interest, we are there forced to acknowledge the power of others and appeal to their standards. We are forced to find or create a common language for purposes and aspirations, not merely to clothe our private outlook in public disguise, but to become aware ourselves of its public meaning. We are forced . . . to transform 'I want' into 'I am entitled to,' a claim that becomes negotiable by public standards. In the process we learn to think about the standards themselves, about our stake in the existence of standards, of justice, of our community, even of our opponents and enemies in the community; so that afterwards we are changed." See too Cass R. Sunstein, "Naked Preferences and the Constitution," *Columbia Law Review* 84 (1984): 1689–1732; "Legal Interference with Private Preferences," *University of Chicago Law Review* 53 (1986): 1129–74; "Preferences and Politics," *Philosophy and Public Affairs* 20 (1991): 3–34; and *Legal Reasoning and Political Conflict* (New York and Oxford: Oxford University Press, 1996). See, finally, Rousseau in the *Social Contract:* "This passage from the state of nature to the civil state produces quite a remarkable change in man, for it substitutes justice for instinct in his behavior and gives his actions a moral quality they previously lacked. Only then, when the voice of duty replaces physical impulse and right replaces appetite, does man, who had hitherto taken only himself into account, find himself forced to act upon other principles and to consult his reason before listening to his inclinations" (I. 8).

52. Arendt refers to some circumstances as "dark times," when "the public realm has been obscured and the world becomes so dubious that people have ceased to ask any more of politics than that it show due consideration for their vital interests and personal liberty. . . . Without a space of appearance and without trusting in action and speech as a mode of being together, neither the reality of one's self, of one's identity, nor the reality of the surrounding world can be established without doubt." Hannah Arendt, *Men in Dark Times* (New York: Harcourt, Brace and World, 1968), 11, and *The Human Condition* (Chicago: University of Chicago Press, 1958), 208. Alasdair MacIntyre regards emotivism as a true description of the contemporary moral world filled with incommensurable values and arbitrary decisions. In that world he thinks we are left with moral utterances reducible to the expression of feeling. Dewey is saying that the emotivist cannot live his emotivism. The issue becomes: which is true, the rational surface or the supposed underlying emotional reality. That will be the question for the next chapter.

53. Krog, *Country of My Skull*, 35. See too *Servicio Paz y Justicia, Uruguay Nunca Mas: Human Rights Violations, 1972–1985*, trans. Elizabeth Hampsten (1989), reprinted in "Nunca Mas Report on Human Rights Violations," in Kritz, *Transitional Justice*, 2: 420, and quoted in Mark J. Osiel, *Mass Atrocity, Collective Memory, and the Law*, 267, n. 77. "The facts do not only speak, they call out in the midst of an intolerable silence, that is being imposed on the immediate past. Silence has become a cornerstone—placed in the past by the dictatorship and in the present by those who believe that it can assure a peaceful future, but the facts, the victims, are there; they speak or call out to us. There is no future in pretending to be deaf to what they are saying."

CHAPTER TWO

1. Michel Foucault, "Space, Knowledge, and Power," in *The Foucault Reader*, ed. Paul Rabinow (New York: Pantheon, 1984), 249.

2. J. M. Balkin, "Ideological Drift and the Struggle Over Meaning," *Connecticut Law Review* 25 (1993): 869–91, at 878.

3. One could tell the story of the pre-1994 struggle as a confrontation between two incommensurable claims about who would replace Jews as the human characters in the biblical story of exodus and redemption. However, once the transition to the new South Africa began, those competing narratives seemed so diverse that there was indeed no common ground, and so these claims lost their political relevance.

4. For an example of someone who could not tell the difference between reasoning and rationalizing, consider this description. Julius "Caesar was insensitive to political institutions and the complex ways in which they operate. . . . Since his year as consul, if not before, Caesar had been unable to see Rome's institutions as autonomous entities. . . . He could see them only as instruments in the interplay of forces. His cold gaze passed through everything that Roman society still believed in, lived by, valued and defended. He had no feeling for the power of institutions to guarantee law and security, but only for what he found useful or troublesome about them. . . . Thus what struck him most about the Senate was the fact that it was controlled by his opponents. It hardly seems to have occurred to him that it was responsible for the commonwealth. . . . In Caesar's eyes no one existed but himself and his opponents. It was all an interpersonal game. He classified people as supporters, opponents or neutrals. The scene was cleared of any impersonal elements. Or, if any were left, they were merely props behind which one could take cover or with which one could fight. Politics amounted to no more than a fight for his rights." Christian Meier, *Caesar*, trans. David McLintock (New York: Basic Books, 1995), 358–59, quoted in Jeremy Waldron, "Arendt's Constitutional Politics," in *The Cambridge Companion to Hannah Arendt*, ed. Dana Villa (Cambridge: Cambridge University Press, 2000), 214–15.

For a sustained argument against drawing a line between reasoning and rationalizing, see Steven D. Smith, *The Constitution and the Pride of Reason* (New York and Oxford: Oxford University Press, 1998). See too Steven D. Smith, "Rationalizing the Constitution," *Colorado Law Review* 67 (1996): 597–621, at 600: "Suppose . . . that something offered as a reason is really a rationalization—so what? One plausible answer to this question might distinguish between the desirability or moral quality of the action and the wisdom or moral quality of the actor. Even if a rationalization can persuasively show that your action was for the best . . . you still do not deserve commendation if you acted for other, less admirable, motives."

Korsgaard explicates Kant's condemnation of deception this way: "Your reason is worked, like a machine: the deceiver tries to determine what levers to pull to get the desired results from you. . . . Lying treats someone's *reason* as a tool." Christine Korsgaard, "The Right to Lie: Kant on Dealing with Evil," *Philosophy and Public Affairs* 15 (1986): 334.

5. Aristotle himself has little to say about the sophists. He talks about them only in *Rhetoric* I.1, II.24, *Ethics* X.9, *Metaphysics* IV, and, most extensively, in the *Topics*. Especially telling is the absence of the sophists from the *Politics*. I am not going to worry here about the relation between Plato's representation of the sophists, and my representation of his representations, and any actual sophists, Greek or contemporary. Plato's *Sophist* is a meditation on the many-sided appearance of the sophist, and the impossibility of capturing the sophist in a definition. It should caution us against any definite statements about the sophists. On Plato's distinction between philosophy and sophistic, see Alexander Nehamas, "Eristic, Antilogic, Sophistic, Dialectic," *History of Philosophy Quarterly* 5 (1990): 3–16, and Thomas Cole, *The Origins of Rhetoric in Ancient Greece* (Baltimore: Johns Hopkins University Press, 1981). The surviving fragments by the sophists themselves are collected in H. Diels and W. Kranz, *Die Fragmente der Vorsokratiker*, 6th ed., 3 vols. (Berlin: Weidmann, 1951–54). Among the literature on the Greek sophists, I recommend Barbara Cassin, *Le plaisir de parler* (Paris: Gallimard, 1986), and *L'effet sophistique* (Paris: Gallimard: 1995). Cassin gives an accurate account of the evidence for what the sophists really said and thought, along with a deconstruction of any attempt to fix such a reality. Other recent scholarship has presented us with a much richer picture of the sophists than we could find in Plato and Aristotle. But the more serious and sophisticated the sophists look, the more striking is Aristotle's dismissal of them. What if Aristotle knew even more about the sophists than we do, and still chose, for his own purposes, not to take them seriously?

6. James B. White, "The Ethics of Argument," *University of Chicago Law Review* 50 (1983): 878.

7. Jeremy Waldron, "The Constitutional Conception of Democracy," in *Democracy*, ed. David Estlund (Oxford: Blackwell, 2002), 51–83, at 74: "The alternative to a self-interest model of politics is not a scenario in which individuals, as responsible moral agents, converge on a single set of principles which add up to *the truth* about justice, rights and the common good. That would not be a credible alternative from a social science point of view. The proper alternative to the self-interest model is a model of opinionated disagreement—a noisy scenario in which men and women of high spirit argue passionately and vociferously about what rights we have, what justice requires, and what the common good amounts to, motivated in their disagreement not by what's in it for them but by a desire to get it right. If we take *that* as our alternative model, we may be more inclined to recognize that real world politics are not necessarily governed by self-interest than if we think the only alternative to the self-interest model is one which has high-minded citizens converging on the truth."

8. White, "The Ethics of Argument," 889.

9. Things are of course more complicated still. Gorgias points to Pericles as an example of the success of rhetoric, and Socrates denies the value of that example (515e–516d). For some of the complications, see Harvey Yunis, *Taming Democracy: Models of Political Rhetoric in Classical Athens* (Ithaca, N.Y.: Cornell University Press, 1996).

10. Sanford Levinson, "The Law of Politics: Bush v. Gore and the French Revolution: A Tentative List of Some Early Lessons," *Law and Contemporary Problems* 65 (2002): 7–39, at 11: "American constitutional lawyers . . . seem to feel relatively few genuine constraints on the kinds of arguments they are willing to make or endorse. It is, I am confident, harder to recognize a 'frivolous argument' in constitutional law than in any other area of legal analysis. Almost all constitutional analysts, as a matter of brute fact, seem committed to a de facto theory of 'happy endings,' whereby one's skills as a rhetorical manipulator of what my colleague Philip Bobbitt terms the 'modalities' of legal argument are devoted to achieving satisfying results."

11. Paul Kahn, *The Reign of Law:* Marbury v. Madison *and the Construction of America* (New Haven: Yale University Press, 1997), 126. "A judge's knowledge of the rule of law functions analogously to a doctor's knowledge of health. The doctor's power is also founded on a claim to special knowledge. When the doctor identifies an injury or a disease, he or she is not simply stating a fact. Rather, he or she is setting forth a predicate for an intervention in the body. Power flows from knowledge, but knowledge is made possible by the openness of the members of the community to this form of power/intervention on their bodies. When we accept the idea of medical expertise, we make possible a certain kind of intervention on our own bodies. And when we are open to this form of intervention, we open a space for medical expertise. To resist the doctor's prescriptive action looks 'irrational.' Indeed, in extreme cases, resistance is taken as a sign of further illness."

12. Kenneth Burke, "The Virtues and Limitations of Debunking," *Philosophy of Literary Form* (Baton Rouge: Louisiana State University Press, 1941; rpt. Berkeley: University of California Press, 1973), 145–46: "We may note the emergence of the debunking attitude in the works of Machiavelli and Hobbes. Machiavelli tended to consider the 'ungrateful, deceitful, cowardly and greedy' aspects of men not as an aspect of their 'fall,' but as the very essence of their nature. Lying was not a deviation from their nature, it was the norm. Beneath this strategy, to be sure, there was a humane motive. Machiavelli felt, I believe, that since virtues are by definition rare, they are a frail structure upon which to build a state. But if you could found a state upon vice, you would have a firm foundation indeed. And in an age of marked instability, Machiavelli was searching vigorously for firmness, a kind of beneath-which-not.

"In brief, the history of debunking is interwoven with the history of liberalism."

13. Much of the recent revival of the sophists depends on seeing them as outsiders challenging existing orders, and thus as inspiration for contemporaries who wish to do the same. David Estlund, "Making Truth Safe for Democracy," in *The Idea of Democracy,* ed. David Copp, Jean Hampton, and John Roemer (Cambridge: Cambridge University Press, 1993), 74: "There is . . . an historical association between the idea of truth as an independent standard of political choices, and the idea of our being constrained by the

authority of a boss. It is possible to see much of the opposition to normative political truth as, at root, anti-authoritarian." For a more sober analysis, see Bernard Knox, *The Oldest Dead White European Males and Other Reflections on the Classics* (New York: W. W. Norton, 1993). See too Lenn Goodman, *In Defense of Truth: A Pluralistic Approach* (Amherst, N.Y.: Humanity Books, 2001), 89: "The Greek Sophists spoke up for relativism because they found a ready market for the claim that conflicting interests deserve recognition—not despite but for their very partiality. Renaissance humanists linked relativism with reason and moderation in a trinity of toleration. But they, like the Sophists, oversold their goods. If reason has no more to offer than a sweet voice, it cannot settle disputes." For a rebuttal of the idea that sophistic, relativism, and postmodernism are inevitably on the side of the oppressed, with the suggestion that such an idea confuses real politics with academic politics, see Ernest Gellner, *Postmodernism, Reason and Religion* (London and New York: Routledge, 1992), to which I am indebted for the observation that "communicate" has become an intransitive verb. Anyone who thinks that relativism is necessarily on the side of human liberation and "essentialism" on the side of oppression should consult the works of Robert Bork, for whom relativism means that there can be no appeal beyond the sentiments of the majority. Or so Bork used to argue before he saw better opportunities in defending natural law.

14. John Searle, "Rationality and Realism: What Is At Stake?" *Daedalus* 122 (1992): 55–84, and *Construction of Social Reality* (New York: Free Press, 1995). Richard Rorty, "Does Academic Freedom Have Philosophical Presuppositions?" in *The Future of Academic Freedom,* ed. Louis Menand (Chicago: University of Chicago Press, 1996), 24: "I take it as a mark of moral and intellectual progress that we are more and more prepared to judge institutions, traditions, and practices by the good they seem to be doing rather than by the philosophical or theological beliefs invoked in their defense. More generally, I view it as a mark of such progress that we are coming to think of such beliefs as abbreviations of practices rather than as foundations for practices, and that we are able to see many different beliefs as equally good abbreviations for the same practice." Similarly, "We did not learn about the importance of [free] institutions . . . by thinking through the nature of Reason or Man or Society; we learn about this the hard way, by watching what happened when those institutions were set aside." See too Joseph Vining, "Legal Affinities," *Georgia Law Review* 23 (1989): 1035–51, esp. 1040: "The world of words, or of texts, comes to lawyer and theologian, as to everyone, tagged with a question. The question is, Will you attend, or not? Are words—if not ignored—to be fought against, manipulated, subdued, reduced? Or do you seek to understand? Do you accept the world of words with faith that it is a world, that there is an it (though I think the English pronoun here is wrong, too much a neuter), or do you proceed doubting that there is anything in words at all?" As Vining also notes, the faith in the world is not ontological or epistemological—*pace* the debates between John Searle and the postmodernists—it is ethical. For a contrary argument in defense of the metaphysical dimension of such disputes, see Lenn Goodman, *In Defense of Truth.*

15. John Dewey, *The Future of Liberalism, Later Works,* vol. 11 (Carbondale: Southern Illinois University Press, 1987), 291. Compare Isaiah Berlin: "The history of thought and culture is, as Hegel showed with great brilliance, a changing pattern of great liberating

ideas which inevitably turn into suffocating straightjackets, and so stimulate their own destruction by new, emancipating, and at the same time, enslaving conceptions." Isaiah Berlin, "Does Political Theory Still Exist?" in *Philosophy, Politics and Society,* 2d series, ed. Peter Laslett and Walter G. Runciman (Oxford: Blackwell, 1962), 19. See too Holmes in *Towne v. Eisner,* 245 U.S. 418, 425 (1918): A "word is not a crystal, transparent and unchanged" but "the skin of a living thought and may vary greatly in color and content according to the circumstances and the time in which it is used."

In important ways, my sense of "argument" or "reasoning" that includes its purposes and other contextual features corresponds to the idea of "refined arguments" as opposed to "source arguments" in Terence Parsons, "What is an Argument?" *Journal of Philosophy* 93 (1996): 164–85. The same "source argument," found in a text, can be interpreted in various ways to yield diverse "refined arguments," and so are liable to different judgments. On the other hand, I think that what I call "ethical criticism" or "ethical assessment" includes both what he calls "interpretation" and "logical assessment."

16. Compare the following two accounts of legal reasoning, one which sees all limitations to an art as restricting, and one which sees the same as liberating. First, Peter Gabel, "Reification in Legal Reasoning" in *Critical Legal Studies,* ed. James Boyle (New York: New York University Press, 1994), 17: "Legal reasoning is an inherently repressive form of interpretive thought which limits our comprehension of the social world and its possibilities." Second, Charles L. Black Jr., *The Humane Imagination* (Woodbridge, Conn.: Ox Bow Press, 1986), 29, 31. "The techniques of our law were sharpened for attaining the sensible, the just result. They are not always adequate to justice, or to the correcting of injustice. There are some musical compositions that you couldn't play on the piano. But I repeat, it is overwhelmingly true that if you seek ye shall find, in the technical weaponry, the means needful for a fair outcome. . . . It is visibly true of law that a really high technical proficiency liberates instead of binds—and this is one of the surest diagnostic signs of art."

17. Guido Calabresi, "Foreword: Antidiscrimination and Constitutional Accountability (What the Bork-Brennan Debate Ignores)," *Harvard Law Review* 105 (1991): 80–151, 132, n. 169. "When I questioned Justice Black on how he could justify his support for the majority opinion in Bolling despite its blatant violation of his own judicial philosophy, he responded as follows: a wise judge chooses, among plausible constitutional philosophies, one that will generally allow him to reach results he can believe in—a judge who does not to some extent tailor his judicial philosophy to his beliefs inevitably becomes badly frustrated and angry. (Justice Black may have been thinking of Justice Robert Jackson, whose basic constitutional philosophy fit more comfortably with the political views of his law clerk, William Rehnquist, than with his own.) A judge who does not decide some cases, from time to time, differently from the way he would wish, because the philosophy he has adopted requires it, is not a judge. But a judge who refuses ever to stray from his judicial philosophy, and be subject to criticism for doing so, no matter how important the issue involved, is a fool."

18. Jeremy Waldron, *Liberal Rights: Collected Papers, 1981–1991* (Cambridge: Cambridge University Press, 1993), 186–87. "A community like the United States cannot found itself on something it takes to be a 'self-evident' truth—that all men are created

equal'—and then go on to say glibly, 'But that's just what we happen to think around here; different attitudes toward equality are distinctive of and valid for different societies.' A person who says anything like that from within our society betrays our norms (and hence our communal identity). . . . He does not keep faith with the *content* of our norm—namely, that it is *all men* (not simply all men who happen to live around here) who are said to be have been created equal."

Cornelius Castoriadis, *The Imaginary Institution of Society* (Cambridge, Mass.: MIT Press, 1987), 350: "The true ground of grand sophistic is the same as the true ground of inherited philosophy: the requirement of tautology. . . . Sophistic posits this requirement bluntly and arrogantly in order to show that it cannot be satisfied; philosophy posits it scrupulously and attempts to satisfy it. This is what makes Aristotle say that the sophist and the philosopher differ only by an ethical choice (*prohairesis*): one can do philosophy only by seeking communication in truth, in one and the same coherent discourse. All the 'refutations' of sophistic and of skepticism that have ever existed have consisted simply in showing that sophistic destroys itself as coherent discourse. . . . These refutations are of no avail against those for whom discourse is only play or warfare—whether they live in fifth-century Athens or in today's Paris."

19. For one of many examples of this topos, see Ronald Dworkin, *Law's Empire* (Cambridge, Mass.: Harvard University Press, 1986), 324: "Legislators can usefully predict how judges will interpret their statutes only if they think judges are using some method of statutory interpretation that is independent of legislator's predictions." See also David Luban, "The Bad Man and the Good Lawyer: A Centennial Essay on Holmes' *The Path of the Law*," *New York University Law Review* 72 (1997): 1547–83, at 1577–78: "Judges puzzled about the law of a case will not answer their questions by predicting their own behavior, especially if the only basis for that prediction is their belief that the law is nothing but a prediction of their own behavior. The problem is not that they can't get the prediction right, but rather that they can't get it wrong: any answer they come up with is the right answer, just because they have come up with it. If law is prophecies of what the courts will do, then court-made law consists of self-fulfilling prophecies." Its general application to human understanding is expressed by Arthur Danto, "Historical Language and Historical Reality," *The Review of Metaphysics* 27 (1973): 257–58. "The beliefs of others are part of the reality we have to deal with when we explain their conduct in the world. We can speak of *their* world meaning only their beliefs about the world. We cannot in the same sense speak of 'our world.' For us, our world is: *the world.* . . . Our beliefs, because we regard them as true, are not thought of as *our* beliefs. . . . What is curious is that in our own case, the distance between ourselves and the world which the concept of truth requires is automatically closed . . . because we do not think of the representation of the world, to which truth properly applies, but to *what* is represented, namely the world." Also Aristotle, *Politics* I.2.1255a32–35: "Our nobles consider themselves noble not only in their own country but everywhere, but they think that barbarian noblemen are only noble in their own country—which implies that there are two kinds of nobility and of freedom, one absolute and the other relative."

20. I. A. Richards, *Science and Poetry* (London: Kegan Paul, 1935), 29: "We believe a scientist because he can substantiate his remarks, not because he is eloquent. . . . In fact,

we distrust him when he seems to be influencing us by his manner." See also Kant: "In view of the malevolence of human nature, which can be seen unconcealed in the free relations of nations (whereas in a condition under civil laws it is greatly veiled by the government's constraint), it is surprising that the word *right* could still not be altogether banished as pedantic from the politics of war and that no state has yet been bold enough to declare itself publicly in favor of this view. . . . This homage that every state pays the concept of right (at least verbally) nevertheless proves that there is to be found in the human being a still greater, though at present dormant, moral predisposition to eventually become master of the evil principle within him (which he cannot deny) and also to hope for this from others; for otherwise the word *right* would never be spoken by states wanting to attack one another, unless merely to make fun of it, as a certain Gallic principle defined right: 'It is the prerogative nature has given the stronger over the weaker, that the latter should obey him.'" Immanuel Kant, "Towards Perpetual Peace," *Perpetual Peace and Other Essays,* trans. and ed. Ted Humphrey (Indianapolis: Hackett, 1983), 116.

21. Quoted in Arthur M. Schlesinger, *The Politics of Upheaval* (Boston: Houghton Mifflin, 1960), 463. See also Thomas More in Robert Bolt, *A Man for All Seasons* (1960), 37: "The currents and eddies of rights, of right and wrong, which you will find such plain sailing, I can't navigate. But in the thickets of the law, oh there I am a forester."

22. Francis J. Mootz III, "Rhetorical Knowledge in Legal Practice and Theory," *Southern California Interdisciplinary Law Journal* 6 (1998): 572. "Many first year law students are troubled by what they perceive to be the wide freedom of judges to decide cases on personal whim and then later to supply adequate legal justification for their decision, but it is no surprise to find that these same students have difficulty formulating a coherent argumentative essay for the final exam. It is easy enough to believe that the law is 'just rhetoric' when reading a case, but the tremendous challenge of confronting a specific legal dispute and arguing persuasively on behalf of a client quickly demonstrates to students that a rhetorical exchange can be extremely demanding because it is so decentering."

23. Robert P. Burns, *A Theory of the Trial* (Princeton, N.J.: Princeton University Press, 1999), 142–43: "Difficult methodological issues may prevent the integration of methods of social science research that explicitly seek to create a 'scientific image' of the jury by discovering quantifiable relationships between certain bits of 'jury behavior' and independent variables of one sort or another. Precisely what those independent variables are makes a great deal of difference, as does the interpretation of the relationship between those independent variables and the dependent variables (jury 'behaviors') they 'explain.' Where the independent variables and the postulated relationship are such that no normative account can be given of that same relationship, difficulties of integration into a normative account are probably insurmountable. These are cases where the independent variables cannot serve as *reasons* or *justifications* within a recognizably normative perspective for the results that form the dependent variables in the 'scientific' account. For example, if social scientists could isolate the variable of the defendant's race and demonstrate its causal effect on verdicts, they would have identified an aspect of jury decision making ripe for reform, not a defensible situated ideal. . . . Certain independent

variables affecting jury behavior may provide a behavioral or causal explanation of an intellectual practice (whether a science or a trial) but not a rational reconstruction of the *validity* of the practice's results."

24. J. L. Mackie, *Ethics: Inventing Right and Wrong* (Hardmondsworth: Penguin, 1977).

25. Onora O'Neill, "Reason and the Resolution of Disputes," *Notre Dame Law Review* 67 (1992): 1376–77: "If the kernel of practical reasoning is a matter of basing one's action and communication on principles that others too can follow, then those who reason must reject strategies which disable others' capacities to follow principles. Some of the principles practical reasoners must therefore reject can be readily identified. For example, principles of destroying or injuring others' capacities for action are in principle unshareable: we cannot expect those whom we intend to destroy or injure to act as they could if not destroyed or injured. Destruction and injury take many forms: violence destroys and injures bodies; coercion undermines the will; deception injures understanding. Each of these has unending variety. Those who make principles of violence, of coercion or of deception fundamental to their conduct of disputes cannot claim to be seeking reasoned resolution to those disputes. Rather they are resorting to methods of settling disputes which, in principle, will bypass the agency and the reasoning of those with whom they are in dispute. If reasoning has to avoid relying on principles that others cannot share or follow, then it cannot be simply a matter of patterning action and communication according to certain formal structures, or of respecting instrumental rationality. Rather reasoned action has to be based on principles of helping to respect and to secure, rather than to damage and destroy, the capacities for action of those with whom one seeks to reason."

26. For details on how advertising works in this vein, see Walker Gibson, *Tough, Sweet, and Stuffy* (Bloomington: Indiana University Press, 1966), as well as many of the works of Kenneth Burke.

27. Machiavelli, *The Prince*, chap. 6. Here is the context of the remark: "All armed prophets succeed whereas unarmed ones fail. This happens because . . . the people are fickle; it is easy to persuade them about something, but difficult to keep them persuaded. Hence, when they no longer believe in you and your schemes, you must be able to force them to believe." Machiavelli, *The Prince*, ed. Quentin Skinner and Russell Price (Cambridge: Cambridge University Press, 1988), 21.

28. Thucydides, *History of the Peloponnesian War*, III. 82.

CHAPTER THREE

1. Ronald Beiner, "Do We Need a Philosophical Ethics? Theory, Prudence, and the Primacy of *Ethos*," *Philosophical Forum* 20 (1989): 235–36. See too W. B. Gallie, *Philosophy and the Historical Understanding* (New York: Schocken, 1964), 24: "The conclusion of a good story—a conclusion which we wait for eagerly—is not something that could have been or should have been foreseen. . . . We can imagine almost any good story being presented, and probably ruined, as either a cautionary tale or as the illustration of a moral homily. . . . In the homily the persons and early incidents of the story will be introduced somewhat in the manner of instantial or factual premises from which,

in conjunction with appropriate wise saws and moral principles, the conclusion of the story—the exemplification of the appropriate moral lesson—can be deduced. But in this process the conclusion will, of course, have lost all its virtue *as the conclusion of the story.* Inevitably, it will have become a foregone conclusion, possibly to be assimilated with moral profit, but certainly not to be awaited with eagerness and excitement."

2. The story about Black recommending the *Rhetoric* to Warren is found in Roger K. Newman, *Hugo Black: A Biography* (New York: Pantheon Books, 1994), and repeated in Ed Cray, *Chief Justice: A Biography of Earl Warren* (New York: Simon and Schuster, 1997), where I first learned of it. I thank Mr. Cray for leading me back to Newman.

3. *Brown v. Board of Education,* 347 U.S. 483 (1954), 495.

4. These questions reenacted the progress of the Civil War Amendments. When the abolition of slavery was proposed, opponents claimed that abolition implied equality which in turn implied "miscegenation." Those who proposed the Thirteenth Amendment were unsure and divided about whether abolition implied equality, and what the content of any such equality would be. Some thought that the provisions of the Fourteenth and Fifteenth Amendments were included in abolition. Others claimed to support abolition but denied that racial equality was either implied or desired. Again, the question is not what is logically implicated, and not what advocates can get away with, but what are the ethical implications of a commitment.

For accounts of the cases that gradually led to *Brown,* see Richard Kluger, *Simple Justice* (New York: Knopf, 1976), along with Mark Tushnet, *Making Civil Rights Law: Thurgood Marshall and the Supreme Court, 1956–1961* (New York and Oxford: Oxford University Press, 1994).

5. On the logical equivalent of a principle of inertia, see Chaim Perelman and L. Olbrecht-Tyteca, *The New Rhetoric: A Treatise on Argumentation,* trans. John Wilkinson and Purcell Weaver (Notre Dame, Ind.: University of Notre Dame Press, 1969).

6. For case-to-case and analogical reasoning, see, among many others, Edward H. Levi, *An Introduction to Legal Reasoning* (Chicago: University of Chicago Press, 1949); Wendy Raudenbush Olmsted, "The Uses of Rhetoric: Indeterminacy in Legal Reasoning, Practical Thinking and the Interpretation of Literary Figures," *Philosophy and Rhetoric* 24 (1991): 1–24; and Cass R. Sunstein, "On Analogical Reasoning," *Harvard Law Review* 106 (1993): 741–91.

7. William J. Brennan Jr., "The Constitution of the United States: Contemporary Ratification," *Interpreting Law and Literature: A Hermeneutic Reader,* ed. S. Levinson and S. Maillou (Evanston: Northwestern University Press, 1988), 15.

See Paul Gewirtz, "Narrative and Rhetoric in the Law," *Law's Stories: Narrative and Rhetoric in the Law,* ed. Peter Brooks and Paul Gewirtz (New Haven: Yale University Press, 1996), 10: "A judicial opinion serves three primary functions: first, to give guidance to other judges, lawyers and the general public about what the law is; second, to discipline the judge's deliberative process with a public account of his or her decision, thus deterring error and corruption; and third, to persuade the court's audiences that the court did the right thing. The opinion usually ends with the words 'It is so ordered,' emphasizing the coercive force that judges wield. But the written justification in the body of the judicial opinion is what gives the order its authority." See also John Rawls,

"The Idea of Public Reason," reprinted from John Rawls, *Political Liberalism* (New York: Columbia University Press, 1993), in *Deliberative Democracy: Essays on Reason and Politics,* ed. James Bohman and William Rehg (Cambridge, Mass.: MIT Press, 1997), 112: "The constitution is not what the Court says it is. Rather, it is what the people acting constitutionally through the other branches eventually allow the Court to say it is." At issue here is how the Supreme Court earns authority, which will be the subject of chapter 5. Similarly, see Bruce Ackerman, "Revolution on a Human Scale," *Yale Law Journal* 108 (1999): 2303. "If lawyers and judges hope to explain to their fellow citizens why the Thirteenth and Fourteenth Amendments are *properly* part of the Constitution, they should be in a position to explain how the Republicans, no less than the Federalists, *earned* the constitutional authority to speak for the People by virtue of their unconventional adaptation of preexisting institutions."

8. D. O'Brien, *Storm Center: The Supreme Court in American Politics* (New York: Norton, 1986), 281.

9. L. A. Powe Jr., *The Warren Court and American Politics* (Cambridge, Mass.: Harvard University Press, 2000), 56: "The Court stated that 'it should go without saying that the vitality of these constitutional principles [from *Brown*] cannot be allowed to yield simply from disagreement with them.' Yet that is what *Brown* II was about: the principles of *Brown* being delayed for an undetermined time because the Court feared the extent of southern disagreement with them. The Court was not willing to say so honestly; therefore, the Court had to offer reasons why delay was acceptable. One reason was that equity was flexible in adjusting private and public needs."

10. Luban sees this as central to the Warren Court's achievement, which he characterizes as rethinking the concept of a right "by rethinking the nature of a remedy." David Luban, "The Warren Court and the Concept of a Right," *Harvard Civil Rights and Civil Liberties Law Review* 34 (1999): 11. Luban sees the Warren Court as moving away from the idea of protecting rights "reactively" to indirect prevention of rights violations before they occur. That is just what the Court achieved in *Brown* by the separation of the finding of injury from the determination of redress. The *Brown* decision does not fit comfortably into Aristotle's three kinds of rhetoric because it is an equitable decision. For details, see Peter Charles Hoffer, *The Law's Conscience: Equitable Constitutionalism in America* (Chapel Hill: University of North Carolina Press, 1990).

11. Paul Kahn, *Legitimacy and History: Self-Government in American Constitutional History* (New Haven: Yale University Press, 1992), 153: "The meaning of the idea of equality upon which the Court began to act in *Brown,* only became clear over the next twenty years." *Brown* is not unique in producing such an ethical surplus. Consider *Griswold,* which saw a privacy right in marriage. It led to *Eisenstadt,* in which unmarried sexual partners were as protected as married people, to avoid discrimination based on marital status. But that means that the place of marriage in the derivation of *Griswold* is lost. Indeed my concept of ethical surplus is a restatement, with I believe a richer intellectual backing, of Douglas's talk in *Griswold* of penumbral rights emanating from constitutional provisions. While Douglas talks about emanations from rights, I see the ethical surplus coming from judicial reasoning. Richard A. Posner, *The Problematics of Moral and Legal Theory* (Cambridge, Mass.: Harvard University Press, 1999), 138, calls the

Brown decision and its *per curiam* successors "disingenuous" because of the initial restriction to education and its quick abandoning of that limit. For an analysis of the language of emanations and penumbras, see Richard Mohr, "Mr. Justice Douglas at Sodom: Gays and Privacy," *Columbia Human Rights Law Review* 18 (1986): 43–110.

12. Frank H. Easterbook, "Levels of Generality in Constitutional Interpretation: Abstraction and Authority," *University of Chicago Law Review* 59 (1992): 362: "Styles of literary interpretation exalt creativity, indeterminacy, novelty. Readers use texts to enlarge their horizons. Judges, by contrast, use texts to impose obligations—to order persons to do things, pay money, go to jail. An approach that helps people broaden their minds does not justify sending them to jail; that depends on the idea that there are rules. 'Let a thousand flowers bloom' is the right cast of mind for literary interpretation; attractive ideas will take root and others wither; it would be silly to have only one 'approved' understanding of a poem or novel. Certainty and uniformity are important in law; our theory of legal obligation does not admit the possibility that one text has many meanings."

13. For that history, see Michael W. McConnell, "Originalism and the Desegregation Decisions," *Virginia Law Review* 81 (1995): 947–1140; Michael J. Klarman, "*Brown*, Originalism, and Constitutional Theory: A Response to Professor McConnell," *Virginia Law Review* 81 (1995): 1881–1936, and then McConnell again in Michael W. McConnell, "The Originalist Justification for *Brown:* A Reply to Professor Klarman," *Virginia Law Review* 81 (1995): 1937–55.

14. Note that this sense of presupposition differs from some uses of the term in logic, in which a presupposition is a basic premise. Michael J. Perry, *The Constitution in the Courts: Law or Politics?* (New York and Oxford: Oxford University Press, 1994), 46: "The ratifiers' expectation that reliance on the death penalty would persist into the future and their decision, given that expectation, to regulate imposition of the penalty, do not constitute a decision to authorize reliance on the death penalty, to *constitutionalize* the death penalty." See too Robert Bork's testimony in his confirmation hearings about *Brown*, in response to a question from Senator Thurmond. "Let me proceed on the assumptions that [segregation] was intended by those who framed the 14th amendment. The rule they wrote was no individual shall be denied the equal protection of the law. They may have written that rule on the assumption—a background assumption—that you could get equal protection or equality with separation or segregation. If they did, then by 1954 it had become abundantly clear that the background assumption was false. At that point the Court is faced with a choice: Does it enforce the rule—equal protection—or enforce the background assumption that the framers and ratifiers made? I think it is clear that you have to enforce the rule, the background assumption being false." *Senate Hearings* at 132, quoted by Philip Bobbitt, *Constitutional Interpretation* (Oxford: Blackwell, 1991), 92.

15. For Lincoln, see Herman Belz, *Abraham Lincoln, Constitutionalism, and Equal Rights in the Civil War Era* (New York: Fordham University Press, 1998); Michael Vorenberg, *Final Freedom: The Civil War, The Abolition of Slavery, and the Thirteenth Amendment* (Cambridge: Cambridge University Press, 2001).

16. MacIntyre, *Whose Justice? Which Rationality?* (Notre Dame, Ind.: University of Notre Dame Press, 1988), 174–75. See too John Dewey, *Human Nature and Conduct:*

An Introduction to Social Psychology (New York: Modern Library, 1930), 216–17: "The poignancy of situations that evoke reflection lies in the fact that we really do not know the meaning of the tendencies that are pressing for action. We have to search, to experiment. Deliberation is a work of discovery. Conflict is acute; one impulse carries us one way into one situation, and another impulse takes us another way to a radically different objective result. Deliberation is not an attempt to do away with this opposition of quality by reducing it to one of amount. It is an attempt to uncover the conflict in its full scope and bearing. . . .

"In short, the thing actually at stake in any serious deliberation is not a difference of quantity, but what kind of person one is to become, what sort of self is in the making, what kind of a world is making."

17. Albie Sachs, "The Constitutional Position of White South Africans in a Democratic South Africa," *Social Justice* 18:33, quoted in Aletta Norval, *Deconstructing Apartheid Discourse* (London: Verso, 1996), 293.

18. H. Jefferson Powell, *The Moral Tradition of American Constitutionalism, A Theological Interpretation* (Durham, N.C.: Duke University Press, 1993), 166: "*Brown*'s greatest long-term intellectual impact arose from the difficulty constitutionalists had identifying the constitutional principles on which it rested. In one sense, the principle of *Brown* was straightforward and widely accepted: outside the white South the decision was generally regarded as morally correct from the beginning. The problem, of course, was that the constitutional tradition's long-standing insistence on the autonomy of constitutional discourse made direct reliance on the case's 'moral goodness' unacceptable to most constitutionalists." More recently, it has again become fashionable to criticize *Brown*, this time because of more general suspicion of the Supreme Court.

19. Kenneth L. Karst, *Law's Promise, Law's Expression: Visions of Power in the Politics of Race, Gender, and Religion* (New Haven: Yale University Press, 1993), 84.

20. "The assertion of that principle at that time, was the word 'fitly spoken,' which has proved an 'apple of gold,' to us. The Union and the Constitution, are the picture of silver, subsequently framed around it. The picture was made, not to conceal, or destroy, the apple; but to adorn, and preserve it. The picture was made for the apple—not the apple for the picture." Abraham Lincoln, *The Collected Works of Abraham Lincoln*, ed. Roy Basler (New Brunswick, N.J.: Rutgers University Press, 1953), 4:240.

21. For the supposed lack of success of *Brown*, see Gerald N. Rosenberg, *The Hollow Hope: Can Courts Bring About Social Change?* (Chicago: University of Chicago Press, 1991).

22. On these grounds, footnote 11 with its reference to Kenneth Clark's dolls does weaken the argument of *Brown*. Making the holding rely on evidence makes it less ethical by trying to make it more logical.

23. David J. Garrow, "From *Brown* to *Casey:* The U.S. Supreme Court and the Burdens of History," in *Race, Law, and Culture: Reflections on Brown v. Board of Education*, ed. Austin Sarat (New York: Oxford University Press, 1997), 77: "Since the Fourteenth Amendment applied its Equal Protection Clause only to the states, and not to the federal government, the *Brown* Court found itself having to identify some non-Fourteenth Amendment constitutional grounds for avoiding the utterly incongruous paradox of striking down *state*-mandated school segregation while not being able to void identical

governmental policy imposed by *federal* authorities. With a doctrinal dexterity that again may be more significant in historical retrospect than it appeared to be in 1954, the Court—lacking any federally applicable equal protection language—unanimously turned to the Fifth Amendment's Due Process Clause."

24. Sunstein's arguments about "baselines" and their political character is apposite here. Cass R. Sunstein, "Legal Interference with Private Preferences," *University of Chicago Law Review* 53 (1986): 1129–74; Sunstein, "Naked Preferences and the Constitution," *Columbia Law Review* 84 (1984): 1689–1732; Sunstein, "Preferences and Politics," *Philosophy and Public Affairs* 20 (1991): 3–34.

25. For example, the theme of Kant's essay "What is Enlightenment?" is the difference between the consequences and implications of my statements for which I am accountable when speaking in a public and in a private capacity. This is the reason the behavior of judges, especially Supreme Court Justices, cannot be predicted from their behavior in other circumstances.

26. Rorty continues: "So injustices may not be perceived as injustices, even by those who suffer them, until somebody invents a previously unplayed role. Only if somebody has a dream, and a voice to describe that dream, does what looked like nature begin to look like culture, what looked like fate begin to look like a moral abomination." Richard Rorty, "Feminism and Pragmatism," *The Tanner Lectures on Human Values,* vol. 13 (Salt Lake City: University of Utah Press, 1994), reprinted in *Truth and Progress: Philosophical Papers,* vol. 3 (Cambridge: Cambridge University Press, 1998), 203. Greater elaborations of this idea can be found in R. G. Collingwood, *An Essay on Metaphysics* (Oxford: Clarendon Press, 1966), and, earlier still, in John Henry Newman, *An Essay in Aid of a Grammar of Assent,* ed. I. T. Ker (Oxford: Clarendon Press, 1985).

27. Alexander Bickell, "The Supreme Court, 1960 Term—Foreword: The Passive Virtues," *Harvard Law Review* 75 (1961): 41–79; and Anthony Kronman, "Alexander Bickel's Philosophy of Prudence," *Yale Law Journal* 94 (1985): 1567–1616.

28. This sense of ethical argument, which centers on the meanings of equality, shows that while the Nineteenth Amendment was certainly never cited in *Brown* and its descendents, the political equality of women was a part of the development of racial equality. It was difficult to argue in the nineteenth century that the Fourteenth Amendment and the Constitution forbade the existence of second-class citizens. Half the nation's citizens could not vote. Women getting the right to vote changed the meaning of citizenship so that there could not be degrees of citizenship, fulfilling or transforming Harlan's claim that there are no castes in America. The meaning of equality changed when women became full citizens, and so the possibilities for racial justice changed as well. To refer again to the last quotation from Rorty, one could say that the meaning of any assertion depends on the competing live possible assertions. Ethical argument is in this regard similar to logical phenomena like inference to the best explanation.

29. Paul Gewirtz, "The Triumph and Transformation of Antidiscrimination Law," in *Race, Law, and Culture: Reflections on Brown v. Board of Education,* 110. For an example of an important, nontrivial decision without an ethical surplus, and indeed without ethical argument, I nominate *Shelly v. Kramer* (334 U.S. 1 [1948]), the case that declared restrictive covenants in housing unconstitutional. Often we complain about decisions

that should be ethical but are not by calling them legalistic. But to call a decision ethical is not necessarily to praise it. The majority opinion in *De Shany v. Winnebago County Department of Social Services* (489 U.S. 189), which denied government responsibility for the beating of a child after repeated reports of abuse, seems to me ethical, concerned with justice and not merely law, and speaking to the wider audiences ignored by *Shelly*. I still think it is a badly reasoned decision.

30. Kahn, *Legitimacy and History*, 154–55. "The Court's desegregation cases cumulatively made clear that the evil targeted in *Brown* was not simply harm to education but discrimination itself. Segregation was not evil simply because of its harmful consequences to some other value, whether educational achievement or economic well-being. *Brown* and its progeny rested upon a substantive concept of equality under which segregation was an evil in itself. The social science language of *Brown*, however, was of little help in explaining the harm that the Court perceived in segregation. The harm worked in the domain of morals, not statistics. The Court needed a new language with which to explain the moral harm. It found that language in the simultaneous development of a right to privacy. Behind the Court's elaboration of a right to privacy stood an idea of the autonomous individual who creates his or her own identity independently of any assertion of public authority. The evil of segregation for the modern Court can best be understood as a violation of this principle of individual autonomy: racial segregation entails a refusal to acknowledge its victims' right to decide their racial or ethnic identity."

See also Karst, *Law's Promise, Law's Expression*, 75–76: "The Warren Court's earliest civil rights achievements can be seen as a redefinition of formal equality that placed officially sponsored racial segregation—even in 'separate but equal' facilities—outside the constitutional pale. Yet, from the 1950s to the 1970s, the need for remedying a wide variety of forms of private discrimination was also recognized; for example, by the Warren Court's decisions relaxing the 'state action' barrier to the assertions under the equal protection clause, by the Burger Court's acceptance of group remedies, and by both Courts' generous construction of federal civil rights laws. These civil rights decisions nourished a countertradition of public responsibility, not just to avoid perpetuating the effects of racial caste but to take positive action to end those effects."

31. David Luban too notes the shift in burden of proof and the corresponding presumptions concerning the behavior of the state and its officials. See "The Warren Court and the Concept of a Right," esp. 20–21.

32. *Brown* also had a less friendly legacy, which I hope to explore elsewhere. Southern legal resistance to *Brown* often took the form of facially neutral laws, such as "pupil placement laws," or redistricting, which did not mention race, whose intention was to maintain segregation. Judgment of the constitutionality of such laws had to turn on their motivation or intention. Such inquiry into intention, although necessary, destroyed one of the conditions of friendship, the ability to treat proffered reasoning as reasoning and not as rationalization.

CHAPTER FOUR

1. Quoted in Bent Flyvbjerg, *Making Social Science Matter: Why Social Inquiry Fails and How It Can Succeed Again* (Cambridge: Cambridge University Press, 2001), 9. See

too Pierre Bourdieu, "Practice has a logic which is not that of logic," *Outline of a Theory of Practice* (Cambridge: Cambridge University Press, 1977), 109.

2. N. MacCormick, "Legal Reasoning and Practical Reason," *Midwest Studies in Philosophy* 7, ed. P. A. French, T. E. Uehling Jr., and H. K. Wettstein (Minneapolis: University of Minnesota Press, 1982), 274.

3. Thus for most of the history of rhetoric, *ethos* is not a mode of persuasion alongside logos and pathos. It is method to be used at the beginning and end of a speech to get the audience's trust and attention, something distinct from the reasoning that is the content of the presentation. See Quintilian, *Institutio Oratoria*, VII.2.8–9 (Loeb Classical Library, Cambridge Mass.: Harvard University Press, 1921, 420–23): "Emotions, as we learn from ancient authorities, fall into two classes; the one is called pathos by the Greeks and is rightly and correctly expressed in Latin by adfectus: the other is called ethos, a word for which in my opinion Latin has no equivalent: it is however rendered by mores, and consequently the branch of philosophy known as ethics is styled moral philosophy by us. . . . The more cautions writers . . . explain pathos as describing the more violent emotions and ethos as designating those which are calm and gentle."

4. Philip Bobbitt, *Constitutional Fate: Theory of the Constitution* (New York and Oxford: Oxford University Press, 1982), 95.

5. While the motivations and directions of her argument are very different from mine, Onora O'Neill develops an analogous argument that the categorical imperative is not merely a principle of morality but of rationality in general in Onora O'Neill, *Constructions of Reason: Explorations of Kant's Practical Reason* (Cambridge: Cambridge University Press, 1989).

6. Charles Taylor, *Sources of the Self: The Making of the Modern Identity* (Cambridge, Mass.: Harvard University Press, 1989), 97: "We can readily see why some people distrust articulation as a source of delusion or fear it as a profanation. . . . It is not mainly because there are so many dead formulations, so many trite imitations, although this is one of the reasons why one may prefer silence. . . . What is worse is that the whole thing may be counterfeited. This is not to say that words of power themselves may be counterfeit. But the act by which their pronouncing releases force can be rhetorically imitated, either to feed our self-conceit or for even more sinister purposes, such as the defence of a discreditable status quo."

7. Julia Annas, "Aristotle on Human Nature and Political Virtue," *Review of Metaphysics* 49 (1996): 731–53.

8. I used this example in *Aristotle's Rhetoric: An Art of Character* (Chicago: University of Chicago Press, 1994). For a similar example, see Michael W. McConnell, "The Selective Funding Problem: Abortions and Religious Schools," *Harvard Law Review* 104 (1991): 989–1050. Aristotle goes on to show how such integrity, the way the good person is "of one mind with himself," exceeds formal consistency. In *Topics* II.7 Aristotle elaborates tests for when the combination of contraries makes a contrariety, and his criteria are ethical. E.g., "'To do good to friends' is not the contrary of 'to do harm to enemies'; for both these actions are objects of choice and belong to the same character" (113a3–5). See also *Ethics* VIII.8.1159b3–12, where good men are consistent, which bad men are not: "Equality and similarity, and above all the similarity of those who are similar in

being virtuous, is friendship. For virtuous people are enduringly [virtuous] in themselves, and enduring [friends] to each other. . . . Vicious people, by contrast, have no firmness, since they do not even remain similar to what they were, but become friends for a short time, enjoying each other's vice."

See also Charles Taylor, "Rorty in the Epistemological Tradition," in *Reading Rorty,* ed. Alan R. Malachowski (Oxford: Blackwell, 1989), 260–61: "We use logical inconsistency to point up and articulate what's wrong with a position, but that's not how we identify it as wrong. For instance, we might say to a holder of a self-indulgent view: 'How nice and convenient! In your artistic and love life, you're always quoting Sartre, and rejecting any human essence. Then when you want to denounce the Junta, suddenly you're talking about their violating this essence. You can't have it both ways.'"

See also Bernard Williams, "Consistency and Realism," *Proceedings of the Aristotelian Society Supplementary Volume* 40 (1966): 19: "The line on one side of which consistency plays its peculiarly significant role is the line between the theoretical and the practical, the line between discourse which . . . has to fit the world, and discourse which the world must fit. With discourse that is practical in these terms, we can see why . . . consistency . . . should admit of exception and should be connected with coherence notions of a less logical character."

And George Eliot, in *Middlemarch:* "It is but a shallow haste which concludeth insincerity from what outsiders call inconsistency." Quoted in Donald Davidson, "How is Weakness of the Will Possible?" *Essays on Actions and Events* (Oxford: Clarendon Press, 1980), 28, n.11.

Note, finally, the way Kant talks about consistency in the *Critique of Judgment:* "The following maxims [of common human understanding] may serve to elucidate its principles: (1) to think for oneself; (2) to think from the standpoint of everybody else; (3) to think always consistently. . . . The third maxim, viz. that of *consecutive thought,* is the most difficult to attain, and can only be attained by the combination of the former and after the constant observance of them has grown into a habit." Immanuel Kant, *Critique of Judgment,* trans. Werner S. Pluhar, with a foreword by Mary J. Gregor (Indianapolis: Hackett, 1987), 160–61; cf. *Kants Gesammelte Schriften* (Berlin: Königlich Preussische Akademie der Wissenschaften, 1908–13), 5:294. See also Kant, *Anthropology from a Pragmatic Point of View,* trans. Victor Lyle Powdell (Carbondale: Southern Illinois University Press, 1978), 228; cf. *Kants Gesammelte Schriften,* 7:96–97. These maxims are not only ethical in that they involve "everyone else," but in that they must engage the character of the thinker, thinking for him or herself as a habit.

9. Bernard Williams, "Conflicts of Values," in *The Idea of Freedom: Essays in Honour of Isaiah Berlin,* ed. Alan Ryan (London: Oxford University Press, 1979), 222; rpt. in *Moral Luck* (Cambridge: Cambridge University Press, 1981), 71–82. See also 224–25: In "tragic" choices, "it must be a mistake to suppose that what we have here is a case of logical inconsistency, such that the agent could not be justified or rational in thinking that each of these moral requirements applied to him. This is to misplace the source of the agent's trouble, in suggesting that what is wrong is his thought about the moral situation, whereas what is wrong lies in his situation itself—something which may or may not be his fault."

10. Christine Korsgaard, *The Sources of Normativity* (Cambridge: Cambridge University Press, 1996), 226.

11. Richard Posner, "The Jurisprudence of Skepticism," *Michigan Law Review* 86 (1988): 860, emphasis mine. The passage continues: "Consistent with this point, the rules on conflict of interest have been growing stricter in lockstep with the decline of consensus in law and the concomitant growth in judicial discretion. The greater the consensus, the easier it is for judges to fix the premises of decision and thus transform the process of legal reasoning into something approximating logical deduction. Because legal reasoning is more powerful in a consensus setting, conflict of interest rules are less needful in that setting to prevent bias from operating."

12. The analysis of authority, which I will consider in more detail in chapter 5, found in Joseph Raz, *The Morality of Freedom* (Oxford: Clarendon Press, 1986), is relevant to this treatment of precedent. See, e.g., 42: "The arbitrator's decision is meant to replace the reasons on which it depends. In agreeing to obey his decision they agreed to follow his judgment of the balance of reasons rather than their own. Henceforth, his decision will settle for them what to do. Lawyers say that the original reasons merge into the decision of the arbitrator or the judgment of a court, which, if binding, becomes res judicata. This means that the original cause of action can no longer be relied upon for any purpose. I shall call a reason which displaces others a pre-emptive reason. . . . Because the arbitrator is meant to decide on the basis of certain reasons, the disputants are excluded from later relying on them. They handed over to him the task of evaluating those reasons. If they do not then deny them as possible bases for their own action they defeat the very point and purpose of the arbitration. They only proper way to acknowledge the arbitrator's authority is to take it to be a reason for action which replaces the reasons on the basis of which he was meant to decide." For more on precedents in reasoning, see Anthony Kronman, "Precedent and Tradition," *Yale Law Journal* 99 (1990): 1029–68.

13. I have offered by own analysis of Aristotle's arguments in "Aristotle's Natural Slaves: Incomplete *Praxeis* and Incomplete Human Beings," *Journal of the History of Philosophy* 32 (1994): 1–22. I will return to the hermeneutics of understanding ancient indefensible arguments for slavery in chapter 7.

Others have pointed out the difference between defending *Dred Scott* today, which could be a pure intellectual exercise made impractical by the Thirteenth Amendment, and defending *Lochner,* which has been rejected but not by constitutional amendment and is therefore still capable of being revived.

14. David Hume, *Essays: Moral, Political, and Literary,* ed. Eugene F. Miller (Indianapolis: Liberty Classics, 1987), 252–53. See too Adam Smith, *The Theory of Moral Sentiments,* ed. D. D. Raphael and A. L. Macfie (Oxford: Clarendon Press, 1976), 17: "To approve of another man's opinions is to adopt those opinions, and to adopt them is to approve of them. If the same arguments which convince you convince me likewise, I necessarily approve of your conviction; and if they do not, I necessarily disapprove of it; neither can I possibly conceive that I should do one without the other." See finally, Lee C. Bollinger, *The Tolerant Society: Freedom of Speech and Extremist Speech in America* (Oxford and New York: Oxford University Press, 1986), 221: "Sometimes . . . even to

consider an idea—especially one we think is dangerously wrong—can lend to that idea an element of credibility, making it thereby more thinkable than it might otherwise properly be, and making ourselves the unwitting instruments of our own loss."

15. Stephen Carter, *God's Name in Vain: The Wrongs and Rights of Religion in Politics* (New York: Basic Books, 2000), 99.

16. David Luban, "Legal Traditionalism," *Stanford Law Review* 43 (1991): 1035–60. Paul Kahn, "Approaches to the Cultural Study of Law: Freedom, Autonomy, and the Cultural Study of Law," *Yale Journal of Law and the Humanities* 13 (2001): 141–71, at 171.

17. Anthony Kronman, *The Lost Lawyer: Failing Ideals of the Legal Profession* (Cambridge, Mass.: Harvard University Press, 1993), 71–72. The passage continues: "The attitude I have in mind . . . might best be characterized as an attitude midway between observation, on the one hand, and identification or endorsement, on the other. To sympathize with the values represented by a particular choice is to do more than observe their association with a given way of life, to take note of the fact that those living the life in question typically affirm values of a certain sort. Taking account of this fact may be a first step toward a sympathetic consideration of these values but is not equivalent to it. Only those who have experienced something of the power and appeal of a value and who understand why others are drawn to it even if they themselves ultimately are not, may be said to have sympathetically considered it—to have *entertained* the value rather than merely noted its existence as an anthropological fact. . . .

"But if sympathy goes beyond mere observation, it also falls short of outright acceptance. It is possible to entertain a point of view without making it one's own, in the sense of giving the values associated with that point of view one's full endorsement. Indeed, where one person actually adopts the values of another as his own, in the way that parents, friends and lovers sometimes do, it is no longer accurate to describe his attitude as one of sympathy, for sympathy—which a person may feel even for those whose values he rejects—does not imply the affirmation of another's commitments and concerns that marks most relationships of this kind. Here, it is more appropriate to speak of love than of sympathy. Love implies a measure of identification, a degree of union, that sympathy does not."

18. For more on this subject, see Wayne C. Booth, *The Company We Keep: An Ethics of Fiction* (Berkeley and Los Angeles: University of California Press, 1988). It is always debatable whether these signs of rationality are in a given case indications of true reasonableness or only its appearance. See also Anthony T. Kronman, who, after citing Aristotle's claim that character is essential to persuasion, and hence essential to the successful lawyer, then faces the question of why the fake appearance of character is not a threat to law and justice: "It might be objected that all anyone really needs in order to be successful in debate is a reputation for practical wisdom and not the trait itself. But a person's character is more difficult to conceal than this cynical advice implies. Our characters reveal themselves in all we do and are open to view, on the public surface of our lives, for everyone to see. Indeed, a person's character is often the first thing we feel with any confidence that we know about him. The reason is that our characters (unlike our beliefs and intentions, which are more easily concealed) have a dispositional dimension—more exactly, they consist in a set of dispositions or habitual desires. What

we desire is generally harder to hide than what we think or intend, and the most difficult desires to conceal are those that have congealed into habits." "Living in the Law," *University of Chicago Law Review* 54 (1987): 869.

See also L. A. Kosman, "Being Properly Affected: Virtues and Feelings in Aristotle's Ethics," in *Essays on Aristotle's Ethics,* ed. Amélie Oksenberg Rorty (Berkeley and Los Angeles: University of California Press, 1981), 113: "One can simulate an action but can only pretend to have a feeling. Thus the mode of inculcation with regard to feelings must be by some other method than that of habituation. There is, in other words, no way to come to feel a certain way by practicing feeling that way, and this is precisely because in some sense our feelings are not in our control. But it is nonetheless possible to engage in a certain range of conduct deliberately designed to make one the kind of person who will characteristically feel in appropriate ways, at appropriate times, and so on."

19. Joseph Vining, *The Authoritative and the Authoritarian* (Chicago: University of Chicago Press, 1986), 54–55: "If the utterer of a statement does not mean what he says with regard to who he is, one may doubt whether he means what he says in the substance of his statement, because, not being who he says he is, and knowing it, he will not easily think and speak as a judge—or a king, or a parent, or whoever it is that he is not. Anyone . . . may, like an actor, imitate a judge, but he will not be a judge, or know what it is really like to be a judge unless he has been one, and that will have been in the past. He will know himself to be an imitation judge when he speaks and there will thus be a constant difficulty in meaning what he says. There is always the danger of breaking into laughter in the midst of his playing or pretense; amusement is at once a signal (to oneself and others), a betrayal, and a protection, as one plays with a role rather than really entering into it."

20. See, along similar lines, the discussions of guilt and dirty hands in Bernard Williams, *Moral Luck,* and Michael Stocker, *Plural and Conflicting Values* (Oxford: Clarendon Press, 1990). Both stress the way, in morally complex and realistic decisions, the rejected reasons do not simply disappear. There is a difference between a reason that is not ultimately decisive and a reason that does not bear considering.

21. See the considerations of *Mozert v. Hawkins County Board of Education* in Stephen Macedo, "Liberal Civic Education and Religious Fundamentalism: The Case of God v. John Rawls?" *Ethics* 105 (1995): 468–96, and Amy Gutmann, "Civic Education and Social Diversity," *Ethics* 105 (1995): 557–79. Gutmann, 566, n. 13: "The Mozert parents . . . generally objected to exposing their children to any ideas or information with which they disagree on religious grounds unless the ideas and information are accompanied by a statement that their religious beliefs are the only true ones." And 571: "The reading classes in Hawkins County schools exposed children to knowledge of different ways of life, but they did not require children to profess belief in what they read. Nor did they try to indoctrinate children into any belief or convince them that any way of life is (or is not) the singularly true or superior one. The *Mozert* parents rejected the relevance of the distinction between exposure to knowledge and inculcation of belief. They claimed that their children were being taught to believe in a way of life by being exposed to it in what they read. They rejected the idea that schools may teach children to understand

and thereby to evaluate different ways of life. They assimilated such teaching to indoctrination into false beliefs."

22. I don't mean this judgment about Bork to be partisan. The same failure of substituting logos for *ethos* could be said about Michael Dukakis. Joseph Vining, *The Authoritative and the Authoritarian*, 156: "Hard and practical men are generally impatient with methodological questions and inquiry into presuppositions. Just tell us what the law says, they growl, and forget the jurisprudence. Thinking themselves realists, they are in fact just the opposite, magicians, believing that the written or spoken word has an independent power, that it can command. But it can issue no commands. Statements of law are not formulae to be conjured with."

See also Robert P. Burns, *A Theory of the Trial* (Princeton, N.J.: Princeton University Press, 1999), 198: "There are subtle though important differences between a purely instrumental (or 'bureaucratic') use of the trial device and the political dimension of the trial. . . . A purely instrumental use of the trial will tend to treat the forms of trial communication solely as means by which the participants reach relatively predetermined ends, with relatively less regard for preserving or respecting the meanings implicit in the ordinary language in which the trial is inevitably carried out. That is what is meant when a procedure is called 'Orwellian' or 'Kafkaesque.' . . . In decision making that respects the political or public dimension of adjudication, there exists a deeper tension—'dialectic,' if you want—between respect for the individual litigant and for the public meanings of the language employed, on the one hand, and, on the other hand, for maintaining the institutional structure that serves interests beyond the courtroom—between, in other words, the 'simultaneous creation of justice and the enabling conventions of justice' [quoting Luban, *Legal Modernism*, 380]. Furthermore, in political decision making, the public identity of the decision-maker is in play in a way that it is not in bureaucratic contexts. Bureaucrats have a Cartesian kind of aloofness from the manipulation of facts and concepts controlling the 'objective' world before them."

23. Robert M. Cover, *Narrative, Violence and the Law: The Essays of Robert Cover*, ed. Martha Minow, Michael Ryan, and Austin Sarat (Ann Arbor: University of Michigan Press, 1992), 144–45. See too Christine Korsgaard, "The Normativity of Instrumental Reason," *Ethics and Practical Reason*, ed. Garrett Culitty and Berys Gaut (Oxford: Oxford University Press, 1997), 215–54, at 248: "The rational necessity of believing the implications of our beliefs can only be explained if we regard believing itself as a normative act. To believe something is not to be in a certain mental state, but to make a certain commitment. It is, we might say, to be committed to constructing one's view of the world in one way rather than another."

24. See Charles Larmore, *Modernité et morale* (Paris: Presses Universitaires de France, 1993), 13–14: "L'idée d'une éthique de la pensée ne devrait pas suprendre. Car il y a non seulment des norms practique concernant comment il faut agir, mais aussi des normes cognitives concernant comment il faut penser. En conséquence, il y a des vertus intellectuelles aussi bien que des vertus morales. Puisqu'il faut toujours agir suivant ses meilleures connaisances, on pourrait aller jusqu'à dire que l'éthique de la pensée constitue le coeur de l'éthique en général, que, comme Pascal l'a exprimé, tout notre devoir est de penser comme il faut."

25. Jonathan Shay, *Achilles in Vietnam: Combat Trauma and the Undoing of Character* (New York: Atheneum, 1994), 209.

CHAPTER FIVE

1. Sources for the three epigraphs are, in order, Robert Weisberg, "Proclaiming Trials as Narratives: Premises and Pretenses," *Law's Stories: Narrative and Rhetoric in the Law*, ed. Peter Brooks and Paul Gewirtz (New Haven: Yale University Press, 1996), 78; Robert M. Cover, "The Supreme Court 1982 Term: Foreword: Nomos and Narrative," *Harvard Law Review* 97 (1983): 45; and David Luban, *Legal Modernism* (Ann Arbor: University of Michigan Press, 1994), 209.

2. Richard A. Posner, "Narrative and Narratology in Classroom and Courtroom," *Philosophy and Literature* 21 (1997): 295. See also 294: "The Supreme Court in *Brown v. Board of Education* was right to forgo a narrative of the history of the oppression of black people in the South, even though that history is the essential background to under-standing the harm of segregated schooling. Such a narrative would have made it even more difficult than it proved to be for the southern states to accept the decision." Paul Gewirtz offers this hypothesis to explain why narrative is so popular now: "The interest in narrative may actually represent a retreat from reformist ambitions in a conservative age—a turn to analyzing form and structure and rhetoric that arises from a frustration with the capacity of substantive legal argument to change the real world of law as one would like, or perhaps even a loss of faith in substantive reform itself." Paul Gewirtz, "Narrative and Rhetoric in the Law," *Law's Stories*, 12.

See too Robert Weisberg, "Proclaiming Trials as Narratives: Premises and Pretenses," *Law's Stories*, 63: "To say that law is narrative is to share in the more general kind of plea that law ought to find some association with literature: the plea is really an expression of hope for spiritual redemption. To utter a popular trope like 'law is essentially narrative' is simply to plead that law be treated as having a spiritual or emotional quality that might redeem the life of lawyers." And 65. "The past decade of law reviews has produced tens of articles that constitute what we might call a genre of narrative affirmance. Typically an article begins by denigrating the supposedly traditional and rarely questioned view that law's authority is objective, deductive, linear, abstract, and acontextual. Next we get an allusion to developments in the social and even natural sciences, where tradi-tional modes of analysis are now understood as forms of discourse, as being 'situated' or 'produced,' as being constructed as rhetoric or literature."

For another useful strategic, and ethically neutral, distinction between the uses of narrative and argument, see Richard K. Sherwin, "The Narrative Construction of Legal Reality," *Vermont Law Review* 18 (1994): 689. "Prosecutors in criminal cases can be quite fond of the logico-scientific story form. It comports nicely with their burden of proof, namely to demonstrate guilt beyond a reasonable doubt. And it carries a solid psycholog-ical insight. Cast into a world of objective truth, where deductive and inductive logic dictates concrete results, jurors may more readily accept their fate: to confirm what has already occurred, and to apply that rules that govern legal outcomes in such situations. Passivity before truth and law, letting the judgment that must come, is a classic (although by no means exclusive) formula for prosecutorial success.

"Of course, jurors may also be led to reject the passive role that the prosecutor may cast for them. Rather than being ruled by fixity and closure, jurors may instead enter a world of possibility and openness. . . . There is a good change that this is the kind of world that the defense's story will presuppose."

3. Terence Ball, "Authority and Conceptual Change," *Authority Revisited, Nomos XXIX,* ed. J. Roland Pennock and John W. Chapman (New York: New York University Press, 1987), 48: "More and more, the expert is in authority because he or she is an authority."

4. Michael Moore, "Authority, Law, and Razian Reasons," *Southern California Law Review* 62 (1989): 833.

5. Richard Kluger, *Simple Justice* (New York: Knopf, 1976), 579.

6. I take "between legitimacy and justice" from Philip Bobbitt, *Constitutional Fate: Theory of the Constitution* (New York and Oxford: Oxford University Press, 1982) and *Constitutional Interpretation* (Oxford: Blackwell, 1991). I will explore Bobbitt's use of that distinction in greater detail in chapter 7. In another idiom, one could substitute for Bobbitt's distinction that found in Perelman between the rational and the reasonable. For a decision to be just, it has to be in the first place legitimate. Similarly, for an argument to be ethical, it has to be in the first place logical. At the beginning of the last chapter it looked as though *ethos* was a threshold condition for logos. We now see that it is the other way around.

7. Kluger, *Simple Justice,* 580. To see this argument as a rhetorical failure is not to make any claims about its impact on the ultimate decision of the Court. Rhetoric is not an art of winning, but of finding and presenting the available and appropriate means of persuasion. It is a rhetorical failure because it must make the Court suspicious of anything further Korman would have to say. In terms of actual impact, this "gaffe" was merely one incident in a larger presentation, and that entire presentation but one of six by defendants in *Bolling* and *Brown v. Board of Education of Topeka,* the case to which it was the companion. I would be amazed to find that Korman's mistake had any impact at all on the ultimate decision. Nothing in my argument presupposes any actual historical significance to this event, but I think it powerfully illustrates the themes of narrative, authority, and *ethos* in rhetorical argument.

8. James Boyd White, *Acts of Hope: Creating Authority in Literature, Law, and Politics* (Chicago: University of Chicago Press, 1994), 125: "The authority [of lawyers and judges] depends upon that of the texts they interpret. Which decisions are entitled to respect, and how much, and what they mean, are of course all open questions; but they are real questions too, and cannot be simply ignored, without erasing what is distinctive, and distinctively valuable, in the law." For a connection between *ethos* and authority, see Peter Brooks, "Storytelling Without Fear? Confession in Law and Literature," *Law's Stories,* 179. In a brief exposition of the classical trio of *ethos,* logos, and pathos, Brooks defines *ethos* as that which "works on the hearer's sense of the speaker's various possible kinds of authority, status as speaker, relationship to the listener, and so on."

9. The narrative transmission of authority has affinity to, but is quite different from, Dworkin's image of the chain novel. I am less concerned with accounting for the growth of the law than its apparent and self-declared continuity. Ronald Dworkin, *Law's Empire* (Cambridge, Mass.: Harvard University Press, 1986), 228–34.

10. Bruce Ackerman, "Liberating Abstraction," *The Bill of Rights in the Modern State,* ed. Geoffrey R. Stone, Richard A. Epstein, and Cass R. Sunstein (Chicago: University of Chicago Press, 1992), 317–48, suggests that it would be argumentatively worse to cite a discredited case, such as *Lochner,* which has not been overruled by constitutional amendment, than a case like *Dred Scott,* which has been overruled. It is part of my present project to show why that assessment misses the point of how arguments are evaluated ethically. While *Dred Scott* no longer has weight as precedent, its use is still an ethical misfire.

11. H. L. A. Hart, *Essays on Bentham* (Oxford: Oxford University Press, 1982), 253. Sometimes this contrast is made in terms of the authority that French laws have over an American tourist vs. the laws of one's own country. If one substitutes the word authority for testimony in the following, Jonathan Adler expresses my point: "Our critical resources are operative in the ordinary acceptance of testimony, and not only in rejection." Jonathan E. Adler, "Testimony, Trust, Knowing," *Journal of Philosophy* 91 (1994): 273. Josiah Royce, *The Philosophy of Loyalty* (New York: Macmillan, 1930), 120, expresses a similar thesis about the object of loyalty: "However much the cause [or principle to which I am loyal] may seem to be assigned to me by my social station, I must cooperate in the choice of the cause, before the act of loyalty is complete."

For a discussion of legal authority that makes a similar point, see Charles Fried, "Impudence," *Supreme Court Review, 1992,* ed. Dennis J. Hutchinson, David A. Strauss, and Geoffrey R. Stone (Chicago: University of Chicago Press, 1993), 187: "I do not believe that a conscientious judge fulfills her role in a hierarchy of courts by seeking to predict how a superior court will rule. Her task is to interpret the superior courts' opinions, and that means taking their text—not the subjective intentions of their authors—and fitting it into the whole body of controlling legal materials, including materials bearing on her subordinate role. It is possible, even likely, sometimes that a superior court's immediately preceding judgment states less than that court's members hope and wish lower courts to do, but the superior judges' own sense of restraint may keep them from putting that wish into words. The lower court judge may predict that her hierarchical superiors will do what she thinks is the wrong thing, but she need not rule as if they had already done it."

See also Joseph Vining, *From Newton's Sleep* (Princeton, N.J.: Princeton University Press, 1995), 63. "When one is asked to 'follow' a statement, one is asked to follow its meaning. The first thing an order giver may be expected to say when things do not go as he expects is 'You fool! I didn't mean that. I meant this. You were wrong. You made a mistake.' If a farmer were to order his man, 'Buy me four sacks of oats for the cattle' and the man were to reply, 'Oats? Don't you mean barley?' the farmer would angrily say, 'Yes, of course I mean barley for cattle. Oats would make them sick.' If the man did not raise a question, or had no chance to question, and there were sanctions for disobedience, would he face sanctions for buying oats or for buying barley?"

12. Robert A. Ferguson, "The Judicial Opinion as Literary Genre," *Yale Journal of Law and the Humanities* 2 (1990): 210.

13. Bernard Williams, "Deciding to Believe," in *Problems of the Self: Philosophical Papers, 1956–1972* (Cambridge: Cambridge University Press, 1973), 136–51.

14. My argument is similar to claims that in ethical choices involving conflict, the rejected reasons are not lost and rejected but can become subsidiary parts of the action chosen, as, for example, when an action is chosen with regret. For details see Michael Stocker, "Dirty Hands and Conflicts of Values and of Desires in Aristotle's *Ethics*," *Pacific Philosophical Quarterly* 67 (1986): 36–61. See especially 37. "The dirty features—the impossible oughts—are double counted. In determining the act to be done, they are taken into account. They tell against the act, but not with enough force to make it overall wrong. However, in focusing on these features as dirty, they are given moral weight all over again, now on their own—as, it seems, reasons against doing that act and as reasons for regretting doing it. They remain dirty even though justified. For good reason, then, Bernard Williams in 'Ethical Consistency' calls them remainders."

15. Robert Hariman, *Political Style: The Artistry of Power* (Chicago: University of Chicago Press, 1995), 178. See too John Leubsdorf, "The Structure of Judicial Opinions," *Minnesota Law Review* 86 (2001): 447–96 at 447: "A judicial opinion tells many stories and speaks with many voices. It is less a single and anonymous utterance of the law than a condensed quarrel."

On the inappropriateness of thinking of such discounting of contrary arguments as insincere, see Kent Greenawalt, *Private Consciences and Public Reasons* (New York and Oxford: Oxford University Press, 1995), 163: "Insofar as the issue is genuine deceit, the problem is largely circular, because so much depends on existing expectations. . . . If citizens expect fully candid disclosure of actual grounds of decision, then restraint in discourse not matched by restraint in decision will mislead. However, if people regard forms of discourse as having particular functions in the political process, they will not necessarily expect that public advocacy will reflect all bases of decision. Let me give two kinds of examples. In most personal conversation and in meetings of some small groups, people (or some people) feel they should include their degree of doubt or confidence about courses of action that they favor, actually stating arguments for the position contrary to that which they take and conceding the weight of those arguments. That plainly is not the approach of most judicial opinion writing, and of most public political discourse. Having decided, people state the arguments in favor of their position with great force and downplay the weight of opposing grounds. This practice is so common, and so commonly understood, that engaging in it is not insincere; no one takes the stated positions as reflecting the true weight of grounds in the speaker's or writer's mind.

"Another feature of legal opinions is that innovative steps are substantially concealed in language that suggests that a principle is already to be found in prior cases. This practice, again, is so common that it is not properly conceived of as insincere."

See too Sanford Levinson, "The Rhetoric of the Judicial Opinion," *Law's Stories*, 187–205.

16. Reva B. Siegel, "In the Eyes of the Law: Reflections on the Authority of Legal Discourse," *Law's Stories*, 225–31, at 226. See too Robert Burt, "Constitutional Law and the Teaching of Parables," *Yale Law Journal* 93 (1984): 475: "The Court is, as many have observed, 'the least dangerous branch,' without direct power to command 'the sword or the purse.' This does not mean that the Justices are without power. It does mean that, when their power is directly and adamantly challenged, they are dependent on

others' acts of faith, of good faith toward them." David Luban distinguishes Holmes's moral philosophy from his judicial *ethos*, a distinction parallel to Justices' appealing to their own "philosophies" and to "the national *ethos*." See Luban, "Justice Holmes and Judicial Virtue," *Virtue*, ed. John W. Chapman and William A. Galston (New York: New York University Press, 1992), 235–64, and "Justice Holmes and the Metaphysics of Judicial Restraint," *Duke Law Journal* 44 (1994): 449–523. Andrew Jackson said, too, that Supreme Court decisions "have only such influence as the force of their reasoning may deserve." President Andrew Jackson's Veto of the Bank of the United States, July 10, 1832.

17. Joseph Vining, *The Authoritative and the Authoritarian* (Chicago: University of Chicago Press, 1986), 168. The entire passage is worth quoting. "A statement is not worked against or around, only to the extent that it is internalized. It is part of one to that extent, animates and directs one's affirmative seeking: one cares about it, believes in it, is committed to it. Indeed, the authoritative statement is a clue to what one oneself believes. Personification, understanding, authority, and internalization flow together. But if one is to be committed to and care about and affirmatively and imaginatively seek what the authoritative voice seeks, one must believe, or assume, that the voice means what it says, that it cares about what it is asking another to seek, that it believes in what it is asking another to believe in. Thus authenticity joins personification, understanding, authoritativeness, and internalization in any sketch of a statement of law or a decision that is to have the force of law—again, not just force, which it may have regardless, but the force of law immediately and thereafter. And with authenticity comes openness, speaking out loud, revealing one's purpose, not holding back and keeping secrets, not manipulating, all that goes under the name of disclosure and that underlies the production of the justifying, explanatory, and integrating texts that are the material for the exercise of legal method."

See too Isaiah Berlin, "Two Concepts of Liberty," in *Four Essays on Liberty* (Oxford: Oxford University Press, 1969), 172, quoting Joseph Schumpeter: "To realise the relative validity of one's convictions and yet stand for them unflinchingly, is what distinguishes a civilized man from a barbarian." To which Berlin adds: "To demand more than this is perhaps a deep and incurable metaphysical need; but to allow it to determine one's practice is a symptom of an equally deep, and more dangerous, moral and political immaturity."

18. Justice Souter captures this sense of ethical authority in his opinion on *Casey:* "Where, in the performance of its judicial duties, the Court decides a case in such a way as to resolve the sort of intensely divisive controversy reflected in *Roe* and those rare, comparable cases, its decision has a dimension that the resolution of the normal case does not carry. It is the dimension present whenever the Court's interpretation of the Constitution calls the contending sides of a national controversy to end their national division by accepting a common mandate rooted in the Constitution." That this obligation to be an authority is an *ethical* obligation to be an ethical authority is recognized by Souter: "The promise of constancy, once given, binds its maker for as long as the power to stand by the decision survives and the understanding of the issue has not changed so fundamentally as to render the commitment obsolete. . . . A willing breach

of it would be nothing less than a *breach of faith,* and no Court which broke its faith with the people could sensibly expect credit for principle in the decision by which it did that" (112 S. Ct. at 2815–16).

19. Thus Kant's *What Is Enlightenment?,* which hopes that we are entering an age in which people think for themselves, spends most of its time distinguishing the times in which what I say will be taken as rational persuasion and when the pure assertion of authority. Thinking for oneself means persuading and being persuaded.

20. Charles Fried, "Constitutional Doctrine," *Harvard Law Review* 107 (1994): 1156. See Vining, *From Newton's Sleep,* 45: "How does one imagine oneself going about following a decision? What are called 'the rules laid down by a decision' are verbal formulations of the reasons relied upon by a decision maker in making the decision. Those reasons are values, importances; any decision maker acting in a particular role necessarily gives relative weights to them in making a particular decision. One follows the decision by focusing upon the values appropriate for that role and discovering the weights used by the decision maker." See too William Brennan's quotation from Learned Hand in "The Role of the Court—The Challenge of the Future," in *An Affair with Freedom,* ed. Stephen Friedman (New York: Atheneum, 1967), 324: "The judge's authority depends upon the assumption that he speaks with the mouth of others, that is to say, the momentum of his utterances must be greater than any which his personal reputation and character can command, if it is to do the work assigned to it—if it is to stand against the passionate resentments arising out of the interests he must frustrate—for while a judge must discover some composition with the dominant trends of his times, he must preserve his authority by cloaking himself in the majesty of an overshadowing past."

21. Hannah Arendt, "What Was Authority?" in *Authority,* ed. Carl J. Friedrich (Cambridge, Mass.: Harvard University Press, 1958), 88.

22. See too the sentence immediately preceding: "A judiciary that discloses what it is doing and why it does it will breed understanding." "Stare Decisis," Eighth Annual Benjamin N. Cardozo Lecture to the Association of the Bar of the City of New York (1949), 31. Quoted in Joseph Goldstein, *The Intelligible Constitution: The Supreme Court's Obligation to Maintain the Constitution as Something We the People Can Understand* (Oxford and New York: Oxford University Press, 1992), 114.

23. Robert M. Cover, "The Supreme Court 1982 Term," 45.

24. H. L. A. Hart, *The Concept of Law* (Oxford: Oxford University Press, 1961), 149–50: "The truth may be that, when courts settled previously unenvisaged questions concerning the most fundamental constitutional rules, they *get* their authority to decide them accepted after the questions have arisen and the decision has been given. Here all that succeeds is success. . . . When this is so, it will often *in retrospect* be said, and may genuinely appear, that there always was an 'inherent' power in the courts to do what they have done."

25. Joseph Raz, *The Morality of Freedom* (Oxford: Clarendon Press, 1986), 35.

26. Mark Tushnet, "Renormalizing Bush v. Gore: An Anticipatory Intellectual History," *Georgetown Law Journal* 90 (2001): 113–25 at 125: "A decision can be justified by the rule of law standing alone only if there are no other reasons justifying the decision."

Paul Kahn, *The Reign of Law: Marbury v. Madison and the Construction of America* (New Haven: Yale University Press, 1997), 106: "Identification of the author of a legal text can have two different effects each in tension with the other. On the one hand, authorship helps to establish the authority—or lack of authority—of a text. The text is seen to share in the status of its author. . . . But authorship is equally a way of limiting a text and its potential impact. Authorship suggests possession: it is uniquely the author's text. An authored text is a localized text. Ascribing authorship to a text is a way of establishing distance between the reader and the text. This distance is the inverse image of the author's identification with the text."

27. Philip B. Kurland, "The Privileges or Immunities Clause: 'Its Hour Come Round At Last'?" *Washington University Law Quarterly* 50 (1972): 405–20; Sanford Levinson, "Constitutional Rhetoric and the Ninth Amendment," *Chicago-Kent Law Review* 64 (1988): 131–61; Kenyon D. Bunch, "The Original Understanding of the Privileges and Immunities Clause," *Seton Hall Constitutional Law Journal* 10 (2000): 321–416.

28. Philip B. Kurland, *Politics, The Constitution and the Warren Court* (Chicago: University of Chicago Press, 1970), 89: "Professor Cox may have been correct when he suggested that: '*Plessy v. Ferguson* was still authoritative when *Brown v. Board of Education* came before the Court,' if by 'authoritative' he meant unreversed. But so, too, was Mr. Justice Clark when commenting on Cox's proposition. He said that *Plessy* was moribund before *Brown* was born. . . . By the time *Brown* was accepted for decision the question was not whether *Plessy* would control but what new rationale would be offered in its place. The fact is that *Plessy* may have been stillborn, for it never developed beyond a fictional excuse for discrimination. The states adhered to the 'separate' part of the doctrine but never took notice of the 'equal' proposition. It was the vast and rapid expansion of the areas of application of the new principle of equality—not its originality—that was the contribution of the Warren Court."

29. C. J. Friedrich, "Authority, Reason, and Discretion," *Nomos I: Authority,* ed. C. J. Friedrich (Cambridge, Mass.: Harvard University Press, 1958), 35.

30. 112 S. Ct. at 2814. For an analysis of *Casey* along similar lines, see James Boyd White, *Acts of Hope: Creating Authority in Literature, Law, and Politics* (Chicago: University of Chicago Press, 1994).

31. Joseph Raz, *Ethics in the Public Domain: Essays in the Morality of Law and Politics* (Oxford: Clarendon Press, 1994), 326.

32. Paul Kahn, *The Reign of Law,* 187: "Sovereignty and interpretation are linked ideas in the Western tradition—both in law and theology. Sovereignty supports interpretation, not as a temporally prior object creating an appearance but as the conceptual framework that creates the imaginative space in which interpretation works. The sovereign never completely shows itself; it is outside the ordinary dimensions of time and space. It is just this extraordinary character of the sovereign that requires an extraordinary relationship between it and the subject: faith.

"The political sovereign is conceived of as that which precedes law and creates law through its word. Constitutionalism understands the singular act of the sovereign to be the creation of a text. To the legal mind, the only cognizable act of which the sovereign is capable is an act of writing. In the beginning was the word. Speaking, the sovereign brought the state into being as an appearance of itself. Were the sovereign to show itself outside of the text, it would displace, not found, a legal order."

33. Kluger, *Simple Justice*, 559.

34. See Robert Kraut, "Love *De Re*," *Midwest Studies in Philosophy* 10 (1986): 413–40, and Amelie Oksenberg Rorty, "The Historicity of Psychological Attitudes: Love is Not Love Which Alters When It Alteration Finds," *Mind in Action* (Boston: Beacon Press, 1986), 121–34.

35. For one example of way institutions and rules can create the conditions in which *ethos* as a function of argument flourishes, see Robert P. Burns, *A Theory of the Trial* (Princeton, N.J.: Princeton University Press, 1999). Burns shows that rational *ethos* functions best when we are not tempted to draw a further inference from the *ethos* of the speaker to some further, "real" *ethos*. See, e.g,. 70: "The few rules surrounding closing [arguments in a trial] situate the trial in a web of public meanings. It is the *lawyer*, not the client, who addresses the jury. He is prohibited from directly expressing his personal opinion on the justness of the cause or the credibility of the witnesses. He must accept the law as given in the instructions and may not paraphrase that law, misstate it, or urge the jury to disregard it. The analogies, allusions, and stories he tells in order to make both factual and normative arguments are all drawn from the jury's common sense. The advocate is prohibited from addressing a juror by name or from urging the jury's self-interest or lessening the responsibility the jury bears by mentioning the possibility of appeals or of commuted sentences. Closing dramatizes the transformation of private desire into public right. When 'I want' becomes 'I am entitled to,' the claimant must submit to the complex public norms by which the latter claims are determined." On the hermeneutics of suspicion more generally, see Paul Ricoeur, *Hermeneutics and the Human Sciences: Essays on Language, Action, and Interpretation* (Cambridge and New York: Cambridge University Press, 1981).

CHAPTER SIX

1. See *Poe v. Ullman*, 367 U.S. 497, 542 (1961): "If the supplying of content to this Constitutional concept has of necessity been a rational process, it certainly has not been one where judges have felt free to roam where unguided speculation might take them."

2. For some helpful recent discussions of trust, see Jonathan E. Adler, "Testimony, Trust, Knowing," *Journal of Philosophy* 91 (1994): 264–75; Annette C. Baier, "Trusting People," *Philosophical Perspectives*, 6: Ethics, 1992, ed. James Tomberlin (Atascadero, Calif.: Ridgeview, 1992), 137–53; Judith Baker, "Trust and Rationality," *Pacific Philosophical Quarterly* 68 (1987): 1–13; Lawrence C. Becker, "Trust as Noncognitve Security about Motives," *Ethics* 107 (1996): 43–60; Bernard Barber, *The Logic and Limits of Trust* (New Brunswick, N.J.: Rutgers University Press, 1983); Ernest Gellner, "Trust, Cohesion, and the Social Order," in *Trust: Making and Breaking Cooperative Relations*, ed. Diego Gambetta (Oxford: Blackwell, 1988), 142–57; Russell Hardin, "Trustworthiness," *Ethics* 107 (1996): 26–42; Karen Jones, "Trust as an Affective Attitude," *Ethics* 107 (1996): 4–25.

3. *Politics* V.11.1313b2–5: Tyrants must guard "against anything that customarily gives rise to two things, high thoughts (*phronēma*) and trust (*pistis*). Leisured discussions are

not allowed, or other meetings connected with leisure, but everything is done to make all as ignorant of one another as possible, since knowledge tends to create trust of one another (*gnōsis pistin poiei mallon pros allēlous*)."

See also V.11.1314a15–29: "Tyranny aims at three things: one, that the ruled have only modest thoughts (for a small-souled person will not conspire against anyone); second, that they distrust one another (for a tyranny will not be overthrown before some persons are able to trust each other—hence they make war on the respectable as being harmful to their rule not merely because they claim not to merit being ruled in the fashion of a master, but also because they are trustworthy, both among themselves and with respect to others, and will not denounce one another or others; and third, an incapacity for activity, for no one will undertake something on behalf of those who are incapable. . . . One might reduce all things characteristic of tyranny to these presuppositions—that they not trust one another, that they not be capable, that they have modest thoughts."

4. Donald Davidson, *Inquiries into Truth and Interpretation* (Oxford: Clarendon Press, 1984), 197.

5. Adam Smith, *The Theory of Moral Sentiments* (1759; Indianapolis: Liberty Classics, 1976), 168. The relevance to trust of this failure of instrumental reason is the subject of Martin Hollis, *Trust Within Reason* (Cambridge: Cambridge University Press, 1998).

6. What Margalit says of self-respect could equally be said of trustworthiness. Avishai Margalit, *The Decent Society* (Cambridge, Mass.: Harvard University Press, 1996), 124: "Although self-respect is an attitude you may have toward yourself, it depends on the attitude of others toward you. This dependence is not merely causal—it does not consist only of the fact that what people think of you, and the way they treat you, affect your own attitude toward yourself psychologically. The dependence is conceptual as well."

7. Sigmund Freud, *Civilization and Its Discontents* (New York: Norton, 1961), 48–49.

8. Annette C. Baier, "Trust and Antitrust," *Ethics* 96 (1986): 231–60, rpt. in *Moral Prejudices* (Cambridge, Mass.: Harvard University Press, 1995), 107: "The persistent human adult tendency to profess trust in a creator-God can also be seen as an infantile residue of this crucial innate readiness of infants to initially impute goodwill to the powerful persons on whom they depend."

9. "To believe, to trust, to rely on another is to Honour him; signe of opinion of his vertue and power. To distrust or not believe, is to Dishonour." Hobbes, *Leviathan*, quoted as an epigraph, Steven Shapin, *A Social History of Truth: Civility and Science in Seventeenth-Century England* (Chicago: University of Chicago Press, 1994), 65.

10. See also Adam Smith, *Lectures on Jurisprudence*, ed. R. L. Meek, D. D. Raphael, and P. G. Stein (Oxford: Clarendon Press, 1978), 352: "It is clearly then natural inclination that everyone has to persuade [which is] the principle in the human mind on which this disposition of trucking is founded. . . . The offering of a shilling, which to us appears to have so plain and simple a meaning, is in reality offering an argument to persuade one to do so and so as it is for his interest. . . . And in this manner every one is practicing oratory on others through the whole of his life." See too *Theory of the Moral Sentiments*, 352: "It requires long and much experience of the falsehood of mankind to reduce them to a reasonable degree of diffidence and distrust. . . . The natural disposition is always

to believe. It is acquired wisdom and experience only that teach incredulity, and they very seldom teach it enough."

11. For something as an object of trust being valued for its own sake, consider the remarks of Charles Fried concerning loyalty. Fried clearly sees loyalty as a matter of *ethos*, not emotion. Charles Fried, *Order and Law: Arguing the Reagan Revolution—A Firsthand Account* (New York: Simon and Schuster, 1991), 189: "I owed loyalty to the President and to my superior in the Department of Justice, the Attorney General. Such loyalty is enjoined both by law and by a proper conception of the President's establishment; it is a matter neither of affection nor of self-interest. It is a moral attitude; the object of this loyalty must be recognized as having intrinsic value, as being worth following for its own sake and in principle. First we judge a thing or a person to be worthy of our loyalty, and then—and for that reason—subordinate our will to it. That is why loyalty makes for dependability, since our choices are determined as long as our minds hold to the same judgment; and that is why disloyalty is also seen as unprincipled, since when we are disloyal we allow a lesser or a private good to determine our action. As Josiah Royce expressed it, loyalty gives a steadfastness of bearing and implies a seriousness of judgment."

12. Steven Shapin, *A Social History of Truth*, 410. "Premodern society managed its affairs in a face-to-face mode. When people assessed the credibility of what they were told, they were able to draw upon the resources of *familiarity.* . . . Knowledge circulated within a system of everyday recognitions, just as the crediting or gainsaying of relations formed the fabric of everyday interaction. Premodern society looked truth in the face."

And 411: "Trust is no longer bestowed on familiar individuals; it is accorded to institutions and abstract capacities thought to reside in certain institutions. The village has given way to the anonymous city, relative simplicity of social structure to relative complexity. We trust the reliability of airplanes without knowing those who make, service, or fly them; we trust the veracity of diagnostic medical tests without knowing the people who carry them out; and we trust the truth of specialized and esoteric scientific knowledge without knowing the scientists who are the authors of its claims. Abstracted from systems of familiarity, trust is differently reposed but vastly extended." For a related argument, see Herbert Morris, "The Decline of Guilt," *Ethics* 99 (1988): 62–76.

13. Just as I do not always want to be trusted, I do not always want to have to trust others. See, for example, Cass R. Sunstein, *Legal Reasoning and Political Conflict* (New York and Oxford: Oxford University Press, 1996), 115: "A special advantage of rules is that because of their fixity and generality, they make it unnecessary for citizens to ask an official for permission to engage in certain conduct. Rules turn citizens into rightholders. Discretion, standards, or factors make citizens into supplicants. Importantly, factors and standards allow mercy in the form of relief from rigid rules. But rules have the comparative advantage of forbidding officials from being punitive, or unmoved, for irrelevant or invidious reason, by a particular applicant's request.

"Compare, for example, a mandatory retirement for people over the age of seventy with a law permitting employers to discharge employees who because of their age, are no longer able to perform their job adequately. If you are an employee, it is especially humiliating and stigmatizing to have employers decide whether you have been rendered incompetent by age. A rule avoids this inquiry altogether, and it might be favored for this reason even if it is both over- and underinclusive. Or consider a situation in which officials can give out jobs at their discretion, as compared with one in which officials must hire and fire in accordance with rules laid down in advance. In the first system, employees are in the humiliating position of asking for grace." For a similar account, see Jeremy Waldron, "When Justice Replaces Affection: The Need for Rights," *Harvard Journal of Law and Public Policy* 11 (1988): 628–47.

14. Baier suggests betrayal, as opposed to mere disappointment, as a test for whether trust is involved. "We all depend on one another's psychology in countless ways, but this is not yet to trust them. The trusting can be betrayed, or at least let down, and not just disappointed. Kant's neighbors who counted on his regular habits as a clock for their own less automatically regular ones might be disappointed with him if he slept in one day, but not let down by him, let alone had their trust betrayed." Annette C. Baier, "Trust and Antitrust," 99. See too the analysis of loyalty in George P. Fletcher, *Loyalty: An Essay on the Morality of Relationships* (Oxford and New York: Oxford University Press, 1993). The middle grounds between trust and suspicion are emphasized in Niklas Luhmann, *Trust and Power* (New York: John Wiley, 1979).

15. Angus Ross, "Why Do We Believe What We Are Told?" *Ratio* 28 (1986): 76–77: "One way of bringing out the difference between our attitude to natural signs and our attitude to language is to ask what view we take of falsehood. Suppose we find a natural sign occurring in the absence of the phenomenon of which it is a sign, say (what looks like) smoke without fire. We may not be pleased to discover that we have been misled, if we have been misled, but *criticism*, at least of the smoke or of what is producing it, will be out of place. If anything it will be self-criticism that is in order: a mental note to more cautious in the future. If someone speaks falsely, however, that *is* a matter for criticism, and for criticism of the speaker, regardless of whether there was any serious risk of our being misled." The difference between believing in a person, which as Ross claims and as I argue, is a moral act, and believing what someone says, which is not, is the difference Aristotle draws in the second chapter of the *Rhetoric* (1355b35–39) between artful means of persuasion, which the speaker must "invent," and inartificial means, which he merely has to use.

For a similar point see Richard Holton, "Deciding to Trust, Coming to Believe," *Australian Journal of Philosophy* 72 (1994): 63–76, at 66: "Why do we not say that we rely on [would-be poisoners] not to poison us? The reason, I think, is that their motivation is insufficiently self-generated." See also 73: "When I trust my friend . . . , I trust her to speak knowledgeably and sincerely. And, because I trust her in these ways, I believe what she says. But none of this requires that I believe that she is knowledgeable or sincere."

16. Angus Ross, "Why Do We Believe What We Are Told?," 72: "The main problem with the idea that the hearer views the speaker's words as evidence arises from the fact that, unlike the examples of natural signs which spring most readily to mind, saying something is a deliberate act under the speaker's conscious control and the hearer is aware that this is the case. The problem is not that of whether the hearer can in these circumstances see the speaker's words as good evidence; it is a question of whether the notion of evidence is appropriate here at all. There is, of course, nothing odd about the

idea of deliberately presenting an audience with evidence in order to get them to draw a desired conclusion, as when a photograph is presented in court. But in such a case what is presented is, or is presented as being, evidence independently of the fact of the presenter having chosen to use them. Speaking is not like allowing someone to see you are blushing. The problem is not, however, that the fact of our having chosen to use certain words cannot be evidence for some further conclusion. Our choices can certainly be revealing. The difficulty lies in supposing that the speaker himself sees his choice of words in this light, which in turn makes it difficult to suppose that this is how the hearer is intended to see his choice."

17. Baier, "Trust and Antitrust," 140. See also 196: "Trusting is taking not-so-calculated risks, which are not the same as ill-judged ones. Part of what it is to trust is not to have too many thoughts about possible betrayals. They would turn the trust into mistrust." As Adler puts it, "our critical resources are operative in the ordinary acceptance of testimony, and not only in rejection." Jonathan E. Adler, "Testimony, Trust, Knowing," 273. See also Michael Wellbourne, "The Transmission of Knowledge," *Philosophical Quarterly* 29 (1979): 5: "I cherish the hope that you will come to believe some of what I am saying, but I should be disappointed, even dismayed, were you to believe it by virtue of believing me. I had rather you believed it on its own merits, because you find the argument convincing. Success in the game I am playing is when I get you to see things my way because the arguments are cogent and the claims compelling. It is not when you accept my pronouncements because I have made them, when you accept them on the basis of my authority by virtue of believing me. The reason is that I am not now in the business of disseminating knowledge but of arguing for a view."

18. Earlier I noted the analogy between the trust that makes any community possible and the charity which Davidson claims makes all communication possible. At this point I think we can see that every community requires trust, but that what form that trust takes, and its relation to evidence, suspicions, burdens of proof, and presumptions can be quite variable with different communities and different purposes. The same, I think, holds for charity. See Steven Shapin, *A Social History of Truth*, 116–17: "If disputatious and wrangling scholars accounted truth well worth the price of social discord, gentlemanly civil society took a radically different view. And if the philosopher's code was 'A friend of Plato but more a friend of truth,' early modern gentlemanly society accounted friendship and practical civil order a far stronger claim than philosophers' truth." One can read Shapin's entire book as an account of the transformations of trust in a community in which the search for truth becomes one of the dominant civil values, rather than a minor one as is usually the case. Shapin's point is that truth is not opposed to civility, except in polemics against scholastics and mathematicians, but that truth becomes a part of civility in a new community. His book is a detailed exploration of a historically significant analogue of my encounter with students, with changing canons of trust and evidence.

19. Niklas Luhmann, *Trust and Power*, 88. See also Martin Hollis, *Trust Within Reason*, 12: "The difference [between the normative and the normal, between what can be relied upon and what can be predicted] will be memorably clear to anyone who reflects on the signal which Nelson sent to the fleet in 1805 at the start of the battle of Trafalgar:

'England expects every man to do his duty this day.' The signal put his trust in their patriotism and sense of duty. Since he thought his sailors the scum of the sea, he may not have expected that they would do their duty, at least without the help of petty officers ready to shoot those disinclined to do so; but he still expected it of them." See too Joseph Vining, *The Authoritative and the Authoritarian* (Chicago: University of Chicago Press, 1986), 53–54: "It might be thought that since a contract written and signed by an authorized agent is the contract of the principal and is enforced against the principal, the same would be true here; but not so. A book written by an agent is not the author's book. It is a ghostwritten book. And a judicial opinion is not held against a judge in the way an agent's contract is held against a principal any more than a ghostwriter's words are held against an author for purposes of literary analysis."

20. This is what Aristotle means when he says: "The polis wishes to be [made] 'out of' equal and similar people to the greatest extent possible" (*Politics* IV.11.1295b25–26). Baier, "Trust and Its Vulnerabilities," reprinted in *Moral Prejudices*, 131: "Trust can coexist, and has long coexisted, with contrived and perpetuated inequality. This may well explain and to some extent justify the distrust that many decent vigilant people display toward any attempt to reinstate a climate of trust as a social and moral good." True; instrumental desire for trust is compatible with inequality. But trust as a good does depend on equality. The more unequal a trusting relationship is, the more it must be instrumental.

21. The paradox that trust should be earned but not demanded and tested shows that trust is a historically variable phenomenon, a fact that philosophical analysis is by its nature always in danger of ignoring. For a legal scholar who does better than many philosophers in this respect see Robert Burt, *The Constitution in Conflict* (Cambridge, Mass.: Harvard University Press, 1992), 150: "In the gentry world, gradations of social authority were clear that social deference was observed; but explicit claims of authority and demands for deference were inconsistent with the etiquette of the regime. The basic ethos of the ideal was that authority came 'naturally' and deference would be offered 'willingly'; to demand social deference would virtually disqualify one's claim for it. The approved form of openly waged social conflict was not between superior and inferior but within the same social rank; and the aim of such conflict was not to establish dominance but to reassert claims of equality within rank. The bitter personal rancor that almost invariably accompanied this intra-gentry conflict arose because personal disagreement seems it imply inequality: if one disputant were right, then the other must be wrong. Conflicts thus quickly became personalized; and these personalized disputes could be successfully resolved only when both parties agreed that neither claimed superiority over the other." See too Locke, *Essay Concerning Human Understanding*, ed. Peter H. Nidditch (Oxford: Clarendon Press, 1975), 4.17.19.686: "*Argumentum ad verecundiam.* The first is, to allege the opinions of men, whose parts, learning, eminency, power, or some other cause has gained a name, and settled their reputation in the common esteem with some kind of authority. When men are established in any kind of dignity, it is thought a breach of modesty for others to derogate any way from it, and question the authority of people who are in possession of it. This is apt to be censured, as carrying with it too much pride, when a person does not readily yield to the determination of approved authors, which is wont to be received with respect and submission by others:

and it is looked upon as insolence, for a person to set up and adhere to his own opinion against the current stream of antiquity; or to put it in the balance against that of some learned doctor, or otherwise approved writer. Whoever backs his tenets with such authorities, thinks he ought thereby to carry the cause, and is ready to style it impudence in any one who shall stand out against them. This I think may be called *argumentum ad verecundiam.*"

22. Lawrence E. Mitchell, "Trust. Contract. Process." *Progressive Corporate Law*, ed. Lawrence E. Mitchell (Boulder, Colo.: Westview, 1996), 194: "Your cannot trust another unless you are, yourself, trustworthy. Our basic understanding of human nature starts with self-knowledge, with an appreciation of what we, as individuals are capable. If I know that I am not capable of being trusted, then I have no reasonable basis for expecting that you, acting reasonably, can be trusted either, and therefore I will not trust you. If nobody views herself as trustworthy, then trust cannot exist."

23. Joseph Vining, *The Authoritative and the Authoritarian*, 43–44: "The chronically manipulative and mendacious may thus be treated as things, to be manipulated themselves. For disclosure, absence of deception, almost defines what it means to be inside rather than outside an entity. It is a doctrine as old as the *Iliad* and as contemporary as the securities law that individuals within an organization—a partnership, a corporation, a public agency, a family—are to be loyal and candid, make full disclosure, not mislead others within the organization. (Those outside do not have the same claim not to be manipulated or deceived.)"

24. For similar arguments, see Elijah Millgram, *Practical Induction* (Cambridge, Mass.: Harvard University Press, 1997), 69–70: "If someone accepts the assertions made by his physics textbook because they were arrived at through the scientific method, he must think that the scientific method would be a legitimate technique for him to apply too." And 118–19: "Suppose that one is interested simply in the pleasure produced, and not in any further desirability the pleasure may indicate, and that one proposes to use the knowledge of what gives one pleasure to put oneself in situations that one will find pleasurable, without regard to the reliability of one's judgments of desirability in those circumstances. That would be a little like putting oneself in the way of a series of well-groomed and sincere-sounding young men with attaché cases, without too much regard to *what* they are likely to persuade one of, just in order to acquire *convictions*. It is evidence of the strategy's incoherence that knowingly putting oneself in the way of acquiring convictions in this manner will impede one's ability actually to acquire them."

25. As Jonathan Shay pointed out to me, this is similar to his thesis that only people who care for themselves are able to care for others. It is also similar to Kant's insight that duties to oneself are the ground of all duties, and to Aristotle's observation that the same faculty (*thumos*) is the cause both of the love of freedom and the power to command others (*Politics* VII.6.1327b24–1328a7). Although the Rhetoric tells us that fear and confidence are contraries, the object of fear is an external object, while the proper object of confidence is oneself and one's abilities. Of course I can fear that I will not be up to a challenge, and be confident that the Cubs will not win the World Series, but fear is naturally directed outward and confidence inward.

26. There is a significant resemblance between this object of our trust and Aristotle's magnanimous man "who thinks himself worthy of great things and is really worth of them" (*Ethics* IV.5.1123b2–3). "If he thinks he is worthy of great things, and is worthy of them, especially of the greatest things, he has one concern above all, . . . the right concern with honors and dishonors" (15–21). And just as Machiavelli tells us that taking responsibility generates trust, so "magnanimous people seem to remember the good they do, but not what they receive, . . . and they seem to find pleasure in hearing of the good they do, and none in hearing what they receive" (1124a13–16). The magnanimous not only has earned trust, but expects to be trusted: "He is open in his hatreds and his friendships, since concealment is proper to a frightened person. He is concerned for the truth more than for people's opinion. He is open in his speech and actions" (1124b27–30). In Stephen Toulmin, *Return to Reason* (Cambridge, Mass.: Harvard University Press, 2001), Toulmin quotes (154), without further citation, Jeremy Bentham: "The best way to influence people is to appear to love them, and the best way to appear to love them is to love them indeed."

27. See especially *Ethics* IX.4.1166a30–33: "It is therefore because the good man has these various feelings towards himself and because he feels towards his friend in the same way as towards himself (for a friend is another self), that friendship is also thought to consist in one or other of these feelings, and the possession of them is thought to be the test of the friend." In *Leadership Without Easy Answers* (Cambridge, Mass.: Harvard University Press, 1994), Ronald A. Heifetz discusses a physician who had to earn the trust of her patient, and he shows how such trust depends on the doctor trusting herself (110): "If she were to communicate uneasiness in her body language or tone of voice . . . she would communicate a lack of trustworthiness. If *she* could not carry on painful conversations with competence, then how could they?"

See also Ernest Gellner, "Trust, Cohesion, and the Social Order," 148: "Specialists *as such,* of any kind, are morally suspect. I was told in the central High Atlas that any clan which acquires the reputation of special wisdom is *therefore* deprived of the vote in tribal elections. Excellence of any kind is a form of specialization and that precludes full citizenship. The unspecialized human being constitutes the moral norm. It is he who can lose himself in a solitary unity, and gladly accept collective responsibility. By contrast, the specialists of the towns, for whom specialization is of the essence, are politically castrated and incapable of cohesion, and hence of self-government. Consequently they are also incapable of governing others."

28. Ernest Gellner, "Trust, Cohesion, and the Social Order," 142: "The notion of trust as something specific within a society, one thing among others, and another, broader version of it, which makes it coextensive with the very existence of a social order. . . . Trust as coextensive with *any* kind of social order is one thing, and trust as something within society, of which sometimes there is more and sometimes there is less, is another."

29. Paul Woodruff, *Reverence: Renewing a Forgotten Virtue* (Oxford: Oxford University Press, 2001), 197–98, locates three degrees of "thickness" for reverence: "too thick, too thin, and just right. Thick respect is a judgment of quality that is supposed to be due only to those who deserve it. Thin respect expresses only equality, and is due to

every human being. But the respect that flows from reverence is a felt recognition of a connection growing out of common practices."

30. William James, "The Will to Believe," *Essays in Pragmatism* (New York: Hafner, 1896), 88–109. See also J. M. Balkin, "Agreements with Hell and Other Objects of Our Faith," *Fordham Law Review* 65 (1997): 1721. "To be faithful to someone or something is simultaneously to have faith in someone or something. Fidelity is a two-way street; it is a relationship between oneself and another. One is faithful to the other in part because one expects the other to be faithful to oneself.

"Of course, one does not know that the other will be faithful, and often the other is not. Thus, faithfulness is also faith in the other's fidelity. To be faithful is to be faithful even though does not know whether the other will live up to the other's obligations. Hence, to be faithful is to trust, to make a leap of faith. Conversely, to be faithless also has a double meaning. It means both to lack faith and to betray a trust. A faithless person both lacks trust and cannot be trusted; she is unreliable and disloyal."

31. Baier, "Trust and Antitrust," 235: Trust "is reliance on another's good will," echoing Aristotle's account of friendship as caring about another's good. According to Socrates, "guardians must be intelligent (*phronimous*) and capable (*dynatous*), and furthermore careful of the interests of the state. . . . One would be most likely to be careful of that which he loved . . . and most likely to love that whose interests he supposed to coincide with his own" (*Republic* III.412c–d).

32. There is a parallel between Aristotle's observation that which qualities make for authority and trust vary with context and Arthur Fine's observation that the qualities that make for objectivity, which is in his eyes a form of trust, also vary with context. Arthur Fine, "The Viewpoint of No-One in Particular," *Proceedings and Addresses of the American Philosophical Association* 72 (1998): 18. Objectivity is "that in the process of inquiry which makes for trust in the outcome of inquiry. Here objectivity is fundamentally trust-making not real-making. . . . There is no list of attributes of inquiry that necessarily make it objective. What counts as an objective procedure is something that needs to be tailored to the subject-matter under consideration in a way that generates trust. It follows that attributes like 'unbiased' or 'impersonal' may be objective here and not there. It also follows that other attributes, like the publicity and democracy that go into libertarian model, need to be topically indexed as well. In every case the question is whether a process marked out as objective makes for trust in the product. According to my Deweyan experimentalism, that is among the things we learn by doing."

33. Josiah Royce distinguishes loyalty from love in a way that suits my demarcation of *eunoia*: "You can love an individual. But you can be loyal only to a tie that binds you and others into some sort of unity, and loyal to individuals only through the tie. . . . Loyal lovers, for instance, are loyal not merely to one another as separate individuals, but to their love, to their union, which is something more than either of them, or even than both of them viewed as distinct individuals." Josiah Royce, *The Philosophy of Loyalty* (New York: Macmillan, 1930), 20. *Eunoia* and justice both figure in Annette Baier's observation that "the best reason for confidence in another's good care of what one cares about is that it is a common good." "Trust and Antitrust," 243. In strategic trust, such

as the trust one has in iterated prisoner's dilemmas, there is no such common good. For the trust I want imputed to me, there is.

34. Anthony Kronman, "Practical Wisdom and Professional Character," *Social Philosophy and Policy* 4 (1986): 204: "There is an important distinction between professionals and technicians. Samuel Huntington has rightly observed that the former notion includes, as the latter does not, the idea of an activity with a self-conscious history or tradition that serves ends widely regarded as essential to the well-being of society as a whole. The notion of a professional includes something more than this, however. To be a professional is to have a certain identity or character, to be a person of a certain sort. An expert possesses special knowledge, but to call someone an expert implies nothing about his character traits or dispositions, about the sort of person he is. When someone describes himself as a professional, he is making a claim not merely about what he knows but also about who he is; considered strictly as an expert, as the possessor of some expertise, a person has no character at all, which is why the perfect expert can never be anything but a tool or instrument for others whose ends pass through him as through an utterly transparent medium that offers no resistance of its own. When lawyers complain that they are not mere tools but professionals bound by an ethic that requires them to behave in certain ways, they are insisting, in effect, on the link between character and professional identity."

35. Anthony Kronman, *The Lost Lawyer: Failing Ideals of the Legal Profession* (Cambridge, Mass.: Harvard University Press, 1993), 72, contains a useful diagnosis of my failure: "The sort of imaginative sympathy that deliberation requires combines two opposite-seeming dispositions, that of compassion on the one hand, and that of detachment, on the other. . . . It is difficult to be compassionate, and often just as difficult to be detached, but what is most difficult of all is to be both at once." In this case, at least, the lack of *eunoia* came from a lack of compassion.

36. "You do not trust a person (or an agency) to do something merely because he says he will do it. You trust him only because, knowing what you know of his disposition, his available options and their consequences, his ability and so forth, you expect that he will *choose* to do it." Partha Dasgupta, "Trust as a Commodity," in *Trust: Making and Breaking Cooperative Relations,* ed. Diego Gambetta (Oxford: Blackwell, 1988), 50–51. See also Nancy L. Rosenblum, "Studying Authority: Keeping Pluralism in Mind," *Authority Revisited, Nomos XXIX,* ed. J. Roland Pennock and John W. Chapman (New York: New York University Press, 1987), 107: "Trust in authority involves personal trustworthiness. In addition to judging formal entitlement and the content of commands, . . . we judge character and intentions. We respond to personal qualities in public officials, beginning with honesty and moving on to more elusive elements of personality like decisiveness or responsiveness. We are always on the alert for signs of hypocrisy, too. These estimates are affective; they may not be reducible to principles at all. And it seems as if judging character is something we are unable to surrender. . . . Moral sentiments apply to character before anything else."

37. Joseph Vining, *The Authoritative and the Authoritarian,* 168: "A statement is not worked against or around, only to the extent that it is internalized. It is part of one to that extent, animates and directs one's affirmative seeking: one cares about it, believes

in it, is committed to it. Indeed, the authoritative statement is a clue to what one oneself believes. Personification, understanding, authority, and internalization flow together. But if one is to be committed to and care about and affirmatively and imaginatively seek what the authoritative voice seeks, one must believe, or assume, that the voice means what it says, that it cares about what it is asking another to seek, that it believes in what it is asking another to believe in. Thus authenticity joins personification, understanding, authoritativeness, and internalization in any sketch of a statement of law or a decision that is to have the force of law—again, not just force, which it may have regardless, but the force of law immediately and thereafter. And with authenticity comes openness, speaking out loud, revealing one's purpose, not holding back and keeping secrets, not manipulating, all that goes under the name of disclosure and that underlies the production of the justifying, explanatory, and integrating texts that are the material for the exercise of legal method." I use the formulation of having a visible insides mindful of the historical variations in what such an expression means.

Allan Silver, "Friendship and Trust as Moral Ideals: An Historical Approach," *Archives Europeenes de sociologie* 30 (1989): 276: "In transcending the unavoidable possibility of betrayal, personal trust achieves a moral elevation, lacking in contractual or other engagements enforced by third parties." And 277: "Understanding others based on interest does not depend on knowledge of their moral qualities or inner attributes—indeed, it is predicated on a universal rather than an individuating model of human nature. Trust represents a moral accomplishment that extends experience beyond the possibilities of extrapolation."

See too Josiah Royce, *The Philosophy of Loyalty*, 30–31: "If I am to know my duty, I must consult my own reasonable will. I alone can show myself why I view this or this as my duty. But on the other hand, if I merely look within myself to find what it is that I will, my own private individual nature, apart from due training, never gives me any answer to the question: What do I will? . . . By nature, then, apart from a specific training, I have no personal will of my own. One of the principal tasks of my life is to learn to have a will of my own. To learn your own will,—yes, to create your own will, is one of the largest of your human undertakings."

38. "Political systems lacking a highly developed bureaucratic apparatus, for example the Greek polis, may prove to be arenas for a broader and more subtle exercise of virtue than anything we can witness in modern Western political life. But for this they pay a very high price; namely, far less freedom to pursue other activities independently of political control." Charles Larmore, *Patterns of Moral Complexity* (Cambridge: Cambridge University Press, 1987), 41. For an example of a treatment of trust that is nostalgic for better, but less rational, times, see Francis Fukuyama, *Trust: The Social Virtues and the Creation of Prosperity* (New York: Free Press, 1995). Fukuyama assumes that the habits on which trust depends are necessarily given instead of functions of purposeful activity, and so the habitual and the rational must be in opposition. If that is the case, then reason must destroy trust. For an identification of the problem without nostalgia, see Alasdair MacIntyre, "Is Patriotism a Virtue?" in *Theorizing Citizenship*, ed. Ronald Beiner (Albany, N.Y.: SUNY Press, 1995), 225: "For precisely the same reasons that a family whose members all came to regard membership in that family as governed only by

reciprocal self-interest would no longer be a family in the traditional sense, so a nation whose members took up a similar attitude would no longer be a nation. . . . Since all modern bureaucratic states tend towards reducing national communities to this condition, all such states tend towards a condition in which any genuine morality of patriotism would have no place and what paraded itself as patriotism would be an unjustifiable simulacrum."

CHAPTER SEVEN

1. Paul W. Kahn, "On Pinochet," *Boston Review* (March–April 1999).

2. John Rawls, "Justice as Fairness: Political Not Metaphysical," *Philosophy and Public Affairs* 14 (1985): 223–51.

3. Michael W. McConnell, "Religious Freedom at the Crossroads," *The Bill of Rights in the Modern State,* ed. Geoffrey R. Stone, Richard A. Epstein, and Cass R. Sunstein (Chicago: University of Chicago Press, 1992), 173, n. 250.

4. Gerald Bruns, *Hermeneutics: Ancient and Modern* (New Haven: Yale University Press, 1992), 11: "What is understood in a text is never reducible . . . to another's meaning, rather what one understands, in the light of another's meaning, is a subject matter. . . . Because of who we are and how we are situated the text has a claim on us, and part of what we understand is the substance and force of this claim, and also how we are going to respond to it." And 65–66: "A text, after all, is canonical not in virtue of being final and correct and part of an official library but because it becomes *binding* on a group of people. The whole point of canonization is to underwrite the authority of a text, not merely with respect to its origin as against competitors in the field—this, technically, would simply be a question of authenticity—but with respect to the present and future in which it will reign or govern as a binding text."

5. E. P. Thompson, *Whigs and Hunters: The Origin of the Black Act* (New York: Pantheon Books, 1975), 263, quoted in Robert M. Cover, *Narrative, Violence and the Law: The Essays of Robert Cover,* ed. Martha Minow, Michael Ryan, and Austin Sarat (Ann Arbor: University of Michigan Press, 1992), 174, n. 5: "Most men have a strong sense of justice, at least with regard to their own interest. If law is evidently partial and unjust, then it will mask nothing, legitimize nothing, contribute nothing to any class's hegemony. The essential precondition of the effectiveness of law, in its function as ideology, is that it shall display an independence from gross manipulation and shall seem to be just. It cannot seem to be so without upholding its own logic and criteria of equity; indeed, on occasion, by actually *being just*." For the complications of constitutional fidelity, see J. M. Balkin, "Agreements with Hell and Other Objects of Our Faith," *Fordham Law Review* 65 (1997): 1703–38.

6. Sanford Levinson, *Constitutional Faith* (Princeton, N.J.: Princeton University Press, 1988). Prior to Levinson is Hugo Black's *A Constitutional Faith* (New York: Alfred Knopf, 1968). See also Paul Kahn, *Legitimacy and History: Self-Government in American Constitutional Theory* (New Haven: Yale University Press, 1992). As Kahn points out, to the extent that reason is sufficient to determine justice, a written constitution becomes unnecessary. The founders described their act of constitution-making as one of deliberation and choice based on reason, but those who come after them seem forced to choose between

obeying either the reason or the will of the founders. While our projects have many affinities, Kahn would find my exposition of rational fidelity overly optimistic.

7. The distinction between contract and constitution, and so between the kinds of interpretation appropriate to each, has been present since the beginnings of judicial review, in *Marbury v. Madison* (5 U.S. at 163, 175), where Marshall says that the Constitution is the vehicle through which the people "establish, for their future government, such principles as, in their opinion, shall most conduct to their own happiness. . . . [It] is the basis on which the whole American fabric has been erected."

8. Kahn, *Legitimacy and History*, 36: "When the issue of slavery became critical to the life of the nation, this idea of exceptionality [of slavery in the Constitution] was threatened. As the nation confronted constitutionally legitimated inequality, the scientific foundation of the whole constitutional edifice came under tremendous stress." For interpretations of the Constitution regarding slavery prior to the Civil War, see William M. Wiecek, *The Sources of Antislavery Constitutionalism in America, 1760–1848* (Ithaca, N.Y.: Cornell University Press, 1977), and Joseph Story, *Commentaries on the Constitution of the United States* (Boston, 1891), 1: 466–71.

Frank Easterbrook, "Text, History, and Structure in Statutory Interpretation," *Harvard Journal of Law and Public Policy* 17 (1994): 17: "Legislation is compromise. Compromises have no spirit; they just are." See too John Paul Stevens, "The Bill of Rights: A Century of Progress," *The Bill of Rights in the Modern State*, ed. Geoffrey R. Stone, Richard A. Epstein, and Cass R. Sunstein (Chicago: University of Chicago Press, 1992), 13–39, for an argument that freedom in the Bill of Rights could not be given an expansive meaning, and there could be no unenumerated rights, until the Civil War amendments, because the legality of slavery prevented wide meanings of freedom.

9. William Lloyd Garrison, *The Liberator*, May 6, 1842, at 3, quoted in James Brewer Stewart, *Holy Warriors: The Abolitionists and American Slavery* (New York: Hill and Wang, 1976), 98–99. See also J. M. Balkin, "Agreements with Hell and Other Objects of Our Faith," 1704: "The social and psychological pressures that arise from the practice of fidelity create three basic kinds of ideological effects. The first is that we will tend to see the Constitution as standing for whatever we believe is just, whether it does or not, and whether it ever will be so. In this way the 'true' Constitution can be separated from any evils of the existing political system. This is a matter of conforming the Constitution to our ideas of justice, and so we might call it interpretive conformation.

"The second possible effect is that we will accept what we think the Constitution requires as being just, or at least not too unjust. In this case we conform our beliefs about justice to our sense of what the Constitution means, and not the other way around. We might call this interpretive coopation. It allows us to pledge faith to the Constitution because we decide that things are not really so bad after all.

"Finally, the practice of constitutional fidelity can affect us in a third way. Immersing ourselves in this practice makes it natural for us to talk and think about justice in terms of the concepts and categories of our constitutional tradition. In this way, the practice of constitutional interpretation can actually skew and limit our understandings about justice, because not all claims are equally easy to state in the language of that tradition."

10. Cass R. Sunstein, *The Partial Constitution* (Cambridge, Mass.: Harvard University Press, 1993), 23–24: "The framers' belief in deliberative democracy drew from traditional republican thought, and . . . departed from the tradition in the insistence that a large republic would be better than a smaller one. It departed even more dramatically in its striking and novel rejection of the traditional republican idea that heterogeneity and difference were destructive to the deliberative process. For the framers, heterogeneity was beneficial, indeed indispensable; discussion must take place among people who were different. It was on this score that the framers responded to the antifederalist insistence that homogeneity was necessary to a republic."

The debate between Habermas and Gadamer, as reported by Richard Bernstein, re-enacts this same dispute over whether *phronesis* requires a background of agreement in order to function. Richard Bernstein, *Philosophical Profiles* (Philadelphia: University of Pennsylvania Press, 1986), 71–72: "Habermas can be used to highlight some of the diffi-culties in the very appeal to *phronesis*. For Gadamer himself has stressed that *phronesis* involves a mediation and codetermination of the universal and the particular. In the context of ethical and political action, by the 'universal' Gadamer means those principles, norms, and laws that are funded in the life of the community and orient our particular decisions and actions. Gadamer stresses how all such principles and laws require judg-ment and *phronesis* for their concrete application. This makes good sense when there are shared *nomoi* that inform the life of a community. But what happens when there is a breakdown of such principles, when they no longer seem to have any normative power, when there are deep and apparently irreconcilable conflicts about such principles, or when questions are raised about the very norms and principles that ought to guide our *praxis*? What type of discourse is appropriate when we question the 'universal' ele-ment—the *nomoi*—that is essential for the practice of *phronesis?*"

11. The distinction between instrumental and constitutive reason, between reasoning as a means to some other end and argument setting its own standards, that we've been tracing all along, is nicely developed in Charles Fried, "Constitutional Doctrine," *Harvard Law Review* 107 (1994): 1145, 1149: "I call the rationality implicit in all these structures [of argument] constitutive, as opposed to instrumental or means-end, rationality. In instrumental rationality an end or value is posited, and all other elements in the argu-ment are judged by whether they best lead to that end or maximize that value. Constitu-tive rationality proposes complex structures in which elements are related according to rules or principles, and it is the resultant whole that satisfies the conditions of this kind of rationality. An activity to which this concept applies I call rationally constituted. Thus, although *following* an argument may be—and, to the extent that it is done for its own sake, clearly is—an example of a rationally constituted activity, the argument itself may express nothing but instrumental reason. The argument that says: if you want to do *X*, you must do *A*, unless *B*, and if *B*, then *C* . . . , is purely instrumental for the goal *X*. So, to the extent that it is like a recipe for *X*, following the argument is not a rationally constituted activity—although it is certainly quite rational. But if getting to *X* by follow-ing the argument is the point of the activity, then that activity is rationally constituted. It is the difference between removing your opponent's pieces from the board by captur-ing them and just putting them in your pocket. . . .

"Judges and publicists have regularly proclaimed some value or goal in the name of the law and sought to bend legal decisions to the service of that goal; this is legal decision according to instrumental rationality. . . . When law just states a desirable, mandatory, or forbidden end, with the steps along the way no more than means for its attainment, then the law operates like a recipe—the whole proof of the pudding is in the eating. In an argument, on the other hand, the proof of the pudding is in the proof."

12. Alasdair MacIntyre, "Epistemological Crises, Dramatic Narrative and the Philosophy of Science," *Monist* 60 (1977): 453–72.

13. Michael W. McConnell, "Originalism and the Desegregation Decisions," *Virginia Law Review* 81 (1995): 947–1139, at 952 n. 16: "Such is the moral authority of *Brown* that if any particular theory does not produce the conclusion that *Brown* was correctly decided, the theory is seriously discredited." See also H. Jefferson Powell, *The Moral Tradition of American Constitutionalism: A Theological Interpretation* (Durham, N.C.: Duke University Press, 1993), 166: "*Brown*'s greatest long-term intellectual impact arose from the difficulty constitutionalists had identifying the constitutional principles on which it rested. In one sense, the principle of *Brown* was straightforward and widely accepted: outside the white South the decision was generally regarded as morally correct from the beginning. The problem, of course, was that the constitutional tradition's long-standing insistence on the autonomy of constitutional discourse made direct reliance on the case's 'moral goodness' unacceptable to most constitutionalists."

14. Philip Bobbitt, *Constitutional Fate: Theory of the Constitution* (New York and Oxford: Oxford University Press, 1982), and *Constitutional Interpretation* (Oxford: Blackwell, 1991). References to these books within my text appear as *CF* and *CI*.

15. It is worth noting that structural and doctrinal arguments are those most absent from the sorts of hermeneutics influenced by Gadamer, who downplays the institutional context of interpretation.

16. For the grounding of interpretation in a theory of interpretation, see E. D. Hirsch, *The Aims of Interpretation* (Chicago: University of Chicago Press, 1976). For the grounding of interpretation in a theory of politics, see Ronald Dworkin, *Taking Rights Seriously* (Cambridge, Mass.: Harvard University Press, 1977).

17. *CF*, 228: "The more carefully we examine the actual uses of the Constitution in constitutional decision, the sharper becomes the conflict between those uses and our requirement that they follow inexorably from a constitutional command." See also Joseph Vining, *The Authoritative and the Authoritarian* (Chicago: University of Chicago Press, 1986), 156: "Hard and practical men are generally impatient with methodological questions and inquiry into presuppositions. Just tell us what the law says, they growl, and forget the jurisprudence. Thinking themselves realists, they are in fact just the opposite, magicians, believing that the written or spoken word has an independent power, that it can command. But it can issue no commands. Statements of law are not formulae to be conjured with." For an opposed point of view, compare Robert H. Bork, *The Tempting of America: The Political Seduction of the Law* (New York: The Free Press; London: Collier Macmillan, 1990), 176.

18. See too Robert Post, "Theories of Constitutional Interpretation," *Representations* 30 (1990): 27: "Arguments about theories of interpretation commonly modulate into

arguments about the inherent 'nature' of the Constitution. To the extent that the three theories of constitutional interpretation [doctrinal, historical, and responsive in Post's own taxonomy] are perceived as incompatible, it is due to the fact that they are seen as flowing from incompatible notions of the Constitution itself.

"But this vision of constitutional authority is fundamentally flawed, for it postulates a form of constitutional authority that is external to the processes of its own interpretation. It imagines that the nature of the Constitution can somehow be determined in a manner which is independent of the practice of constitutional interpretation, and that the practice is therefore logically controlled by this antecedent determination of constitutional authority. But a better account of the practice of constitutional interpretation would situate constitutional authority instead in the *relationship* obtaining between participants in that practice and the Constitution. Paradoxically, then, constitutional interpretation is not merely about the Constitution but about the more radical and profound question of how we stand in connection to the Constitution."

19. This reversal is a modern working out of the problem about justice posed in *Republic* II. Justice may come into existence because of the need for cooperation in the division of work, but true justice makes such divisions among natures possible.

20. Vining, *The Authoritative and the Authoritarian*, 224. See also Jerold S. Auerbach, "What Has Teaching of Law to do with Justice?" *New York University Law Review* 53 (1978): 457–74.

21. John Dewey, *Essays in Experimental Logic* (Chicago: University of Chicago Press), 311.

22. Cass R. Sunstein, *The Partial Constitution*, 119.

23. Kahn, "On Pinochet," *Boston Review*: "We create law in order to achieve a just political order. If we are to see ourselves in the legal order, that order must hold forth a normatively attractive vision. Legal discourse is, therefore, unavoidably a moral discourse in its foundations. We expect modern constitutions to include guarantees of human rights because this is the dominant moral discourse today. We are mistaken, however, if we believe it is the content of the values, rather than the law's constitutive character within the community, that supports the compelling claim made upon individual citizens. It is not the case that liberal democratic regimes everywhere can claim our sacrificial support; expressing correct moral values does not allow a state to draft noncitizens. We may contribute sympathetically to the causes with which we agree, but we do not think that state should compel sacrificial acts for other political communities, regardless of our agreement with their values."

24. Post's "responsive" mode of interpretation has many similarities to Bobbitt's "ethical." This mode is necessarily self-conscious and pluralistic; it necessarily distinguishes legitimacy from justification. See Robert Post, "Theories of Constitutional Interpretation," 29–30: "Responsive interpretation is unique, for it alone explicitly thematizes this relational nature of constitutional authority. Both historical and doctrinal interpretation purport to submit to a Constitution whose authority is independent and fixed, either in the preexisting consent of the ratifiers or in the preexisting rules of controlling precedents. Although this submission is illusory, it is an illusion capable of disarming dissent. Responsive interpretation, however, disavows this illusion, and frankly locates constitutional authority in the relationship between the Constitution and its interpreters. As a

consequence responsive interpretation generates an intense and singular kind of political dynamics."

CHAPTER EIGHT

1. For a few examples of the discovery of the disunity of practical reason, see, first, Alexis de Tocqueville, *Democracy in America,* ed. J. P. Mayer (New York: Vintage, 1945), 2:54–55: "In the moral world everything is classified, coordinated, foreseen, and decided in advance. In the world of politics everything is in turmoil, contested and uncertain. In the one case obedience is passive, though voluntary; in the other there is independence, contempt of experience, and jealousy of all authority."

Next, C. S. Peirce, "How to Make our Ideas Clear," *Collected Papers,* ed. Charles Hartshorne and Paul Weiss (Cambridge, Mass.: Harvard University Press, 1931–60), 5: 405: "The first thing that the Will to Learn supposes is a dissatisfaction with one's present state of opinion. There lies the secret of why it is that our American universities are so miserably insignificant. What have they done for the advance of civilization? The English universities, rotting with sloth as they always have, have nevertheless in the past given birth to Locke and to Newton, and in our time to Cayley, Sylvester, and Clifford. The German universities have been the light of the whole world. The medieval University of Bologna gave Europe its system of law. The University of Paris and that despised scholasticism took Abelard and made him into Descartes. The reason was that they were institutions of learning while ours are institutions of teaching. In order that a man's whole heart may be in teaching he must be thoroughly imbued with the vital importance and absolute truth of what he has to teach; while in order that he may have any measure of success in learning he must be permeated with a sense of the unsatisfactoriness of his present condition of knowledge. The two attitudes are almost irreconcilable."

See, finally, Learned Hand. "You may take Martin Luther or Erasmus for your model, but you cannot play both roles at once; you may not carry a sword beneath a scholar's gown, lead flaming causes from a cloister, Luther cannot be domesticated in a university. You cannot raise a standard against oppression, or leap into the breach to relieve injustice, and still keep an open mind to every disconcerting fact, or an open ear to the cold voice of doubt. I am satisfied that a scholar who tries to combine these parts sells his birthright for a mess of pottage; that when the final count is made, it will be found that the impairment of his powers far outweighs any possible contribution to the causes he has espoused. If he is fit to serve his calling at all, it is only because he has learned not to serve in any other, for his singleness of mind quickly evaporates in the fires of passions, however holy." Learned Hand, "On Receiving an Honorary Degree," in *The Spirit of Liberty,* 3d ed., ed. Irving Dillard (Phoenix, 1960), 138, quoted in Philip B. Kurland, "The True Wisdom of the Bill of Rights," in *The Bill of Rights in the Modern State,* ed. Geoffrey R. Stone, Richard A. Epstein, and Cass. R. Sunstein (Chicago: University of Chicago Press, 1992), 8.

2. First published as "A Pragmatist View of Rationality and Cultural Difference," *Philosophy East and West* 42 (1992): 581–95, and then reprinted in Richard Rorty, *Truth and Progress: Philosophical Papers,* vol. 3 (Cambridge: Cambridge University Press, 1998), 186–202.

3. In *Aristotle's Rhetoric: An Art of Character,* I show how Aristotle's warnings against excessive precision are really cautions against reducing deliberative rationality to a professional technique detached from character. That is one important instance of the way technical rationality can become irrational.

4. The lack of unity among the three kinds of rationality is noted at the beginning of Alasdair MacIntyre, *Whose Justice? Which Rationality?* (Notre Dame, Ind.: University of Notre Dame Press, 1988), 2: "Disputes about the nature of rationality in general and . . . practical rationality in particular are apparently as manifold and as intractable as disputes about justice. To be practically rational, so one contending party holds, is to act on the basis of the costs and benefits to oneself of each possible alternative course of action and its consequences. To be practically rational, affirms a rival party, is to act under those constraints which any rational person, capable of an impartiality which accords no particular privileges to one's own interests, would agree should be imposed. To be practically rational, so a third party contends, is to act in such a way as to achieve the ultimate and true good of human beings."

5. "Protestantism has a double (and somewhat contradictory) role: it makes men instrumentally rational in handling things, and non-instrumentally honest in their dealing with each other." Ernest Gellner, *Plough, Sword and Book: The Structure of Human History* (Chicago: University of Chicago Press, 1988), 106. See also Keith Baker, *Condorcet: From Natural Philosophy to Social Mathematics* (Chicago: University of Chicago Press, 1975), 75: "Princes and powers are led to favor the advancement of sciences for their utility. Once regarded as an essential part of education, knowledge of the physical sciences forms in the people the habit of accurate, methodical, critical reasoning. . . . Thus Condorcet not only posited a relationship between scientific advance and social welfare. He also insisted that scientific progress necessarily entailed the rationalization of the whole social order." Of course there are powerful arguments, such as Hayek's, that there is an essential connection between liberalism and capitalism. I neither endorse nor dismiss such arguments, but I do think that that connection depends for its success on intellectual as well as material preconditions. Those conditions are my subject here. See F. A. Hayek, *The Constitution of Liberty* (Chicago: University of Chicago Press, 1960); *Law, Legislation, and Liberty: A New Statement of the Liberal Principles of Justice and Political Economy,* vol. 1, *Rules and Order* (Chicago: University of Chicago Press, 1973), and *Law, Legislation, and Liberty: A New Statement of the Liberal Princples of Justice and Political Economy,* vol. 2, *The Mirage of Social Justice* (Chicago: University of Chicago Press, 1976).

6. See also his "Thugs and Theorists: A Reply to Bernstein," *Political Theory* 15 (1987): 564–80. For a clear statement of the common story that instrumental rationality developed in opposition to a more substantive kind of rationality, see Charles Taylor, "Justice After Virtue," *After MacIntyre: Critical Perspectives on the Work of Alasdair MacIntyre,* ed. John Horton and Susan Mendus (Notre Dame, Ind.: University of Notre Dame Press, 1994), 19: "Reason is no longer defined substantively, in terms of a vision of cosmic order, but formally, in terms of the procedures that thought ought to follow, and especially those involved in fitting means to ends, instrumental reason: the hegemony of reason is consequently redefined, and now means not ordering our lives according

to the vision of order, but rather controlling desires by the canons of instrumental reason."

7. John Dewey, *Freedom and Culture* (New York: Capricorn Books, 1939), 173.

8. Richard Rorty, *Contingency, Irony and Solidarity* (Cambridge and New York: Cambridge University Press, 1989), 29: "The wonder in which Aristotle believed philosophy to begin was wonder at finding oneself in a world larger, stronger, nobler than oneself. The fear in which [Harold] Bloom's poets begin is the fear that one might end one's days in such a world, a world one never made, an inherited world. The hope of such a poet is that what the past tried to do to her she will succeed in doing to the past: to make the past itself . . . bear *her* impress." Compare Allan Bloom, *The Closing of the American Mind: How Higher Education Has Failed Democracy and Impoverished the Souls of Today's Students* (New York: Simon and Schuster, 1987), 35, who thought that religious wars were proof that partisans took "their beliefs seriously," and conversely that the lack of people dying, and killing, for ideas means that ideas are no longer central to their lives. The idea that religion is succeeded first by philosophy and then by irony sounds more like Comte than Dewey to me. See too Rorty, "Pragmatism as Romantic Polytheism," in *The Revival of Pragmatism: New Essays on Social Thought, Law, and Culture*, ed. Morris Dickstein (Durham and London: Duke University Press, 1998), 21–36.

9. John Dewey, *The Problems of Men* (New York: Philosophical Library, 1946), 12–13: "The word 'relativity' is used as a scarecrow to frighten away philosophers from critical assault upon 'absolutisms.' Every class interest in all history has defended itself from examination by putting forth claim to absoluteness. Social fanaticisms, whether of the right or the left, take refuge in the fortress of principles too absolute to be subject to doubt and inquiry. The absolute is the isolated, is that which cannot be judged on the ground of connections that can be investigated." And 13: "Not 'relativity' but absolutism isolates and confines. The reason, at bottom, that absolutism levels its guns against relativity in a caricature is that search for the connection of events is the sure way of destroying the privileged position of exemption from inquiry which every form of absolutism secures wherever it obtains."

10. For some historical reflections on the connection between pluralism and pragmatism, see my "Why Pluralism Now?" *Monist* 73 (1990): 388–410.

11. Dewey, "Anti-Naturalism in Extremis," *Partisan Review* 10 (1943): 37. But see Rorty, *Contingency, Irony and Solidarity*, 189: "A belief can still regulate action, can still be thought worth dying for, among people who are quite aware that this belief is caused by nothing deeper than contingent historical circumstances."

12. Gellner, *Plough, Sword and Book*, 252: "How can a society which commends and inculcates both individualism and instrumental rationality, and which in fact could not function without them, nevertheless also hope to maintain solidarity and cooperativeness?"

13. The most famous complaint is found in Mary Ann Glendon, *Rights Talk: The Impoverishment of Political Discourse* (New York: Free Press, 1991). Recall a quotation I used in the first chapter, from John Dewey, *The Quest for Certainty* (New York: Capricorn Books, 1929), 260: "In justifying our actions and our requests to one another we normally make our case by explaining why it is that we want a certain thing rather than merely citing

the fact that we do prefer it and indicating the strength of our preference. In a situation in which there is real disagreement over what is to be done, to be willing to say only, 'I prefer . . .' amounts to deliberate incommunicativeness or even imperiousness."

14. John Dewey, *The Public and Its Problems* (Chicago: Gateway Books, 1946; first published, Henry Holt, 1927), 50–51: "Toleration in matters of judgment and belief is largely a negative matter. We agree to leave one another alone (within limits) more from recognition of evil consequences which have resulted from the opposite course than from any profound belief in its positive social benificence. As long as the latter consequence is not widely perceived, the so-called natural right to private judgment will remain a somewhat precarious rationalization of the moderate amount of toleration which has come into being."

15. Richard Rorty, "Solidarity or Objectivity?" in *Post-Analytic Philosophy,* ed. John Rajchman and Cornel West (New York: Columbia University Press, 1985), 8 See too Rorty, "A Pragmatist View of Rationality and Cultural Difference," 193: "Dewey's attitude toward the idea that philosophers might provide foundations for social practices resembled that of Wittgenstein, who said, in reference to the Frege-Russell notion that the foundations of mathematics can be found in logic, 'The *mathematical* problems of what is called foundations are no more the foundations of mathematics for us than the painted rock is the support of the painted tower' (*Remarks on the Foundations of Mathematics,* 8:16). In other words, the philosophy of X (where X is something like mathematics, art, science, class struggle, or postcolonialism) is just more X and cannot *support* X—though it may expand, clarify, or improve X." That seems to be a significant role of philosophy, although probably not for philosophy departments.

16. Richard Rorty, "The Priority of Democracy to Philosophy," in *The Virginia Statute of Religious Freedom,* ed. Merrill Peterson and Robert Vaughn (Cambridge: Cambridge University Press, 1988), and reprinted in Alan R. Malachowski, *Reading Rorty* (Oxford: Blackwell, 1989), 279–302, at 293.

17. In *Employment Division v. Smith* (494 U.S. 872) the Supreme Court ruled that Native Americans who ingested peyote for religious reasons were not exempt from laws prohibiting narcotics. In *Goldman v. Weinberger* (475 U.S. 503) the Court held that military regulations against non-uniform head coverings included yarmulkes worn by Jews for religious reasons. What Major Goldman saw as a religious obligation, the Court saw as a preference.

18. Sidney Hook, *Pragmatism and the Tragic Sense of Life* (New York: Basic Books, 1974), 20: "Intelligence may be optimistic when it deals with the control of things but the moral life by its very nature forbids the levity and superficiality which has often been attributed to the pragmatic approach by its unimaginative critics."

19. William James, *Some Problems of Philosophy,* in *Writings, 1902–1910,* ed. Bruce Kuklick (New York: Library of America, 1987), 979–1105, at 1019. The quotations are from Royce, *The Philosophy of Loyalty.*

20. It is only since *Brown* that the Supreme Court has been regarded as the sole "forum of principle," with the rest of the government working to satisfy popular desires. We shouldn't forget that for much of American history, the entire government, and not just the Supreme Court, was "countermajoritarian" and at least potentially prin-

cipled. Cass R. Sunstein, *The Partial Constitution* (Cambridge, Mass.: Harvard University Press, 1993, 145–46: "Ronald Dworkin defended an active role for the judiciary on the theory that the Supreme Court is the 'forum of principle,' countering the horse-trading characteristic of interest-group politics. But the Court was never intended to be the only principled institution in American government. Nor has it been the only such institution in our history. On the contrary, the major reflections of principled deliberation in the American history have come from Congress and the President, not the courts. In the twentieth century the labor movement, the New Deal, the environmental movement, the deregulation movement, and the women's movement are simply a few examples." To this passage, Sunstein adds a footnote to Ronald Dworkin, *A Matter of Principle* (1985), with a further note also citing Alexander Bickel, *The Least Dangerous Branch* (1958) and Michael Perry, *The Constitution, the Courts, and Human Rights* (1982).

21. John Dewey, *The Public and Its Problems*, 142. "Symbols control sentiment and thought, and the new age has no symbols consonant with its activities. Intellectual instrumentalities for the formation of an organized public are more inadequate than its overt means. The ties which hold men together in action are numerous, tough and subtle. But they are invisible and intangible. We have the physical tools of communication as never before. The thoughts and aspirations congruous with them are not communicated, and hence are not common. Without such communication the public will remain shadowy and formless, seeking spasmodically for itself, but seizing and holding its shadow rather than its substance. Till the Great Society is converted into a Great Community, the Public will remain in eclipse. Communication can alone create a great community. Our Babel is not one of tongues but of the signs and symbols without which shared experience is impossible."

22. Claude Lefort, *Democracy and Political Theory*, trans. David Macey (Minneapolis: University of Minnesota Press, 1988), 39. The quotation from Lefort is the epigram to Robert Post, "Theories of Constitutional Interpretation," *Representations* 30 (1990): 24. "What is authoritative is neither more nor less than our common commitment to the flourishing of the mutual enterprise of nationhood. . . . The radical and paradoxical implication of this perspective is that the Constitution explicitly loses its character as a specific document or a discrete text. It becomes instead, as Karl Llewellyn bluntly put it, a 'going Constitution,' a 'working Constitution' which has a content that 'is in good part utterly extra-Documentary,' and which represents the '*fundamental* framework' of the 'governmental machine.' In this way the Constitution is transformed into what Kant might call the 'regulative' idea of the enterprise of constitutional adjudication, the 'imaginary focus from which the concepts' of that enterprise 'seem to proceed, even though there is nothing knowable at that focus.'

"The Constitution as a regulative idea defines the *telos* and shape of constitutional interpretation; it demands a continual effort to articulate the authority of our 'fundamental nature as a people' and hence concomitantly to summon 'us to our powers as co-founders as to our responsibilities' in the full knowledge that 'how we are able to constitute ourselves is profoundly tied to how we are already constituted by our own distinctive history.'" The quotations are from (1) Karl Llewellyn, "The Constitution as an Institution," *Columbia Law Review* 34 (1934): 14–15, 26; (2) J. N. Findlay, *Kant and the Transcendental Object: A Hermeneutic Study* (Oxford, 1981) 241; and (3) Hanna Pitkin, "The Idea of a Constitution," *Journal of Legal Education* 37 (1987): 167–69.

23. Dewey, *Freedom and Culture,* 103: "It is not accidental that the rise of interest in human nature coincided in time with the assertion in political matters of the rights of the people as a whole, over against the rights of a class supposedly ordained by God or Nature to exercise rule. The full scope and depth of the connection between assertion of democracy in government and new consciousness of human nature cannot be present without going into an opposite historical background, in which social arrangements and political forms were taken to be an expression of Nature—but most decidedly not of human nature.

"Regard for human nature as the source of legitimate political arrangements is comparatively late in European history; that when it arose it marked an almost revolutionary departure from previous theories about the basis of political rule and citizenship and subjection—so much so that the fundamental difference between even ancient republican and modern democratic governments has its source in the substitution of human nature for cosmic nature as the foundation of politics."

And *Freedom and Culture,* 124: "Because of lack of an adequate theory of human nature in its relations to democracy, attachment to democratic ends and methods has tended to become a matter of tradition and habit—an excellent thing as far as it goes, but when it becomes routine is easily undermined when change of conditions changes other habits."

24. Dewey, *Liberalism and Social Action* (New York: Capricorn, 1963), 60: "The conditions that generate insecurity for the many no longer spring from nature. They are found in institutions and arrangements that are within deliberate human control. Surely this change marks one of the greatest revolutions that has taken place in all human history. Because of it, insecurity is not now the motive to work and sacrifice but to despair."

25. See John Dewey, "Anti-Naturalism in Extremis," 32: "Naturalism finds the values in question, the worth and dignity of men and women, founded in human nature itself, in the connections, actual and potential, of human beings with one another in their natural social relationships. Not only that, but it is ready at any time to maintain the thesis that a foundation within man and nature is a much sounder one than is alleged to exist outside the constitution of man and nature."

See also John Stuart Mill, *The Subjection of Women,* in the *Collected Works of John Stuart Mill,* ed. J. M. Robson (Toronto and Buffalo: University of Toronto Press, 1984), 21:272–73: "What is the peculiar character of the modern world—the difference which chiefly distinguishes modern institutions, modern social ideas, modern life itself, from those of times long past? It is, that human beings are no longer born to their place in life, and chained down by an inexorable bond to the place they are born to, but are free to employ their faculties, and such favourable chances as offer, to achieve the lot which may appear to them most desirable."

Similarly, for today rather than the middle of the nineteenth century, see Stanley Cavell, *Must We Mean What We Say?* (Cambridge: Harvard University Press, 1976), xxii: This is "a moment in which history and its conventions can no longer be taken for granted: the time in which music and painting and poetry (like nations) have to define themselves against their pasts; the beginning of the moment in which each of the arts becomes its own subject, as if its immediate artistic task is to establish its own existence."

26. I avoid the more convenient locution, "deliberation about ends," to avoid arguments about whether such a thing is possible under Aristotle's meanings of deliberation and end. In Aristotle's *Ethics* I believe that he means what he says in saying that we only deliberate about means. But none of that affects the points at issue here. For a sustained argument about deliberation about ends, see Henry Richardson, *Practical Reasoning About Final Ends* (Cambridge: Cambridge University Press, 1994).

27. The first quotation is from Charles S. Peirce, "Ideals of Conduct," *The Collected Papers of Charles Sanders Peirce*, 8 vols., ed. Charles Hartshorne, Paul Weiss, and Arthur Burks (Cambridge, Mass.: Harvard University Press, 1931–58), 1:615. The second is from Charles S. Peirce, "Review of *Clark University, 1898–1899*," *Science* (April 20, 1900), 620–22, quoted in Richard Bernstein, "The Lure of the Ideal," *Peirce and Law: Issues in Pragmatism, Legal Realism, and Semiotics,* ed. Robert Kevelson (New York: Peter Lang, 1991), 29–44, at 31.

But while Peirce cautions against assimilating practical reason to science, he also thinks that prudential thinking suffers from the same ills Dewey ascribes to it. They differ on science as a cure. See his "Science and Continuity," *Collected Papers*, 1:61: "One of the worst effects of the influence of moral and religious reasonings upon science lies in this, that the distinctions upon which both insist as fundamental are dual distinctions, and that their tendency is toward an ignoring of all distinctions that are not dual and especially of the conception of continuity. Religion recognizes the saints and the damned. It will not readily admit any third fate. Morality insists that a motive is either good or bad. That the gulf between them is bridged over and that most motives are somewhere near the middle of the bridge, is quite contrary to the teachings of any moral system which ever lived in the hearts and conscience of a people. . . . It is not necessary to read far in almost any work of philosophy written by a man whose training is that of a theologian, in order to see how helpless such minds are in attempting to deal with continuity. But continuity, it is not too much to say, is the leading conception of science."

28. Rorty's own argument against the Romantic reduction of principles to preferences can be found in "The Priority of Democracy to Philosophy," 288.

29. John Dewey, *Individualism Old and New* (New York: Capricorn, 1962), 160–61. See too Oliver Wendell Holmes Jr., *The Essential Holmes: Selections From the Letters, Speeches, Judicial Opinions, and Other Writings,* ed. with an introduction by Richard A. Posner (Chicago and London: University of Chicago Press, 1992), 218: "If a man has the soul of Sancho Panza, the world to him will be Sancho Panza's world; but if he has the soul of an idealist, he will make—I do not say find—his world ideal. Of course, the law is not the place for the artist or the poet. The law is the calling of thinkers. But to those who believe with me that not the least godlike of man's activities is the large survey of causes, that to know is not less than to feel, I say—and I say no longer with any doubt—that a man may live greatly in the law as well as elsewhere; that there as well as elsewhere his thought may find its unity in an infinite perspective; that there as well as elsewhere he may wreak himself upon life, may drink the bitter cup of heroism, may wear his heart out after the unattainable."

30. Dewey, *The Problems of Men,* 158. See too *Reconstruction in Philosophy,* enlarged ed. with a new introduction by the author (Boston: Beacon Press, 1948), ix: "The reconstruction to be undertaken is not that of applying 'intelligence' as something ready-made. It is to carry over into any inquiry into human and moral subjects the kind of method (the method of observation, theory as hypothesis, and experimental test) by which understanding of physical nature has been brought to its present pitch.

"Just as theories of knowing that developed prior to the existence of scientific inquiry provide no pattern or model for a theory of knowing based upon the present actual conduct of inquiry, so the earlier systems reflect both pre-scientific views of the natural world and also the pre-technological state of industry and the pre-democratic state of politics of the period when their doctrines took form."

See also Dewey, *Logic: The Theory of Inquiry* (New York: Henry Holt, 1938), 494: "An approach to human problems in terms of moral blame and moral approbation, or wickedness and righteousness, is probably the greatest single obstacle now existing to development of competent methods in the field of social subject matter."

31. Dewey, *Liberalism and Social Action,* 44, 46.

32. Ibid., 46–47.

33. The seminal work here is Steven Shapin, *A Social History of Truth: Civility and Science in Seventeenth-Century England* (Chicago: University of Chicago Press, 1994).

34. Richard Rorty, "Hermeneutics," *Synergos* 2 (1982): 1–15.

35. C. S. Peirce, *Collected Papers,* 2.635.

36. Dewey, *Freedom and Culture,* 145–46.

37. Ronald Dworkin, "The Forum of Principle," *A Matter of Principle* (Cambridge, Mass., and London: Harvard University Press, 1985), 33–71, originally published in *New York University Law Review* 56 (1981); John Rawls, *Political Liberalism* (New York: Columbia University Press, 1993), 231.

INDEX